CONTESTING ISLAM, CONSTRUCTING RACE AND SEXUALITY

Suspensions: Contemporary Middle Eastern and Islamicate Thought

Series editors: Jason Bahbak Mohaghegh and Lucian Stone

This series interrupts standardized discourses involving the Middle East and the Islamicate world by introducing creative and emerging ideas. The incisive works included in this series provide a counterpoint to the reigning canons of theory, theology, philosophy, literature, and criticism through investigations of vast experiential typologies—such as violence, mourning, vulnerability, tension, and humour—in light of contemporary Middle Eastern and Islamicate thought.

Other titles in this series include:

Gilles Deleuze, Postcolonial Theory, and the Philosophy of Limit, Réda Bensmaïa
The Qur'an and Modern Arabic Literary Criticism: From Taha to Nasr, Mohammad Salama
Hostage Spaces of the Contemporary Islamicate World, Dejan Lukic
On the Arab Revolts and the Iranian Revolution, Arshin Adib-Moghaddam
The Politics of Writing Islam, Mahmut Mutman
The Writing of Violence in the Middle East, Jason Bahbak Mohaghegh
Iranian Identity and Cosmopolitanism, edited by Lucian Stone
Continental Philosophy and the Palestinian Question, by Zahi Zalloua
Sorcery, Totem and Jihad, Christopher Wise
Orientalism and Imperialism, Andrew Wilcox
Traces of Racial Exception, Ronit Lentin
Transgression and the Inexistent, Mehdi Belhaj Kacem
Plural Maghreb: Writings on Postcolonialism, Abdelkebir Khatibi
Revolutionary Bodies, K.S. Batmanghelichi

CONTESTING ISLAM, CONSTRUCTING RACE AND SEXUALITY

The Inordinate Desire of the West

Sunera Thobani

BLOOMSBURY ACADEMIC
LONDON • NEW YORK • OXFORD • NEW DELHI • SYDNEY

BLOOMSBURY ACADEMIC
Bloomsbury Publishing Plc
50 Bedford Square, London, WC1B 3DP, UK
1385 Broadway, New York, NY 10018, USA
29 Earlsfort Terrace, Dublin 2, Ireland

BLOOMSBURY, BLOOMSBURY ACADEMIC and the Diana logo
are trademarks of Bloomsbury Publishing Plc

First published in Great Britain 2021
This paperback edition published in 2022

Copyright © Sunera Thobani, 2021

Sunera Thobani has asserted her right under the Copyright,
Designs and Patents Act, 1988, to be identified as Author of this work.

For legal purposes the Acknowledgements on p. viii constitute
an extension of this copyright page.

Series Design by Catherine Wood
Cover image: Inordinate Desire, mixed media on paper (© Arax Nazari)

All rights reserved. No part of this publication may be reproduced or transmitted
in any form or by any means, electronic or mechanical, including photocopying,
recording, or any information storage or retrieval system, without prior
permission in writing from the publishers.

Bloomsbury Publishing Plc does not have any control over, or responsibility for, any
third-party websites referred to or in this book. All internet addresses given in this
book were correct at the time of going to press. The author and publisher regret
any inconvenience caused if addresses have changed or sites have ceased to
exist, but can accept no responsibility for any such changes.

A catalogue record for this book is available from the British Library.

Library of Congress Cataloging-in-Publication Data

Names: Thobani, Sunera, 1957-author.
Title: Contesting Islam, constructing race and sexuality: the inordinate
desire of the West / Sunera Thobani.
Description: New York: Bloomsbury Academic, 2020. |
Series: Suspensions: contemporary Middle Eastern and islamicate thought |
Includes bibliographical references and index.
Identifiers: LCCN 2020032494 (print) | LCCN 2020032495 (ebook) |
ISBN 9781350148093 (hardback) | ISBN 9781350198715 (paperback) |
ISBN 9781350148109 (ebook) | ISBN 9781350148116 (epub)
Subjects: LCSH: Civilization, Western–Islamic influences. | East and West. |
Islamic countries–Relations–Western countries. |
Western countries–Relations–Islamic countries.
Classification: LCC CB245.T485 2020 (print) | LCC CB245 (ebook) |
DDC 909/.09821–dc23
LC record available at https://lccn.loc.gov/2020032494
LC ebook record available at https://lccn.loc.gov/2020032495

ISBN: HB: 978-1-3501-4809-3
PB: 978-1-3501-9871-5
ePDF: 978-1-3501-4810-9
eBook: 978-1-3501-4811-6

Series: Suspensions: Contemporary Middle Eastern and Islamicate Thought

Typeset by Deanta Global Publishing Services, Chennai, India

To find out more about our authors and books visit
www.bloomsbury.com and sign up for our newsletters.

In memory of my mother, Roshan
The strength of her spirit runs through my life every day, in ways that even I don't quite understand.

CONTENTS

Acknowledgements — viii

INTRODUCTION — 1

Chapter 1
THE IN/HUMAN SUBJECT — 37

Chapter 2
WESTERN CONSTITUTIONS: RELIGION, RACE AND COLONIALITY — 77

Chapter 3
SEX/UALITY IN THE ISLAMIC ORIENT — 107

Chapter 4
FEMINISM AT WAR — 139

Chapter 5
REMAKING THE WEST: SOVEREIGNTY, WHITENESS AND
THE JUDEO-CHRISTIAN — 169

Notes — 193
Bibliography — 232
Index — 253

ACKNOWLEDGEMENTS

This work began in an entirely unanticipated manner. Following the 9/11 attacks, I made a speech at an anti-violence feminist conference urging women's organizations to oppose the then looming invasion of Afghanistan, and the war on terror in general. The hatelash that followed – a small taste of things to come – pushed me into a deeper and far lengthier study of the issues mentioned only briefly in that speech. This book is the result of that larger study; it has pulled me in directions I had never before imagined taking.

The journey has been long and hard, but also exhilarating at precisely the right moments. The arguments presented here are not palatable to many: I have lost friends and colleagues along the way. But I have also been met with unbelievable generosity from family and friends, from previously unknown fellow travellers, who have given me such comforts – big and small – that they continue to enrich my life beyond measure. Exactly the right person showed up, exactly the right experience had to be undergone, exactly the right reference came my way at exactly the right moment on this journey. Serendipity? Coincidence? Fate? What I do know is these gifts I would have never been fortunate enough to receive had I not travelled this particular path.

My deepest thanks go to Malinda Smith, Shelina Kassam, Hanifa Kassam, Dana Olwan, Sedef Arat-Koc, Mustafa Koc, Suvendrini Perera, Sara Ahmed, Meyda Yeğenoğlu, Mahmut Mutman, Nadera Shalhoub Kevorkian, Cavlan Erengezgin, Yuezhi Zhao, Radha D'Souza, Aziz Choudhry, Huma Dar, Seemi Ghazi, Benita Bunjun, Parin Dossa, Simrita-Gopal Singh, Farah Zeb, Itrath Syed, Farida Akhtar, Farhad Mazhar, Fatima Jaffer, Zool Suleman, Habiba Zaman, Susan Boyd, Dara Culhane, Jin Haritaworn, Geeta Sondhi, Akbar Thobhani, Monya Thobhani, Zaibby Sheikh, Rabab AbdulHadi, Nahla Abdo, Sami Zubi, Michelle Hartman, Shimona Sharoni, Mridula Thanki, Imtiaz Popat, Alnoor Gova and many others for standing with me during some of the most difficult challenges I have faced working on this project. I was fortunate enough to be invited as a Visiting Scholar and Speaker at a number of institutions while I was working through the ideas presented in this book. I am deeply thankful for the warm generosity, and spirited exchanges, I experienced at each of these sites. Again, I was lucky enough to have spent just the right amount of time during these visits and learn enough about the conditions, debates and concerns relevant to my study unfolding there to see how directly and intricately these were interconnected. I would like to thank all the colleagues and friends who facilitated my visits to Bilgi University, Delhi University, Jawaharlal Nehru University, Aalochana, the London School of Economics, UBINIG, the Indian Institute of Advanced Studies, Pune University, Banaras Hindu University, University of Dhaka, *Jamia Millia Islamia* University, University of Westminster,

Concordia University, McGill University, Duke University, the Doha Institute for Graduate Studies, Syracuse University, and the Communication University of China.

Sitara continues to be my guiding star, my sisters Munira and Karima have loved and supported me in ways too deep to untwine, in the ways only sisters can. David Hacker and Christopher Schweitzer have been incredibly generous, welcoming me without reservation whenever I arrived on their doorsteps. The warm-heartedness of all our extended families, Thobanis, Jiwanys, Hackers, Coxalls, Imirsids, Kassams, have provided me with care and sustenance, including much good food and too much good cheer, during the writing of this book. 'This book of yours, when *will* it be finished?', my aunty Laila admonished me far too many times to count, keeping me plodding on even during those times when I just wanted to run away from it. I thank you all, from the bottom of my heart.

This study would not have appeared as a book without the labour and support of Cavlan Erengezgin and Faisal Nahri, who went well above and beyond the call of duty in helping me clean up and format the manuscript to meet various deadlines. The comments of the anonymous reviewers helped me sharpen my focus and analysis; I am grateful for the time they have taken to read my work. Many thanks to Jason Mohaghegh and Lucian Stone, the Series Editors for *Suspensions: Contemporary Middle Eastern and Islamicate Thought*, for their enthusiastic support for this work. At Bloomsbury Press, Liza Thompson and Lucy Russell have been terrific to work with, their assistance has made the publication process so much smoother for me. My thanks also to the Design and Production Teams.

Arax Nazari's painting, which appears as the book's cover, captures perfectly the issues, relations and histories of violence studied in this book. I am very thankful for her generous consent for the use of this work.

I have received funding for this project from the Social Science and Humanities Research Council, UBC Hampton Fund, as well as UBC VP – Research Fund. I am grateful for this support.

The following publishers have kindly given their permission for reprinting early versions of the arguments presented in this book as cited below: *Feminist Theory*, *borderlands*, *Hypatia*, University of Toronto Press, Routledge and Between the lines. I would like to thank them for this support. A very special thank you to Copyright (c) 1970, 1992, Betty Shabazz and Pathfinder Press for use of Malcolm X's quote, and the *Journal of Islamic Sciences* for use of Talal Asad's quote, that are the epigraphs to this book.

All under-readings, over-readings, misreadings and outright errors are, of course, my responsibility. I knew I was venturing far afield: this had to be done.

Journals

'The Secularity of Empire, the Violence of Critique: Islam, Race and Sexuality in the Politics of Knowledge Production', *Hypatia: A Journal of Feminist Philosophy*. Vol. 32, No. 3. (Summer, 2017) 715–30.

'Empire, Bare Life and the Constitution of Whiteness: Sovereignty in the Age of Terror', *Borderlands*, Vol. 11, No. 1, (2012). 1–30.
'White Wars: "Western" Feminisms and the "War on Terror"', *Feminist Theory*, Special Issue. 8(2). (August, 2007). 169–85.

Book Chapters

'Race, Sovereignty and Empire: Theorizing the Camp, Theorizing Postmodernity', Bakan, A. B. and E. Dua (eds.) *Theorizing Anti-Racism: Linkages in Marxism and Critical Race Theories*. Toronto: University of Toronto Press (2014) 280–310.
'Vigilante Masculinity and the War on Terror', Tareq Y. Ismael and Andre Rippon (eds.) *Islam in the Eyes of the West*. London: Routledge (2010) 54–75.
'White Innocence, Western Supremacy: The Role of Western Feminism in the "War on Terror"', Razack, S., M. Smith and S. Thobani (eds.) *States of Race: Critical Race Feminism for the 21st Century*. Toronto: Between the Lines (2010) 127–46.

I believe in a religion that believes in freedom. . . . Any time I have to accept a religion that won't let me battle for my people, I say to hell with that religion.

Malcolm X[1]

The struggle for encouraging public virtue is opposed to an overriding interest in material accumulation, in securing what one enjoys as an individual against others who might covet what one owns. Fear is the dark side of greed, but greed isn't simply 'inordinate desire', it indicates the disease of a world in process of dissolution. Opposed to it is political struggle in a cause that transcends the fear of death and loss. This kind of politics does not accept the liberal state's claim to secular neutrality. Politics in this sense arises out of a desire to extend and defend a democratic ethos (that seeks to connect through relations between living things), rather than the liberal democratic state (that seeks to homogenize all that is subject to it). It is only struggle as a moral/religious effort (jihad), a struggle without fear of death but not a struggle for death, that can sustain a concern for the enhancement of common life for Muslims and non-Muslims, animals and humans, and that can confront contemporary global disasters generated by the lust for material gain and military power.

Talal Asad[2]

---

1. Malcolm X, *By Any Means Necessary* (Pathfinder, 1992).
2. Talal Asad, 'Muhammad Asad, Between Religion and Politics', *Islam & Science* 10, no. 1 (Summer 2012): 77–88.

INTRODUCTION

The quotes that open this book allow a glimpse into the temporal and spatial reach of Islam, and into the dynamic relation of the Muslim to this tradition. These comments also offer the faint outlines of a genealogy of the Muslim, and of their fraught relation to the West: '. . . when we accept Islam as our religion, that does not mean we are religiously wrong to reject the man who has exploited us and colonized us here in this country', Malcolm X noted.[1] Clearly, for this Muslim, there is no contradiction between Islam and the struggle against Man, a Western construct, who has everywhere wrought war, exploitation, and global disasters.

Islam and the figure of the Muslim make an uncanny appearance at crucial moments in the making of this West. Whether in the spectre of the Anti-Christ, false prophet or demonic blasphemer; Moor, Saracen or Turk; Oriental, Semite or Muselmann; or more recently, terrorist, Jihadi, Hijabi or radical Islamist, the constancy of this phenomenon is staggering.

This book is a study of the place of Islam and Muslims in the cultural-political formation of the West. In particular, it focuses on race and religion, gender and sexuality, those axiomatic relations which, although defined in various fields of contemporary scholarship as central to the constitution of the sovereignty, identity and subjectivity of the West, are rarely brought together in the same analytic frame. It is the contention of this work that the relations of power that have produced the 'West' found concrete expression in a striking desire for, as well as intense animosity towards, Islam and Muslims. Indeed, attempts to neutralize the power of Islam and thwart the ambitions of Muslims to realize futures oriented towards justice have been a structuring feature of the West in previous historical junctures; this is also the case in the politics of the present.

Using the war on terror as my point of entry, and contextualizing its reconstitution of the West in the *longue duree*, the chapters of this book examine how Islam and Muslims are pivotal to its making at each historical juncture. This introductory chapter begins with a broad outline of the conditions – contemporary and historical – that map the terrain of my study. I then discuss how the war on terror revealed not just the extent of the economic–political crisis of Western-capitalist globalization and its critical theoretical–political traditions but also the ongoing Muslim resistance to the futures charted by Western post/modernity. The final section of the Introduction presents the main contributions of this book to contemporary debates on the secular and the religious, on the sexual and the philosophical, by highlighting their linkages in an ongoing attempt to subjugate Islam and discipline Muslims into the racial and sexual regimes of the West.

From the vantage point of two decades of the global war, it is evident that the power of the West, such as it is, relies on the containment of at least two contesting forces: Islamist/Muslim resistance and anti-racist/colonial resistance. Although these are often treated as oppositional forces, I attend to the convergence between them by interrogating the popular representation of the first, Islamist/Muslim resistance, as rooted in 'religious' difference, and conversely of the second, anti-racist/colonial resistance, as arising from a strictly 'secular' politics. Situating race and religion in the same analytic frame, and defining their relationship as constitutive, not only overlapping, I unearth their doubled constitutionality within, and with the West. That is, I demonstrate how race and religion are mutually constitutive, and also how their nexus is constitutive of the West itself. Moreover, this nexus is thoroughly saturated with specific ideas about sex, gender and sexuality.

The construction of Islam as a 'religion of violence' and the conflation of Muslim with 'terrorist' during the early phase of the war on terror has received considerable attention. What has been less studied is how these constructs reworked the idea of the West as a cohesive entity, how they sutured over the ruptures wrought by capitalist globalization and particularistic Western nationalisms, evident in anti-globalization movements; these constructs also redefined gender/sexual egalitarianism into the distinctive cultural property of the West. Consequently, the relations among the contending constituencies within the West were reconfigured as were its global alliances and enmities. The war on terror thus gave new content, character and meaning to the idea of the West even as the crisis sparked by its invasions, occupations and proxy wars led to the undoing of an international order that had been in place since the mid-twentieth century.

Yet public discussion regarding the return of 'religion' to 'politics', the realm of the secular, in the early decade of the new millennium obfuscated what is a fixation with Islam and the 'threat' embodied by its adherents. As noted by Sayyid, 'Secularism as a discursive regime deals not with "objective reality" but with a specific constructed version of its object. It generates Muslims as permanently transgressive subjects, whose religious essence is constantly being undermined by the temptations of the political. As a consequence, Muslim politics becomes either a purely empirical designation or an illegitimate articulation.'[2] For all the talk of the return of 'religion', the numerous 'wars on terror' – global, national and local – demonstrate that it is Islam that is branded by Western nation-states and their allied regimes as a threat that is existential in nature, global in scope and apocalyptic in ambition.

If the 'threat' of religion pivots on Islam as absolute alterity, the issue of race has not been evacuated from this 'enemy' that is defined as global in reach. Indeed, the reworking of racial politics in the global war had consequences that would extend well beyond its initial racialization of Muslims, as well as of Islam, as evidenced in the subsequent rise of white nationalist movements across the West.

The crisis set in motion across the Muslim world by the global war was soon enough compounded by the crisis of whiteness within Western nation-states as ultra-right nationalist movements began the undoing of its liberal–democratic institutions. This phenomenon is widely defined as a populist expression of the economic anxieties of the working and middle classes 'left behind' in the institutions dominated by neoliberal-multicultural elites. The erosion of living standards and increasing poverty that resulted from decades of privatization is identified as sparking the racial resentments harnessed by right-wing populists whose objective it is to reinstate the white supremacist order. But this perspective delinks these white supremacist politics from the earlier assertions of Western cultural superiority by liberal, multicultural and left forces; it also glosses over the political impact of the defeats of the Western alliance in Afghanistan, Iraq and elsewhere in the last two decades of the war.

Moreover, the global war's construction of the figure of the Muslim as a fanatical enemy of modern values isolated Muslims from mainstream white communities *as well as* other communities of colour. This sequestering of Muslims as singularly backward looking and culturally oriented towards 'terror' drew many people of colour communities into the discourse of the global war, allowing them to claim greater proximity to the West on the basis of this shared antipathy towards Islam. The resulting demonization of Muslims *as* Muslims, however, proved to be the thin edge of the wedge that subsequently unleashed state and vigilante violence to further engulf Black, people of colour and Indigenous communities.

The West has, of course, never been a monolith. Its meaning, identity and culture are disparate and internally riven (white supremacist versus multiculturalist, neoconservative versus social democratic, etc.). The idea of the West also shifts in relation to the contestation of its power by the different communities seeking release from its suffocating grasp, including the colonized and Indigenous peoples of every continent. It is also the case that Western nation-states now face unprecedented competition *on their own grounds* from an economically vibrant China intent on extending its sphere of influence and a politically emboldened Russia contesting the US domination of the greater Middle East and Europe. Yet it is in 'Islamic terror' that the West identifies its existential foe; it is with regard to Islam that the most frenzied passions of the Western alliance are unleashed.

If war with 'Islamic terror' is the grounds for the contemporary reformation of the West, what are the historical antecedents to this relation of violence? What underlying logics and submerged histories are expressed in such emergence of Islam at the centre of Western cultural politics in the twenty-first century? In what registers has this relation of enmity been forged in the past?

In his study of liberalism and Islam, Joseph Massad shows how Islam is at the heart of Europe and has shaped its political culture. His argument is that it was in the projection of illiberalisms onto Islam since the eighteenth century that Europe constituted its 'liberalism'. Islam thus 'resides inside liberalism', it marks the difference and identity of Europe, and its claims to superiority. Constructed as intolerant, violent and so on, that is, the antithesis of liberalism, Islam came to symbolize the attributes that were disclaimed by the West. Massad's work demonstrates how the construction of Islam as illiberal functions in the global war, particularly with regard to the gender and sexual 'freedoms' proffered by liberalism. Moreover, he points out that Europe's Others also included Orientals,

Africans, Native Americans and Indigenous peoples to argue that these are all 'internal' to Europe by way of their exclusion. My argument, however, is that Islam has been constitutive of the West since its very inception, and not just by way of a relation of exclusion. Hence, the scope of this work has a longer historical span; it also argues that *racial* as well as *religious* enmity with Islam gave shape, form and content to the West, in gendered as well as sexual terms.

The foundational religio-racial logics of Western self-formation were fixated on Islam and centuries in the making, so that its hatreds of Muslims were already well in place by the late-eighteenth- and nineteenth-century construction of Europe's liberalism and its relations with its multiple others. These foundational logics of the West form a blueprint, an underlying pattern and structure, so to speak, of its self-making at successive stages. Moreover, the West's relations to its numerous Others is structured by their asymmetrical positioning within the national and global hierarchies instituted by Europe.

The role of Islam, and of religion, in the making of Europe has also been discussed, most famously, by Carl Schmitt, Jacques Derrida and Gil Anidjar, whose work informs numerous critical traditions. Schmitt used the concept of 'political theology' to underscore how Christian concepts continued to inform Western secular ideas and politics. He noted how Christendom's early wars with Islam initiated the rupture between theology and politics in the making of 'Europe'. Derrida took up Schmitt's ideas to show how war with 'the enemy' was the grounds for the emergence of Europe, for how Europe thinks itself, for the emergence of 'the political'. However, Derrida also drew attention to a lapse in Schmitt's distinguishing of the theological from the political, so that Islam is treated as a 'political' as well as a 'non-political' enemy of Europe.

Drawing on both Derrida and Schmitt, Gil Anidjar has studied the history of 'the enemy' in the making of Europe, in the making of its political philosophy. Drawing a distinction between the enemy and the other, he argues that Europe constructed both Jew and Arab as 'enemy', so that the relation of enmity came to 'constitute the condition of religion and politics'. Anidjar argues that the Jews were constructed as the 'internal', 'theological' enemy while the Arabs were constructed as the 'external', 'political' enemy; both were hence constitutive of Europe.[3] Moreover, having distinguished itself from both, Europe made this relation of enmity 'invisible' to itself. Anidjar goes on to analyse Derrida's *Politics of Friendship*, and its reading of Schmitt's distinction between theology and politics, to mean that, 'without an enemy, Europe would be a subject that "would lose its being-political"', that Europe '"would purely and simply depoliticize itself"' in the absence of war. Indeed, Anidjar further argues that in Schmitt's view,

> Europe, and with it, the political, 'nothing more and nothing less than the political as such . . . would no longer exist without the figure of the enemy', without *this* figure of the enemy that is Islam. If such is indeed the case, it would demonstrate, were it still needed, that Islam is not only at the source of 'our history', but also that it is one of the 'conditions' of the history that I am trying to read, that is, the history of the enemy, the Jew, the Arab.[4]

Islam is defined here as the condition of possibility for the politics – and political history – of Europe.⁵ What this concept of 'politics' might look like in an Islamic context is not a question that is taken up in this framing of 'Islam'.

Although such critical perspectives can help unpack the place of Islam in the making of Europe, it is notable that they take for granted a pre-existing 'Western' theological community that transforms itself into a political one in the war against Islam. Nor do they engage the Islamic tradition itself, or with Muslims as historical subjects. The 'Islam' and 'Moslem/Arab' they reference are thus neither substantive nor historical *in their own terms* or in any meaningful sense; lacking content, Islam and Muslims thus remain spectral, reduced to a backdrop in the central drama of Europe's self-making at the fraught interstices of its – always incomplete – theological/political binary, stuck between religion and politics. Although Derrida underscores the constitutive role of war with Islam in the political formation of Europe, towards the end of his life he nevertheless called for supporting those Muslims who advocate secularization of the Muslim world, as I discuss in more detail later in this book. Ian Almond included Derrida in his study of the 'new' Orientalists, noting that "what we have in Derrida's treatment of Islam is a proliferation of the different identities, each one the response to a certain textual need."⁶ My reading of Derrida's comments on Islam and Muslims certainly concurs with this view.

Anidjar's analysis of the Jew as Europe's enemy presents a complex reading of this figure, who, as he notes, is also often an Arab. But the figure of the Muslim is repeatedly collapsed into that of the 'Arab', it acquires no specificity in its own terms, or in its relation to Islam, in his work. The gesture of recognition is thus simultaneously a gesture of erasure. Yet the multifaceted relations of heterogeneous communities of Muslims to Islam are rooted in histories, visions, conflicts, hopes and desires that do not arc towards the West, its modernity or even its postmodernity. In short, the self-identification of these Muslims *as Muslim* matters.

Eschewing approaches of recognition-as-(non)engagement with Islam which dominate much critical scholarship on the global war, and which rarely move beyond Europe's self-referentiality, my study brings critical traditions rooted in anti-colonial and anti-racist praxis in dialogue with critical studies of Islam. Addressing specific aspects of the Islamic tradition that are relevant to my study, and centring histories of the racialization/colonization of Muslims, the relation of *this* Muslim to Islam is foregrounded in my reading of the Western tradition which relegates the Muslim to the status of phobogenic object and marks Islam for obliteration.

The depiction of Islam and the figure of the Muslim as demonic can be traced to St. John of Damascus (749) in what became "the first great Summa of theology to appear in the East or the West"; this work considered Islam to be heresy and its Prophet an evil imposter.⁷ Pope Urban II proclaimed Muslims 'an accursed race utterly alienated from God' against whom he launched the First Crusade (1095); these constructs are a landmark in the making of 'Europe'.⁸ In the Iberian Reconquista, Muslims were cast as *Saracen* and *Blackamoor*, racial degenerates whose perversity was carried in the blood; the destruction of Muslim rule and the presence of Islam in *al-Andalus* enabled the formation of the early-modern European nation-state.[9] The *Oriental* and *Semite* were produced as figures of despotism and degradation in the production of the global colonial order.[10] In the Nazi death camps, the appellation *Muselmann* was invoked by Jewish survivors to signify death, this figure subsequently traversed into the Zionist ideology of the Israeli settler state.[11] In the contemporary moment, the *Jihadi*, the *Hijabi* and the *radical Islamist* are routinely identified as the embodiment of global 'terror'.

These figurations of Islam and the Muslim have functioned in different ways at different moments in Western history – neither their content nor the needs of the moment were static. No less pertinent, these constructs were forged in tropes that are recognizably 'sexualized' and 'gendered' in their invocation of particular kinds of desire – fascination, fear, horror and attraction. Indeed, the overdetermination of Islam in racial/sexual tropes fetishized the figure of the Muslim as the site of a primal evil characterized by sexual barbarity, with the capacity to overwhelm the Christian subject's sensibilities and values. As this Christian, man and woman, gave concrete shape and meaning to such constructs in the attempt to 'protect' themselves from this phantasmal Islam, they 'Westernized' themselves in practices that led to the fusing of their sociocultural and politico-libidinal energies. The endurance of such fixation with Islam and the figure of the Muslim is evident in the transformations in sexual-gender politics set in motion by the war on terror which realigned relations between the state and its nation, the nation and its subject, and the West and the rest.

Furthermore, studies of the early-twentieth-century anti-colonial and anti-racist movements, which I consider antecedents to contemporary Islamic resistance, have generally overlooked the role of Islam. These movements compelled a transformation of the white supremacist global order in the post-Second World War period, yet much of this scholarship treats the gains made by colonized peoples in acquiring a measure of access to liberal rights, and to the reconfigured international order's signal institution, the United Nations, as a largely secular story.

The political ascendance of the United States in the remaking of this global order reshaped the racial politics of that nation as well as the international order with the effect of derailing the revolutionary potential of anti-colonial and anti-racist movements.[12] The assimilationist direction of US-dominated capitalism instituted a racial liberalism which fractured the radical internationalism of the Non-Aligned Movement following the Bandung conference (1955); such assimilation also countered the growing Soviet and Chinese influence in the Third World. During this period, Islam was either banished from the public sphere or defined as requiring modernization in the secularizing politics of most Muslim majority countries. This modernizing approach towards Islam as 'religion' – that is, a sphere disassociated from state, politics and economy – was led and internalized by Westernizing elites across Muslim societies.

Inclusion in this Westernizing liberal order through the extension of civil and political rights to previously enslaved and colonized populations also redefined white racial tolerance as normative to the new international order. In the settler colonial societies, including the United States and Canada, the development of multiculturalism led to shifts in their modality of governance of Indigenous, Black, Asian, Latino and other 'internally' racialized populations.[13] The resulting assimilation of these peoples into Western societies became internally and structurally linked to the destruction of the radical potential of the Third-World project.

The niceties of these liberal political concessions were shunted aside by the war on terror. Its targeting of the figure of the resisting Muslim revealed the hollowness at the core of multicultural inclusion as well as national independence, whose unravelling had escalated during decades of neoliberal globalization. The limits of the gains made by Muslim and other people of colour within the liberal international order *as well as* the depth of their integration into neoliberalism were demonstrated by the war on terror, which instituted violence as the modality of governance of Muslims. Such overt reiteration of older colonial/racial forms of governance, what Mbembe has named *necropolitics*, stripped Muslims of the liberal rights enshrined in the political-juridical order; the explicit sanction of 'new' invasions and occupations by the most powerful Western and non-Western nation-states made such violence the basis for the reorganization of their alliances. Moreover, the inscription of Islam as the sign of 'global terror' made the adherence of Muslims to Western values and cultural practices the *only* condition for their 'right to have rights', to use Arendt's words. The older racial binary between civilization and barbarism that had been discredited in the mid-twentieth century was thus reinstated by situating the figure of the resisting Muslim, marked for elimination, at the centre of the remaking of the international order.

Yet even as this war destroyed one post-independence state after another, Afghanistan then Iraq, soon followed by Libya, the US-led alliance's inability to win these wars galvanized epochal movements in these regions, including in Egypt and Syria, the most powerful of these led by Islamist forces. An array of Islamist movements – no doubt divided in their vision of Islam, in their historical specificities, in their ideological approaches and political commitments – led the insurgencies that challenged the Western invasions, occupations and proxy wars, throwing into disarray the post-independence regional balance of power, the global repercussions of which remain unpredictable. Indeed, the geo-strategic import of the Middle East, Central Asia, North Africa, and their control by native authoritarian regimes whose rule is underwritten by their Western allies, has only magnified as the global war expanded into newer territory and terrains, including sub-Saharan Africa and South Asia.[14]

The ramifications of the global war are also to be found in the growing divides within Western corporate, political and media elites. As the US-led alliance lurched from one monumental disaster to another, its Islamophobic and racist politics grew in intensity across Western nation-states; the simmering rage of white supremacists was harnessed by ultra-right movements to confront the ambitions and domination of their inclusionary and multiculturally minded neoliberal elites. Transforming the 'internal' national political landscape, this rise of xenophobic politics and extremist movements plunged the Western liberal–democratic order itself into an unprecedented 'internal' crisis.[15]

The effects of the ominous shifts mentioned above remain yet to be seen, but these are redefining trans/national alliances and enmities, forms of subjectivity and sovereignty in a fairly profound manner. What is clear is how deeply these effects are infused with the underlying racial/religious logics and gender/sexual politics of the long histories of the West. Yet it would be a mistake to take the contemporary expression of these logics and politics as being either the same as their earlier iterations, or as entirely novel.

Resistance to Western powers as well as their native enforcers reshaped the relations of Muslims to the West, especially after the Iranian revolution. The international crises sparked by such resistance also had transformative effects on social movements inside Western societies. The 'freedoms' offered and deployed by the neoliberal order to old and new formations of the left, to feminist, gay rights and other social movements, as well as to Indigenous, Black and people of colour communities promoted an assimilationism that has had considerable impact. Many of these communities, however, were to be caught in the backwash of the war on terror as well as its anti-Islamic ideologies. The seduction of these communities and movements into Western horizons eroded their liberatory ideologies and radical internationalism. This assimilation has been called into question by the racial violence now increasingly waged within the West, as it has by the Islamist/Muslim resistance that is not amenable to incorporation into either the hegemonic or counter-hegemonic orders of the West.

In the chapters of this book, I study particular aspects of Western cultural politics and processes of identity-formation to examine how these found expression in relation to Islam, and how they remain enmeshed in the religio-racial logics and psychosexual desires that constitute post/modern sovereignty and subjectivity. These logics, and their attendant forms of desire, I argue, are centred on phantasmic constructs of Islam and fetishization of the figure of the Muslim.[16] For the constitution of the Muslim as a phobogenic-cum-erotic object reveals more about the desires and obsessions that structure the psycho-social universe of Western subjects than it does about the Islamic tradition, or indeed about the historical experience or even contemporary practices of heterogeneous Muslim communities.

The attributes presently ascribed to Islam in the onto-epistemological traditions and political structures of the West bespeak a full-blown Islamophobia that has overtaken other elements of the Orientalist discourse. Yet such amplification of anti-Islamic praxis reveals just how tenuous is the West's hold over the global order. Its inability to destroy the power of Islam in shaping Muslim imaginaries has rendered Western power highly volatile and utterly unstable.

The Phobogenic object

I began this study with the following observation: power is exerted in myriad ways, the tradition of the wretched of the earth has demonstrated for some time now.[17] Those who fail to comprehend its shifting configuration do so at their own peril. Judicial and extrajudicial execution, pre-emptive and counter-insurgency wars, torture, occupation, collective punishment, mass rape, dispossession and destruction of family, home and community, these have been a staple of colonial regimes for centuries. As Fanon argued, the tradition of the wretched recognizes full well *how* these techniques of power *produce* these communities as such; Fanon also recognized how the violence of these techniques compels these communities into resistance. Yet the ideology of the global war reframed the Muslim – male as well as female – into such a charged object of fear and hatred that their status as emblematic of the wretched of the earth became obscured in the collective aversion directed towards them.

In the critical political and philosophical traditions of the West, however, power has been redefined as productive and performative, functioning in a manner that leaves its operations undetected.[18] Invasions, occupations, stress positions, death squads, vigilantes and mercenaries – these apparently remain foreign to the issues of concern in these traditions. This is not to say that the Western politico-philosophical tradition is not itself under a certain kind of stress; it is only to note that this stress, if one may call it that after Abu Ghraib, is of a different order. The stress – one might even call it a crisis – faced by the critical Western tradition arises from a phenomenon that remains unanticipated in its analytic frame – the resistance of its constitutive Enemy/Other.

How, then, to contend with the workings of power at a juncture wherein the discourse of terror has reshaped its prime modality of expression? How to account for the *fear* as well as the *desire*, the *revulsion* as well as the *pleasure* articulated to this modality?

The entanglement of rage, desire and terror became particularly acute in Western self-making as its combined forces remain unable to contain the power of Islam, or to assert control over Muslim societies. Despite the vast and unparalleled military, political and cultural resources amassed by Western nation-states, they have yet to bring Afghanistan or Iraq under their control. Or Palestine, Iran, Egypt, Libya, Yemen, Somalia, and the list goes on.

As mentioned above, the war's institutionalization of violence to destroy Muslim resistance revealed how fictive was their status as juridical, that is, politically legible human, subjects. The inscription of Islam as a stultifying force, religion of cultural barbarism, constructed this Muslim as embodiment of evil, hence the origin, cause and recipient of violence. The illusion that the wretched of the earth had secured access to the coveted status of the Subject in the post-independence world was thus dispensed with.

The evolving nature of this Western antipathy towards Islam came into sharp focus as the civilizational binary on which it relies was first imposed in the Bush Administration's clash of civilizations; refined in the neoliberal Obama Administration's slightly more nuanced distinction of 'good' from 'bad' Muslims; and then recast in the white supremacist policies – 'radical Islamic terror' – of the Trump Administration. The political fixation on the figure of the Muslim thus remained a constant feature. This thrusting of Islam into the position of the enemy of the human, along with the realignment of racial politics in the demonization of the resisting Muslim, also revealed the crisis in Western critical theory as the various trajectories that have underwritten the binary proved unable to engage Islam or Muslims *on their own terms*.

Contemporary Muslim resistance is rooted in earlier struggles against European empires, as noted above. However, the Islamic aspect of this resistance was eclipsed by the institutionalization of secular nationalism in the post-independence state, whether in its liberal, socialist or authoritarian manifestation. The global war demonstrates that older strategies of Islamic resistance did not die out, nor did they remain static; these clearly require sustained attention.

Scholars of the Middle East and the larger Muslim world generally identify the Islamic revolution in Iran as a turning point in the post-independence politics of Muslim resistance, a phenomenon commonly designated 'political Islam'.[19] The term speaks of a 'return' of Islam to the public realm of 'politics', it treats this as an unwelcome 'mix' that many consider historically regressive and reflective of the failure of Muslims to come to terms with the progressive, modern and secular age. The Iranian revolution, as well as other Islamist struggles, the popular argument goes, are driven by a pre-modern fanaticism, by the rage of disaffected and alienated Muslim men who grasp onto a fundamentalist version of their faith in a hopeless attempt to return to the glories of the past.

Yet attending to the historicity and particularity of these movements and politics points to a very different set of factors at work. The extent, range and form of Muslim resistance, as discussed more fully in the following chapters, is a far more complex phenomenon than its derision as backward-looking fundamentalism presents the case to be.

For one thing, the values, intellectual work and aspirations of the earliest proponents of Islamist movements were forged within the anti-colonial, nationalist and anti-racist politics of their times. Inspired by these forms of Islamic resistance, contemporary Islamist movements seized the political momentum at the end of the Cold War to challenge the symbolic and cultural geographies bequeathed them by European powers, as in the Sykes-Picot agreement and the Balfour Declaration. The designation of this resistance as fanaticism also obscures the point that contemporary articulations of Islamist politics have emerged in engagement with neoliberalism and capitalist globalization. Similarly, the Islamist awakenings in the Middle East and North Africa can be read as reactive to the war on terror. *But this is not all that they are.*

How far this Islamist resistance may have shifted the balance of power at the national, regional as well as international levels may not yet be entirely clear. What is clear, however, is that this Muslim resistance situates Islam firmly on the horizon of the possible political futures of the Muslim world.

Furthermore, this Islamist resistance is actively shaped by Muslim women, in its earlier anti-colonial and anti-racist articulation as in its present resurgence. Colonial powers considered their access to Muslim women as key to their control of the societies they colonized, a strategy well documented in studies of the various European empires, particularly the British and the French. In the case of Algeria, Fanon dissected colonial attempts to control Muslim women. He also discussed their crucial role in the success of revolution, with many of the women unveiling themselves to fight the French occupation. During the 1970s–80s, Leila Ahmed found young Muslim women in Egypt to be engaged in what she called 'a quiet revolution'; these women redefined the practice of veiling to signify their rejection of Westernization, a phenomenon found to be the case also in the Iranian revolution. These Muslims reworked Islamic values and practices as inspiration for their rejection of capitalist materialism and the growing corruptions of the secular state and elites. Islam, as these women experienced it, shaped their commitment to realize justice for their communities and for themselves.

In similar fashion, Miriam Cooke found that Muslim women were drawn into Islamist movements by 'the symbolic capital provided by the Qur'an and Traditions, or the authenticated sayings and deeds of the Prophet Muhammad that form the basis of Islamic law' and by their 'unprecedented importance' in the Islamic discourse. Embracing this discourse, these women were 'inventing ways to navigate between forced changes necessary for survival, a critique of globalized modernity, and a viable means of self-projection that retains dignity, morality and integrity'.[20] Claiming their own 'religious authority and social power', Muslim women were remaking their status within particular national and transnational contexts, as well as within global politics.[21] In the case of Turkey, Nilüfer Göle has shown how working and middle-class Muslim women used the practice of veiling as an assertion of their identity as *Muslim women* to make their claim to the public spaces previously denied them within the secular political, social and educational institutions of a modernizing society.[22] The Islamic resurgence has had a likewise galvanizing effect on Muslim women in the United States and other parts of the West to confront the Islamophobic and racist violence directed at their communities in the global war, but more on this later.

This post-independence resurgence of Islam shaped not only the politico-cultural context for the 9/11 attacks but also the subsequent uprisings across the Muslim world a decade later. In the case of the Islamists, their politics were shaped by the strategic alliances as well as violent conflicts between and within their movements, some linked to Iran and/or Turkey, others to al-Qaeda, many divided among themselves. These divisions were compounded by the post 9/11 transformation of al-Qaida; the strategies used by the Taliban; the rise of ISIS-Daesh; the role of Hezbollah in the carnage unleashed by the Assad regime against the Syrian population; the Saudi-led war in Yemen; the election of Hamas in Gaza; the blockade of Qatar, all developments that reflect the deep divisions as well as shifting alliances among the various Islamist movements and organizations.

The different trajectories of these Islamist responses, collusions and reversals sharply divided the Muslim world.[23] Although Islamist movements adopted various – even contradictory – strategies of resistance, these often proved highly controversial across the Muslim world. For example, the violence of ISIS, its enslavement and sexual exploitation of Yazidi women, appalled Muslim populations in the region and beyond, as did the destruction of Sufi shrines, sectarian attacks on minorities, violence against Muslim women. The shock waves these events sent throughout the Muslim world, including in the diaspora, will be of immense and no doubt lasting consequence. As the battles between the various

Islamist, secularist and nationalist revolutionary and counter-revolutionary forces rage on, the Islamic tradition and forms of Muslim being are being transformed no less profoundly than is the idea of the West.

With regard to Western epistemological traditions, however, the global war threw into sharp relief the depth of their investment in the idea of the West. This proved to be the case even with regard to critical theory, that radical element in the Western philosophico-political corpus influenced by Marx's searing critique of capitalism. Reworking the 'old' Orientalist and racializing constructs of Islam into the 'new' discourse of Islamic terror, developments within critical theory demonstrated how deeply this tradition was tied to its Eurocentric moorings. Critical theorists addressed various aspects of the global war: some exposed the illegalities and corruptions of the national security state while others focused on unpacking US imperialism, yet most of this work demonstrated an inability to move beyond Eurocentric frameworks.

The long-standing view among left and critical theorists has been that anti-racist politics amount to little more than an identitarian distraction, misguided if not outright reactionary, unless articulated in the former's languages and politics. This perspective has started to change with the glaring escalation of racial violence and white supremacist politics, and with the intensification of the resistance organized by the Black Lives Matter and other anti-racist movements. Yet the refusal to rethink their Eurocentric paradigm leaves these critical theorists even less equipped to engage critical race theory, or the Islamist intellectual traditions, than were their early-twentieth-century counterparts in taking up the revolutionary anti-colonial and anti-racist critiques of the time *on their own terms*.[24] Instead, left and critical theory contributes in its own fashion to cement dominant constructs of Islamic resistance as medieval fanaticism – if not outright fascist – in toto.[25] No less significant, left and critical theorists remain largely silent on, or reduce to tokenistic reference, the vital contributions of the radical Black, Indigenous and Third World – including Muslim – traditions to the development of Euro-American high theory, whether in its leftist, critical, feminist or poststructuralist variant.[26]

Poststructuralists and postmodernists – who pronounced the end of metanarratives upon being confronted by the Other's metanarrative of the colonial/racial underside of modernity – charted new ground in the global war in their reiteration of the abstractions and universalizations that are the staple of the Western tradition. These practices are expressed in the development of concepts such as 'bare', 'precarious', 'grievable' and 'disposable' life. Their newfound fixation on the acute vulnerability of the Subject is formulated in alignment with the dominant framing of the global war, these concepts overlook the religio-racial specificities of the catastrophic brutalizations of the present. While such developments advance representations of the Westernizing subject as essentially innocent, they also attribute irrational violence to the hate-filled Muslim.[27] It is ironic how closely such self-representation within critical theory mirrors the sense of victimization articulated to the white nationalisms of the ultra-right.

Dominated by intellectuals who overlook the particularity of their own whiteness, of their own positionality within their nation-state, and of the rootedness of their epistemic traditions within Western power, these theoretical advances render illegible the anti-colonial and anti-racist politics of the resisting Muslim. Moreover, these disciplining concepts soon became indispensable to governmentality, as is well recognized by those Islamists who argue that at the heart of their opposition to Western power is 'the western process of thinking – how it [the west] "thinks about thinking"'.[28]

In the case of the feminist tradition, this hit an impasse during the closing decades of the twentieth century when its poststructuralist variant pronounced the impossibility of the feminist political project. This development was, among other things, a reflection of the (non)engagement of Western feminists with the anti-racist and anti-colonial *feminist* challenges to hegemonic feminism's universalizing claims and ambitions.[29] As a distinct and cohesive field of intellectual thought and political activism, feminism centres the primacy of sex/gender in shaping the social world. This privileging, as feminists of colour were quick to point out, comes at the expense of universalizing white feminism while rendering its own racialization invisible. The concept of intersectionality as developed within Black feminist theory was used by these critiques which drew attention to how race, class, nation and so on, are crucial elements in the construction of gender and sexuality, yet western feminists' recent adoption of intersectionality focuses only on class, gender and sexuality, while race and colonialism continue to be sidelined.[30]

The ongoing feminist refusal to rethink the feminist tradition through sustained and substantive engagement with the divides of race, coloniality, nation and so on, keeps the orientation of feminist futures within the orbit of Westernity. Moreover, the feminist insistence on reading what are basically Western constructs of patriarchy and heteronormativity as transhistorical and transcultural allow Western feminist appropriation of the historical experiences, struggles and consciousness of Indigenous, Black and Third-World women to bolster hegemonic narratives of white gendered/sexed victimhood. By shunting aside the perspectives, politics and priorities of heterogeneous women's communities across time and space, the majority of which have been forged in abolitionist, anti-colonial/racist and Indigenous traditions, dominant feminism's colonizing practices allows this to be represented as the singular emancipatory politics for 'woman'. The core feminist stance, that is, that feminism is the only legitimate politics up to the task of 'saving/liberating' women inevitably leads to the construction of Muslim women, among others, as always-already failed gendered objects – they may be *female*, they may aspire to the status of Woman-as-Subject, but they are not *feminist* – unless integrated through the idiom of feminism into Westernity.

The situation is not quite so bleak in the anti-colonial/racist traditions that still remain rooted in their earlier revolutionary antecedents. Indeed, the work of these Indigenous, Black and other anti-colonial thinkers, including Muslim, remains the most promising of attempts to rethink the structure of war-making in late-capitalist coloniality. Even this field can be perilous, given that the 'chronic drift of theory towards Europe' is difficult to resist; the danger remains acute that 'a single-minded dimensionality, one that while having a compassionate eye towards its Other, is still incapable of de-totalizing our intellectual production and immunizing the discipline against surrendering once again to the good old gravitational pull of Eurocentrism'.[31] The discipline in question here is Comparative Literature, but the critique is equally applicable across the social sciences and humanities.

Postcolonial theory, with its invaluable attention to ongoing forms of coloniality in pre- and post-independence nationalist politics and culture, unfortunately has little to say about the transformative potential of *contemporary* Islamist movements.[32] In other words, postcolonial theory 'is still operating within the limits of colonial history and has not yet gone beyond a parasitic form of critique'.[33] As a consequence, despite 'its roots in the colonized Arab world (Fanon, Said, Memmi)', postcolonial theory has not been immune to 'the siren call of Eurocentrism', such that most scholars from the colonized world 'are left with nothing but footnotes of our histories'.[34]

Critical race theory – defined here as rooted in the abolitionist and anti-colonial/anti-racist traditions, not the self-admittedly reformist project of Critical Legal Studies – faces similar peril.[35] Shaped by earlier revolutionary politics that were internationalist in their outlook and scope, this tradition's founding figures identified race as produced by/in the violence of slavery, colonial genocide, dispossession and indentureship; race was here considered foundational to the making of the global capitalist order.[36] The vision and revolutionary praxis of the early theorists linked the revolutionary movements in the Americas with the pan-Africanist and pan-Asian anti-colonial struggles. That radical tradition was overrun in the post-independence and post-Civil Rights era by a liberal anti-racism, such that an integrationist ethos made significant inroads. Consequently, critical race theorists seem to have largely washed their hands off the possibility of revolutionary internationalism, and off the labour of imagining a solidarity that is global in scope. In its contemporary iteration, critical race theory has been integrated into the post-independence nation-state system, for the main; it has yet to come to terms with the eclipse of its earlier revolutionary drive, let alone with the contemporary phenomenon of revolutionary Islamist politics. The figure of the Third World revolutionary may well have all but disappeared from the political field, and the revolutionary potential of the Islamist goes at best, ignored, and at worst, caricatured as fanatical hatred.[37]

A significant challenge is how hamstrung critical race theory is by the secularist field in which it has historically developed, and within which it remains entangled. Faced with the apparent choice of engagement with Islam and resisting Muslims, or (by default) with Westernizing culture and values (even if the promise of these have yet to be fulfilled), the dominant trend within critical race studies has been to yield to the latter's secularizing paradigm.

It is, however, important not to loose sight of how some critical race scholars working with/in left and feminist/queer traditions are pushing these to their limits; it is in this work that one finds the cutting edge of these traditions. Interrogating the effects of the now entrenched liberalism within these 'progressive' fields, these critical race scholars eschew the privileging of the national frame – with its rights-based framework – as the means to radical change. Yet even here one finds, with relatively few exceptions, a reluctance to take up the question of religion *in its relation* to race. Overlooking this relation, in my view, leaves the sharpest of critical race theorists trapped in the field of Western secularity which, as I argue in this book, reproduces the very racial coloniality this tradition so adamantly opposes. Secularism, as Talal Asad has persuasively argued, is best approached as a political doctrine of modern governance,[38] yet most critical race theorists assume the secular to be a self-evident, penultimate principle for social transformation as they overlook its historical role in reproducing colonial/modernity.

Islam, in short, is often a blind spot for even the critical scholar/activists most committed to confronting Western imperialism and building solidarity with Muslim communities under siege. While they contest the racialization of Muslims, the issue of Islam itself goes unaddressed. This situation is mirrored in the field of Islamic Studies, where a singular focus on Islam as 'religion' leads to the neglect of race and coloniality. Indeed, the designation of Islam as 'religion' is itself a colonizing gesture. As a result, ahistoric and un-self-reflexive approaches to the category 'religion' are hegemonic, such that most debates focus on the hermeneutic in/accuracies of contemporary Islamist readings of the Qur'anic text and the *hadith* tradition.

In the process, the historical experience of heterogeneous communities of Muslims, like the dynamism of their relation to Islam, goes unexamined. The disciplining of Islam/ic Studies into the Westernizing academic apparatus through essentializing approaches to 'religion' is not unrelated to the earlier attempts of European powers to domesticate and neutralize the transformative power of Islam. That the 'goodness' of Islam is now adjudicated even in the field of Islamic Studies by the willingness of Muslims to subjugate themselves – their hermeneutics, values and practices – to Western cultural and epistemological traditions speaks to such historical continuity.[39] The unquestioning adoption of Western conceptual frameworks in the study of Islam has put this field on 'the path of intellectual slavery' in the estimation of an erudite scholar of Islam.[40]

Perhaps it is in the epistemological-political field that the global war has enjoyed its greatest success. This is far from insignificant, for it includes the widespread conflation of 'radical Islam' with 'terror' that has normalized the militarization and securitization of the nation-state system and sanctioned violence in the governing of Muslims. The dissemination of the above mentioned discursive practices across the political, cultural and academic fields may well prove to be among the most lasting accomplishments of the global war. The crystallization in these fields of the idea that an ahistoric fanaticism distinguishes Islam, and that this is the threat embodied by resisting Muslims, mobilizes public support for violence as an *ethical*, even if sometimes regrettable, inevitability.

The intimacy of terror, the power of desire

The war on terror marks a new juncture in the formation of the West, its forms of sovereignty and subjectivity. Many studies are now available of this war, many also link this to the crisis of contemporary capitalist globalization.[41] *Confronting Inordinate Desire* is distinguished by its centring of the imbrication of Islam and

Muslims in the socio-economic, psychosexual and political-epistemological processes that constitute the West. Moreover, I track these processes by attending to how they are infused with desires, phantasies as well as hatreds fixated on Islam and Muslims which are rooted in the idea of the West since its very inception and which have animated the making of its subjects, nations and states.

I began this study with these initial questions: How are Muslims and Islam represented in North American mainstream media coverage of the war on terror? What (in)securities and (in)stabilities can be discerned in the constructs of the 'West', 'Islam', 'terror', 'sex' and 'race' that shape these depictions? What kinds of masculinities and femininities are deployed through such exertions of power?

But as I started working with these questions, the impact of left, feminist and queer politics and cultural production on mainstream media became immediately evident. Interesting enough, the ideas and perspectives emanating from these 'progressive' sectors seemed all too often to share the core assumptions of the neoconservative architects of the war, particularly with regard to 'the' West (vulnerable), Islam (fanaticism) and Muslims (hate-filled, misogynist, etc.). My study thus expanded organically to focus on when, where and how the assumptions informing these progressive interventions (public statements, political campaigns, scholarly writings, online and digital postings, documentaries, films, television shows and radio interviews, etc.) dovetailed with those of ruling elites, particularly in their assertion of Western cultural superiority. Tracking the scope and sites of this convergence led me to study the historical antecedents of Western self-formation. Once I began working with this larger timespan, all directions seemed to me to point towards Islam, and the figure of the Muslim, as the focal point of Western antipathy. This study is the result of my work within this broader framework, its main contributions are clustered around four interlinked arguments: (i) the early Latin-Christian fixation with Islam shaped the religious as well as racial logics of Western self-making, such that Islam became the organizing principle of the emergent West; (ii) early Christendom's ideas about women and sex were 'Westernized' through the projection of sexual monstrosity onto the Muslim, such that these constructs shape the gender and sexual regimes of the West; (iii) the transformation of feminist and queer politics through the gendering of Islamophobia is incorporating women as well as gender and sexual minorities into the Westernizing/colonizing regime of power; (iv) and the war on terror has consolidated the reformation of the West as Judeo-Christian – in secular *as well as* religious terms – in a relation of enmity with Islam.

My first set of arguments arises from rethinking the formation of the West in light of Latin Christendom's desires as well as antagonisms towards Islam, and from questioning the dominant tendency to treat 'Europe *and* Islam' as a relation between two independently and fully formed antagonists. Most scholarship on the topic defines 'Europe' as a transparent – in geographical, religious or sociopolitical terms – entity, as sui generis, a self-generating formation that emerged upon the decline of the Roman empire through forces and processes that were largely internal.[42] Islam, on the other hand, is defined as 'religion', one that originated in the Arabian heartland and was codified in a distinct set of laws and culture to be found across a conglomeration of Islamic empires and societies. In this familiar narrative, Europe is considered exceptional for developing its entrepreneurial and innovative spirit[43] through a modernity whose foundation is 'the' political-secular. Europeans came to dominate Islamic/Muslim empires as a result of the former's inner dynamism and the latter's innate cultural stagnation, with Islamic inertia having stalled sociopolitical as well as scientific-technological advancement.[44]

This narrative carried over into much of the scholarship on the global war.[45] That Orientalists such as Bernard Lewis and Samuel Huntington would reinvigorate the West/Islam binary, and that this framing would be materialized by the Bush Administration's war on terror may be less surprising than the reproduction of this binary in a conversation between Derrida, the founder of deconstruction, and Mustapha Cherif, a scholar of Islam. The exchange between them focused on how to reconcile this binary, it is worth a close read. Offering as alternate to the Islam/West binary the idea of the 'northern' and 'southern' shores of the Mediterranean, which is defined as a 'divided unity', the exchange as recounted in the text, *Islam and the West*, demonstrates how firmly fixed remains the binary throughout the conversation. Instead of being dislodged, the binary was re-inscribed in geographical fashion. Derrida's reluctance to address his own relation to the Muslim (he refers to the name 'Arab' instead) despite repeated and direct questions, particularly in light of his self-naming as 'Arab', is a point to which I return later in this book.

In place of the binary formulation of 'Europe and Islam', I trace the embryonic emergence of 'Europe', that is, 'the West', in the late-medieval/early-modern Crusades against Islam. It was through these wars that the power of Latin Christendom was extended and consolidated over the Christianizing community that would be constituted as 'Europe'. Islam was thus formative – as object of desire and hatred– of Latin Christendom, and subsequently, of Christian-Europe. Furthermore, Islam was the structuring principle of this Europe at key junctures in its subsequent incarnations, namely, in the Iberian Reconquista that defeated Muslim rule in 'Europe' and facilitated the emergence of the early modern state; in the colonial period wherein the subjugation of the Islamic empires led to the global domination of the European empires; in the imposition of the secularizing nation-state system across the post-independence Muslim world concurrent with the founding of Israel as a Jewish state, whose colonization of Palestine destabilized the Middle East; and most recently in the global war against 'radical Islamic terror'. The corresponding figuration of the Muslim at these junctures include the Anti-Christ and blasphemer; Saracen and Moor; Oriental, Semite and Muselmann; and Jihadi/terrorist. Each figure functioned within a particular kind of religio-racial logic to shape these specific junctures.

Latin Christendom's successive waves of antipathy towards Islam and Muslims extended the former's reach and power into and across 'Europe', for this entailed the Christianizing of the heterogeneous populations thus drawn into its domain. The Latin Papacy's configuration of Islam as demonic heresy is well documented,[46] as are its condemnations of Islam's Prophet as a satanic imposter and Muslims as followers of the 'false' Prophet. In such a casting, 'Mohammedism' (as Europeans named Islam well into the twentieth century) was less a 'religion' than a satanic plot. Pope Urban II's launch of the Crusades (1095) to conquer Christianity's 'holy lands' in the East then under Muslim rule underpinned the consolidation of the power of the Latin Papacy over Eastern Christianity and advanced the Christianization of a Europe-still-to-come.[47] And although the Latin Church demonized the category 'Muslim' in crusading against them, Muslims neither demonized Christianity nor considered the Crusades an existential war, for Islam revered Jesus as a prophet and Muslims well recognized the differences between the Byzantine Christians (Rum) and the Latin ('European') Christians (Franj).[48]

While the Crusades, particularly the Fourth, continued the attempt to destroy Muslim rule, these wars allowed the cleansing of what the Latin Church considered the 'contaminations' of the Eastern Church, then based in Constantinople, as well as the Jewish 'heresy'. The Crusader wars lasted over several centuries during which period they galvanized the communities, men and women, who would identify themselves as 'Christian', and later as 'Europeans', and reshape accordingly their identities, cultures, political affiliations and forms of social being and belonging. The creation of a new order was underway and the Crusades 'represented Western or Latin Christendom's attempt to seize control of the perceived core of the known world. . . . Here begins the first endeavour by a representative of (a still barely self-conscious) Europe to transform the continent into the world's axial civilization. Here begins the quest for subjective Eurocentrism.'[49] This 'Europe', however, was itself being brought into being, not simply becoming 'self-conscious' of itself.

The Latin Church's pronouncements that shaped the Crusader imaginary into the later Middle Ages continue to inform contemporary representations of Islam in significant ways (i.e. the idea of the clash of good and evil; the image of a 'false' Prophet in the Danish cartoons; the idea that Islam and Muslims have taken what rightfully belongs to the West, such as oil in the Middle East and the land 'promised' to Israel, etc.). Moreover, the racializing symbolism of these Crusader constructs would become absorbed into the political philosophies and scientific theories of modernizing Europe. While it is certainly indisputable that the language and meanings ascribed to 'race' and 'religion' during the Crusades differ significantly from their later treatment within Western modernity, the alterity itself, and its key characterizations as conceived of in the early Latin-Christian theological imaginary, reverberate into the present.

The designation of Islam as existential enemy made it the organizing principle of the collective consciousness of this 'new' entity, Europe, in religio-racial terms. With Latin Christendom's ideas about 'heresy/evil' and 'satanic/demonic' materialized in the phantasmic figure of the Muslim, this figure gave concrete shape and meaning to Europe's ideas about itself. The theological-racial matrix that mapped Latin Christendom's identity on the symbolic plane was thus literally mapped onto the geographical plane, as in the invasions of the 'holy lands' and the subsequent destruction of Islamic rule in *al-Andalus* with its expulsions of Jews and Muslims which produced this geographical 'Europe' as a religious configuration. The subsequent Orientalization of Islamic empires and acquisition of control over their territories; the expulsion of Islam from the public realm in the post-independence secularization of Muslim societies; and the wars presently associated with 'terrorist havens' and protecting 'homelands' all mapped out this symbolic alterity onto the territorial plane.

My contention here is that along with everything else that Islam is, it remains *the organizing principle* of the West in existential terms, of its identity, values and culture. Moreover, the sets of associations – religion, culture, language, body, geography, nation, civilization and so on – that shaped the modern concept of 'race' also found meaning in and through this Western relation of enmity with Islam. These foundational logics – at the nexus of race with religion – became a blueprint of sorts for the successive reformulations of this West.

The religio-racial logic that structured early Europe was a dynamic that shifted in relation to the changing conditions that shaped and are reflected in the major developments that mark the history of its formation. 'Race' and 'religion' thus remained mutually constitutive in shaping this Europe's ideas about the ordering of the world – human salvation and damnation; human evolution and degeneracy; freedom and despotism – within its theological, biological, cultural and civilizational paradigms. This conjoining of race and religion is evident in the contemporary idea of the West as a historically cohesive and contiguous *political-cultural* entity, with an overall consistency even if the entity is internally riven (by religious, racial, gender, national, class and imperial conflicts and rivalries). The idea of the cohesiveness of 'the' West holds considerable political sway in the present, as does its reduction of Islam and the figure of the Muslim to a death-centred ethos. Such equations attest to the longevity of the early ideological underpinnings I am outlining in broad strokes here and will discuss in more detail in the following chapters.

If the socio–cultural imaginary of the novel formation was centred on an amalgamation of ideas about religion and race, these ideas were explicitly gendered and sexualized. Gender was 'one of the primary ideas around which medieval society was both structured and imagined', Lambert has found in her study of the period; Crusades literature 'participates in this ordering of its world' by, for example, transforming the definition of the knight 'from a merely military description to a highly charged socio-political role' and by redefining the idea of 'poor' such that this term was 'not simply concerned with wealth or even the possession of ready cash, but carries a range of social and religious meanings'.[50] The meanings of sex and gender were shifting during this period, especially given the often fervent participation of Christian women in these early wars against Islam.

The issue of gender brings me to the second cluster of arguments made in this book, which centre on the gender and sexual regimes of the West. The gender and sexual constructs of Europe, I argue, can be tracked to early Christendom's identification of the 'evil' of Islam as located within sexual degeneracy. These ideas about Christian chastity and sexual virtue during this period, and the necessity to guard these from the Saracens, sexualized the Muslims as constitutionally perverse. The gendered/sexual formation of Latin Christendom reflected, of course, a particular Christian tradition, its beliefs and practices, yet the production of these *as* European, that is, their 'Westernization', was mediated by the eroticization of the Muslim as a figure of sexual and gender depravity. Such Christian preoccupations – recall that sex had already been conflated with sin, sin with woman, and repression of both with salvation in this tradition – shaped the lens through which Latin Christendom framed Islam. Not surprising, this lens incited a great deal of horror at what these Christians deemed to be sexual monstrosity. Sexual temptation, it should be remembered, was earlier equated with devilry in this theological paradigm, and fixing this evil onto the figure of the Muslim confirmed the 'truths' of the Christian faith, which considered sexual chastity (i.e. repression) as the highly fraught path to Christian deliverance. Muslims – considered the embodiment of the satanic sexual conspiracy against God – threatened the Christian not only with sexual corruption, but through this, with eternal damnation.

It is indeed striking how often gender and sex feature in the early Christian depictions of Muslims, such absorption would only become more intense as Europeans ventured deeper into the 'East'. Statements of revulsion at the corporeality and carnality of the Muslim are abundant in the historical record and predate by centuries the 'invention' of 'Sexuality' which Foucault located in the late eighteenth and nineteenth century. These early statements, which became authoritative over time, signal more than a projection of Christian sexual anxiety onto Muslims. Inciting desires as well as revulsions, the texts reveal an implicit recognition that Christendom's regime of heterosexual chastity and binary gender order was an anomaly, seemingly at odds with the practices among heterogeneous Muslim communities. The zeal with which the early Christian commentators – followed later by European explorers, traders, missionaries, travellers, colonial administrators, governesses, anthropologists and so on – felt compelled to express outrage at what they deemed 'Eastern' barbarism suggests how deeply destabilizing were their encounters with Muslim societies.

Drawing on scholarship that interrogates the binary organization of sexuality and gender, I argue that it was in its wars with Islam that the sexual and gender regimes of a particular Christian tradition became *Europeanized*, such that 'Islamic' sexual degeneracy was the primal scene for the formation of the *westernizing* gendered and sexualized subject: '[T]he time in which you are living is an effeminate one, weak like a woman, and it also inclines to oppose injustice, which is attempting to destroy justice in Lord's vineyard', Hildegard of Bingen warned the King of Germans, Conrad, during the Crusades.[51] The German Abbess, believed by her many followers to be a Prophetess, is identified as an early feminist icon by Christian and spiritually inclined feminists.

Philip, the Count of Flanders who went to Jerusalem to crusade as penitence for his sins, wrote to the Abbess asking for advice on undertaking the perilous journey. Philip's sins included complicity in the murder of a knight, beaten to death for sexual impropriety. Hildegard's advice was to go, fight and 'hold out against the infidels' as long as possible.[52] As Tessera explains in her study of the exchange between the two, the Abbess 'urged the count of Flanders to reflect on *infidelitas*: this condition embodied in the pagans' fighting against Christ and his church as instruments of the devil, was a visible symbol of the sinful condition marking humankind as a whole after Adam's fall, and marking every human being who was determined to depart from God by his own will'.[53] The influential Hildegard thus promoted the Crusades as the opportunity for Christian redemption from their sins of the flesh, not to mention from the sin of murder; in her view, '[t]he count of Flander's own story followed the symbolic pattern of Adam's fall too'.[54] This opinion was 'also announced all over Western Christendom by Bernard of Claivaux's well-known epistle 363 when he preached the Second Crusade'.[55] The Crusades thus offered these Christians the chance to purge themselves of prohibited desires and atone for sexual sins through the projection of the condition of sinfulness itself onto the Muslim.

The idea of Muslim existence as this-worldly manifestation of sin produced this figure as primarily sexual; in this Western gaze, sex, or more to the point, sexual degeneracy, became the defining aspect of Muslim life. Crusader wars were hence entangled with the sexual/gender purification deemed essential by Latin Christendom to the spiritual redemption of the Christian world. The war with Islam thus gave the violence itself an erotic and sexual charge, for it made the killing of Muslims a means for the conquest of the crusading Christian's own sexual desire. The emergent theologio-social imaginary was thus a peculiarly sexualized landscape in which early Western ideas about gender and chastity were fused with desire for the conquest and extermination of the Muslim as an act of sexual purification. At a later juncture, these ideas would travel into the Protestant/bourgeois values of monogamous heterosexual respectability and become an essential element of modernity's calculations of ab/normality, morality, health, hygiene and so forth. These discourses of sexual respectability and unhealthy transgression would also carry over into the biological-scientific discourses of secularism even as the fixation with sexuality infused ideas about Oriental degeneracy and despotism.

The fascination with 'Islamic' sexual perversion and gender disorder has found expression yet again in contemporary constructs of the cultural barbarism and innate homophobia of the Muslim male and the sexual imprisonment of the veiled Muslim female. The reworking of the idea of Muslim perversity in the global war continues to be disseminated in public, political and scholarly debates that contrast 'Islamic' sexual repression with the 'sexual freedom' that is now considered a core Western trait. The phantasm of the Muslim thus looms over each phase in the transmutation of Western sexual/gender politics – whether as hyper-sexual 'Mohammedan', virile Moor, impotent Oriental or homophobic Islamist. My point here is that the transit of Crusader expressions of Christian gender/sexual ideologies, values and anxieties into those of Europe was never a matter 'internal' to the West, shaped *only* with regard to relations between Christian/European men and women. Indeed, relations between Christian men and women were reworked in their collective sexualization of Islam and of the figure of the Muslim. These early practices laid the groundwork for the development of the gender and sexual regimes of the West at later junctures.

My reading of a number of early Christo-European statements shows that the sexualization of the Muslim began with the Prophet of Islam himself, and it was articulated in 'heterosexual' as well as 'homosexual' terms. The statements are permeated with horror at the physicality and sexual potency projected onto the Black/brown Muslim body; they would become regulatory with the deepening, over time, of their integration into the theological and political imaginary of a Europe-in-the-making. The almost verbatim expression of sexually phantasmic projections onto the Muslim one finds in these texts come down through generations of European intellectual thought; the reworking of these constructs can therefore be taken as pedagogical practice, their invocation of horrors at the Muslim body as steeped in all manner of sexual-gender travesties was part of the Westernizing mechanism.

Consider one such example, penned by Hrostvitha of Gandersheim, who described in lurid terms the existential threat presented by the Muslim male to Christian chastity in *al-Andalus*, that is, within territorial 'Europe'. The tenth-century Christian nun is often taken to be a feminist foremother. In her poem glorifying the martyrdom of a Christian boy, Hrosvitha presents a phantasmic image of King 'Abd ar-Rahman as 'stained with bodily lust', his sword 'aflame' as he sets out in hot pursuit of the Christian boy, Pelagius.[56] Describing in graphic detail the struggle between the Muslim king and the Christian boy, the nun valorizes the boy's sexual chastity as evidence of his 'love of God' and denounces the king's (homo)sexual desire as confirmation of his satanic nature. The poem is fuelled by, and in turn fuels, Christo-European phantasies about Muslim men as perverse sexual aggressors, in clearly identifiable homo-heterosexual registers. The poem implicitly speaks of the nun's sense of her own, and of the Christian community's, sexual vulnerability in the face of the sexual threat being collectively projected onto the 'evil' Muslim king, imagined as irresistibly attracted to Christians.

That such texts were penned by Christian women as well as men is no insignificant matter. The women's statements point to a gender alliance, a 'sexual' coming together, so to speak, of Christian women with men. With the labour of both conjuring these sexual phantasms, one finds their works encoded with expressions of sexual and erotic desire in the idiom of dread, fear, excitement and terror. The range and tenor of such statements, and the extensive period over which they were produced, archives the processes by which these Christians were constituting their 'religious' subjectivity *as* gendered and sexual, their chastity and spiritual purity threatened on the terrain of the religio-racial 'difference' of the Muslims. The projection of grotesque virility onto the male Muslim body transformed it into a site for the working out of the specific sexual enticements to be constrained, the chastity to be cultivated, publicly at least, as the means to Christian salvation. At a later stage, the ambition would be to adhere to civilized and modern codes of sexual conduct. The figuration of the Muslim that comes down these centuries is that of an unnaturally potent sexual object, an anxiety-producing threat that elicits the authors' – and their audiences' – defence of their own identity into the rigidly gendered and sexual binaries that would characterize the West.

Moreover, these sexual phantasms of Muslims foreclosed their access to the respectable manly and womanly virtues being produced as distinctive of the chaste, moral and civilized life. Exalted as the civilizational property of the West, the constructs of 'masculinity' and 'femininity' one finds in these texts are saturated with Christian-Europe's religio-racial values. Muslims were hence always already produced as sexually perverse, their 'masculinity/femininity' always already detestable in these representational strategies.

Feminist historians have studied the participation of Christian women in the Crusades as well as the Reconquista. They have found that these women organized military/religious orders during the Crusades and worked to inspire, support and care for male Crusaders; the women also took over, established and expanded economic activities in the territories previously held by Muslims, as in *al-Andalus*.[57] Reading the historical accounts of these women in the eleventh to thirteenth centuries against the grain demonstrates how, as their activities aided and shaped the construction of Europe-as-Christian, they simultaneously fashioned the women's identities as victorious, albeit gendered, subjects of the new order.

In the colonial period, European women would seek, and acquire, access to the erotically charged Black/brown Oriental/Muslim body, male and female, through the politics of feminism. European women travellers, for example, supplemented the late-eighteenth- and nineteenth-century Orientalist narratives of the gendered/sexual life of Muslim/Orientals that were produced by European men, Meyda Yeğenoğlu has argued. Extending Said's reading of Orientalism by attending to its 'latent' as well as 'manifest' aspects, Yeğenoğlu studies the narratives produced by Western women in Turkey during the Ottoman Empire. Using their own gender identity to enter the inner spaces of the harems, European women contributed to the exoticization and eroticization of the Muslim woman, seen by many of the writers as then enjoying greater sexual freedoms than European women. These women writers, influential and well connected in their own circles, thus extended the reach of their male compatriots, Yeğenoğlu argues. In the process, the women expanded their own gendered power over the Muslim world, male and female, through the politics of Western imperialism as well as feminism.

The Western preoccupation with the 'sexuality' of Muslims remains unabated as is evident in the cultural politics of the global war. What distinguishes the contemporary fixation with revealing the 'truth' of Islamic culture in the sexual/ gender perversions of Muslims is that disgust and contempt have become the dominant mode of Western erotic expression. Correspondingly, the idea of the sexual chastity of the Western subject, particularly 'woman', has been supplanted by the idea of sexual and gendered 'freedom' as crucial to the emancipation of this subject, an ambition defined as sorely lacking in the case of the Muslim woman.

The extent to which fascination with the 'sex' of Islam shapes the treatment of Muslims is evident in the sexual brutalization of the Muslim body at Abu Ghraib; the defence of gender/sexual freedoms against the 'threat' of Islam; the hijab bans; the focus on the sexual frustration of the female suicide bomber; the de-radicalization projects aimed at young Muslim women, and so forth. Yet despite the constancy of public displays of the forms of violence and disciplinary practices employed to teach Muslims, *male as well as female*, lessons in 'civilized' sexual and gender attitudes, unpacking how Islamophobia organizes the linkages between Western gender regimes and its technologies of war has yet to enter the Western feminist/queer analytic and political project.

Said argued that the Orient was 'feminized' within the Orientalist discourse, but the complexities of the gender/sexual politics to which he pointed have yet to be fully explored. Gender/sexual constructs certainly provided the architecture for the Orientalizing imaginary, but their binary casting, like their formulation of masculinity and femininity as oppositional and conflictual, was, of course, rooted in a *particular* Christo-European ordering of social life. This binary was universalized by its institutionalization in the administrative structures of the colonial bureaucracy, and later in the post-independence state as Muslim societies were drawn further into the orbit of Western power by projects of modernization. That this binary is now taken for granted as the normal order of life even by Muslim communities, feminists, scholars of Islam and historians of the Muslim world attests to the powerful hold of Western sexual culture over the global imaginary. Islam can only feature as sexual deviance in such an imaginary.

The gendered formation of the Orient/al was, in many ways, a paradoxical affair. The Muslim male was emasculated as impotent and effete, but this construct was in uneasy tension with this figure's simultaneous hyper-masculinization as bestially endowed and rapacious. Said's observation of what he considered the 'feminization' of the Orient/al is likewise complicated, for colonization entailed the racial domination of the Muslim man –*as male* – by the European Man. Departing from Said, my argument is that the gender/sexual dimensions of Orientalism relied on the constitution of the Muslim male *as a figure of failed manhood*, a failure marked simultaneously by *excess* as well as *lack* of proper masculinity. Both deficiency and surfeit function as measures of inadequacy in relation to the masterful and controlling masculinity of Man, the Western Subject.

In other words, the masculinity of Man, the politicized human subject, was racially constituted in the global field as regimented and regimenting, weaponized and prosthetic. To read the subjugation of the Oriental/Muslim male as his 'feminization' is to overlook how Western masculinity itself was constructed as the universal mark of Man in relation to the inadequate masculinities He discovered across the global field; His bringing under control these 'Other' males who were not quite as highly evolved confirmed His own masculinity. The subjugation of the Muslim male was thus in his production in the register of *masculinity* as a failed specimen. If the evolution of Western Man was confirmed in his superiority over savage male life forms, the inferiority of the Muslim male lay in his (perpetual) inability to rise to the former's exalted status. The Muslim male thus symbolized a savage (Islamic) manliness within the phallogocentrism of the West.

Yet Said's point regarding the feminization of the Orient does provide an important clue in thinking through how 'femininity' itself became associated with the condition of colonial subjugation and occupation. If 'feminization' symbolized the condition of colonization, this postcolonial condition could not have been the same as the pre-colonial 'femininity' of 'the' Muslim woman. In other words, the femininity ascribed to the Orientalized Muslim woman – the outcome of colonization-as-feminization – cannot be uncritically subtended into the pre-colonial Islamic world. My proposition is that the colonial invocation of an abject Islamic 'femininity' can therefore be more accurately described as the inscription of Europe's religio-racial power in a *gendering* idiom. This fixing of the Oriental(ized) female as perversely gendered (exotic, promiscuous or abject) constructed her as a particular kind of target for control in colonial discourses, albeit such control was represented as a form of 'freedom'. In my view, it would be a misreading to take the 'femininity' produced through colonization (conquered, subjugated, submissive, etc.) as the expression of innate Muslim 'femininity', as a pre-existent condition in the Islamic world. Interrogating the production of this 'femininity' in colonial discourses allows for a critical rethinking of the impact of the gender/ing sexual/izing regimes of the West in the historical construction of the status of 'the Muslim woman' as abject, a condition which is presently attributed to 'Islamic' misogyny.

The cultivation of properly feminized roles for Oriental/Muslim women was a key concern of colonial administrators and missionaries; the task was undertaken by European women as well as men. In the coveted positions of missionaries, governesses, writers, teachers and so on, Western women were incorporated into the civilizational mission and granted considerable authority and force. From these positions, they represented the power of the West and legitimized it in gendered terms. Constituting themselves as modern women gave them access to such power, and in the process, access to the Muslim male and female. One sees a parallel with contemporary feminist reconstruction projects.

European women eventually carved out an extensive public role for themselves in the governing, educating and modernizing of Muslims, particularly in disciplining the females into the gender/sexual norms of the West. The point here is that with 'gender' being the site for the articulation of colonial 'difference', Muslim women, like the men, were produced as failed gendered subjects, a condition inherent to their racialization. The histories of nineteenth- to mid-twentieth-century colonial societies demonstrate how serious a project was the 'feminizing' of the Oriental/Muslim woman, which entailed disciplining her into Western norms of domesticity, heteronormativity, reproduction, hygiene, child-rearing and so on.

A particular obstacle encountered by Westerners in the 'feminization' of the Muslim female, that is, in her transformation into a facsimile of the Western Woman, was, of course, the act of veiling. This has since become a symbol of oppressed femininity, of sexual slavery and misogynist violence in the global war. The contemporary preoccupation with unveiling, firmly tied by feminists to the 'liberation' of the Muslim woman from Islamic culture, is hence but a contemporary articulation of the long-standing Western mission to civilize Muslims. The veil, considered to conceal the inner 'truth' of Islam, is seen to make inscrutable the 'real' nature of the Muslim woman. In her refusal to unveil, that is, to be subjected to the scopic regime of the *phallic* order of a West that insists on her 'feminization', this Muslim woman remains undisciplined, impenetrable, that is, *unfeminizable.*

The colonial inscription of the meaning, roles and values of sexual/gender relations incorporated Muslim men and women, families and communities, into the alien and alienating forms of 'femininity' and 'masculinity'. Nationalist reformers enthusiastically took on this project of incorporation by advocating the development of 'modern' man and woman, companionate marriage, and other Westernizing norms, albeit to different ends. As postcolonial scholars have demonstrated, nationalist reformers became particularly invested in constructing the 'new' woman – traditional yet modern – out of the remains of the colonial order.[58] This colonial imperative is also discernible in the abundant contemporary feminist, queer and human rights campaigns which extend the Westernizing gender/sexual regimes deeper into the lives of Muslims.[59] It should be noted here that Muslims are considered delinquent subjects not only in queer registers, but also with respect to heterosexuality, for Muslims have yet to meet the standards for heterosexual normativity in the Western adjudication of Islam (i.e. harems, men with four wives, genital mutilation, etc.).

The deficiencies of Muslims in this regard are even now considered innate to Islam in Western discourses of sex and gender. The earlier imposition of these genitally oriented discourses in the Orient locked Muslim males and females in a gender binary that remade relations among them as conflictual and oppositional, in nature and in their socio-economic interests, setting them on a collision course. Muslim women's well-being could now be defined as *naturally* in conflict with that of Muslim men, and *naturally* allied with those of Western women, in colonial as well as feminist discourses so that both elicit particular kinds of attention and labour.

The issue of feminism brings me to the third cluster of arguments made in this book. Gender moved to the centre of global politics as the Bush Administration made 'saving' Afghan women a foreign policy objective.[60] Most feminists and human rights advocates largely welcomed this development, while those opposed to US imperialism were alarmed that the Administration had 'hijacked' feminism to advance its neoconservative objectives. My reading of a range of feminist engagements with the war on terror – expressed in campaigns, theoretical treatises, popular books, political statements, films, documentaries and so forth – lead me to conclude otherwise.[61] Feminist rhetoric most certainly permeated the post-9/11 political language of the US and allied states, the argument that the war would 'liberate' Afghan women proved highly persuasive in mobilizing Western publics, especially women, to support the invasion of that country. The US state's (proto) feminist rhetoric also enabled the Western alliance to identify women's equality as a core Western value, in relation to a 'terroristic' Islam which promoted the hatred of women. However, the argument that feminism was 'hijacked' could not account for why and how feminists themselves were advocating and mobilizing public support for the war, why secular forms of misogyny receded into the background, or why feminists endorsed and deepened the idea that women's equality was a paramount Western value and that this was the key factor in the invasion and occupation of Afghanistan. Indeed, as I have argued elsewhere, the feminist contribution to the demonization of Islam and Muslim men as hyper-misogynist actually grounded Islamophobia within feminist politics to legitimize a racial-colonial war.

The idea of global sisterhood was also recuperated by many feminists to mobilize women's support for the war. As the notion of a common cause between Western and Afghan/Muslim women in opposing 'global patriarchy' became popular, campaigns against Islamic backwardness and the misogyny of Muslim men was picked up by numerous women's organizations while campaigns against US state violence disappeared from view. Such a global sisterhood had previously been discredited by Black, Third World, Indigenous and other feminists of colour who argued that any feminist solidarity based on such a notion only served to obscure the privileged position of Western women within the gender-racial hierarchy. The reinvigoration of global sisterhood by white feminists, a number of women of colour pointed out, not only popularized the idea that feminism (global sisterhood) was an 'antidote' to Islamic backwardness, it also dovetailed with the foreign policies of the Western alliance by extending the war's Islamophobic discourse. Some anti-racist and postcolonial feminists even linked such feminist support for 'fighting Islamic misogyny' to the 'saviour complex' that had shaped earlier Western feminist interactions with Third World women, a phenomenon famously dubbed the 'toxic effect' of imperialism by Gayatri Spivak.

I take up these feminist interventions in the war not to rehearse the critique of 'imperialist feminism' that was so richly developed by anti-colonial and anti-racist feminists in the decades preceding the global war.[62] Nor am I interested in critiquing the feminist politics of solidarity that reiterate a moribund sisterhood which allows white feminists to appropriate the experiences of Third World, Indigenous, Black and other women of colour to bolster their own claims of gendered victimhood. These critiques are certainly worth studying, particularly given the growing number of Muslim feminists who now embrace such outdated notions of sisterhood in their designation of Islam and Muslim men as incorrigibly misogynist and queerphobic.[63] Instead, my study of feminist and queer engagements with the global war interrogates what these reveal about the present state of feminist and gender/sexual politics. My readings of these politics demonstrates that feminist engagement with the war has grounded the idea of Western cultural superiority within the terrain of gender/sexual politics. I argue that this intervention has enabled feminist and queer politics to be situated at the forefront of the ideology of the global war, in political as well as epistemic terms. In other words, feminist and queer discourses have become strategic components of the colonial/imperial discourse of the global war and in the process, reinvigorated the relation of feminists to Western nation-states.

This realignment of feminism with the idea of Western exceptionalism arises from the profound crisis that arose within feminist politics during the closing decade of the twentieth century. The crisis was sparked by, among other developments, the contestation of the power of Western feminism to speak for all women by Black, anti-racist, Third World and Indigenous women's movements. These counter-hegemonic feminist politics laid bare the conviviality between Western feminism, colonialism and multicultural neoliberalism.[64] The universalization of (white) feminist politics, these critiques charged, aligned white women with the structures of power that oppress and exploit racial minority women in the West, and the majority of the women in the Global South. Read in this light, the Islamophobic discourse of the global war presented an opportunity for Western feminists to reclaim their lost ground by inscribing feminism, and gender and sexual egalitarianism, as the cultural property of the West and thereby override the growing counter-hegemonic critiques they faced. Feminist representational strategies and theoretical reworking of gender politics in the global war, I therefore argue, re-stabilized the idea of the West, reenergized its racial/colonial ideologies in gendered idioms, and enabled feminist and queer activists to represent themselves as embodiment of the highest values of Western culture.

The feminist gendering of the war on terror reasserted the authority of Western feminism over the struggles of Other, including Muslim, women, and in the process, countered the anti-racist deconstruction of the idea of the West. Consequently, feminists were soon on the front lines of the ideological as well as geographical battlefields of the global war. The feminist gendering of Islamophobia not only echoed the anti-Islam polemics of the early Christo-European women, often in very similar, if not the same, language, it also enabled feminists to explicitly re-Westernize themselves by shunting aside anti-racist/colonial politics in a moment of global crisis. The state and vigilante violence that feminist advocates of the global war have helped direct towards Muslims, male as well as female, has not been of much concern within feminist debates to date.

Western feminists, however, have had to contend with the anti-imperialist and anti-Islamophobia activism of Muslim/Islamist women following the launch of the war. Consequently, some feminists responded by giving new life to outmoded constructs of Islamic 'barbarism' while others developed novel concepts to respond to the shifts in national and global political cultures. Many of these feminist concepts, such as 'new Semitism', 'gender apartheid', 'precarious life', 'grievable life' and 'feminist foreign policy', now dominate the feminist and queer analytic field. These theoretical developments are defined in this book as gendered advances within the *Westernizing* religio-racial praxis being tracked in this book, for they have produced a new lexicon for feminist and queer intellectual and political activism which, while extending the epistemological reach of the Western tradition, also situates feminist and queer subjects at its forefront. Feminist epistemic practices now regularly represent the gendered/sexual Subject (woman, queer) as embodiment as well as champion of the tradition's highest values.

These developments in feminist and queer politics pivot on their construction of Islam as a gender/sexual threat and can be tracked on two fronts: first, in the feminist representation of the white gendered/sexual Subject as 'precarious', 'vulnerable' to Islamic terror on the basis of her gender identity, not political affiliations; second, in the racializing – if not outright racist – representation of Muslims as sexually repressed, of Muslim women as passive objects of rescue and of Muslim men as hate-filled misogynists. These representations simultaneously produce the feminist/queer subject as the 'real' target of irrational Muslim violence and project the extension of Western gender/sexual norms as the 'solution' to the present global crisis.

These feminist and queer representational strategies obfuscate the colonial/racial divide reinstituted by the global war, they also mystify the Westernizing impetus embedded in contemporary feminist thought and praxis. I show how this is the case by presenting a reading of an exchange among a number of scholars/public intellectuals on issues and events explicitly related to the global war. Critiquing how feminist intellectuals take up and negotiate Muslim-centred, anti-Islamophobia and anti-racist critiques of the war's ideologies and practices by locating themselves squarely within the Western tradition, I argue that even as they draw upon its authoritative power, they rework the tradition itself to neutralize these anti-racist critiques. Given the high political stakes of the issues taken up in this exchange, my focus is on how the epistemic authority of the Western tradition is reasserted in the register of feminist and queer politics to derail critiques of this tradition. Such feminist reworking deepens the colonizing drive of the West, it also empowers the feminist/queer subject to speak in its name to reinstate her position of privilege.

In the case of Muslim feminists, my study finds that many adopted westernizing feminist approaches to denounce Islam and Muslims. Advancing their own inclusion into Western nation-states through what they present as 'insider' accounts of Islamic cultural barbarism, such Muslim feminist engagements display a remarkably unself-reflexive embrace of bourgeois values and politics to project cultural backwardness onto their lower-/middle- and working-class co-religionists. Reading these Muslim feminist approaches in the context of the class struggles within Muslim societies shows how the now dominant representations of the majority of Muslims as culturally backward is the condition that makes possible the Muslim feminist's representation of her own identity as 'modern' and 'civilized'.

Representing themselves as 'insiders' to the Muslim world, many Muslim feminists claim an authoritative position to express their conviction in the superiority of Western values by way of their emulation. This 'insider' position was previously known within the anthropological tradition as that of the native informant, it is now much celebrated within feminist and human rights circles as the 'authentic' voice with direct access to the truth of Islam. Where the mid-twentieth-century Islamists (Sayyid Qutb, Ali Shariati, Zaynab al-Ghazali, etc.) engaged with revolutionary Third World as well as Marxist thought, and with the gender politics of their times, to think through and rework their postcolonial allegiance to Islam, the popular interventions of Muslim feminists studied in this chapter lack such rigorous engagement with even feminist, let alone anti-colonial or anti-racist feminist, critiques. Instead, their sensationalist accounts of rape and sexual violence condemn all Muslims as misogynists and remain mired in an un-interrogated investment in liberal feminism.

The labour undertaken by contemporary feminists – Western and Muslim – to discipline Muslims into Westernity has produced feminism as the *only* legitimate grounds on which the Muslim woman can be recognized. Western feminist interventions that seek to disrupt the dovetailing of feminist politics with imperialist power are few and far between[65]; these are relegated to the margins of feminist politics as intellectual curiosities. As such, they are unable to gain traction enough to disrupt the hegemonic feminist narrative of Islamic barbarism.

In short, if the feminist contribution to the Islamophobic discourse upholds Western cultural politics as oriented towards gender-sexual equality, it does so to leave the colonial/racial politics of the war unaddressed. This is the case even as the white supremacist backlash in the US turned on feminists and blew apart the racial liberalism which had shaped that nation-state's politics. The overt anti-feminism of these ultra-right forces has left feminists in a state of turmoil, such that many are turning even more strongly to a defence of Western liberalism.

The fourth and final set of arguments in this book centre on the formulation of Western identity, culture and politics as Judeo-Christian – in *religio-racial* as well as *secular-cultural* terms – in the global war. This transformation entailed the reconfiguration of Jews as essentially white and Western, of Islam as singularly anti-Semitic, and of Muslims as the enemy of Judaism, along with Christianity, secularism and modernity.

The assimilation of Jews into whiteness began to take shape in the post-Holocaust remaking of Euro-America. The integration of European Jews into US whiteness is evident, Brodkin Sacks argues, in what she identifies as their construction as 'model middle-class white suburban citizens'.[66] She credits this transition of European Jews into whiteness to the upward class mobility of Jews and other 'Euroethnics' within an expanding post-war US economy that offered new opportunities for education, employment and professional advancement; changing immigration policies; and most important, the GI Bill of Rights (1944) which functioned as an immense 'affirmative action' program. I want to suggest that such narratives are but partial accounts of Jewish socio-economic and political advancement, which became a central component of the post-war narrative of Western exceptionalism. For this opening up of whiteness and nationality to American Jewish communities – a pattern replicated across European nation-states – took place in conjunction with, and was constitutive of, the formation of the West itself as Judeo-Christian in the post-Holocaust era.

If the Holocaust was a seminal moment that laid bare the genocidal consequences of the historical enmity of Christian-Europe with Judaism-Jews, it was also a moment that ruptured this relation of enmity by subsequently enabling the acceptance of Jewish survivors into Western nation-states, by recasting them as Europeans, citizens and nationals, that is, Westerners. This momentous transformation can be discerned in the post-Holocaust acceptance of Euro-American Jewish communities as culturally, racially and religiously compatible with the West, and in the post-Holocaust foundation of the nation-state of Israel through the colonization of Palestine and its peoples. The condition of possibility for these changes, I argue, is to be found in the Nazi camp, and more specifically, in the 'hidden' yet omnipresent figure of the *Muselmann*.

Until well into the mid-twentieth century, Western identity and culture were defined as a conglomeration of Christian, white, Aryan, liberal and secular in contrast to Orientals and Semites, that is Muslims and Jews, as well as Black, Indigenous and other 'degenerate' races. These forms of alterity gave ideological content and material grounding to the self-constitution of the modern West, particularly with regard to the 'Orient', as Said, Massad and others have discussed. Drawing on their work, my reading of the culmination of the Christo-European animosity towards the Jews (commonly identified as beginning with their 'rejection' of Christ as Messiah) in the Holocaust attends to the religious as well as racial logics at work in the Nazi camp.

As is well documented, Jewish communities were subjected to religious persecution as well as racial hatred in Europe throughout its history. Discrimination against them was codified in the laws, policies and practices of Europe's modern nation-state from its inception (from the expulsions of Jews from *al-Andalus*, to recurrent anti-Jewish pogroms, to the rejection of the European Jews fleeing Nazism, etc.). Anti-Semitism towards the Jews was thus a constant feature in Euro-American history leading up to the Holocaust, despite short periods of respite and notwithstanding the accomplishments of individual Jewish intellectuals, scientists, doctors, entrepreneurs and so forth.

Anidjar has analysed the historical construction of the Jew and the Arab as enemy of a Europe that constituted itself as 'political'.[67] To recap his argument, the Jew was defined as an internal-theological enemy ('enemy of Christ') and the Arab the external-political enemy (the Crusades) in Europe's making of itself. Yet in interrogating this relation of animosity towards Jews, Anidjar stops short of studying how that enmity was transformed into affinity, in religious as well as political terms, such that the figure of the Jew became integral to the formation of the West and its domination of the post-independence global order. Unfolding over half a century, this change altered quite fundamentally the cultural, political and religious values and identifications of Euro-America, as well as its racial politics and forms of whiteness as inclusive of 'Jewish-ness'. These affiliations were also remade at the global level with Israel now a crucial partner in the remaking of the international order. The very identity of the West was itself thus transformed as Judaism became part of the intellectual heritage of the West, a valuable source of its cultural identity, and a strategic partner in the making of its future, a partnership cemented in the global war on terror. Indeed, Jews have been neither the 'theological' (see, for example, Christian Evangelical fixation with eschatology, Christian-Zionists, etc.) nor the 'political' (Israel as the only 'democracy' in the Middle East, a socialist experiment, etc.) enemy of the West for some time now. These changes, however, had a deadly repercussion for the figure of the Muslim, for it is this figure who came to stand as the singular *existential* enemy – in religious, racial, cultural as well as political terms – and thus ground the formation of the West as Judeo-Christian.

Studying the two sites vital to the making of the Judeo-Christian – first, the reshaping of Jewish identity in the Nazi camp; and second, the reshaping of the Middle East by Israeli settler colonialism – I highlight how these transformed the relationality between the figure of the Jew and of the Muslim, and of both to the West. Departing from Anidjar, I define the camp's violent internal splitting – within the figure of the Jew – of the 'European' from the 'Oriental' as a fundamental remaking of Jewish identity, thereafter binding it to the West and its whiteness. At the centre of this rupture stands the figure of the *Muselmann*, the name given to those Jews on the verge of death in the camp; this was a figure of decay and horror. In the post-Holocaust period, the figure was projected onto the Palestinian, who, like the *Muselmann*, was reconfigured in the Israeli imaginary as the sign of death

– that is, 'terrorists' bringing about their own deaths and 'anti-semites' who would bring death to the Jewish people.

The coming integration of Europe's Jews into whiteness is signalled in this figure of the *Muselmann*, which fractured the category 'Semite/Oriental'. *Muselmann* was the term used in the camp by the Jewish inmates as well as the Nazi guards to refer to those who were on the verge of death. Reading Giorgio Agamben's work on the 'remnants of Auschwitz' against the grain demonstrates that this figure did much more than define the relation of the Jewish survivors of the camp to those who perished there. Agamben identifies this *Muselmann* as a 'limit figure', a figure crucial to understanding the fraught issue of morality and ethics within and beyond the camp.

Asking why it was the case that *Muselmann* was the name given to the Jews who perished in the camps, I make the case that this figure symbolizes the split that sundered apart the European from the Oriental *within* the Jewish inmates, that is, it represents the split between the 'European' and the 'Semite' in the identity of the Jews in the camps. The figure of the *Muselmann* thus became available as the lone signifier of religio-racial degeneracy, the quintessential death-oriented Oriental, to the Jews who clung to their European identity to survive the horrors of the camp. Consequently, the Jews who survived the camp did so as Europeans; they subsequently entered into whiteness and as such acquired/were granted the status of the sovereign Subject, while the Jews who perished did so as *Muselmann*, the figure of racial decay and symbol of the death of the 'Oriental Jew'. The previous racial designation of the Jew-as-Oriental was thus projected solely with full force onto the figure of the Muslim. Although internal to the Jewish self, this split reveals not only the religio-racial politics of the Nazi genocide but also the deadly nature of the religio-racial politics that were to afterwards be directed towards the Muslim/Arab in the colonization of Palestine and the destabilization of the Third World.

The post-Nazi resolution of the crises of Western anti-Semitism in the acceptance of European Jews was accompanied with the founding of the Israeli state. This new nation-state enabled Europe to cleanse itself of its responsibility for the genocide of the European Jews, it also ensured the new settler colonial outpost would counter the then unfolding Arab – and larger Third World – revolution. The establishment of the Israeli nation-state was thus of apiece with the shifting religio-racial politics of Europe, it was also of apiece with the extension of Western power into a Middle East that was in the throes of anti-colonial revolutionary change.

With the racial embrace of the Jews and the creation of the Israeli nation-state, the Palestinian/Muslim/Arab was designated the singular repository of 'anti-Semitism', as both Said and Massad have argued; my debt to Said's and Massad's work on Palestine runs throughout my study of this monumental shift in the historical formation of the West. The deadly political violence within Europe that congealed in the figure of the *Muselmann* marks a crucial moment of rupture in the identity, culture and politics of the West, its effects would reverberate deep into the Middle East to split and counter the revolutionary politics of pan/Arab, pan/

Islamic and pan/Asian nationalism as well as the larger Third-World project. The defeat of this Third World project set the stage for the subsequent neo-liberalization of the global economy and the intensification of the Western penetration of the Middle East, Africa and significant parts of South and Central Asia.

European anti-Semitism reached unprecedented levels in the Holocaust to create an epic crisis *within* Europe, that this crisis occurred in the same moment as anti-colonial and anti-racist movements gained political clout across the colonial order and within Euro-America to challenge the white supremacist discourses of the West is no coincidence. These movements shattered the West's self-proclaimed racial-moral authority as well as its political legitimacy: the significance of this factor is neglected in much of the Holocaust scholarship. This is not the case with scholars working within anti-colonial and critical race traditions, but their work is either silenced or pushed to the margins.[68]

The view that Jewish presence polluted a West that identified itself as Christian *and* Aryan, secular *and* liberal, informed state policy, public culture, as well as popular sentiment across the Euro-American world as anti-colonial movements were gaining ground. Although the level of anti-Jewish hostility and tolerance undoubtedly varied and fluctuated across these nation-states, the genocidal politics of the Nazis were forged in this larger context, shaped as much by the colonial interests as the religio-racial logics of Europe. The fascist variant of these ideologies that exploded with such force within Europe thus drew upon centuries of anti-Jewish pogroms as well as the colonial genocides, and also directly involved the entire colonial world, along with what would become the global superpowers, the United States and the Soviet Union, into the Second World War. The industrialized killing of six million European Jews; the deaths of millions of other Europeans including other racial and sexual 'degenerates', gays and lesbians; the mass starvation of Eastern Europeans; the anguish of the camps' survivors; the politics of the collaborationist regimes; the destruction of European communist movements, these were among the major legacies and traumas of the Nazi regime within Europe. This genocide had an indelible effect on Jewish consciousness, history, identity, politics and culture, and the Holocaust came to be defined as the single most powerful racial tragedy of Europe, beyond comprehension and compare, by European Jews as well as non-Jewish Westerners. The racial-colonial amnesia infusing such a designation of the Holocaust ruptured the previous Jewish solidarities with anti-colonial and anti-racist movements and wrote out of the historical record the devastating effects of this war on the nascent Third World.

The de-Orientalization of the Jew and the re-Orientalization of the Muslim as the 'real' figure of racial-political degeneracy shaped the post-Holocaust remaking of the Western order, they seeped into the anti-Arab racisms harnessed by Israel to counter the Palestinian struggle and by the West to advance the politics of oil. The religio-racial processes of settler colonialism and imperialist exploitation thus set in motion would eventually culminate in the war on terror. For the development of the Israeli nation-state relied not only on the ongoing genocide and dispossession of the Palestinians, but also on the migrations of Euro-American Jewish settlers into this site after the European empires had been compelled to withdraw from the region. The Palestinians, thrust into the condition of statelessness and transformed into the object of Israeli/Zionist hatred, were emblematic of colonized populations but were instead construed as hate-filled anti-Semites and Muslim fanatics. The integration of the US and European Jews into whiteness, the advancement of Euro-Israeli settler colonialism into Palestine, and the undermining of the post-independence nation-states, with their vision of South–South alliance, were thus processes that were internally and inextricably linked.

At a moment when Euro-American nation-states faced the powerful 'internal' challenge of anti-racist and communist movements and that of decolonization from the Third World, the establishment of Israel introduced a disruptive Western-oriented presence in the resource-rich and strategically located Middle East, a region that was itself in turmoil as mass movements struggled for Pan-Arab/Asian/African, and Islamic, unity. The support of Euro-American nation-states for the Zionist project was thus with a long-term view to securing its influence, now under US leadership, over these regions. The combined effects of the subsequent Israeli wars of aggression, the politics of oil (with a collaborationist Saudi Arabian regime at the centre), and Western covert action (including, for example, the overthrow of Mossadegh in Iran, Allende in Chile, Sukarno in Indonesia; the assassinations of Patrice Lumumba, Malcolm X, Martin Luther King Jr. and others; and the blockade of Cuba after the missile crisis, among other such interventions) derailed emergent possibilities for decolonization in the region and beyond for decades to come.

US involvement in the Middle East during the second half of the twentieth century, its access to, and control of, the region's vast oil reserves in the context of the Cold War only magnified the import and significance of its support for Israel. Moreover, as McAlister has shown, the Middle East had even earlier become essential to the cultural processes involved in the making of US national and Christian identity, for in the US nationalist imaginary, this region was the birthplace of Christianity and the site where the 'truths' of the biblical narratives were 'seen' and 'confirmed'.[69]

Israel's occupation of Palestine redefined the political landscape of the Middle East, introduced new sources of conflicts which redirected political priorities, resources and alliances in the region (in the Arab-Israeli War, invasion of Lebanon, the two Intifadas, the Gaza war, etc.). Despite the ongoing Israeli seizure of territory, and its invasions and wars in the region, it was the Palestinian/Arab/Muslim who was identified by the Western powers as the source of a conflict supposedly rooted in ancient hatreds and innate anti-semitism. In the Western imaginary, the Palestinians' struggles against occupation and for the right to return, and the larger Muslim world's against imperialist domination were, particularly after the Islamic Revolution in Iran, constructed as caused by Arab cultural backwardness, Islamic fundamentalism and Muslim racial degeneracy. This was a view confirmed by what experts soon described as the rise of 'political Islam'. The formation of the Palestine Liberation Organization, the Iranian revolution, the emergence of Hezbollah in Lebanon, the growing strength of the Muslim Brotherhood in

Egypt and the formation of Hamas in Gaza, were all responded to within Western nation-states by their conflation as Islamic/Muslim fanaticism. Israel remained the privileged lens filtering Western engagement with these developments across the Muslim world, whether these societies were led by religious or secular forces, whether they be authoritarian, nationalist, socialist or Islamist in scope, whether they worked within the sphere of electoral politics or took to armed struggle.

The coming together of Euro-American (Christian-secular) and Zionist (Jewish-secular) identity in the figuration *Judeo-Christian* aligned these at a crucial moment that otherwise portended a serious setback for the Western domination of the Middle East, Asia and Africa. Upon the defeat of the Third World project, the transition of the global economy to neoliberalism escalated the integration of key secular-nationalist states as well as authoritarian regimes in the region into the US sphere of influence; Islam was politically isolated and the figure of the Muslim transformed into 'the' enemy of democracy and development, of socio-economic progress and human rights.

In this context, the Islamist recuperation of Islam from the ossifying tendencies inherent to the secularizing post-independence status of 'religion' to which it had been subjected by nationalist, socialist as well as monarchical-authoritarian regimes fuelled Muslim opposition to US-led globalization, to the ideological-political incursions of the Soviet Union and to the neo-colonial regimes that were now vital to policing the post-independence world. In the West, the relation of the Muslim to Islam was now defined as the chief obstacle to 'peace', 'security' and 'democracy', particularly after the end of the Cold War. The challenge from the Islamist movements was thus not only to the Western powers, as has been noted by critical scholars of these regions, but also to the nativist authoritarianism that worked to suppress, ossify and neutralize Islam to advance Westernity as the region's projected future.

The stage was thus set for the events that would lead to the defeat of the Soviet Union in Afghanistan and establish the Islamic resurgence as a formidable challenge to Western power. Concomitantly, Israel's occupations and expansionary ambitions in the Middle East ensured the region remained a vital battlefront for the West. Israel's religio-racial alliances, governing mechanisms and military-policing strategies made it a well-funded test site for the development and marketing of the technologies of occupation, terror and war. The fortification of Western identity, culture and politics as Judeo-Christian – in its philosophico-epistemological as well as war-making aspects – reflects the developments that have taken place in international as well as national politics during the late twentieth century, changes that tapped into – even as they remade – the underlying religio-racial logics that are still the bedrock of Western self-formation.

I have in this Introduction, albeit in very broad strokes, outlined the theoretical issues, historical processes and power relations that shape the parameters of my study of Islam and Muslims in the formation of the West. The chapters that follow address specific aspects of this formation to illustrate how its cultural politics are anchored in its long-standing phantasms of Islam and spectral figuration of the

Muslim to evacuate them from history and politics, law and morality, and thus confine them in the dehumanization that shapes Western modernity's deathworlds.

Chapter 1 introduces – and reworks – key concepts drawn from the theoretical traditions that inform my study. This is followed in Chapter 2 with an examination of the mutually constitutive relation between 'race' and 'religion' at key historical junctures in the formation of the West. Showing how this religio-racial nexus pivoted on early Christo-European conceptions of Islam and Muslims, I trace how these constructs were integrated into Western modernity's political-philosophical traditions. Chapter 3 studies the Western fascination with sex and gender, the lens through which Islam was viewed by Latin Christian men and women. This chapter analyses how ideas about gender-sexuality shaped the phantasy-desires of a variant of Christianity that were transmuted into the gender-sexual regimes of the West, such that Muslims became always-already perverse objects in heterosexual as well as homosexual registers. The 'failures' of Muslims to properly 'feminize' and 'masculinize' themselves is the view that even now shapes Western gender/sexual politics and their related forms of violence: these are also analysed in this chapter. Developments within feminist politics in the global war is the subject of Chapter 4, which shows how feminism has been incorporated into, and in turn advances, the Islamophobia that is at the centre of global political discourses. The gendered and sexualized desire for Western cultural supremacy permeates contemporary articulations of feminist and queer theory, such that their reworking of the Western epistemological tradition has redefined the feminist and queer Subject as emblematic of this superiority. The final chapter, Chapter 5, attends to the contemporary remaking of the West as essentially Judeo-Christian and simultaneously secular and white. The chapter revisits studies of the Holocaust as well as the founding of the state of Israel in historic Palestine as a counter to the revolutionary politics of Pan-Arab nationalism and Third World decolonization. The religio-racial logic of power that runs through this new figuration of the West has made 'religion' and 'race', 'sovereignty', 'secularism' and 'subjectivity' – like 'gender' and 'sexuality' – concept-practices of its colonizing modernity and organizes its ambition to subjugate Islam and destroy Muslim resistance.

Yet the global war is also a reminder of the limits to Western power. The war's expansionary drive reveals the extent to which the West still has to contend with Islam, whose power to inspire Muslims remains clearly undiminished.

Chapter 1

THE IN/HUMAN SUBJECT

Unlawful enemy combatant

These three words instituted a distinct status in international politics and law that would have catastrophic effects on Muslim societies, far beyond those caught in the immediate zones of the war on terror. Fanon may well have described the event as bringing into being a new sub-species of colonized life: the alchemy of Western paranoia re-ontologizing the post-independence figure of the Muslim into that of the 'terrorist'. While critical scholars were quick to describe the development as exclusion of Muslims from the rights of citizenship, the transformation heralded a far deadlier remaking of the law itself and a deeper incorporation of the figure of the Muslim into the formation of Western identity, culture and politics.

Each element of the designation – 'unlawful', 'enemy', 'combatant' – destroys the post-independence gains, such as they were, of Muslim societies to reconstruct them as the very *antithesis* of the modern social order, threatening the destruction of law and politics, ethics and morality, that is, the values and institutions that produce and sustain 'human' life. The designation materialized *in law* the spectral clash between innocence (West) and evil (Islam) by fixing the Muslim as an illegitimate being, now stripped of 'the right to have rights' in Arendt's words. Doing away with the protections enshrined in Habeas Corpus and the Geneva Convention, the designation became a pronouncement of death.[1]

The re-signification of the Muslim put in motion a transformation in racial-gender politics. So, for example, US Special Forces were trained in target practice at a military base with the use of cardboard cut-outs of veiled Muslim women.[2] This use of the veil by the US army occurred in tandem with the images of Muslim women that flooded the media. The veil, an 'icon of intolerable difference',[3] thus gave concrete shape to the abstract construct of the 'global terror threat'. These images brought into sharp focus, even as they reconfigured, the Muslim woman as a particular kind of deadly presence. Locked into the nebulous zone of 'global terror', she now personified the condition of 'evil' against which were to be mobilized the resources of the West. The primal battle between civilization and barbarism as conceived of by neoconservatives and Orientalists thus linked the Western Subject's right to life, democracy and freedom with the destruction of the phobogenic object, the Muslim, as *Black widow, jihadi bride, female suicide bomber, hijabi* and so on.

Likewise, images of bearded and turbaned man – wielding a sword, a rocket launcher, an assault weapon or the Qur'an – became pervasive in the news media and popular culture as Muslim males between the ages of 15 and 45 were officially designated terror suspects. In short, the dissemination of such images helped demolish the idea that the Muslim – male or female – deserved the right to have rights.

International law and the sovereignty doctrine that informs it are rooted in colonial ideologies, Antony Anghie has argued, for their development was historically centred on the concept of 'culture'.[4] Modern forms of sovereignty and law, he demonstrates, emerged in the theological-political relations among European sovereigns who battled each other to extend their power over the territories and peoples they conquered. Muslims, 'Saracens' and 'pagans' in the terms then used by Latin Christendom, were depicted as culturally condemnable at the originary moment of the sovereignty doctrine as is evident in the following comments by Francisco de Vitoria, the Spanish Catholic philosopher:

> And so when the war is at that pass that the indiscriminate spoilation of all enemy-subjects alike and the seizure of all their goods are justifiable, then it is also justifiable to carry all enemy-subjects off into captivity, whether they be guilty or guiltless. And inasmuch as war with pagans is of this type, seeing that it is perpetual and that they can never make amends for the wrongs and damages they have wrought, it is indubitably lawful to carry off both the children and the women of the Saracens into captivity and slavery.[5]

These remarks by Vitoria, who is credited with producing the first text of modern law and called the 'father' of international law, clarify that the waging of war by Europeans transformed all 'pagans' and 'Saracens' into enemy-subjects who could be lawfully captured, enslaved, raped, pillaged and so on, 'whether they be guilty or guiltless'. The category *illegal enemy combatant* re-institutes just such a status in international law.

The early European states did not recognize the practices, systems and dictums organizing the social order in the territories they 'discovered'. Instead, they overrode these by designating the societies lawless and primitive, their peoples as living in a condition of savagery, to colonize them. The modern concept of sovereignty hence became infused with these religio-racial discourses of the Christo-European states as the concept of culture constructed the 'difference' that marked the colonial divide. This idea of culture bound international law to imperialism, and Anghie shows how it has continued to reshape international law at critical moments of historical change, from the sixteenth-century colonization of the Americas and the Treaty of Westphalia (1648) into the twentieth century, including the Congress of Berlin, the League of Nations and the global institutions of the new international economic order.

The war on terror, Anghie argues, is the most recent iteration of this relation between international law, imperialism and lawlessness, for the originary impetus within the sovereignty doctrine is evident in the war's culturalizing ideology. The occupations of Afghanistan and Iraq, like the incarceration and deportations of Muslims in the West, were based on the construction of Islamic culture as sanctioning terrorism, with Muslims constructed as terrorists (even if suspects) who lived in terrorist havens, organized sleeper cells and suicide bombings, radicalized their youth and so on. Anghie's larger argument was that the colonial logic infusing the system of international law made the Third-World state uniquely vulnerable, as was evident in its destruction in Iraq.

The racial/colonial logic running through international law found new expression after the First World War, Anghie argues, in the League of Nations that was formed to establish a new relation between European empires and their colonies. Now designated 'backward territories', the cultural divide was preserved in contrasting these with the achievements of the 'advanced' countries. With the Ottoman Empire placed under the Mandate System of the League, this is how the imperial powers envisioned the 'sovereignty' to be granted in the new system:

> What we want to have in existence, what we ought to have been creating in this time, is some administration with Arab institutions which we can safely leave while pulling the strings ourselves; something that won't cost very much, which Labor can swallow consistent with its principles, but under which our economic and political interests will be secure.[6]

Anghie's study of the historical evolution of sovereignty, although not specifically focused on 'religion', points to how Muslims were being configured in this system of international law over the centuries, and to how 'Islamic culture' was being institutionalized as 'barbaric' and 'backwards'. The present 'cultural' incommensurability of Islam with 'modern' law and sovereignty has thus been centuries in the making, wherein the production of the Muslim as object of racial-cultural 'difference' became a structuring principle of the Christocentric European legal universe. This principle has, of course, shaped not only Western sovereignty but also its subjectivity. One presently finds the sovereignty doctrine at work in the secular-political discourses of foreign policy, national security, immigration and border control and so on. These policies are saturated with the earlier Christian idea of states of innocence and states of evil, of precarious subjects of salvation and demonic bodies of condemnation: these ideas function to construct the Western Subject as oriented towards futurity and the Muslim towards an essential primitivity.[7]

The global war's violent reconfiguration of the Muslim as religio-culturally alien to the status of the sovereign subject thrust her back into the state of pre-modernity (i.e. Islam), into anachronistic time/space (Islamic culture). The *niqab*, the *hijab*, the *turban*, became signs alerting the sovereign Subject to this Muslim's invasion into the modern spaces of democracy, choice and freedom.[8] The war's demarcation of the Western Subject as life-oriented in opposition to the death-oriented Muslim thus reordered relations not only between this Subject and the Muslim but also between the Western state and this Subject; in the process, the war gave new content – characteristics, attributes, qualities and so on – to this Subject's identity and culture.

In the sections that follow, I work though a number of theoretical traditions and concepts used in my study of the contemporary remaking of Western sovereignty and subjectivity. Beginning with a brief outline of the processes of the dehumanization of the Muslim set in motion by the global war, which I read by way of Fanon's theories of race, violence and colonialism, I highlight the point that although he formulated these in the context of the Algerian revolution, Fanon has little to say about Islam. I address this lacuna by bringing studies of Islam as well as of Islamic anti-colonial resistance, in Algeria and elsewhere, into my reading of Fanon. Turning also to Said's critique of Orientalism, I interrogate the secularist investments in his work. My discussion of Islam argues that an anti-essentializing and historicizing approach to Islam as well the experiences of Muslims is crucial to avoid Orientalizing both. Centring processes of colonialization and racialization, I also explore the gender-sexual dimensions of these phenomena. Throughout the remainder of the chapter, I map out how vital remain the insights of the revolutionary anti-colonial and anti-racist traditions in unpacking the effects and the ramifications of the global war and its remaking of relations of power.

The death-dealing subject

It did not take long for the category *unlawful enemy combatant* to transform the legal, political and cultural landscape. For example, it was not considered outside the realm of the reasonable that the architect of the US strategy in Iraq and Afghanistan, General Stanley McChrystal, worked with a 'handpicked collection of killers, spies, geniuses, patriots, political operators and outright maniacs'.[9] Such a teaming of patriots and geniuses with killers and maniacs was considered both pragmatic and inevitable, given the 'evil' nature of the enemy. The General was particularly lauded for 'his single-minded success in a narrow but critical mission: manhunting',[10] a 'mission' that was extended across the Middle East, Central Asia and North and sub-Saharan Africa under successive US Administrations.[11] Indeed, the killing of Osama bin Laden was just such a 'manhunt'.

One does not, of course, hunt Man. Nor, for that matter, Woman. The signifier 'Man', extended to 'Woman' with the advent of feminism, speaks to the sovereignty of the modern Subject – the embodiment of reason, locus of the social contract, whose political agency is reflected in liberal–democratic rights and freedoms. As a citizen, this Subject is the measure of civilized society, the anchor of the political legitimacy of the state. 'Manhunter', on the other hand, bespeaks the coloniality that is constitutive of Man; these interpellations point to the racial logics that underwrite the extent of the power of the sovereign Subject, the right to kill.

McChrystal, Head of the Joint Special Operations Command (JSOC) in Iraq that was described as a 'killing machine',[12] was celebrated as a 'warrior-scholar' who 'moved easily from the dark world to the light'.[13] As intelligence officers who worked with him noted, the General 'had an encyclopaedic, even obsessive, knowledge about the lives of terrorists', and that 'he pushed his ranks aggressively to kill as many of them as possible'.[14] The directive to exterminate 'as many of them as possible' during the Bush Administration has been well documented. Pre-emptive killing of 'terror suspects' also became central to the Obama Administration's war strategy,[15] the president himself finalized the weekly *kill lists* that subjected Muslim communities to the terrorizing drones that could strike anywhere, in any unguarded moment.[16] For its part, the Trump Administration turned over this power to kill to the Generals by giving them direct control over US war strategy, unhindered by presidential or civilian oversight; official release of public information related to the killing of 'terrorists' was ended by this Administration.[17] Western public indifference rendered these killings banal, unworthy of mention, but analysing the impact of such practices on the formation of Western subjects yields important insights.

The status of the human – in political not 'only' biological terms (some scholars conceive of this as the distinction between bios and zoë[18]) – was initially available to the Christian, later to the European, and later still to the Westerner conceived of as white in the historical formation of the West. This is the Subject endowed with power over the Muslim in the global war; the accusation 'terror-suspect' transformed this Muslim into the prey of this Subject.[19] The linking of anti-terrorism measures to immigration and refugee policy extended the reach of this Subject within the nation as well as at the global level by conflating the *unlawful enemy combatant* with the *immigrant* and the *refugee*, likewise racially coded categories. The non/citizen status of the brown/Black Muslim within *as well as* outside the Western nation-state's borders could thus be conflated.

The 'man' living under occupation is no such entity, Fanon argued, for the racial/colonial order transformed the Black/brown 'man' into the 'artefact' of the white.[20] In his critique of modernity, Fanon argued that racial dehumanization precluded the possibility of reciprocity between the Black/brown man and the Man who is the subject of the West. '[The] Black man has no ontological resistance in the eyes of the white man', Fanon concluded, for the former has to contend with 'two frames of reference within which he has had to place himself', his own 'metaphysics' (that is, 'his customs and the sources on which they were based') and the 'civilization that he did not know that had imposed itself on him'.[21] Reduced to an object by the destruction of his 'metaphysics', the Black/brown male, Fanon stated 'is not a man' – an observation arising as much from his own experience as that of his Algerian, that is, Muslim/Arab/African, patients.[22] Moreover, being reduced to the racial object sparked contradictory impulses among the colonized which ranged from psycho-affective affiliation with the colonizer to rage against colonial subjugation. These impulses, Fanon argued, flowed from the condition of violence that destroyed the status of the colonized as human subject, a violence enfolded into 'postmodernity' in what Mbembe has defined as 'necropolitics'.[23]

Moreover, Fanon argued that the political subjugation and material deprivation that were the effects of colonization could not be isolated from the psychosexual aggression entailed in this condition. While the decimation of the languages, values and practices that shaped the historical consciousness of colonized peoples – their being-for-themselves – reduced them to the status of a 'thing', to be captured, classified, remade or exterminated, their psycho-cultural alienation was shaped also by politico-sexual depersonalization in this modality of (non) existence. The transformation of this 'thing' into a new kind of being relied on a radical, humanizing praxis with the potential to recuperate the shattered humanity of the colonized, claimed Fanon, in his defence of the Algerian revolution. This revolution he famously defined as emblematic of the larger anti-colonial Third World revolution.

The occupations and wars of the early twenty-first century speak to the prescience of Fanon's insights and warnings, particularly with regard to the development of national consciousness, a perilous phase which he described as full of pitfalls. The nationalist politics of post-independence states, argue postcolonial scholars, so thoroughly imbibed colonial ideologies that the practices of the post-independence state mirrored those of the colonial state. The corruptions and violence of the post-independence regimes, so evident across the Middle East and most parts of the Third World, demonstrate just how pathological were the forms of 'nationalism' they instituted. Yet these pathologies of modernization did not destroy the resilience of subjugated populations, a resilience that included also various forms of Islamist mobilizations, the extent of which was revealed by the global war. This resilience once again opened up the horizon of possibilities for the futures of late-capitalist modernity.

Yet, inspired as he was by the transformative potential he saw in the Algerian resistance, and committed as he remained to defend armed struggle against colonial occupation, Frantz Omar Fanon, who helped found the publication, *El Moudjahid* for the National Liberation Front (FLN),[24] did not, perhaps could not, account for the role of Islam in the revolutionary tradition that was, for him, the beacon for *les damnes de la terre*.[25] Fouzi Slisli has noted that Fanon, that most insightful theorist of the colonial order, did not see that the 'spontaneity' of the rural peasantry, which he considered a distinctive – and decisive – factor in the Algerian revolution, was no such impulsive phenomenon. What Fanon experienced, and theorized, as spontaneity, Slisli argues, 'belong[s] to a distinctly Islamic anti-colonial tradition that, by the time Fanon was writing, had been in existence for a century'.[26] The revolutionary impulse of the Muslim peasantry that so impressed itself upon Fanon was given shape by the organizing principles of an Islamic anti-colonial praxis that had earlier been led by radical Sufi Shaykhs, by the organizations they founded and the traditions they developed (1832–47).

Slisli's contention is that the organizing of the masses that Fanon considered vital to the success of the Algerian revolution had become, by the mid-twentieth century, a combination of Islamic and Marxist 'systems of organization'. The majority of the Algerian population was deeply rooted in the Islamic tradition, which meant that the reach of the revolutionary leadership's secular, Third World and Marxist politics remained limited.[27] As Slisli further argues, despite being staunch secularists themselves, the Algerian leadership with whom Fanon allied himself nonetheless named themselves the *Moujahidine* as they articulated their politics to an Islamic idiom which had the power to galvanize the revolutionary energy of the Algerian masses against the French occupation.[28]

Under the leadership of the Qadiriya Sufis, including 'Abd al-Qadir al-Juzayri, their earlier resistance to the French had unified the Algerian as a people (1832–1947).[29] It was as *amir al-mu'minin* ('commander of the faithful') that Shaykh al-Juzayri, trained in Islamic/Sufi traditions, took the oath of allegiance from the tribes who allied themselves to his leadership; the Shaykh also appointed marabouts and established lodges for the Qadiriya order, thus establishing a 'rudimentary' state as he organized the Jihad against the French.[30] Nor was Algeria the only such case. In Libya and in the Sahara, it was the Sanusiya Brotherhood who fought the French, as was also the case with the Italian invasion. The Sanusiya worked with the Bedouin leadership to establish the Sufi lodges that functioned as 'centres of resistance' while providing vital services to the needy. Vikor has found that within such instances of anti-colonial organizing across North Africa, 'religious structures and personal resources were deployed in a novel form as required by the new situation' that was colonial rule.[31] Likewise in Palestine, it was Shaykh 'Izz ad-Din al-Qassam – from whom the armed wing of Hamas takes its name – who led the first rebellion (1936–9) in a political resistance that did not separate Islam from, nor consider this to be in conflict with, anti-colonial nationalism. In Algeria, as elsewhere in the colonized Muslim majority world, anti-colonial radicals found their inspiration in Islam to fight to make justice moral and substantive, rejecting Western law and politics as 'simply unjust' on both counts.[32]

Fanon's secularist commitments, as those of his revolutionary comrades, are eminently clear in his politics and writing, yet his willingness 'to devote his life to a liberation struggle that arguably had as its end goal an Islamic state' is not an insignificant – albeit curiously overlooked – matter.[33] Of course neither the FLN nor Fanon envisioned their objective to be the establishment of 'an Islamic state'. Indeed, Fanon's humanist commitments – which were revolutionary, not the now hegemonic humanism of Western liberalism – ring clear in his radical vision, as does his strident rejection of any 'return' to pre-colonial nativist traditions. But the hopes, desires and expectations of the Algerian masses, not to mention the anxieties and policies of the French administrators, may well have been another matter, as suggested in Slisli's reading of Islam as 'the elephant in the room' in Fanon's anti-colonial praxis.

Consider also the following. The Tunisian nationalist leader, Habib Bourguiba, defined as 'a political epiphany' his experience of the uproar against the 1930 International Eucharistic Congress held in Carthage for the centennial of French rule in Algeria; French officials regarded pan-Islamic politics and movements in Algeria, as elsewhere in North Africa, with such concern that they often attempted to restrict pilgrimage to Mecca well into the twentieth century; colonial authorities repeatedly attempted to incorporate Muslim leaders and Islamic institutions into the structures of colonial governance; they also sought to isolate and destroy the more radical of these; and radical Muslim leaders, including the Jihadi leader, Abd al-Karim, were expelled to other French colonies, including Reunion (1926).[34] Islam was hardly a spent force in North Africa, as these examples demonstrate. Marnia Lazreg has also observed that 'religion became the single most important element in the French administration's efforts to control the Algerian people between 1830–1962'.[35] Not only did the French seek to absorb Shari'a into their governance structures, but the 'obsessive preoccupation' of the French administration with Islam was such that it inadvertently 'politicized the Algerian people's Islamic identity'.[36] In light of these examples, the early as well as later phases of anti-colonial resistance in Algeria, and the post-independence Algerian state's response – the infamous coup – to the electoral victory of the Islamic Salvation Front (FIS) point to a far more complex configuration of political ideologies at work than is suggested in Fanon's analysis of the revolution. The response of significant sectors of the Algerian masses – *as Muslims* – to the French occupation, as well as their resistance – *as Muslims* – to incorporation into Westernity was clearly a major destabilizing force in the colonial as well as post-independence period.

Fanon was no doubt aware of the power of Islam to inspire anti-colonial praxis, an awareness that is implicitly present, even if explicitly unexamined, in his perceptive essay, 'Algeria Unveiled'.[37] The essay is focused on the role of the veiled Muslim/Algerian woman at the height of the Algerian revolution, suffice it to note here that in spite of his understanding of the critical role of these un/veiled Muslim women in the resistance, Fanon, much like his revolutionary comrades, could not see beyond the secular as the grounds for revolutionary agency. This may be too obvious a point, but it must be made: Fanon's ideas about revolutionary politics implicitly mirror – even if by omission – the colonial framing of Islam as a relic of the past and secularism as the single path to modernization. This frame will be interrogated in the chapters that follow, where I take up Fanon's insights into the racial-sexual pathologies generated by the colonial order.

The nexus of race with religion was a crucial factor in the making and organization of the colonial order – studying this nexus requires an interrogation of Fanon's near silence on Islam. This religio-racial nexus is discernible once again in the global war's fetishization of the figure of the Muslim and attempts to neutralize Islam. For many of its followers, this tradition continues to offer another world beyond the dehumanization and alienation of post/colonial-modernity.

Oriental inscriptions, secular erasures

Said, like Fanon, mentioned Islam in his study of Orientalism, but this tradition did not feature substantively in his analytic frame. Said did, of course, critique the post-1967 coverage of Islam in the US media,[38] and Courville reads him as not only identifying with the Islamicate but also considering Islam as perhaps compatible with secular–democracy (2005). Moreover, Said also stayed away from explicit and substantive engagement with the issue of race, although he often mentioned it in passing and was hardly oblivious to its effects. His focus was on the critique of culture; the politics of Orientalism as the cultural-epistemological site for the construction of the 'difference' of the West; and Palestine. Yet the Oriental was a stock figure in the interconnected Western discourses not only of culture but also of race, religion and nation in the period of interest to Said, and as significant, this figure was also previously encoded as the Saracen, the Moor, and so forth. In my reading of Said's work, I therefore subtend his insights into Orientalism to revisit earlier moments of Western self-formation in which the major representational tropes and political concerns he studied are not only clearly discernible but, as is the case with Orientalism, pivoted quite explicitly on Islam and the figure of the Muslim.

As noted in the introduction, the figure of the Muslim anchored, not to mention vexed, the imaginative powers of the West, whether in the pre-/early-modern constructs of *Saracen*, *Pagan* and *Moor* or the modern categories of the *Turk*, *Semite*, *Oriental* and *Muselmann*, all precursors to the contemporary figuration of the *Jihadi* and the *hijabi*. Evident also in these tropes is a projection of Western desires as well as anxieties and ambitions. Much as the Orient/al became the point of reference for the Western constitution of itself as a cohesive entity, so does the trope of the barbaric Muslim presently function in assertions of the religio-racial identity of the West, notwithstanding the disparate and conflicting interests that crosscut it.

Revisiting the earlier figurations of this Muslim demonstrates that although its specific content varied over time, what did not change is the logic of alterity embedded within it, a logic dense with intermingled ideas about racial degeneracy and satanic devilry. The affective reach of Latin Christendom's designation of Islam 'as a monstrous evil and curse on humanity' concocted by 'a charlatan, a womanizer, an opportunist, . . .some sort of imposter, a false prophet' not only endured, but deepened over the centuries to shape the Orientalist paradigm.[39] The absolute difference projected onto Islam in these theologically derived constructs made the later tradition a slate for the inscription of Western anxieties and phantasms, as well as desires and pleasures in the colonial era. As the early projections acquired a tactile globality to become a powerful force which shaped the cultural politics of the West, they also traversed into its modern epistemic traditions.

Orientalism clearly drew upon and reconstructed such older cultural-racial alterity, the discourse was also explicitly concerned with 'religious' difference. Yet Said's staunchly secularist paradigm led him, like many postcolonial scholars who follow in his wake, to take secularism as the *only* ground for *critique* of this discourse, and hence the only basis for emancipatory politics.[40] These secular assumptions and investments have been challenged in the critical study of Islam as well as in the study of 'religion'; recent scholarship points to the trenchant and devastating critiques of injustice, inequality, violence and cruelty, including within the Muslim world itself, that have been inspired by Islam as a historical tradition.[41] Interrogating Islamic orthodoxies of all sorts, scholars have opened up new pathways for thinking about the tradition itself as well as its potential to inspire radical social change. I draw on this body of work to highlight the historical scope and depth of the present enmity towards Islam, and to underscore what such violence portends for Muslim communities, which now extends beyond the scope of Orientalism. I also draw on recent studies that have deconstructed the category of 'religion' from a wide array of theoretical perspectives, some secular, others not, which also point to the dangers of taking the category as transparent in meaning.

Islam, race, Orientalism are all invoked – intermingled, conflated, substituted – in the cultural politics of the global war. However, the dominant construct of Islam and the Muslim as death-oriented points to how the representational strategies tracked by Said were overtaken by the hatreds that animate Islamophobia.[42] Previously an element of Orientalism, Islamophobia has become an amalgamation of disgust, fear and bravado centred on ideas about cultural barbarity, gender-sexual perversity and religious depravity. These ideas incite scorn, fascination and revulsion in the projection of phantasmic perils onto 'radical Islamic terror/ists'[43]; it is therefore worth attending to what these caricatures, and debates about their in/accuracy, actually do.

With the early Muslims constituting themselves as a powerful – albeit internally fractured – community with universalist ambitions upon the death of Prophet Muhammad, Islam rose with stunning rapidity out of the Arabian heartland and across Asia and Africa. Attending to the early development of the tradition points to the agency of Muslims in giving the tradition concrete shape and form, even as the tradition itself shaped the agency of these Muslims as historical beings. The traditions associated with the formation of the West, however, did not engage with these actual historical experiences of Islam as lived by heterogeneous Muslim societies.

As is well known of the Prophet of Islam, he declared the revelation he received to be the true monotheism, its earlier expression in Judaism and Christianity having gone astray.[44] Islam was accepted by him and the early Muslims (his wife Khadija being the first, his cousin and son-in-law Ali Ibn Abi Talib the second) as the revelation of creation rooted in a vision of a merciful, compassionate and just divine power in action, *ar-Rahman ar-Rahim*. Muslims were those who willingly 'surrendered' (as translated by Mohammed Asad) or 'delivered' themselves (as read by Joseph Massad) to this divine-cosmic power for guidance. Moreover, in proclaiming his own Prophethood, Muhammad ibn 'Abdullah paid reverence to the status of the earlier Prophets during his lifetime. But, he did insist, that like himself the other Prophets were mortal.[45] Notably then, neither the revelations he received nor the Prophet's practices demonized Judaism or Christianity; Islam thus did not close itself off from its pre-Islamic past.[46] Instead, this past was valued, many of its practices integrated into the Islamic tradition (the Hajj, for one example). Moreover, the Islamic revelation was seen as a divine gift not only to the early Arab-Muslims but to all humanity.[47]

Islam's creation narrative defined human life as brought into being from a single *nafs* (translated as clot, breath or soul), with the creation of the first human followed immediately by that of its mate (*zawj*); no mention is made of a sex/gender order or hierarchy in this originary moment.[48] The only distinction of note made among humans in the Qur'anic text is that between 'believing men and women' and 'non-believing men and women', as Barlas reads this.[49] The distinction is predicated on human praxis, she argues, it is not ontologically derived nor does it connote spiritual capacity or material rank. The distinction itself is clearly unstable, for believers could well turn into 'non-believers' and non-believers into 'believers'. Further, in what many scholars call the 'radical egalitarianism' of the Qur'an, women, children and slaves within the hierarchically organized Arab society - a condition named *jahiliya* - all have 'legal capacity'; the idea of any 'lesser' form of humanity, as innately or ontologically stunted, is absent.[50] 'Believers' are referred to as *mu'minun*, and as the Prophet repeatedly reminded his followers, the ethical practices of non-Muslims were worthy of greater respect and emulation than the immoral behaviour of Muslims.[51]

In keeping with this approach, the *ummah* was defined as an open-ended community, not bound by birth, tribe, nation, language or blood; any 'non-believer' could become Muslim upon recitation of the *shahada*.[52] As part of the *ummah*, Muslims were required to pay the *zakat* while non-Muslim *dhimmis* (that is, 'followers of earlier revelation') were required to pay *jizya*, a tax, for living under the protection of Muslim rulers; *dhimmis* were governed by their own institutions, laws and values.[53] The designation of Jews and Christians as *ahl al-kitab* (the term is generally translated as 'people of the book', but Asad translates this as 'followers of early revelation'[54]) recognized their status as defined within their own traditions, not on ontological grounds. Scholars of the Islamic tradition generally concur that although the Qur'an 'insisted that its message was simply a "reminder" of truths that everybody knew' and sanctioned specific forms of protection for Jews and Christians, the Qur'an most likely 'would have endorsed . . . all rightly guided religion that submitted wholly to God, refused to worship man-made deities, and preached justice and equality came from the same divine force'.[55] This early period of Islamic history, most scholars also concur, was shaped by the Prophet's cultivation of the Qur'anic radical egalitarianism to challenge the prevailing norms of his society. Advocating for the entitlements and protection of widows, orphans and the enslaved, he attacked the wealth, power and hierarchal structure of Arab society. With 'Muslim' symbolizing, and predicated upon, lifelong practice of piety and ethical behaviour, the identity itself had no fixity or stability of meaning in itself as such but instead demanded ongoing justice-oriented praxis.

Islam thus offered a very specific modality of being to believers for grounding the transcendent in the everyday. The notion of a 'chosen' people was dispensed with; Muslims were not chosen, they had to choose and live out the commitment entailed in this choice. Nor were Muslims offered 'salvation', *being* Muslim entailed the ongoing praxis of *becoming* Muslim. Islam did not define 'Allah' in anthropomorphic terms; the pre-Islamic past was treated as living and dynamic, the future likewise unbounded, which meant that past, present and future are interlinked for Muslims in their embodied, ritual practice of daily life. The only legitimate means for a society of the faithful is the practice of justice, compassion and mercy, which oriented the community towards futurity. Indeed, most scholars are in agreement that justice is the overriding principle within the Qur'an.[56] As Reeves has noted, 'With a following of oppressed women, restless slaves and poor people no longer content to be poor, Islam was already beginning to pose a threat to the rich and powerful' in its early days.[57]

Islam's claim on old origins and new futures, by way of *as-Siraat al-Mustaqim*, presented the emergent tradition as simultaneously a return to 'true' monotheism and as such, encompassing the 'real' message of the earlier Prophets.[58] Such foundational principles were at odds not only with the claims of Jewish (the Covenant) and Christian (Salvation) exceptionalism; incidentally, these principles would also be in conflict with the later Enlightenment narrative of Progress as rupture with, and transcendence of, everything past.

The historical record demonstrates that such insurgent Islamic claims were not well received. The Meccans responded to the Prophet's message with contempt and antipathy; the Qur'anic inclusiveness offered by the Prophet in his relations with Jewish communities, as with Christians and other Arabs, was spurned. War would become inevitable.[59] The early Muslim community's conflicts with the Meccans, the Jewish communities in Medina (which aligned with the Meccans), and the Muslim armies' conflicts with Christians in Syria soon after the Prophet's death altered the trajectory of Islam along with that of the region, and well beyond it.

As is also well known, the Muslim community quickly fractured over the question of leadership with the passing of the Prophet, and then yet again over issues of governance as well as the interpretation of Islam itself. Yet Rahman has pointed out that even before the Prophet's passing,

> Islam had developed its major characteristic: the establishment of the community (*Umma*) of the faithful expressing the moral and spiritual quality of its faith through a variety of institutions backed by a governmental organization. But, at the same time, in this entire complex, the Community remained as something more basic than either the state organization or, indeed, the institutions themselves.[60]

This 'something more basic' was the community's 'conscious acceptance' of 'its status as the primary bearer of the Will of God', argues Rahman. Whether 'Allah' translates seamlessly into the Christian/modern concept of 'God' is, of course, contested. What is less contested is that the designation Muslim does indeed speak to a relation – individual as well as collective – to Islam that has endured over the centuries, such that through periods of accomplishments, failings and catastrophes, the tradition continues to inspire those who claim to live and die by this relation.

The growing power of Muslims and their spread of Islam made it a regional, then global phenomenon; this ascendance was aided by, but not reducible to, the weaknesses in the empires on either side of the Arabian heartland, the Byzantine and Sassanid. With the fall of both, the early Muslims integrated into the expanding Islamic framework many of the systems and institutions of law and administration, as well as cultural, social and linguistic traditions, of the peoples they encountered and absorbed into the *ummah*, which 'conferred upon the Islamic civilization its distinctive character, and which, expressing the fundamental moral ethos of Islam, has provided the real constitution, as it were, of the Muslim state and defined its limits'.[61]

During these rapidly unfolding developments, the relation between the community's leadership (defined as 'politics' in the Western tradition) and practice of the dynamic Islamic tradition ('religion') was repeatedly contested, fractured and redefined, often violently so. But, as Rahman argued, the Muslim state that emerged from this fraught and complex history maintained its 'Islamic framework' as 'political leaders' negotiated the defining of the tradition by 'religious leaders' who remained – for the main – outside the state.[62] During this period, as 'Islam broke many regional and civilizational barriers producing numerous new social and cultural hybrid forms which while undeniably Islamic, were also unquestionably Arab, Indian, Chinese, Turkish and African',[63] the tradition attracted significant numbers of Jews and Christians who abandoned their faith for the new tradition.

By the year 750, the Abbasids had overthrown the Umayyads to become the rulers of the major portion of the Muslim world. In this capacity, they initiated a 'dazzling intellectual renaissance' in supporting a 'systemic programme' to translate the major texts of other languages (from Iran, India, Greece) into Arabic, which in turn sparked major intellectual advances in Islamic philosophy, the arts and the sciences.[64] As Egger points out, this flowering of knowledge across the Muslim world was in 'sharp contrast to contemporary Western Europe, where Charlemagne was struggling to find people who could read'.[65] Yet the rule of the Abbasid Caliphs went into a period of decline as a result of internal disintegration and decentralization; their rule was definitively ended with the destruction of Baghdad (the Abbasid capital) by the Mongols (1258). The corruptions of the institutions of rule during this period did not go unchallenged from within, for the decentralized system of these 'empires' ensured multiple sites of authority.

A number of significant developments took place during the Abbasid period that are pertinent not only to Islamic history but to the contemporary practices and perspectives of Muslim societies. First, the three key branches of Shi'ism acquired their particular form during this period; second, the development of the *hadith* tradition helped to shape an explicit Sunni 'consciousness'; third, the four juristic traditions were consolidated; and fourth, the Sufi tradition found its unique shape.[66] These developments were to have a transformative effect across the Muslim world, and in the relations of Muslims to 'Islam' itself. At a later stage, the catastrophic effects of the colonization of most of the Muslim world would not leave Islam itself unaffected.

Talal Asad has counselled caution in approaching Islam as a 'religion', for this is a 'normalizing' concept that is Western and Christocentric in origin. Earlier, Marshall Hodgson had noted the limitations of defining 'Islam' as 'religion': he used the term 'Islam/ic' 'casually both for what we may call religion and for the overall society and culture associated historically with the religion'.[67] Debates about how to adequately define the complexities of the revelation-concept-praxis 'Islam' and 'Islamic' continue to rage in the present, as in for example, the use of world systems theory to move beyond the conceptualization of 'Islam' as either a religion or a civilization[68] and the contesting meanings ascribed to the tradition by various contemporary Islamist movements.

The very broad sketch provided here speaks to the need for greater engagement with Islam, on its own terms and histories, as well as with the experience, hermeneutics, perspectives and histories of the multifaceted world of Muslims. The imposition of the category 'religion' onto Islam evacuates the tradition itself and these histories: it 'freezes' Islam, so to speak, in the Orientalizing frame. Not only does this designation redirect Islam and Muslims towards Westernization and drain the tradition of its dynamism, it renders invisible the meanings made of the tradition in the spatial and temporal specificities of heterogeneous Muslim experience. The imposition of the category 'religion' onto Islam is itself a colonizing gesture, I argued earlier, for this disciplines 'Islam' into Westernizing discourses to manage it all the better. The Islamic term *din* far exceeds, of course, the diminishment encapsulated in the term 'religion'.

Islam/ic matters

In contrast to the conventional situating of Islam in the longer tradition of monotheistic religions ('the Abrahamic', for example), the Qur'an and the Prophet's practice made a clear distinction between Islam and the earlier traditions.[69] This 'newness' of Islam was emphasized by Fazlur Rahman who, distinguishing the 'actual doctrine' and the ideal/theoretical 'religious plane', made the case that

> Muhammad's monotheism was, from the very beginning, linked up with a humanism and a sense of the social and economic justice whose intensity is no less than the intensity of the monotheistic idea, so that whoever carefully reads the early Revelations of the prophet cannot escape the conclusion that the two must be regarded as expressions of the same experience.[70]

Rahman's identification of social-economic justice as the overriding concern in the Qur'anic revelation is supported by critical scholar in the field, among whose ranks are also to be found the Muslim women scholars working on 'woman-centred' readings of the sacred text.[71] These latter readings of the Qur'an also stress the 'newness' of Islam's treatment of the 'woman question', a question all Muslims are now compelled to address given the Western construction of Islam as 'misogynist'. I shall return to this point in a following section, here let me continue with a number of other factors that have been identified by scholars of Islam as distinguishing this tradition from its predecessors.

In Muhammad Asad's view, the Qur'an is distinct 'fundamentally from all other sacred scriptures' for 'its stress on *reason* as a valid way to faith, as well as its insistence on the inseparability of man's daily actions and behaviour, however "mundane", from his spiritual life destiny'; the text is thus marked by 'its constant interweaving of spiritual teachings with practical legislation . . . a guidance not only towards the spiritual good of the hereafter but also towards the good life – spiritual, physical and social – attainable in this world'.[72] This emphasis on *reason* has been taken up in a particularly fruitful manner by Ahmed, whose reading of Islamic philosophy led him to argue that for the Islamic philosophers,

> the cosmos/God's creation is an expression and enactment of (God's) Reason: it is God's Reason that courses through the (philosophers') cosmos – one might say that, for the philosophers, Reason is the infrastructure of the cosmos – indeed it is the fact that the cosmos is an expression of Reason that makes the truth of the cosmos accessible and intelligible by Reason.[73]

Ahmed tracks how Muslims developed a range of hermeneutical approaches to understand creation, the sacred text and the nature of Prophethood, and how the philosophers among them 'subjected[ed] the Qur'an to the higher, prior and universal primacy of Reason'.[74] It is Ahmed's view that for the Islamic philosophers, 'Reason, in other words, *is* Revelation'.[75] Moreover, such privileging of reason was only one among a range of interpretive traditions developed by Muslims, for even the philosophers rejected neither the Islamic tradition nor the ritual practices proscribed in the Shari'a even when they very clearly privileged reason over Prophethood.

Recent critical scholarship of Islam is, in many ways, indebted to Talal Asad's groundbreaking interrogation of what it is that constitutes 'the object of investigation for the anthropology of Islam'; he made the case that 'religion' is a concept that was 'integral to modern Western history' but presents 'dangers in employing it as a normalizing concept when translating Islamic traditions'.[76] Asad famously rejected the idea of 'religion' as a 'universal' category, for this is a concept inadequate to the task of explicating the phenomenon it names, which is rooted in the various cultural specificities of its own origins.[77] Reading the concept of religion as informed by the specific experience of Christianity, and highlighting the heterogeneity that is found among Muslim communities in their practice of 'Islam', Asad argued that Islam is best approached as a *discursive tradition* 'that connects variously with the formation of moral selves, the manipulation of populations (or resistance to it), and the production of appropriate knowledges'.[78] In so doing, he rejected the approach popular among scholars of Islam who classified this into 'Little' and 'Great', or 'orthodox' and 'unorthodox' traditions.

Defining as problematic the tendency to consider that 'the beliefs and practices of a Muslim are sufficient to define what Islam is', Asad pointed out this 'ignores the fact that a subject's beliefs about the beliefs of *other* Muslims are part of his or her beliefs, and as such they enter into complicated social relations (real or imagined) with other subjects and therefore belong to a form of life'.[79] Attending to the differences and disagreements among Muslims thus requires as much attention as do the 'variety of beliefs and practices' they have in common, argues Asad, for 'disagreement presupposes some kind of shared framework (even when this isn't entirely clear to those who disagree) that has temporal dimensions'.[80]

Asad's critique of the employment of the concept 'religion' as transhistorical and transcultural deconstructs this as an essentializing practice. The anthropological investment in the concept 'religion' is particularly problematic in his view, for this tradition treats 'religion' as a typology of a totalizing phenomenon which can be used to hierarchically rank societies from 'primitive' to 'advanced' based on their beliefs and practices. The logic of racial difference informing such a hierarchy among 'religions' is evident.

In contrast to this dominant approach to the study of Islam, Asad privileged the temporal and embodied experience of Islam of Muslim communities, their hermeneutic practices and forms of reasoning to engage the Qur'an, and the institutions they developed within their communities. From such a perspective, he argued, Islam can be thought of as an embodied tradition that brings together discursivity with materiality 'through the minutiae of everyday living'.[81] Islam is here defined as 'a tradition of Muslim discourse that addresses itself to conceptions of the Islamic past and future, with reference to a particular Islamic practice in the present'.[82] In his reading of Asad's early work, Iqbal underscores Asad's proposition 'that in tradition, the present is always *at* the center, tradition is not defined *by* the present. Hence the need to "unthink" the language that limns that present and its impasses.'[83]

More important, Asad's view is that in such nuanced approaches to study Islam, 'it will be the practitioners' conceptions of what is *apt practice* and of how the past is related to present practices, that will be crucial for tradition, not the apparent repetition of an old form.'[84] Yet the search for de-historicized repetitive practice remains the fixation of most anthropological, as well as religious studies and other disciplinary approaches to Islam and Muslims. Asad's treatment of the Islamic tradition as dynamic and changing, as a linking of the past to the future, questions the absolutist and essentialist distinctions routinely made between 'classical' and 'modern' Islam in contemporary scholarship, including in the field of Islamic Studies. Asad's approach likewise rejects the popular claim that there is no 'Islam' as such, only multiple and plural 'Islams'.[85]

Following Asad's lead, Salman Sayyid's study of Islam in the post-independence world likewise approaches this as a discursive tradition. Islam, Sayyid argues, offers an alternate universal to that of the West and, as such, poses a profound challenge to the ambitions of the West. Defining Islam as a 'master signifier', he describes this as a 'crucial nodal point' which grounds a number of discourses, including *fiqh* (Islamic jurisprudence), Sufism, Islamism, as well as the originary 'classical' tradition.[86] All are Islam, Sayyid argues, all find meaning in their temporal specificity, yet none exhausts the 'meaning' of Islam. Moreover, as he explains, 'the various attempts to reinterpret and re-articulate Islam already carry within them traces of previous articulations and interpretations, to the extent that all attempts at re-articulation must begin where the last articulation left off'.[87] Sayyid's reading draws a link between the late-nineteenth- and early-twentieth-century articulations of Islam, their anti-colonial investment, and the contemporary articulation of Islamist thought and praxis within neoliberal globalization.

The relation between Islam as 'signifier' and its various 'signifieds' carries previous historical traces, but this relation itself is established and produced through political action, argues Sayyid. Raising the question of what it is that Islam actually founds, he points out that the answer can only be tautological, for Islam 'founds a community of those who subscribe to it: Islam founds the Muslim *Ummah*. In this act of founding, Islam is the means by which a community is unified and established: the unity of a "Muslim" community comes from retrospectively constructing its identity, through the use of Islam as a nodal point'.[88] As a 'nodal point' then, Islam gives meaning to various discourses even as it constitutes them as a unified field.[89] Islam thus becomes the 'name' by which the community founds and unites itself; what ties this particular community to the larger *ummah*, as community-in-common, 'is their invocation of the name of Islam' in their lives and practices.[90] Moreover, the relationship of these communities to Islam is 'unlike any other relationship between any element and Muslims since, within the discourse of Muslims, Islam occupies a privileged space'.[91]

What makes Islam distinct in Sayyid's view is that despite its multiple and multifaceted articulations, these all maintain the specificity of 'Islam', what he calls its 'thing-ness'. The relation then between Islam as master signifier (open, dynamic, contestable, uncontainable, hence ultimately unsignifiable) and its various (signifying) discourses, for example Islamism, is mutually constitutive, 'both Islam and the identity of Islamism are transformed as Islamists attempt to articulate Islam to their project'.[92] In other words, as master signifier, Islam defies being reduced or constrained to a singular 'essence', a monolithic discourse or a static form. This inter-discursivity means that contestation over Islam's meaning is inevitable for those who seek to tether this – master signifier – to any one particular tradition, Sayyid argues. Rather than a return to idealized origins, Islamists who take up Jihad can be considered to be engaged in a 'democratization of Islam, accomplished by its fragmentation of traditional forms of religious authority and the dispersal of their elements into a potentially endless series of recombinations'.[93] This view is, clearly, not without controversy.

With regard to 'Islamism', Ovamir Anjum's analysis of the political activism of reformist Islamist movements in the Arab Spring, including the Muslim Brotherhood in Egypt, finds their engagement with the 'densely elaborated discursive tradition' to which they align their vision and politics to be quite limited.[94] Anjum's point is that for the moderate Islamists, that is, those 'committed to working within the nation-state system', an over-reliance on a charismatic leader who is a 'master at synthesis and compromise' and on a form of political activism that is not deeply informed by the historical tradition of Islam has led to detrimental consequences for their movements. He finds an 'intellectual deficit' in the framing of their movement by these Islamists, while their 'deeper reformist discourse' draws 'selectively' upon the Islamic tradition and is oriented towards modernist conceptions of political and social justice, despite their scepticism towards the latter. These movements are therefore 'devoid of a well-grounded vision of Islamic politics',[95] Anjum argues, for these reformists 'relate to it [the historical Islamic tradition] in order to reform and transform it, rather than be deeply transformed *by it*.⁹⁶ Curtailed by their inability to undertake 'sustained investigation of either tradition', that is, the Islamic tradition or modernity, reformist Islamists are unable to realize their promise to their constituencies nor are they particularly effective in keeping at bay attempts at the radicalization of their own movements by other Islamists.

In Anjum's assessment, these moderate Islamists have 'weakened' the rich and deeply grounded discursive tradition of Islam as a result of their superficial familiarity and intellectual weakness, with the result that their own politics are likewise undermined. The intellectual dimension of the Islamic tradition matters, as does its impact on the making of subjects, such that, as Anjum argues, 'discursive depth and personal and political transformation of subjects ought to count for more'.

While Asad's critique of anthropological accounts that locate Islam on the bottom of the hierarchy of 'religion' has been taken up by critical scholars, the category of 'religion' itself continues to remain dominant and used in ways that are problematic. Islam continues to be designated among 'world religions' in most studies of the tradition, as well as in the contemporary attempts to build 'interfaith' dialogue among religious communities that is the 'progressive' project. However, as is the case with the category 'religion' (Asad, Mandair, etc.), the idea of 'world religions' has also been deconstructed within critical work.

The 'invention' of world religions, Masuzawa argues, was linked to Europe's colonial ideologies and conquests. The 'discovery' of the 'ancient' 'origins' of the traditions and languages of peoples in the 'East' during the nineteenth century threw European intellectuals into a conundrum: How to account for Christianity in this larger historical frame, and how to define the European heritage that they considered self-evidently superior? Their 'invention' of 'world religions' in a classificatory system ranking these traditions hierarchically enabled a reconfiguration of Christianity as a 'universal', rational religion, not a 'Semitic' tradition, especially in contrast to Islam which became tied to racial and linguistic particularity and defined as quintessentially Semitic. Read in this light, Asad's argument that the category 'religion' is informed by Christianity as the model needs to be pushed further, for the very concept of 'religion' encodes the colonizing and racializing logics of European intellectual traditions and colonial classificatory systems. Here, Arvind-Pal Mandair's deconstruction of 'religion' in his study of the Sikh tradition makes an invaluable contribution, for he identifies colonialism as the historical condition that made possible the emergence of the concept of 'religion' and its imposition into the vernaculars of colonized peoples.

Provocatively asking whether the category 'religion' is actually translatable in the native traditions of colonized peoples, Mandair draws attention to the pitfalls inhering in the category itself. Taking Mandair's question seriously reveals how a deeper scrutiny of the category 'religion' destabilizes this term when applied to Islam. Bringing together these various critiques of the concept of 'religion' (i.e. Asad, Mandair, Masuzawa, etc.), particularly their demonstration of its link to colonialism, my approach is to take the imposition of the category 'religion' onto Islam as an assertion of colonial violence (epistemic, ontological, existential and material) that subjugates, truncates and redirects the dynamism and plenitude of Islam to extend Western power over the Muslim world as well as the Islamic tradition. In such a re-designation of Islam as a 'religion', scholars as well as Muslim communities come to accept a highly mutilated and diminished conception of this tradition. Put differently, the application of the category 'religion' to Islam functions to colonize the tradition and reproduce a racializing logic that constructs it as deficient.

There is yet another trajectory in the historical development of Islam that is directly relevant to my study of the nexus of 'religion' and 'race' in the colonizing practices of the West, this is the tradition as developed by Black American Muslims. Given that the Black Islamic tradition explicitly foregrounds race in the relation of these Muslims to Islam, and to non-Black Muslim communities, it has much to teach the latter about the Islamic tradition itself as well as the systemic relations among race, slavery, colonization and 'religion', in the United States and the global order.

Sherman A. (Abdul Hakim) Jackson points to the significance of the Black Muslim experience in the United States in developing the tradition of Islam as a 'God-centred' resistance to anti-Black racism. Rejecting universalizing approaches to Islam that elevate the tradition in the Arabian heartland, Jackson identified this practice as allowing non-Black Muslims to claim greater ownership of Islam. In the process, these Muslims marginalize the Black Islamic tradition as well as Black American Muslims to reproduce the anti-Black racism that is a core feature of the racial structure of US society. The opening up of US immigration policy in the 1960s led to increased migration from Muslim majority countries, he notes, but with these Muslim communities defining their own tradition as 'universal', they obscured the historical roots of Islam in the United States as well as the contemporary presence of the Black American Islamic tradition.

Drawing on the thought of Ibn Taymiya, the thirteenth-century Islamic scholar, Jackson rejects the idea that there can be a uniform experience of Islam to argue 'that there is no "real", "true", or "authentic" Islam apart from the historical instantiations (read interpretations) of the religion in the world'.[97] The idea of a universal Islam is itself based on a 'false universal', a move by which 'history [is] internalized, normalized, and then forgotten as history'.[98] This idea does, however, allow non-Black Muslim communities to elevate their own experience and to dismiss Black American Islam as a localized, particular form. As these non-Black Muslims expand their power to 'define' Islam, they also extend their racial privilege by further marginalizing the Black American Muslim community, such that the former's critiques of the West do not include confrontation with, but rather reproduction of, race and anti-Black racism. As Jackson rightly points out, the role of Black American Muslims in the development of the Islamic tradition, and it's contesting of the racial structure of US society, is no insignificant aspect of the tradition.

It should be remembered that Islam arrived in the Americas in 1492, with the Spanish conquistadors. Among the crew of Christopher Columbus were those 'Muslims who had been forced to profess the Christian faith', but as Gomez notes in his study of this period, 'it is highly probable that Islam remained embedded in their souls'.[99] During the fifteenth and sixteenth centuries, many enslaved Muslims were brought from West Africa to the Americas in the transatlantic slave trade. More numerous and better organized in the Caribbean and Brazil, the highly 'visible' and 'threatening' presence of these Muslims' was met with the most 'severe political repression' of the state, with the result that Islam 'faltered' during this period, argues Gomez. In what would become the United States, he finds that Muslim communities were 'comparatively quiet and compliant: their legacy survived a temporal interim until the early twentieth century, when the fortunes of Islam were revived by way of the rise of nationalist sentiment'.[100] Indeed, 28 per cent of the present US population that identifies as Muslim are Black Americans.[101]

In the mid-twentieth century, the leaders – including Malcolm X – of what Gomez describes as 'Islamic-like movements' and what Jackson calls Black American Islam 'forged indissoluble bonds with nationalist expressions, providing a vehicle through which certain Islamic ideas could be introduced and disseminated'.[102] The argument Gomez makes is that the turn towards Islamic (Sunni) orthodoxy by Black Muslims was shaped by 'variegations' in Islam's earlier historic presence in the United States. Daulatzai's study of Black Islam during the mid-twentieth century highlights the impact of this tradition in the overall development of Black radical thought and politics, for there is 'a rich and compelling history between Blackness, Islam and the Muslim Third World, a history and legacy that provides a powerful challenge to the post-9/11 era and the election of Obama'.[103]

In the case of Malcolm X, who also took the name Al-Haj Malik Al-Shabazz, his challenge to white supremacy like his reshaping of the Black radical tradition transformed the US political arena. Malcolm X's relation to Islam was a crucial factor in the development of his ideas about race and religion, Islam and politics, for he saw no contradiction in his resistance to white supremacy and his commitment to live his life as a Black Muslim. Conversion to Islam was 'a central part' of Malcolm X's recovery of his Black identity and history, for in this re/turn to Islam, he 'reclaimed the power to redefine oneself, to change from a "slave name" to the "X" (the unknown) and then to the "original" Muslim name. Islam became a vehicle for Malcolm and other Black converts to reject the master narrative of slavery – and by extension America – to redefine themselves from property to person, from slave to human'.[104] Given that the relation between Blackness and Islam 'is rooted in Black resistance to New World Slavery', that is, to the very foundation of US nationhood, this relation creates 'a tremendous amount of anxiety within the larger U.S. national imagination, as it continues to circle and even haunt contemporary ideas and debates around U.S. political culture'.[105] Malcolm X's political legacy was certainly not confined to the United States, nor has it been erased. Black American Islam challenges the liberal framework that is now dominant and functions to integrate Black Americans into US nationalism. The Black Islamic tradition aligned Black Muslims directly with the internationalism of the anti-colonial and anti-racist movements of the 1960s, its potential to do so again cannot be dismissed.

Jackson's critique of the problematic racial – and racist – politics of non-Black Muslims, and not only within the United States, is one that is echoed in other studies of the racializing processes entailed in the making of 'moderate' Islam in the United States and elsewhere. The impetus to advance a 'moderate' form of Islam gained political momentum in the global war, particularly in the desire of many liberal Muslims for inclusion, respectability and upward class mobility within US society. Yet the quest for such inclusion overlooks not only the entrenched racial divides within US society as Jackson argues, it also neglects the tenuous positioning of (non-Black) Muslims of colour themselves within this racial hierarchy. Given the war's deepening of this racial order, Muslim attempts to make Islam respectable directly counter the revolutionary Black Islamic tradition, which is explicitly abolitionist and anti-racist. In contrast, the 'racial strategies of action' to further the assimilation of Muslims into US nationalism range from 'white/colour-blind acculturation' to 'black appropriation' and even compromised forms of 'brown solidarity'.[106] Moreover, the bid to recast Islam as moderate neglects the deep class divides within Muslim countries and communities as well as the highly exploitative effects of neoliberalism's shrinking of the public sector which has had devastating impact on Black and other people of colour communities, Muslim as well as non-Muslim.[107] Moreover, the role of Black Muslims in the development of abolitionist politics, anti-racist and anti-colonial politics, is as underappreciated within Islamic Studies as it is within critical race studies.

My discussion of Islam has thus far focused on a number of critical, and influential perspectives that challenge dominant practices by advancing counter-hegemonic approaches within the tradition itself. Yet even these critical approaches are contested by Shahab Ahmed who asked the seemingly obvious question, *What is Islam?* Ahmed's response to the question is one of those paradigm-shattering events that lays the foundation of a radical rupture within Islamic Studies.

Ahmed identified a number of seemingly transgressive practices among Muslim communities which are nevertheless treated as 'Islamic'. Centring these practices – which have been defined as 'un-Islamic' or simply overlooked – in his work, Ahmed shows how these have been and continue to remain temporally and spatially widespread despite apparently controverting what have been determined to be the essential Islamic injunctions. Such practices include the Islamic philosopher's valorization of intellectual thought above revelation in pursuit of the 'higher truth'; the Sufi commitment to transcendence of the self in the intoxicating experience of 'one-ness' with truth; the drinking of wine and celebration of the state of intoxication; the recitation of Islamic love poetry, with its decidedly homoerotic tenor; the Islamic arts that depict human figures; the notion that divine illumination is to be found in all beings, which opens up the possibility of relativism, not to mention pantheism. Such practices are not marginal, Ahmed notes, they have shaped the mainstream of Muslim life and were sanctioned by highly respected and much beloved Islamic thinkers, poets, artists and jurists across the expansive post-classical Islamic world, the Balkans-to-Bengal complex as he names it, which encompassed parts of Eastern Europe, across North Africa and into the Middle East, to South and Central Asia. How to account for these irreverent practices, which most scholars treat as either aberrations or dismiss as not 'real' Islam? Ahmed's answer is that these practices are themselves *constitutive* of Islam, they give Islam its particular meaning, form and expression in the lives of Muslims as *historical* subjects.

In Ahmed's view, Muslims have experienced Islam on multiple dimensions and in starkly different ways. Islam can thus be understood as

> the hermeneutical engagement with different sources of Revelation (Pre-text, Text, and Con-Text) by different epistemologies in different disciplinary projects, each issuing in different Truths and Meanings of Revelation that are *spatially arrayed* in a social *hierarchy* of truth and in a social *exteriority-interiority* of truth – that is, in acknowledgedly different forms and calibrations and isotopes of truth for different persons and places.[108]

Such an expansive understanding of Islam sheds new light on the ongoing Muslim contestations of the meaning of Islam; it also demonstrates that the power of Islam has never been containable in rigidly, closed-off systems that are passed off as essential elements of the tradition.

Ahmed's groundbreaking work, unfortunately, does not locate these formations of Islam in relation to colonialism or the global capitalist system, whether in periods of Muslim ascendance or in moments of crises. Nor did Ahmed directly address the occupations, wars, securitization and white supremacy being instituted as explicit responses to this dynamic Islam and Muslim presence, which cannot but impact the epistemological practices adopted within Islamic Studies. How contemporary Islamic traditions take up the challenge Ahmed's work presents remains to be seen. He has however, undoubtedly expanded the horizon of possibilities for Muslims to rethink their collective pasts in envisioning their Islamic futures.

Among scholars who study contemporary Muslim responses to occupation and imperialism, the work of historian and scholar of Jihad, Faisal Devji, provides interesting insights into how Muslims have reinterpreted their tradition accordingly. It should be noted here that the concept of *revolutionary violence*, which shaped the anti-colonial politics of Third-World movements (defended so passionately and eruditely by Fanon), is not far removed from the concept of *Jihad* as espoused by Islamist radicals. In the views of some of these Islamists, Devji has found, 'Muslims are not members of a religious group so much as the contemporary representatives of human suffering'.[109] Islamism and globalization exist on the same temporal and spatial plane, Devji notes, so that if neoliberalism integrated previously peripheral regions into the global economy, the operations of Islamists began the integration of some of these peripheral regions into the larger Islamic world. Citing the example of al-Qaeda's attacks on the US embassies in Kenya and Uganda, Devji argues that the event 'integrated the region [East Africa] within the global networks of militant Islam as much as it integrated it within a global security regime administered by the United States'.[110] Afghanistan is another case in point, where the defeat of the Soviet occupation by the Afghan and other *mujahidin* escalated that superpower's disintegration and hastened the end of the Cold War.

As is well known, the Islamic militancy led by al-Qaeda against the Soviet Union then turned against the United States; what is less well known is that the rhetoric of its Islamist leadership was rife with concerns about 'humanism', 'humanitarianism' and 'human rights', Devji has found. Such messages speak to the multifaceted threats that these *Jihadis* identify as emanating from 'the avarice of states and corporations that happen also to threaten Muslims around the world'.[111] Nuclear apocalypse and environmental collapse were explicitly identified among these threats. In this discursive universe, Devji argues, the Muslim functions as archetype of a suffering humanity such that 'for the militants among us, victimized Muslims represent not only their religion so much as humanity itself'.[112] These Islamists' rhetoric, Devji argues, leads to them to conclude that '[t]hose who defend Muslims, then, automatically protect the common interests of humanity'.[113]

A similar analysis of Islamist discourse is to be found in Crooke's work, who argues that the crucial factor at work in shaping their politics is a contestation of the meaning of the 'human'. Islam, Crooke writes with regard to the Islamist movements in Egypt, Iran, Palestine and Lebanon, inspires social bonds based on justice and egalitarianism as the means for the community to access, and experience, the divine.[114] Their resistance to Western domination, he explains, 'was jolted into existence by the trauma of social engineering, ethnic cleansing, political disruption, repression and massacres that were the direct consequence of the western experiment in exporting to Muslim societies its vision of economic market-based life, freed from social and political control'.[115]

Can this Islamist conception of a 'suffering humanity' be another name for *the wretched of the earth*? The parallels between the 'new' humanism glimpsed by Fanon as the potential embedded in revolutionary anti-colonial praxis and the Islamists' reworking of the category 'Muslim' to encapsulate the idea of an exploited global humanity are striking. Where Fanon's attention was focused on the racializing principle of a colonial world that gave rise to the secularist desire for an end to the violence, the imbrication of this racial order within 'religion' – more precisely, Islam – is highlighted by this *Jihadi* tradition, inspired by his/her relation to Islam to struggle in the name of a 'suffering humanity'.[116] How does this Islamist militant, as was the question faced earlier by the Third-World revolutionary, negotiate the catastrophic consequences of the violence that dehumanizes and dispossesses this suffering humanity? How to confront and transform the status of the Muslim from phobogenic object to human being? If the global war reminds its 'enemy' populations that religio-racial and imperial might determine the 'right to be human',[117] the daily brutalization of Muslims reminds these same populations of the immense capacity of Islam to humanize these Muslims and inspire the realization of its humanizing values.

Hence even as the global war extends the condition of coloniality, its dialectic of violence is such that this simultaneously fuels the historical consciousness of the Muslim and reinvigorates her relation to Islam. As the brutalized Muslim insists on justice in a rapidly disintegrating world order, one that is changing on condition of her dehumanization, her quest leads her closer towards the tradition that reaffirms her life, her being, her humanity. This vision of justice is one for

Judeo-Christian secularity: The highest stage of religion?

> At first thought it might seem strange that the anti-Semite's outlook should be related to that of the Negrophobe. It was my philosophy professor, a native of the Antilles, who recalled the fact to me one day: 'Whenever you hear anyone abuse Jews, pay attention, because he is talking about you.' And I found that he was universally right – by which I mean that I was answerable in my body and my heart for what was done to my brother. Later I realized that he meant, quite simply, an anti-Semite is inevitably anti-Negro.[118]

As both Fanon and his professor recognized, racism and anti-Semitism were deeply intertwined in the political cultures of the West into the mid-twentieth century. Yet the contemporary charge of anti-Semitism, more often than not, is made against Muslims, particularly anti-Zionist, anti-Islamophobia and anti-racist activists. Indeed, in the discursive framing of the global war, it is Muslims who are regarded as constitutionally anti-Semitic and virulently anti-Jewish. This is particularly so with regard to the issue of Palestine.

Well into the twentieth century, Christianity and Judaism were defined as antithetical, even enemy, traditions in Western politics and culture. If the old Christian accusation that Jews were responsible for the death of Christ shaped European antipathy towards Jews, the philosophical-political traditions of modernity characterized Judaism as a religion of servility and racial degeneracy. The modern state's institutionalization of these constructs fed the many irruptions of public violence against Jewish communities, such that scapegoating and discrimination was politically sanctioned. As scholars have noted of this history, '[r]ather than receding as time passed', anti-Semitism towards Jews 'increased during the last quarter of the nineteenth and the first half of the twentieth century'.[119] Moreover, this anti-Semitism 'contains religious, racial, economic and political manifestations'.[120] Even when these Jewish communities 'experienced rising toleration and emancipation' to become 'members of the highest echelons of the economic, social, cultural and political elites' as during the period 1791–1870, anti-Semitism was not 'completely eradicated'.[121] Indeed, organizations such as the Anti-Semites League, officially founded to fight 'Semitism' (1879), actually increased ideological and political antipathy towards the Jewish communities of Europe.[122]

Anti-Semitism surged to unprecedented levels in Europe after 1933, following 'the successful Bolshevik Revolution in Russia, the post-World War I collapse of empires, and the toppling of the world economy', so that 1939 was the 'eventful year [that] witnessed the outbreak of World War II and a qualitatively new phase in anti-Semitism leading to the near-annihilation of European Jewry'.[123] Beller points out that 'European history appeared to show that attitudes toward Jews were quite capable of benevolent *change*', and that Jews were 'increasingly accepted as a part of English society' in the nineteenth century, such that Benjamin Disraeli's prime ministership (1874) 'was seen by many as a sign of British enlightenment concerning Jews'.[124] Yet despite periods of such 'benevolent' change, anti-Semitism remained an entrenched feature of European culture: it would irrupt with devastating consequences for European Jews in the Holocaust.

The anxieties provoked by modernization also led to the escalation of anti-Semitism in Europe, Brustein points out. He identifies a number of additional factors such as popular resentment at the upward social and economic mobility of Jewish communities which led to 'anomic stresses', and scapegoating, ethnic prejudice and backlashes in response to state reforms to counter anti-Semitism.[125] Important as these explanatory factors are, Brustein argues, they are limited due to a lack of national comparative studies, especially given the variations in national cultures. He also identifies 'deterioration in a nation's economic well-being, the impact of increased Jewish immigration, the growth of popular support for the political left, and the extent to which leadership of the political left was identified with Jews' as relevant to the periodic resurgence of anti-Semitism.[126]

A number of significant – and well-documented – factors are, however, typically excluded from most discussion of European anti-Semitism; these have been addressed by a handful of scholars. First, the category 'Semite' which shaped the racial imaginary of Europe encapsulated the Muslim as well as the Jew, as did the category, 'Oriental';[127] second, the nexus of race and religion that shaped the Euro-American order was interlinked with the global-colonial order then dominated by Europe;[128] and third, the genocide of European Jews was undertaken *by the same* Europe responsible for earlier, as well as, contemporaneous genocides across the colonies in the Americas, Asia and Africa.[129] The post-Second World War elevation of the Holocaust as a singular event (i.e. genocide without compare) rendered illegible Europe's genocides across the colonies. This singularity severed the structural connection between the genocides in the colonies and within Europe itself, its impact is now evident in the deeply damaged possibilities for anti-racist alliance between these Jewish communities and people of colour, within Western nation-states or across the Middle East, and in the integration of Euro-American Jewish communities into the West.

Discourses of Orientalism and Semitism overlapped and were intermingled to construct Jews and Muslims as threats – albeit of different sort – to the religious sanctity, racial purity and sociopolitical interests of a West that identified itself in Christian (Protestant/Catholic) terms into the mid-twentieth century. This religious identity overlapped with the identity of the West as simultaneously secular, which had became more prominent since the late nineteenth century as Christianity was relegated to a second-order characteristic of a Europe that now increasingly defined itself as heir to ancient (Hellenic) Greece. Indeed, the secular-political sphere generally acceded to the theologio-cultural domination of public life by the Christian ethos, which the concurrent integration of Orientalist logics and anti-Semitic politics into scientific discourses also served to uphold.

The above characterization of the West shifted dramatically in the war on terror, as Western identity became redefined as Judeo-Christian, in secular as well as religious terms. This development, of course, unfolded in relation to an Islam construed as *singularly* and *quintessentially* anti-Semitic, a construction that not only obscures the notoriously anti-Semitic history of the West but also projects this violent history onto Muslims as foundational to their being. Although these changing identifications, affiliations and animosities were in the making over the second half of the twentieth century, they were cemented by the global war. Studying the conditions that led to the reformation of the West as Judeo-Christian and secular, and the dissociation of the figure of the Jew from the categories 'Oriental' and 'Semite' this entailed, is crucial to understanding the Islamophobia that is the organizing feature of global politics in the war on terror.

It is well documented that Jews held a high status in *al-Andalus* in the pre-modern period; they were among the Muslim world's most renowned scholars, including Maimonides, who is credited with having 'codified Jewish doctrine' and who served as the Sultan's personal physician.[130] This would change with the expulsion and forced conversions of Jews and Muslims after the fall of Granada, a 'pet project of the Spanish Inquisition, headed by Father Tomas de Torquemada... who believed that as long as the Jews remained in Spain, they would influence the tens of thousands of recent Jewish converts to Christianity to continue practising Judaism'.[131] Among these expelled Jews, 'the most fortunate' found refuge in the Ottoman Empire, where they were 'warmly welcomed' by the Ottoman Sultan.[132] These anecdotes speak to a past in which the fate of Jewish communities within territorial Europe was tied to that of Muslims, a past in which the destruction of Muslim rule had severe consequence also for the Jewish communities in Europe. The expulsions sealed the fate of relations among and between Muslims, Jews and Christians in Europe over the next five centuries, and as some scholars note, undergirded the making of Europe as Christian (now including the 'pagans' who were then also being converted). The signs 'Islam' and 'Judaism' were thus internally linked in the making of the West as Christian and soon enough, as modern.[133]

Said's work tracked how the Orient/al was discursively constructed during the late eighteenth and nineteenth centuries, and Masuzawa shows how the category 'Semite' was created in the field of philology during this very period. These categories functioned in excess of ethnic and linguistic content as they also codified racial, religious, national and geographic difference.[134] The significance of the period in which these discourses and categories emerged, a period in which the power of the Islamic empires was being undermined, eroded and hollowed out to eventually lead to their dramatic collapse by the post-independence era, cannot be overlooked; these categories and associated discourses were part of the European assault on the Islamic powers whose decimation was key to the expansion of Western domination over the global order. The categories 'Semite' and 'Oriental' – contrasted with 'Aryan' and 'European' – drew on earlier Christian ideas about Jews and Muslims but configured them anew to signify the 'degraded consciousness' and 'inferior nature' that would bespoke the secular processes of racialization within the Euro-America imaginary and helped accomplish such decimation of the Islamic powers.[135]

The myth of the 'Aryan', Figueira argues, 'displaced the Jews from their central position on the world stage'.[136] Whereas Judaism was the undisputed precursor of Christianity, the myth of the Aryan allowed Europe to cut itself free from this history and 'construct an ideal imaginary past' which assigned Jews to a 'subaltern role in history'.¹³⁷ Masuzawa, Bernal and others have illustrated how the category Aryan allowed a making of older origins and was associated with the Western claim to Hellenic Greece as Europe's glorious and ancient 'heritage', a gesture that allowed Western cultural identity to be reconstructed as older than Christianity and rooted in the Greek philosophical tradition. Christianity was to be thus recast as a 'spiritual' influence on this West, while the origins of its scientific and political cultures were attributed to the ancient Greek philosophers.

In his reading of the category 'Semite', Massad emphasizes the point that the opposite of this category is not the 'anti-Semite' but the 'Aryan'. Massad's point here is that 'Semitism' came into existence as a relation of alterity to *Aryanism*, not *anti-Semitism*, as is the widespread perception in the present. Indeed, Said considered Semitism to closely resemble Orientalism, for he argued that 'The Oriental and the Semite, the Orientalist and the anti-Semite, Orientalism and anti-Semitism are therefore second selves to one another, doubles and mirror reflections that must always be read and seen in tandem'.¹³⁸ During the early twentieth century, anti-Semitism 'would continue to focus on the figure of the Jew while its double, colonial Orientalism, would focus on the Arab and the Muslim, often conflated as the Semite of choice', according to Massad.¹³⁹ He goes on to underscore the point, 'Semitism has always been anti-semitism'.¹⁴⁰ I draw on Said's and Massad's reading of these discourses in my analysis of *how* the category 'Semite' underwent an internal split during the Nazi period such that European Jewish communities were subsequently reconfigured as racially white, with the figure of the Muslim being fixed as both quintessential Oriental and anti-Semite.

Most scholars of the Holocaust define the Nazi camp as the site of death.¹⁴¹ The horrors of the camp are well documented, and I draw on Agamben's work on Auschwitz in my reading of the camp to highlight the link between the terror of the camp and the religio-racial logic of power of Western self-formation. While most certainly the site of the mass racial murder of European Jews, the camp however became subsequently a site for the racial remaking of Jewish communities in Europe as white and Western. For the Jewish survivors of the camps were integrated into Euro-American nations and into citizenship, they were thus endowed with the status of Subject and 'the right to have rights' in the post-Nazi period. Further, the establishment of the state of Israel in historic Palestine extended this 'right' as also the right to kill, to colonize, to dispossess. This post-Holocaust reworking of Western religio-racial politics transmogrified the catastrophic violence of the Nazi camps into the catastrophic violence of settler colonialism imposed onto the Palestinians. The effects of these shifts within and beyond Europe speak to how religio-racial violence remained at the forefront of the remaking of the post-Second World War international order which ostensibly heralded the age of 'liberalism', of 'decolonization'.

The coming realignment of the nexus of religion and race is suggested, even if somewhat obliquely, in Freud's description of Europe as 'our present-day white Christian civilization'.¹⁴² Important insights into the unfolding alliance among Christianity, Judaism and Zionism during the period are provided by

Massad, who argues that an equivalence was being drawn at the time in the United States between certain religious traditions and political democracy, such that Protestantism, Catholicism and Judaism became redefined as 'the religions of democracy', setting the stage for the coming political alliance among their adherents.[143] The publication of *The Religions of Democracy: Judaism, Catholicism, Protestantism in Creed and Life* (1941), supported by the National Conference of Christians and Jews, is identified by him as seminal in the 'institutionalization of the new hyphenated connection between Judaism and Christianity'.[144] In this context, Massad explains, 'American secularism was considered completely compatible with their religious commitments, and these three "religions" were redefined as essentially liberal and nationalist (American) in their sentiments and values, given their purported respect for the rights of individuals and their opposition to tyranny'.[145] This 'American creed' was 'exported to post-Nazi Europe', and by the end of the Cold War, focused its attention fully on Islam as a shared threat.[146] As Beller has also observed, 'protecting' Jews served an important doctrinal function for Christians. Despite the long-standing strain of 'anti-Judaism' that prevailed in Christian doctrine since Paul's writings, Beller's argument is that Jews were 'held in a subordinate and wretched state in order to act as evidence of the consequences of their blindness toward the truth of Christ's divinity . . . so that they could eventually act as witnesses, at the Second Coming, to that truth'.[147] As the only religious 'minority' whose presence is necessary for the realization of this Christian future, Jews hold 'a *central* role, as the Chosen People of the one God'.[148]

The establishment of the state of Israel was of apiece with these developments. In Massad's view, Palestine became the battlefield for the 'Semites' who went the way of Europe (that is, the Zionists) and for the 'Semites' who refused to do the same (the Palestinian/Arab/Muslim). In these post-Nazi reiterations of Christo-Judaic religious-cum-secular politics, Islam was also redefined, as a religion of terror and hatred. Islam is hence paradoxically the alien *and* the animating force in these realignments.

The 'splitting' of the category 'Semite', as I demonstrate, can be traced to the Nazi camp, where this rupture was accompanied by a splitting also of the category 'Oriental'. The testimony of the Jewish survivors of the camps reveal the deadly consequences of these processes for Jewish communities at the time, the war on terror provides a glimpse into their devastating consequences for Muslims. For these fracturing processes set in motion an assimilatory impulse towards Jewish peoples which became linked to a reassertion of the colonizing impulse; both found expression in opposition to Muslims that would eventually lead to the political and social destruction of their status as is now so graphically symbolized in the category *unlawful enemy combatant*.

Such violent destruction of the humanity of the Muslim is inseparable from the religio-racial inclusions of the sign Judeo-Christian. The eschatological and white supremacist forces energized by these assimilations and destructions can be observed in the alliance forged by US Christian Evangelicals with US and Israeli Zionists. The strength of this political alliance, intensified by the Trump presidency, which gave carte blanche to the Israeli colonization of Palestine and its violence against Palestinians by endorsing the unrestrained building of settlements on occupied territory, transfer of the US embassy to Jerusalem, imprisoning of the population of Gaza, realignment of the political alliances of the Gulf states, not to mention the elevation of Israel as the laboratory for war and the deadly technologies of 'slow' genocide.

The erotics of terror

In the aftermath of the invasion of Iraq, a post featuring a young man who identified himself as a US soldier and a guard at Abu Ghraib appeared on YouTube.[149] Boasting about his exploits, he described his pleasure in torturing Iraqis and raping a fifteen-year-old girl. Turning to a companion (present in the post) the young man asks, 'What's the big deal in making a Haj[j]i walk around like a dog and bark?' As is well documented, instructions for the treatment of detainees included sexual humiliation as well as treating them like animals by using dog collars and leashes, making them crawl on the floor, etc. Many soldiers were reported in the media to refer to killing Iraqis as 'lighting up a haj[j]i'.[150]

The *Hajj* is a religious obligation for Muslims, who consider this a reminder of the 'egalitarian nature of Islam and its universalism'.[151] Drawing millions to Mecca every year, completion of this sacred journey is 'the apex of Muslim spiritual experience', it bestows the status of *Hajji* on Muslims as public recognition of 'their engagement with and experience of the completeness of a life of faith'.[152] In the Islamic mystical tradition, the *Hajj* is described 'in a language full of symbols and tropes . . . as a mystical journey towards God'.[153] As Asad explains, faith 'is not a singular epistemological means that guarantees God's existence for the believer' in the Islamic tradition, rather, it is 'the virtue of faithfulness toward God . . . a disposition that has to be cultivated like any other, and that links one to others who are faithful, through mutual trust and responsibility'.[154] Miriam Cooke has defined this ritual as the keeping of faith and the building of trust within the community, it 'may be interpreted as something other than the exceptional gathering of different races, ethnicities, and cultures in two Arabian cities. It can be seen rather as an occasion when Indonesians, Americans, and Senegalese join their Arab "cousins" to make the sentimental journey "home" to Mecca, a return they anticipate five times a day when they orient themselves for prayer'.[155] This most revered of Islamic ritual links the Muslim to the transnational *ummah* in a shared relationship to the transcendent; it is also a reminder of Islam's reverence for pre-Islamic practices.

Not insignificant, the *Hajj* is also experienced as transformative of the *Hajji*'s political values and social relations. So deeply affected was Malcolm X by his encounters with 'white' Muslim pilgrims that he returned to the United States with a radically altered view of the prospect for reconciliation between Black and white Americans. Previously convinced that whites were incapable of overcoming their racism, he came to believe that reconciliation was not only desirable but also a real possibility.[156] The siege of *al-Masjid al-Haram* in Mecca (1979) by Muslims attempting to overthrow the Saudi regime illustrates the radical possibilities that may emerge in the event itself.[157]

The scorning of this widely respected status of the *Hajji* as akin to that of a dog in the YouTube post was, likely unbeknownst to the young man, in keeping with a long-standing Western tradition of stripping Muslims of their humanity. Believing his actions would not upset 'anybody', the young man in the YouTube post described how he used plastic to choke Iraqi men, and how he raped and then pimped a young Iraqi woman to other soldiers. In his view, 'they are all guilty. They should have kicked Saddam Hussein out themselves. Instead we are doing the job. We are losing men ... anyone with a fucking rag on their head is fair game.'[158]

The pleasures and contempts described by the young man –incited by torture, rape and pimping – were intermixed, arising as much from service in the war as from brutalizing and killing Iraqis. The Western male power expressed here is likewise intermingled, arising from the belief in US invincibility and Muslim disposability. The young (raped) Iraqi woman subsequently hanged herself, the soldier/rapist informed his audience nonchalantly, going on to explain that as rape is stigmatized in Iraqi society, '[s]he would have been stoned to death anyway'.

Whatever the man's (lack of) understanding of Iraqi law, society and culture, or of Islamic rituals, he seemed unperturbed by the fact that rape in conflict zones is a war crime, and that rape of a minor is a crime even in the United States. The staging of such a public performance speaks to the man's lack of concern regarding legal repercussion or social ostracism. The self-proclaimed rapist clearly believed that whatever he *had* done to the young Iraqi woman could not be compared to what Islam/Iraqi men *would have* done to her.

My recounting of this video post is not, of course, to suggest that such online performances be taken at face value. As an emergent social media in the global war, YouTube rapidly transformed from 'an eccentric technique' into a transnational platform for 'public displays of emotion prompted by suffering', the platform became 'literally, a digital interpellation'.[159] The shift in public discourse following 9/11, that is, 'from an unquestionable faith in the moral imperative of state power towards a more nuanced view of the ramifications of the attack in terms of individual responsibility' was 'picked up' by YouTube[160] as a seductive medium for the venting of private and public emotions, grievances and frustrations. Given the platform's then early evolution as part of the 'consumption oriented personally liberating modern technologies' that encourage 'a sense of narcissistic pseudo-individuality',[161] the online post should *most certainly not* be taken as confirmation of this man's service in the US army, or at Abu Ghraib, or even perpetration of the acts of violence he described.

Yet overlooking the similarities between the claims in this digital post and the case of the twenty-two-year-old US soldier convicted of the rape and murder of a fourteen-year-old Iraqi girl and her family in Mahmudiya would be equally problematic.[162] The post also echoes the experience of another US soldier in Afghanistan who admitted that, along with members of his combat team, he had 'set up and faked combat situations so that they could kill civilians who posed no threat to them'.[163] This soldier was shown in a photograph 'posing with the corpse of a young Afghan boy as if it were a hunting trophy';[164] indeed, US soldiers were also reported to keep 'body parts of their victims, including a skull, as souvenirs'.[165] The parallels between the YouTube post and these documented crimes by US and other allied soldiers cannot be lightly dismissed. At the very least, the post is a chilling reminder of how the global war feeds the fertile imagination and fantasy lives of young Americans whose desires were articulated to the politico-sexual landscape patrolled by their uniformed compatriots in Iraq and Afghanistan.

Race and religion fuse with sex and violence in these incidents, and their recounting shapes the imaginary of this Western Subject, who feels personally called upon to mete out 'punishment' to the Iraqis/Muslims, male and female, he fantasizes as deserving of this. Predictably enough, the threat of such violence from those on the lookout to 'retaliate' against Muslims remains real enough, especially given that the assumptions underlying such representation of Muslims continue to be disseminated on a daily basis in media, politics and culture.

The experience of the violence of the war as personal pleasure was shared by other, far more powerful men, including the US Defence Secretary. Then commander of a Marine Division in Iraq that led the assault on Fallujah, General Mattis expressed his delight in killing Muslim men to 'save' Muslim women. 'Actually it's quite fun to fight 'em, you know. It's a hell of a hoot. It's fun to shoot some people. I'll be right up front with you. I like brawling', he told an applauding audience.[166] The General was earlier reported to have proclaimed with much pride to his command that 'The Marines have landed, and we now own a piece of Afghanistan'.[167] While in Iraq, the advice he gave to his soldiers was to '[b]e polite, be professional, but have a plan to kill everybody you meet'.[168] Celebrated as 'a warrior's warrior', General Mattis was appointed by President Obama to head US Central Command and oversee military operations in Afghanistan, Pakistan and the Middle East;[169] he went on to serve as President Trump's Secretary of Defence. Much like the young man in the YouTube post, the General justified the killings of Afghan men that so delighted him in a religio-cultural-sexual frame, 'You go into Afghanistan, you got guys who slap women around for five years because they don't wear a veil. . . . You know, guys like that ain't got no manhood left anyway. So it's a hell of a lot of fun to shoot them.'[170]

The tropes peppered in such comments are a staple of the Orientalist imaginary, namely, the oppressed/passive Muslim female, the misogynist/fanatic Muslim male, the heroic white Man and the (absent) liberated (unveiled) Woman against whom is measured the status of the Muslim woman. The dialectic of desire and disgust at work in these tropes point to how the figure of the Muslim female as an abject object mediates the desire of the white Man who would save her, and how the phantasy of her unveiling/rape mediates his murderous relation to the Muslim male, a figure he desires to exterminate.

These gendering/sexualizing mediations and relations of power are graphically evident in the forms of dehumanization visited upon the Muslim men, women and children at Abu Ghraib, where the brutalization of the Muslim body involved its sexualization and bestialization it, its smearing with (fake) menstrual blood and adorning in women's underwear.[171] The Taguba Report documents the brutalization of Muslim women as well as the men, among the cases it recorded was an incident in which US soldiers rode an elderly Iraqi woman like a horse and raped her anally with a baton.[172]

Such merging of sexualization with bestialization in the treatment of Black/brown Muslim bodies gave shape and content to the gender-sexual politics of the global war. The practices described above reconfigure 'Islamic terror' into 'Islamic sexual perversity' in the register of gender to map out and organize the psycho-existential *distance* of the properly gendered and sexed Western Subject. Concurrently, the Muslim is transformed from 'terrorist' to sexual degenerate, hence perversely gendered; 'terrorism' itself is here shorn of 'political' content to become redefined as sexual repression and gender hatred. Public exposure of the torture prompted some hand wringing, but little interrogation regarding the construction of 'Islam' as sexual degeneracy or Muslim masculinity as 'perversity', let alone the sexual fixation of Western Subjects with this phobogenic object. The design of the sexual torture by academic and military experts who determined 'Islamic culture' to be inherently sexually repressive did not lead to much investigation of what the sadistic violence reveals about the forms of knowledge production that give rise to such 'expertise'.

The presentation of the Abu Ghraib torture as isolated, even aberrant, allowed the perception to grow that the United States and its allies had moved beyond the mass brutalities documented during the early and chaotic phase of the war, a perception that is debunked as soon as one attends to the Trump Administration's public endorsement of torture and sexual violence, police brutality, vigilante violence by armed white militias, the Muslim Ban, incarceration of migrants and their children. More ominously, the promotion of those US citizens, including women, who oversaw the torture and committed the war crimes demonstrates the ample rewards to be accrued through these practices.[173]

Such sexual-racial violence, it is my contention, points to how the global war reshaped the sense of what it means to be 'Western', to be Man and Woman, not to mention Queer, in the twenty-first century. The intimate desires, phantasies and pleasures incited in the war's cultural politics have reshaped this Subject's experience of her sexual-gender identity, and agency, as reliant on her ties to the Western-ness which now intrinsically includes the sexual denigration of Muslims and the right to dominate, if not destroy, the resisting Muslim. The public sanction of this subject's sense of self reinvigorates her psycho-affective attachment to Western power, to the state and nation, in terms of her sexuality as well as political allegiance. The war's animation of the desires fuelling her subjectivity is shaped by, and reshapes, the complex interaction between the sexual, the existential, the cultural, the political and the corporeal. The imbrication of these desires makes them almost impossible to disentangle, their saturation with the violent tendencies of the state accordingly reshapes her subjectivity as well as sovereign status as Subject: what is the global war *really* about – oil, minerals, resources? Payback for 9/11? Political domination? Destruction of terror? Fighting Islam? Sexual/Gender 'freedoms'? Human civilization? Defence of culture?

Given the inseparability of the sexualized and eroticized expressions of desire recounted above with the logics of imperial power, it bears remembering that earlier as well as more recent histories of European empire building were likewise animated as much by the pursuit of forbidden pleasures as by the material wealth to be extracted from those 'distant' lands in the 'East'. Desire infusing profit.

Anne McClintock's study of the 'porno-tropics of desire' argued that the repressed sexual desires of Europe were projected onto the Orient, such that the 'uncertain continents', that is, Asia, Africa and the Americas, 'were figured in European lore as libidinously eroticized'.[174] Other scholars have also addressed the role of sexuality in shaping the imperial ventures of Europe; many identify rape as a popular practice-trope defining colonial conquest and racial enslavement, as well as territorial invasion and occupation.

The main focus in these studies, however, has been on masculine desire and male sexuality, those scholars who attend to the role of European women in shaping these imaginaries and desires have argued that the women laid claim to the masculine subject position in order to do so. My study of this underlying structure of colonial desire demonstrates that the subject position of Woman, including the feminist, was also mapped out in European women's engagement with these sexualizing racial/colonial ideologies. Suffice it to note here that this structure endured into the post-independence period, it has since remained neither static nor become defunct. As active agents, sometimes even absent presence, Western women have been at the centre of these 'porno-tropics of desire'.

In a study of European expatriates working in post-independence Congo, Hendriks finds that the porno-tropics identified by McClintock, that is, 'a *construct of the imagination* firmly anchored in the western mind, enabling Europeans to *project* "repressed sexual desires" on strange continents', remains very much alive.[175] His study of the phenomenon among a group of Western male expatriates questions the idea of an *a priori* 'shared imagination' among them. His finding is that '[T]he ambiguities of white erotic desire' at work in this situation made for a complex mix,[176] for the 'erotics of ravishment' among the men is 'not a mere replica of a past colonial structure of desire'.[177] Noting there was more talk about sex than its actual practice in the men's lives, Hendriks delineates 'a "porno-tropic" dimension in everyday conversations' that was at work even when 'actual sex' was absent.[178] These white men were fixated on what they termed the 'ugliness' of the Congolese women, who were in close proximity, to hold onto their desire for the female ideal, the white women who were absent and unavailable, as their survival strategy. These men phantasized about white women, who although 'unattainable' in these circumstances, had a powerful presence in their imagination. Centring their everyday conversations about sex by elevating the sexual/physical virtues of white women (in calendar photographs, pornography, etc.), these white men denigrated the physical qualities of the Black women around them. The absent white woman was not a symbol of sexual morality here, Hendriks argues, instead 'she appears as an explicitly eroticized object in itself, arousing fantasies of white-to-white sex that strongly contrasted with the interracial dialectics of desire and disgust'.[179]

I have discussed earlier how the unveiled white Woman is the ideal of gender/sexual emancipation in the ideology of the global war, she is also the measure of the sexual degradation of the Muslim woman, as demonstrated in the General's comments discussed above. Moreover, the heroic masculinity to which he gave expression is explicitly genitally oriented, his own sexualization as masterful infuses the idea of the 'enemy' as a sexual brute. This heroic masculinity was incited by the rape script of the war (the veil as signifier of sexual slavery, unveiling as sexual freedom). The Muslim women's sexual availability through unveiling confirms his identity as man-with-manhood, unlike the 'unmanned' Muslim male. Other examples of these gender/sexual politics abound in political culture: the British prime minister taunted an ex-Head of the British armed forces by commenting that the latter 'lacked "the balls" to take military action in Syria that could have prevented the rise of Islamic State', going on to declare that 'If they had the balls, they would have gone through with it';[180] Bill Maher, the popular US television show host, tweeted this message during the Israeli war in Gaza (Operation Protective Edge, 2014), 'Dealing w/Hamas is like dealing w/ a crazy woman who's trying to kill u – u can only hold her wrists so long before you have to slap her'.[181]

The phallic imaginary at work in these instances is rooted in a representational system that earlier allowed Europeans to project particular modalities of the 'masculinity' and 'femininity' that they considered proper, and thus discover the perversions of the same in the 'East'. One finds a similar dynamic at work in the representational structure that shapes contemporary practices, in the incitationary declarations of perverse masculine and feminine forms among Muslims (men-without-manhood; veiled-hence-rapeable females; crazed women who are not women at all but terrorists; men who dress like women, etc.). These projections cannot but construct the figure of the Muslim as perversion of the (Western) gender/sexual order that is considered universal, the construction of such perversity in turn functions as invitation to assertions of the heroic masculinity and femininity rooted in Western power.

As the Orientalism studied by Said thus gave way to existential disgust – in sexual/gender and religious/racial idioms – towards Muslims and Islam, the earlier construct of the Muslim as a sexually monstrous object was politically re-centered. Moreover, the 'department of thought and expertise' Said studied is now advanced in the 'newer' interdisciplines (feminist, women's, gender and sexuality studies, along with terrorism and security studies, etc.) concurrently with the older traditional disciplines (psychology, anthropology, sociology, political science, etc.); in the public arena, these ideas and constructs are prominent in the flourishing cultural industries (cinema, media, fashion, magazines, on-line, etc.). Said recognized that Orientalism encapsulated attraction as well as horror, temptation as well as revulsion, it is now revulsion – as political, state sanctioned practices – that are the dominant mode of Western erotic expression toward the Islamic world.

Where these expressions could earlier be found on a continuum which encapsulated the range of 'cultural' despotisms to be found across the 'Orient', the present organization of revulsion is focused firmly on Islam. Such recuperation of Islamophobia from within historical discourses has reshaped older Western representations of peoples of colour as uncivilized-in-common to isolate Islam and the Muslim. Here too, the politics of gender and sexuality are at work as Muslims are derided in dominant as well as minority communities for their backwardness, repressive gender/sexual beliefs, self-inflicted ghettoization, radicalization of children and so on. The dominant gender/sexual order is thus policed also by non-Muslim communities of colour as they too operationalize their own cultural distance from Muslims, and in this manner, move into greater proximity to Western culture.

Let me return to the idea of sexual degeneracy and gender perversity in the comments of the General cited earlier: 'You go into Afghanistan, you got guys who slap women around for five years because they don't wear a veil. . . . You know, guys like that ain't got no manhood left anyway. So it's a hell of a lot of fun to shoot them.'[182] Here, the symbolic castration of the Muslim male unable to control his 'woman' is taken to its logical conclusion, death, by the Western Man. The pleasure experienced in this expenditure of violence against the 'man-without-manhood' is as much psycho-erotic as it is religio-racial and military-imperial. David Eng has defined *racial castration*, the phenomenon by which the white man *refuses* to see the penis (manhood) of the Asian man, as the means to stabilize the white man's own masculinity and heterosexuality. This refusal to accept the manhood of the Afghan man illuminates the interface between sexual domination and colonial occupation in the cultural politics of the war.

The trope of the Muslim male-without-manhood confirms the heroic masculinity considered normative of Western Man, the man-with-manhood; this trope also transforms the male-without-manhood into a 'thing', an object available to the *real* man to do with as he determines. Not insignificant, in the decidedly homoerotic tenor that permeates the pleasure expressed by the General, the phantasy of the Muslim male-without-manhood fixes him to his perverse genitality, this male's (absent)manhood locks him in a condition of (lost) masculinity. It is this lack that confirms the Western Man's manhood as potent and active. The violent heterosexual desire also at work here – the General's concern is to 'save' (possess?) the Muslim woman, imagined as rape-able, as 'slapped around' – is to be realized in the act of killing the Muslim male.

The phantasy of unveiling the Muslim woman is linked to the idea of sexual possession, scholars have argued in other contexts.[183] Here one sees the means of such possession to be the commandment of death for the Muslim male. The phantasizing of the veiled Muslim woman as the *possession* of the Muslim male speaks to the phallogocentrism of the West, the act of unveiling this woman as the *destruction* of the power of the Muslim male speaks to its colonizing logic. The coming together of the two presents the Muslim woman as ripe for liberation through the intervention of the *real* Man who will turn her into a *real* – that is, unveiled – woman; the killing of the man-without-manhood is the condition for such access to the Muslim woman. The unveiling and the killing work together to secure Western masculinity as heroic: they also confirm normative femininity as equally Western. The phantasy of the abject Muslim female is thus both incitement *and* alibi to rape and murder, such is the primal scene of Western Subject-formation in the global war. The scene echoes and reworks the sexualizing-colonizing discourse that remains saturated with the religio-racial logic of difference.

The antagonism of Man towards the impotent Muslim male is to be resolved by the transformation of the veiled Muslim woman into a facsimile of the Western Woman in this scenario. Such feminization of the Muslim female is thus to be accomplished in her replication of gendered Western sameness. Although seemingly absent from this scene, the Western Woman hovers above it. This Woman's presence – whether absent or present – is omnipotent, for she need not even figure directly in the gendered equation as she stands outside and above it as the un/spoken gender Ideal. For the Muslim female, it is her distance from this Woman that charts her 'unfreedoms'. The Muslim woman thus serves as the object mediating this libidinal economy of sex and death, the Muslim woman's escape lies in her embrace of Western femininity/feminism. How the Western Woman, the Subject of feminism, enacts her own positionality in this primal scene of Western self-formation can be glimpsed in the anti-veiling campaigns of the present, and even more starkly, in Abu Ghraib.

It is in this power to hunt, subjugate or kill the Muslim male that Man articulates his sense of himself as subject, globally tactile, simultaneously *national* and *Western* in this war. Neither the 'masculinity' nor 'femininity' of Muslims is – indeed, can be – of the same quality as that of Wo/Man.

The global war has demonstrated that the white Woman is not immune from the desire for access to the Muslim female, to unveil her, or from the pleasures of castrating the Muslim male. The historical antecedents of such female desire can be traced to the gendered and sexual self-making practices of Christian women as they constituted themselves as Christo-European subjects in the originary moment of Western self-formation. Sexual anxieties are rife in the authoritative statements of Christian men as well as the women, such apprehensions, fears and pleasures shaped the phallic order of the emergent entity. The complex nature of this sexualizing impetus has entailed the projection of a phantasmic 'manhood' onto the Black/brown Muslim male – hyper-virile or grossly impotent – at different historical junctures, in turn provoking its own forms of anxiety and insecurity, attractions and revulsions. The masculinity of Western Man is presently no less burdened with this historical fascination with the 'monstrous' masculinity of the Black/brown male.

Fanon identified the transformation of the Black/brown male into the artefact of the white man as central to the organization of the colonial order, a condition he observed also in European culture's 'imago' of the Black man that reduced him to a 'penis'. Upon encountering this 'imago', Fanon argued, 'one is no longer aware of the Negro but only of a penis. He *is* a penis'.[184] The attractions provoked by such an 'imago' destabilize Western masculinity, leaving it in a state of existential insecurity and competition. Such sexual imagery and the insecurity it induces is documented in Aldrich's study of homosexuality during the colonial period. European men's encounters with Arab/Muslim males sometimes aroused a fear of being 'impaled' by the latter, he finds, citing the work of Jean Hervez (1922), a French author writing under this pseudonym. Hervez claimed that Arab prisoners were well known for engaging in same-sex relations with Indians and Europeans,¹⁸⁵ going on to report that 'Those who employ them know their vice, and this will sooner or later bring them to court where they use violence on a partner who is recalcitrant not because of prudishness but for fear of being impaled'.¹⁸⁶ Fanon's psychiatric practice in Algeria confirmed his observation that

> [T]he white man is convinced that the Negro is a beast; if it is not the length of the penis, then it is the sexual potency that impresses him. Face to face with this man who is 'different from himself', he needs to defend himself. In other words, to personify The Other. The Other will become the mainstay of his preoccupations and desires.¹⁸⁷

Fanon made the crucial distinction between the physical organ, the penis, of the colonized man, and its symbolic casting in the Western imaginary. The phallic potency conferred upon this organ convinced the Western Subject, consumed by such 'preoccupations and desires', that the bestial nature of the Black/brown male is rooted in his *sexuality*. The horror/desire thus channelled towards the physicality of this Black/brown body is constitutive of the racial architecture of the Orientalist – now the Islamophobic – episteme, which grounds its constructs of 'civilized' and 'bestial' masculinity as was so murderously demonstrated at Abu Ghraib. In the case of the United States, the 'imago' is also deeply rooted in the nation's cultural memory and politics, it shaped the violent heterosexual as well as homoerotic impulses that are historically tied to the institutions of racial slavery-lynching, Indigenous genocide, indentureship of racial migrants, and imprisonment of countless Black men, women and children.¹⁸⁸ The myth of the Black rapist gave this imago wider currency in US culture and politics, argued Angela Davis, as she tied this to the effects of the Vietnam War as well as white feminist politics.

The ambivalence that runs through this sexual/racial fascination of Western Subjects surfaced immediately following the 9/11 attacks. The most watched videos were reported to be those depicting the Middle East as 'a highly romanticized landscape of mystery, a hotbed of lust and carnal indulgence, paradoxically symbolized by the image of submissive, veiled women'; to go 'kick butt' in Afghanistan was the most popular political sentiment expressed in this moment of national crisis was to go 'kick butt' in Afghanistan.¹⁸⁹ The expression of this collective will-to-retaliate as 'kicking butt' presents the national impulse in the sexual/gender idiom of castrating the Jihadi/terrorist. After all, it is not 'real' men who get their 'butt' kicked. The sexualizing imaginary was evident across a remarkable range of ideological/political divides 'internal' to the West, two examples will suffice to demonstrate its cultural embedded-ness. In a provocative essay written shortly after 9/11, French philosopher Jean Baudrillard described the catastrophic attacks and the collapse of the Twin Towers as a *castration* of the most potent symbols of US power.¹⁹⁰ Juan Cole, scholar of the modern Middle East and US foreign policy, described the US reliance on 'Islamist oil' as having a *castrating* effect on the nation.¹⁹¹ Baudrillard and Cole were highly critical of US foreign policy, which makes their use of such sexualizing imagery all the more striking.

The contemporary realignment of Western gender and sexual politics with the politics of the nation-state has been taken up in insightful ways by queer scholars of colour.[192] In *Terrorist Assemblages* for example, Jasbir Puar argues that the idea of US exceptionalism was redefined in the aftermath of 9/11 to incorporate homosexuality, along with heterosexuality, as characterizing the nation's enlightened values and identity. Puar traces this incorporation of homosexuality in the political, media and activist discourses that valorized gay American men – serving in the military, for example – in a rhetoric of heroic nationalism, what she and other scholars name 'homonationalism'.[193] A normative white gayness-queerness was thus enfolded into nationhood to advance US imperialism abroad by marking its difference from the figure of the terrorist as sexually repressed homophobe.[194] Massad has also studied the emergence of the 'gay international' during this period, by which he means a network of Western queer activists who advanced their own political status through their campaigns to 'rescue' gay Muslims in the Middle East. Haritaworn takes this analysis further by unpacking how the paradigm of 'hate' – a hegemonic construct within white queer activism – produces some 'queer lovers' as 'colourful' in contrast to the many 'hateful Others', primarily Muslim and other Black/brown bodies, who are racialized as violent homophobes.[195] Demonstrating how the 'hate crime' sticks to the racialized Muslim body, Haritaworn argue that this construction condemns Muslim and other racial minorities to the deathworlds of the global war. These insights are taken up in the pages that follow, but my focus is on delineating the antecedents of such Muslim-centred sexualizing constructs not only at earlier moments of Western self-formation but in the very construction of the gender and sexual regimes of the West. My argument is that the Muslim was always already a figure of failure in the register of heterosexuality as well as homosexuality, masculinity as well as femininity in these regimes, which incited desires centred on these very 'failings'.

Yet the overpowering of the Islamic/Oriental world, to possess that which the Muslim male supposedly 'owned' (potent appendages, submissive females, vast harems, boundless sexual virility, armies of sexual slaves, ostentatious ornamentation, etc.) became an obsessive ambition of European explorers, travellers, armies, writers as well as colonial administrators and other such, male as well as female, during the eighteenth and nineteenth centuries. Many of these Westerners would go 'native' in the colonies by adopting the dress, ornamentation, affectation, lifestyle, cuisine and so on of Muslim elites; the replication of these modes of bearing and social intercourse by European men and women was a perennial concern of colonial administrators.[196] At a later date, such acquisitiveness became available to the European middle-class and working-class households, transforming their consumption patterns, food tastes, aesthetic styles along with their sense of entitlement.[197]

Such desire for possession, appropriation, consumption of the Islamic 'Orient/al' was spurred by its exoticization and sexualization in the literary and related cultural industries of the West, including print and news media, magazines, films, pantomimes, plays, romances and novels. Incitement of such desire sat in uneasy tension with revulsion at the Muslim's simultaneous dehumanization as impotent, decrepit, tradition-bound despot. Ruled by his vulgar sexual passions, the Muslim male could thus be imagined as perverse, crudely animalistic in his appetites and unable to resist his irrational impulses – inspired by 'Islam' – which rule as well as unman him, leaving him ineffectual and powerless, depending on the historical context, political conditions and geographical setting. The Oriental/Muslim woman was likewise fetishized as either sensually profligate, sexually irrepressible and emotionally immature or as sexual slave, oppressed gender or hated female.

Ultimately though, with both the Muslim male and female defined as bereft of higher virtues, this gendering and sexualization of the world of Islam meant that acquisition of the chaste and refined masculinity or femininity of Christo-Western subjects was foreclosed to the Muslim. His/her hold on these qualities was always-already tenuous, it required constant observation, surveillance, improvement, policing. It should be remembered that the earlier European relation to the Oriental/Islamic world was shaped in a relation of envy and attraction at a time when Muslim empires were ascendant or at the peak of their power in terms of wealth, knowledge, and cultural and artistic accomplishments. The United States, however, encountered this world in a condition of post-coloniality wherein the Muslim world was in serious and severe decline. By the time the United States became the dominant capitalist power, the Islamic world had been ravaged by the colonial plunder and degradation which reshaped its forms of governance and subjugation. Disgust, not envy, became the driving impetus in the US-centred erotics of Western power.

Contemporary iterations of 'Islamic culture' as misogynist and sexually repressive, woman hating and homophobic draw on the historical relations of force invested in the production of the failed 'masculinity' and 'femininity' of Muslims to rationalize the violence visited upon them. The religio-racial logic embedded in such violence ensures the impossibility of Muslim attainment of the subject position of Man, Woman or Queer as organized within the Western gender/sexual regimes.

The point of note here is that historicization of the construction of masculinity and femininity as properties of the Western Subject, and its contextualization within the global field allows a de-naturalization of the Western gender/sexual regimes that are now widespread across the Muslim world. Questions can thus be raised about the interests served when the sexual brutalization of Muslim men is deemed necessary or rendered irrelevant, or when this brutalization is defined as the condition for the gender emancipation and sexual liberation of Muslim women and gender/sexual minorities. Given that sexual violence has long been an essential aspect of conquest, enslavement and colonization, and that this violence has shaped modes of dehumanization as well as subjectification, attending to the specificities of such brutalization sheds light on the shifting nature of the sexual/gender regimes imposed on Muslims in the form of subjugation as well as 'emancipation'.

Fears, desires, phantasies, anxieties – indeed the psychic landscape of Western subjects – are deeply imbricated with/in coloniality and its processes of racialization, argued Fanon. Western domination, he further noted, was sexual and erotic in nature, not only economic and political. What are the ramifications in the present of these past histories in which regimes of gender and sexuality were imbricated within race and religion? Contesting the *colonizing* dynamic inherent in the gendering as well as sexualizing systems of the West has yet to be taken up by feminists, Western or Muslim. As for Islamic Studies, Westernizing gender/sexual politics have become normalized, feeding contemporary narratives of Islamic cultural barbarism. Unpacking the psychosexual dimensions of the religio/racial nexus that continues to give meaning to gender and sexual subjectivity through the prism of a phantasmic 'Islam' is clearly an urgent task.

In this chapter, I have outlined some of the key theoretical traditions, concepts and debates that inform the chapters that follow. The notion of benevolent leadership that informed the idea of the West after the mid-twentieth century was shattered in the destruction of the twin symbols of US power in the world-changing event that was 9/11. These attacks echoed and amplified the anti-colonial and anti-racist critiques of Western power that had earlier emanated from across the colonized world. In this historical context, the global war can be read as an attempt to contain, suture over, and reverse the politically and psychically destabilizing effects of the 9/11 attacks and of the older critiques of Western power.

Drawing on the traditions of anti-colonial and anti-racist thought and practice, my study centres Islam and Muslims to show how central they remain to the ongoing formation of the West, to its foundational nexus of race and religion, gender and sexuality. Effectively Westernizing themselves in relation to 'Islamic terror', the contributions of disparate constituencies, including feminists, to the construction of the figure of the Muslim as a deadly threat helped crystallize the new allegiances and alliances of this West.[198] Yet the anxieties and fissures that shape this entity – the focus of the theoretical traditions upon which I draw – are also being intensified, their political charge exacerbated, as evidenced in the explosion of the white supremacist angst unleashed by the failures of the Western alliance to win its war on the global front. The theoretical context presented here is elaborated upon in the rest of this book.

Chapter 2

WESTERN CONSTITUTIONS

RELIGION, RACE AND COLONIALITY

Political conflicts over the meaning and consequence of the relations between religion and secularism, race and imperialism, are contentious within Western and global politics, particularly so with regard to Islam and Muslims. As the catastrophic effects of the invasions, occupations and displacements of the global war, and its securitization of the nation-state system demonstrate on a daily basis, the conflation of 'religion' with 'race' has produced Islam and the Black/brown/Muslim as the singular 'enemy' of Western culture and values. Cast in the trope of the Jihadi/Hijabi terrorist, the Muslim is situated in the cross hairs of the anti-terror laws, border control and policing apparatus of the state. Such positioning has also made Muslims targets of the racial hatreds of the patriotic nationals who consider Islam an affront to their sensibilities and a threat to their existence.

In this chapter, I study the intersection between modernity's concepts of 'religion' and 'race' to unpack how its foundational values, identities and affiliations were constituted *as Western* in relation to its construction of Islam as existential alterity. Such projection of enmity onto Muslims set in motion processes that would ultimately lead to the ascendance of the West and the systematization of its onto-epistemological tradition at the global level. Yet despite the shifts in power signalled by these developments, Islam exceeded these attempts at its containment in the rubric of 'religion' and 'race'. One argument to be developed in the following sections is that the attempt to reduce Islam to the status of 'religion', like that of Muslim to 'race', remains now, as in the past that I am studying, an incomplete albeit a death-dealing practice.

With few exceptions, which will be discussed later in this chapter, contemporary scholarship – including the interfaith variety – defines Christianity, Islam and other such, as religions among others; the former are also defined as world religions. Scholars who study the relation between religion-theology and politics do so mainly under the rubric 'political theology'. As discussed in a recent collection of essays on the subject, the term 'political theology' refers to the working of religious concepts within political theory, to the permeation of the field of politics with religious thought, ideas, practices and institutions.[1] A 'sectarian' approach is also identified in the collection, defined as theologically grounded engagement with political questions, an approach which is considered either 'a pseudo-academic field founded on beliefs of the supernatural' or 'a second-order religious discourse' focused on Christian concerns and behaviour.[2] This 'sectarian' approach is largely dismissed as irrelevant, a curiosity perhaps, in the secular disciplines.[3]

Advocating a more nuanced approach to 'political theology', one informed by studying 'the conjunction of the two . . . to explore the difficulties involved in each', Vincent Lloyd argues that this would shed light on the 'complicated genealogies' of theology as well as politics.[4] Such an approach would interrogate the *a priori* acceptance of 'theology' and 'politics' as transparently and self-evidently pertaining to separate, and oppositional, realms of social life and experience. My interest, however, is in how these key concepts of modernity – 'theology', 'religion', 'race' and 'politics' – emerged historically from that branch of Catholic Christianity (Latin Christendom) which, through its wars with Islam, became dominant in/over Europe and was subsequently integrated into the early-modern state and its empire.[5] For in the historical production of the bifurcated relation of 'religion' to 'politics', a number of key ideas, concepts and assumptions developed within Latin Christianity that would become reiterated into Enlightenment philosophy and in the political discourses of secularism. In other words, studying the historicity of the relation between 'religion', 'politics' and 'philosophy' dispels the popular idea that the Western tradition expelled religion from the field of politics to become modern and secular.

A significant advance in the study of the vexed relation between religion and politics is to be found in Arvind-Pal Mandair's study of post/colonialism and the development of Sikhism in South Asia, wherein he deconstructs the idea of 'religion' as it emanated from within the Western philosophical tradition. Debunking the notion that 'religion' – a concept which defines 'a set of beliefs and practices supposedly found in all cultures' – was a universal phenomenon, Mandair points out that this concept emerged only during the nineteenth century, in a period of heightened European colonial and military expansion.[6] Prior to this period, he argues, the concept of 'religion' was not to be found in South Asia; Mandair's project is to interrogate the contemporary enunciation of Sikh/ism as a 'religion' and 'identity'.

Practices of translation were central to effective governance and the administration of the colonial world, and such translation took place on the terms developed by, and within, the Western politico-epistemic tradition. Mandair argues that this relation of colonial domination gives rise to the central problem presented by 'cultural' translation. His argument here is that in the absence of the conditions required for actual translation to take place between cultures with radically different praxis in their forms of being, the colonial encounter produced a 'representation of translation' that was to become accepted as *actual* translation. In other words, the colonial relation compromised the possibility of actual translation. Consequently, as the Western concept of 'religion' became indigenized by native elites and integrated into societies that previously had no such concept, an 'active forgetting' of the 'gap' that exists 'between there *not being* a lexical term "religion" and *there being* "religion"' effectively displaced the possibility of 'real translation' between the West and the colony with that of the 'representation of translation' as such.[7] Colonized societies came to enunciate 'their' religion and (religious) identity as comparable with, hence similar to, other such 'religions' and 'identities' as they internalized the Western representational schema. In this manner, native elites entrenched the 'representation of translation' by treating it as *actual* translation, an impossibility given the imbalance of power.

The by now well-entrenched idea within Islamic Studies as well as in Muslim societies that Islam is, like Christianity, one among the 'religions' of the world can be taken as an instance of this 'representation of translation', or more accurately, of the impossibility of translation in the condition of colonial post/modernity. The routine translation of the Islamic term 'Din' into the concept 'religion' can then be read as the passing off of the 'representation of translation' as actual translation, a repetition of the colonizing practices being critiqued in this book. This practice precludes the possibility of reading Islam *on its own terms*, even by Muslims themselves.[8]

Mandair's insightful reading of the (im)possibility of cultural translatability within conditions of coloniality is highly relevant to the violence of the global war. But the question of race, which is here considered crucial to the war's organization of colonial relations of force, remains peripheral in Mandair's analysis. The production of race, as discussed in the previous chapter, is a foundational condition of the colonial, and now the postcolonial, order; race is also structurally foundational to the development of modernity's philosophical and political traditions.

Rejecting the idea that a radical break occurred between 'religion' and 'secularism' to distinguish the Western tradition, Mandair's argument is that there 'is the essential – i.e., ontotheological or metaphysical – continuity between different moments in the Western tradition: specifically, the Greek (onto: being), the medieval-scholastic (theo-), and the modern humanist (logos or logic)'.[9] He argues further that this 'ontotheological matrix effectively took on the role of a blueprint for domination encoded in the structures of thought, practice and order necessary for the maintenance of Empire in the nineteenth century', such that 'this very matrix continues to be replicated and repeated in the postmodern incarnations of Empire, such as global capitalism'.[10] Mandair's use of the matrix, *onto-theo-logical*, moves beyond the 'political theology' frame, yet it overlooks the crucial role of Europe's racial politics in the making of the 'ontotheological' matrix that he charts out in his reading of the Western tradition's making of the concept of 'religion'.

Asad also, as discussed in previous chapters, problematizes the concept of 'religion' for being shaped by Christian ideas, beliefs and practices. He has defined secularism as a doctrine of governance, and as such, identified this as the ground from which the sphere of 'religion' was delimited within modernity. Mandair's argument is somewhat different, for he defines the very idea of 'religion' as an alienating concept, an external imposition that not only truncates but remakes in an entirely different form the tradition of the Other. In other words, rather than debate the merits of what is proper for inclusion in the category of 'religion' in various contexts, Mandair questions the category itself by historicizing it as a key element in the colonial apparatus. Read in this light, the concept of 'religion', and not just that of secularism, functions as a Western – and Westernizing – concept that is absorbed – by way of the colonial encounter – into the cultures, traditions, identities and societies that had previously never employed it yet came to 'own' such a concept. As Mandair notes, this absorption of 'religion' into the native lexicon led to the 'birth of a new subjectivity' in a 'one-way process of transmitting ideas, doctrines and values' rather than in coeval cultural exchange.[11]

Drawing on Mandair's insights into postcolonial theory, religion and continental philosophy, I bring these in dialogue with critical race theory and its imbrication in anti-colonial politics in what follows. Adding another layer of complexity to unpack the 'onto-theo-logical' matrix as outlined by Mandair, I show how this requires reformulation once race enters the analytic frame. The engulfment of Islam through imposition of the category 'religion' reveals this to be a racializing/colonizing practice that functions to contain the radicalism of the Islamic tradition.

Western/izing onto-epistemologies

'Ontotheology', as Mandair explains the term, 'refers to a way of thinking about determinate religions in terms of their classification within a particular order of civilization, a process that is entirely governed by theologio-political considerations.'[12] Hegel is identified as a key figure in developing the concept of 'religion' with its classificatory hierarchy, an endeavour that was sparked by the crisis of Europe's 'discovery' of the 'antiquity' of Oriental cultures and civilizations. This development, Masuzawa also explains in her study of the making of 'world religions', presented a challenge to the relatively recent conception of 'history' within biblical narratives. Defining Oriental 'religions' – with their older cosmologies, chronologies and histories – as 'nature' religions, European scholars (Hume and Hegel, to Comte, Durkheim, Spencer, Fraser, Mueller, etc.), considered its 'Western' form, Christianity, the most highly evolved and advanced of the lot, a true 'world' religion.[13] This classification of religions will be further dealt with below; here, let me draw attention to how the racial politics of Europe infuse the very idea of a 'hierarchy of religions' in the 'onto-theo-logical' matrix by attending to race, for the latter's constitution was very much a factor in the production of the former (the larger matrix as well as the hierarchy of religions).

The 'ontotheological' matrix studied by Mandair begins with ancient Greece as the originary site ('onto', that is, 'being') of the Western tradition, but this convention is a fairly recent development, as argued within critical race theory. The association of the West with an 'ancient' Greek tradition as the 'origin' of Europe's own philosophical and political traditions has been critiqued as a racializing move that helped construct the white supremacist ideology, identity and politics of Europe. Europe's affiliation with 'ancient' Greece was 'discovered' during the colonial period, that is, at a moment when this helped redefine its claims of civilizational and racial supremacy in relation to its subjugation of African and Asian (including, of course, Muslim) civilizations. A major contributor to this critique of the construction of Western origins as rooted in 'ancient' Greece is Cheikh Anta Diop, who, in his early work on 'The African Origins of Humanity', rejected the biblically informed 'Hamitic thesis' that Africans were the descendants of Ham. In unpacking Europe's racial ideologies, Diop's work also rejected the then popular idea that the accomplishments of 'ancient' Egypt could be explained by the idea that different racial 'stocks' had populated Africa, and that ancient Egypt was home to a superior race. Diop famously defined ancient Egypt as thoroughly African in his work which advanced the thesis of a collective African civilization that was the cultural basis for African unity.[14] Following Diop, a number of scholars identified what they called the African *and* Asiatic 'roots' of classical Greek and Egyptian civilization, and in the process, challenged European racial theories that wrote Africans out of both this history and civilization. Martin Bernal followed with his argument that it was during the eighteenth and nineteenth centuries that the Westernization of 'ancient' Greece was accomplished in a reclaiming that severed this tradition from its African and Asiatic roots to produce a Western 'classical' Greek tradition that was redefined as self-originating and self-generating. It was in this manner, Bernal argued, that the 'Hellenic' foundation of the Western tradition was secured; not surprising, he was pilloried for this work.[15]

These decades-old critiques of the idea of ancient Greece as the unadulterated Hellenic foundation of the secular West pointed to how the notion subtends and extends a racial genealogy for Europe's whiteness, a process that historically unfolded in tandem with European colonization across the world.[16] Such self-serving Hellenization of its past confirmed the racial supremacy of the West by tethering it to the older philosophico-political traditions to expunge the African and Asiatic ancestry of 'ancient' Greece and to erase the Islamic role in the construction of this 'classical' tradition. The fraught political relation of Greece to the Ottoman Empire during the period when such theories of pure Western origins were being advanced should not be forgotten, nor should the earlier contributions of Islamic scholars in reworking and passing on the Greek tradition.

It is not insignificant that 'the stimulation of an intellectual awakening in thirteenth-century Western Europe' has been credited to the prominent Islamic scholars whose works were translated after the capture of Toledo (1085):

> The Muslim scholars whom the Latins respected the most included Ibn Sina (known in Europe as Avicenna, famous for his philosophical texts and his medical encyclopaedia, which was used in European universities into the seventeenth century), ar-Razi (Rhazes, medicine), Ibn Rushd (Averroes, philosophy), al-Ghazali (Algazel, philosophy), al-Khwarizmi (Algorismi – the origin of *algorithm* and algebra), and Ibn al-Haytham (Alhazen, optics).[17]

The subsequent European appropriation of the Greek tradition for the former's racializing logics entailed the eclipsing, if not erasure, of these Islamic traditions and scholars whose work had actually made available the Greek texts to Western

Christians in the Toledo translations of the twelfth and thirteenth centuries.[18] After the fall of the Roman Empire, Greek and Latin thought were all but lost to 'Europe'; clerics mainly read the Bible. Although some of the Greek texts had been preserved in the Byzantine Empire, the main interest there was in the Christian writings and the truths of the Bible. Not so for the Islamic philosophers and scholars of the various Muslim empires, who set about collecting, studying, engaging, reworking and thereby advancing, the major works of Greek philosophy within an Islamic context.[19] The Abbasid Caliphs, 'rivalled only by the Chinese imperial court for grandeur and spectacle' had begun 'a systematic program of translating scientific, mathematical, medical and philosophical texts from other languages into Arabic. This intellectual enterprise resulted in a dazzling intellectual renaissance in which the contributions of India, Iran, Greece and Rome were not only preserved, but synthesized and reworked into novel patterns'.[20] This 'intellectual enterprise' made possible the later discovery and adaptation of these texts by 'Europe' in the late-medieval and Renaissance periods, revolutionizing what became reconfigured as 'the' *Hellenic-Western* tradition. 'The achievements of Muslim science, for a time the wonder of the Western world and the widespread source of emulation among medieval Latin scholars, were quickly submerged under the weight of the broader anti-Islam discourse', Lyons argues, as the Renaissance humanists dismissed this Islamic tradition in the early fourteenth century.[21] It is thus possible to trace a racial, as well as theological, logic of difference at work in the construction of the Western tradition, that is, in its development of the idea of the 'West' as projected back from Christian European (theo-racial) onto an ancient Greece now identified as white (onto-racial) and simultaneously projected forward into secular modernity (logos-rational-racial). The historical relations, exchanges, interminglings and reworkings of these various imbricated 'classical' traditions clearly run deep: yet attending to these connections would lead to a reordering of the (political-chronological) trajectory of the 'theo-onto-logical' Western tradition, which remained permeated throughout with racial as well as religious considerations, anxieties, desires and interests.

This European enmeshment of 'race' with 'religion' made Afro-Asiatic histories as well as Islamic intellectual traditions disappear; here, it is useful to recount Hammill's and Reinhard Lupton's observation that 'Political theology is not the same as religion', rather, '[p]olitical theology reflects and feeds on a crisis in religion'.[22] They identify the Reformation as the origin of this crisis, Mandair situates it in the European encounter with South Asian and other 'ancient' civilizations. My focus, however, is in tracking the ramifications of an earlier historical moment in the making of this West, for the period between the seventh and thirteenth centuries precipitated a seminal crisis for the Christians who witnessed Islam's spectacular advances and saw a contesting modality for the ordering of human society as well as its relation to the transcendent divine. The turmoil and failures of the Crusades, to which Latin Christendom turned in order to destroy the insurgent tradition, was the context for the subsequent destruction and erasure of Muslim power and presence within 'Europe' itself. The crisis within Christianity that resulted from those earlier failures was also no doubt a factor in compounding the internal divisions and challenges to Catholicism that are reflected in the rise of Protestantism. The point is these 'religious' conflicts had deeply embedded racial dimensions and were shaped by developments within the larger global order.

The racial dimension is evident in the construction of the Umayyads, Almoravids and the Almohads, who established and extended Muslim rule in the Iberian Peninsula, *al-Andalus* (Spain and Portugal) since the eight century, conceived of as Moors and Saracens. These Muslims established what can be defined in present terms as multi-racial, multi-religious cosmopolitan societies in which the arts and sciences flourished within territorial 'Europe'. The various wars they fought with Christian kingdoms through the ensuing centuries, along with their growing internal divisions, contributed to the weakening and eventual expulsion of these Islamic powers.[23] In the fifteenth century, Ferdinand and Isabella of Castile cemented their relationship with the Latin Church to fight these Muslims and after the fall of Granada in 1492, forcibly converted or expelled Muslims and Jews from *al-Andalus* in the process of Christianizing 'Europe'. If the Crusader wars had been the condition of possibility for the consolidation of the power of the Latin Church over/in 'Europe', the merging of Papal authority with the power of the Iberian state laid the foundation of the modern nation-state as a religio-racial and colonial entity. For 1492 marks also the voyage of Columbus, sponsored by the same Crown of Castile, that begins the colonization of the Americas. The Latin Christian antipathy towards Muslims within 'Europe' shaped a racial animus that destroyed the cosmopolitanism of the Islamic *taifas* in *al-Andalus*, wherein Muslims, Jews and Christians had intermingled socially, culturally, intellectually to create what has been described as 'the ornament of the world'.[24] This antipathy, armed with its racial-cultural sovereignty doctrine sanctioned by the Pope, was brought into the colonization of the Americas. Thus was the modern nation-state brought into being.

Coming on the heels of this Reconquista, the European 'discovery' of what the Christians defined as the 'New World' led to the extension of their control across the Americas through the genocide and enslavements of the Indigenous peoples, racialized as 'savage' and without 'religion'. This colonization opened the door to the rapid economic expansion of Europe, further underwritten by the transatlantic slave trade. Invigorated by the wealth that now poured into Europe, its early-imperial nation-states financed and advanced their naval technologies, expeditions, explorations and armies.[25] Such inauguration of the modern capitalist world economy, institutionalized Europe's religio-racial and class hierarchies over the following centuries. Accumulation of the wealth and resources of the Americas and Africa set the stage for the next phase of European development, the colonization of most of Asia and Africa.

As the power of the Euro-Christian states expanded eastwards and southwards, they encountered once again the powerful Muslim empires, from North and West Africa to the Middle East and Persia, from South to South East Asia, to parts of China and Russia. Put differently, wherever their explorations and adventures in the 'East' led them, Europeans confronted the power of Islam. The development of the settler colonies in the Americas and the transatlantic slavery, in international trade from the Mediterranean to the Atlantic, led to the production of commodities for mass consumption which overtook the trade of luxury goods from the Levant. These developments transformed the world economy in favour of the Western nation-states. Not insignificant, these global shifts also brought about a far-reaching 'internal' transformation of Europe itself.

The world-changing events and encounters outlined above were fundamentally reshaping Western ideas about 'religion' as well as 'race', their nexus tipping in one or the other direction spatially as well as temporally. Concurrently, relations of power within and between the societies and peoples that became integrated into global capitalism shaped its relations of violence and subjugation, exploitation and domination, as well as subversion and resistance. Europe's religio-racial 'purification' remained, however, mythical and incomplete since the Ottomans were simultaneously expanding their empire into Eastern Europe (1370–1629), eventually ruling almost a third of *this* Europe. Nevertheless, as the Latin Papacy put its seal of approval on the religio-racial genocides, slavery and colonial expansions, and as the Protestant challenge to the power of the Catholic Church grew stronger, not only did Christianity rupture further from within, so did the older traditions and relations in the world over which Europe now asserted its power.

The sixteenth-century Reformation quickly spread over northern Europe and its Puritan ethics, ideas and practices have been credited with the development of capitalism and modernity, particularly in the United States; the rise of the bourgeoisie with its individualist ideologies redefined the pursuit of profit and possessions as a theological endeavour and the sign of grace.[26] The power of the Catholic Church was to diminish with the successes of Protestantism, buttressed by the materialist philosophy of Spinoza, Machiavelli and Hobbes; new forms of power now articulated to Christian conceptions of 'religion', 'nature', 'time', 'war' and 'politics' as now pertaining to separate/d realms of social, political and religious life. The 'tyranny' earlier projected onto Islam by Latin Christendom was now projected by Protestants onto the Catholic Church, with lasting consequence for a West thus being reconfigured.[27] These splits within Christianity occurred in tandem with the political—economic conflicts among European nation-states. Yet İyigün has found in his study of the 'internal' (Protestant vs Catholic) and the 'external' (Moors, Turks) conflicts of Europe that 'internal' feuds tended to lessen considerably during periods of war with the Ottoman Empire, and that Protestants gained considerable advantage in capitalizing on such complacency.[28]

The development of these new ideological currents – Catholic and Protestant/Reformism as well as the Renaissance – and their conceptions of theology, politics, nature and race, like their definition of the relation between the modern state and the individual, thus unfolded and found expression in relation to Islam and Muslim empires. Europe's internecine religious wars broke out with renewed ferocity once the treaty between the Hapsburgs and the Ottomans was signed, with the Hapsburgs and the Catholic establishment now turning on the Protestants. But the Protestants had by then 'become a much more formidable opponent' such that the eventual signing of the Peace of Westphalia (1648) made religious 'pluralism', that is, Catholicism and Protestantism, 'the accepted norm'.[29] I have already discussed how the concept of culture infused this construct of modern sovereignty and international law to mediate the relations of dispossession between the Western states and colonized peoples.

The Ottoman, the Safavid and the Mughal 'empires' were powerful formations during this period, but as mentioned earlier, the colonization of the Americas was to eventually transform this situation. The settler colonies in the Americas, the plantation system, and the colonization of Asia and Africa, all fuelled the destruction of Indigenous economies and the industrialization of Europe, developments which put the Muslim empires on the defensive as they gradually lost power within this ascendant capitalist system to eventually become decimated by its colonizing modernity. By the late eighteenth and early nineteenth centuries, the economic transformation and the consolidation of bourgeois power over European nation-states gave the West a decisive edge. This brief sketch serves only to point to the larger context for the related shifts in the religio-racial nexus of power, with race at its forefront at certain moments and religion at others.

Although defined as a product of early modernity, the concept of race, Ania Loomba notes in her study of early-modern Europe's 'vocabularies of race', had 'religious underpinnings' that are traceable to the Crusades:

> each side was composed of diverse peoples, and yet, each was also understood as a distinct group – the Saracens were identified by their allegiance to Islam and the Franks by their belief in Christianity. Religion was seen to confer certain moral as well as physical traits: thus Christians regarded Saracens as not only unreliable but also 'dirty' and often represented them as literally black.[30]

Moreover, Blackness was understood during the medieval period in overlapping ways, 'one, in which it signified monstrousness, bestiality, and godlessness, the other in which it signified religious difference, especially Islam.'[31]

Glossing over the ambiguities and contradictions within such depictions of Blackness and Islam can be problematic, for Loomba also notes that such racializing designations were often bifurcated with 'Blackness' identified also with 'godlessness' to signal the difference of 'class, culture and location' of non-Muslim Blacks from those Black Muslims who were defined as having 'religion'.[32] The expansion of the transatlantic slave trade would further transform the construction of 'Blackness' with far-reaching consequence as the distinction between having and not having 'religion' was also changing.

The 'East' that was long associated with Islam in Christendom's medieval myths and shaped its psychic landscape was also associated with 'Blackness', it was a complex mytho-geographical figuration that was considered 'a dangerous region, where Islam flourished and monstrous races multiplied and thrived. . . . Muslims were ... portrayed as black, dog-headed and ugly. There was a widespread association of Saracens and Cynopheli.'[33] Tolan's study of the Western representation of Islam and Muslims argues that the 'Saracen' was the 'most vivid avatar' of the Muslim: this figure was at the heart of Europe's anti-Islamic polemics.[34]

The medieval notion that the evil of Islam was evident in the 'bodily difference' of Muslims received empirical verification in the narratives of those Christians who travelled to the 'East' and came back claiming to have seen the monstrous pagans in the flesh. Latin Christian identity was thus coded as not only unlike that of Muslims – brown and Black – but also unlike the 'eastern' Christians, the Byzantines, identified as heretics corrupted by their presence in the 'East'. Christo-Europe's separation from 'non' Europe took place in terms that not only exceeded religion and race by conflating these with geography, even as such distinctions in turn relied on the remaking of religion, race as well as geography. Early Christo-Europe thus had a ready racial vocabulary with regard to Muslims which was extended in the distinctions Christo-Europeans made between the human, the monstrous and the bestial in other sites; these distinctions also crossed over into early modernity's theories of alterity and enmity. Shaping the mythic 'internal' cohesion of Europe, Latin Christendom's racializing vocabulary eventually evolved with, and into, the secular and biologically determinist 'scientific' discourses of modernity which also conceived of the West as a cohesive entity.

The race of religion

The Latin Christian concept of salvation went beyond the question of 'religion', for it carried ideas that would shape the modern concept of race and its ideas about the human self. So, for example, this theological tradition's 'symbol of divinity' was also 'a vehicle through which to conceptualize the human self', for the idea of the perfection of God was linked with the idea of the perfection of the Christian self as the 'true' self.[35] In relation to this Self, the non-Christian was considered 'untrue', steeped in evil, sin, abnormality and so forth. The Christian dichotomy 'between people who were saved, those with grace, who had a special relationship with God and who participated in the truth, as opposed to those who were out of grace, who were not saved, and who did not participate in the truth' has been associated with ideas about human evolution as well as Anthropology's later production of Europe's 'human Others' in contrast to the 'true' Western self defined as rational and civilized in this secular discipline.[36]

J. Kameron Carter makes the interesting argument that Christian theology provided the 'inner architecture of modern racial reasoning' and thus shaped how Man came to be defined within modernity as a 'racial being'.[37] He traces the 'genesis' of modern racial discourse to the Christian severance of their roots within Judaism, and in particular, to the extrication of Christ from his 'Jewish flesh' as Jesus. This entailed both the construction of Jews as a 'race' apart from Christians-as-Europeans and the association of Judaism with the 'East', transforming Judaism itself into a zone of inferiority. The first move saw Europeans defining themselves as Christian through a 'racial imagination', and with the second move, this 'racial imagination became a white supremacist one'.[38] Hence, argues Carter, race and white supremacy were co-constitutive within the Christian tradition well before the advent of modernity. This theologio-racial configuration was subsequently integrated into modernity through the political imaginaries of the Enlightenment thinkers, including the most prominent among them, the German philosopher Immanuel Kant. Carter's identification of the 'inner architecture of modern racial reasoning' at work within early Christianity demonstrates how closely race and religion were already theologically tied in this tradition; his study of the subsequent linkages between Christianity, whiteness, slavery and Black Christianity in the United States overlooks the key role of the Christian wars with Islam in producing these connections such that the actual making of 'Europe' is taken for granted in his work.

Walter Mignolo has also linked the modern-secular concept of race directly to Christianity, but at a later historical moment. He points out that the idea of 'race' came into circulation at different historical moments in different parts of Europe. The concept was used much earlier in the 'old' world than it was in the 'new'. In Germany and France, the idea of race developed during the Enlightenment, corresponding 'in time and in space with the New World Order that emerged after the American Revolution in 1776 and the French Revolution in 1789',[39] but in Spain and Portugal, the concept had been in circulation several centuries earlier, specifically during the Reconquista and the Renaissance (fourteenth to seventeenth centuries). The Reconquista marks a significant moment in the emergence of the idea of race, Mignolo argues, for the Spanish term 'razza' defined race as carried in the 'blood'. This conception of race was articulated at the time within a Christian paradigm, and '[w]hat secular science and philosophy did in the nineteenth century was to translate and adapt the racial system put in place by theology in the sixteenth century'.[40] To take Christianity's concept of salvation as strictly 'religious', as symbolizing an other-worldly realm, is to miss the point that by 1492, Latin Christianity's identification of the 'true' Christian was unambiguously defined as 'blood purity'.

Yet this idea of race as 'blood purity' was not without its own conundrums. The conversion to Christianity that was demanded of Muslims and Jews by the Spanish crown as the price for their continued presence in Europe presented a paradox, for such conversion threatened to undermine narratives of innate racial difference. Loomba, for example, points out that conversion had the potential to reveal that the difference of race was actually porous. For with conversion came the implicit promise of recognition of the 'humanity' of the convert, a humanity that was linked to descent from Adam in Christian terms; but 'in practice, the idea of a common descent was complicated by ideologies of bodily difference, and particularly by blackness'.[41]

The idea that the 'old' Christians were defined by 'blood' and therefore were distinct from the newly converted was one response to the unsettling effect of conversion. The 'blood'-centred concerns regarding the intermingling of race and religion are evident also in the Spanish Inquisition (1480), which was waged, among other things, to protect the 'purity of blood' of the Christians. Although 'the idea that religious faith was manifested in "purity of blood"' had a powerful hold, 'converts could hardly prove their purity of blood and many fled the country'.[42] This 'inner' and therefore 'purer' difference of blood was treated as manifest in the 'outer' difference of 'colour'; in both cases, however, 'race' was construed as divinely ordained. Such anxieties regarding the possibility that the 'true' religious self might be claimed by the racial degenerates identified by their external difference therefore ran through the idea of 'razza' as 'blood purity'.

The idea of 'blood' has played a significant role in the making of the Christian community, Anidjar has also pointed out. He complicates the theological understanding of 'blood' by asking 'What is the community made of?' The answer, he argues, is that the community 'has been held to be *made of one shared substance*', that is, blood.[43] Whereas blood – as the basis for family, community, nation – is 'erroneously presumed to be ancient and universal, that communities partake, or understand themselves to partake, of one substance', Anidjar demonstrates that within the Christian theological frame, 'blood' is treated as an external essence which becomes internal. This is evident in how 'the sharing of blood fostered by the Eucharist gave rise to the community of blood, from which was extrapolated a universal anthropology'.[44] The belief, widespread during the Middle Ages, that Christians shared a community that was defined by blood 'is accordingly at the center of the "papal revolution", the disciplinary revolution that recasts and refigures first the body mystical as the visible body of the church's members; second, the earthly authority of the pope (the Crusades); and third, the community of Christians as united in the pure blood of Christ'.[45] In the medieval era, blood – and bloodlines – determined how community and kinship were formed, and it is here that 'blood' becomes crucial to the ideas of race and nation as 'a political hematology as well as a hematocentric embryology, a conception of kinship based on consanguinity'; blood henceforth becomes the substance that 'drenches . . . representations of the body politics'.[46] The significance of such a conceptualization of 'blood' is to be found not only in Christian theology, for Anidjar goes on to demonstrate that 'blood' was a 'privileged element' in shaping modernity's concepts of capital, state and nation, not to mention in the development of modern medicine. Yet the instability of Christian concepts of race were to become no more stable in the modern concept of race within the sciences, which also grappled with the physical as well as cultural manifestation of 'race' well into the twentieth century.

The theological contribution to the concept of blood-as-race was twofold, Mignolo explains in his analysis of how race functioned in the 'Black Legend', a European phenomenon that defined the Spanish as themselves racially contaminated due to their close association with the Moors, the Muslims.[47] As Mignolo puts it: 'First, Spain, and later England and France, distinguished themselves from the Muslims (in the north of Africa) and the "Turks" in the East (the Ottoman Empire); Second . . . England distinguished itself from the Spaniards, who, the English said, had Moorish blood and acted as barbarians in the New World.'[48] Although Spain, England and France all distinguished themselves from the Muslims, race now became the strategy deployed by Western Europeans to claim that the Spanish had imbibed the 'Moorish' propensity for violence, expressed in their cruelty towards Indigenous peoples in the Americas. Given that the Spanish and the Sicilians, as well the people of the Balkans, had intermixed with Muslims for centuries, and as a result these communities could not be easily separated in 'racial' terms, the 'Black Legend' produced a 'racial' separation between and among Christians by treating race itself as transferable-by-association with Muslims.

The conversions and expulsions of Muslims and Jews from Spain, as Mignolo rightly notes, became internally linked in Europe's self-constitution in the 'old' and the 'new' worlds: all would henceforth be situated hierarchically within a classificatory system that tied the Mediterranean to the Atlantic in the sixteenth century. This system was 'controlled by Christian theology as the overarching and hegemonic frame of knowledge';[49] the Christian enmity with Islam that had shaped this 'frame of knowledge' carried over into the 'new world as Europeans attempted to keep Islam out of the "new world"'.[50]

The theologically infused racializing logic that structured this ideological European expansion from the 'old' into the 'new' worlds found novel expression at an earlier moment that would prove formative in the making of the new global order. This world-transforming event was the auction of 235 African slaves that was organized by the Portuguese (1444).

The Portuguese, Hortense Spillers has argued, 'probably gain the dubious distinction of having introduced black Africans to the European market of servitude'; these Portuguese 'encounters with "Moors", "Mooresses", "Mulattos" and people "Black as Ethiops"' are well recorded.[51] The auction in question has been studied at some length by Jennings, who describes it as a 'deeply Christian' ritual that signalled 'Portugal's arrival as a world power'.[52] Present at the auction was the Portuguese prince, Infante Henrique (Prince Henry), as was his chronicler, Gomes Eanes de Zurara (c. 1410–1474), who recorded the event. This first-hand account of the slave auction is steeped in Christian theological imagery, Jennings argues; it is also significant in that its author uses racial categories to represent, condone and justify what is clearly understood to be a divinely ordained Christian form of slavery.

Zurara's (or De Azurara's) description of the event notes the heterogeneity that is on display among the enslaved Africans as he 'invokes . . . a scale of existence, with white at one end and black at the other end and all others placed in between'.[53] The bodily difference between 'Europeans', 'Africans' and 'Indians' was previously recognized, and such 'difference' was linked to geography by the early Westerners, Jennings notes. However, the significance of Zurara's account, in Jennings' view, is that as the chronicler records these distinctions, their associations and their meanings become located in a racial hierarchy that is classified, organized and managed by the European. Jennings' reading of this event presents it as a seismic shift for its 'reconfiguration of space and bodies, land and identity . . . as a theological operation', and as such, it marks 'the crossing of a threshold into a distorting vision of creation'.[54] Jennings defines this 'distortion' as one that 'will lodge itself deeply in Christian thought, damaging doctrinal trajectories' for the future to come.[55]

In her reading of this event, Spillers argues that here 'we observe males looking at other males' as this Christian gaze 'transforms the "pagan" into the "ugly"'; on display then, is how 'human beings came up with degrees of "fair", and then the "hideous", in its overtones of bestiality as the opposite of "fair"'.[56] Spillers' point regarding European males 'looking' at the Other, that is Black/brown males, informs her crucial insight that the Black body, in being likened to beastliness, becomes an 'altered human factor' that 'renders an alterity of European ego'.[57] The Moor/Mulatto/African/Ethiop is collapsed in this inscription of the Black/brown body as bestial, 'the opposite of "fair"', she notes.

Zurara, like many Christians after him, cast the suffering of the slaves as a 'passion play' as he draws a parallel between the Crucifixion and the suffering of the slaves, as he compares the pain of the slaves to that of Christ, according to Jennings.[58] Considering himself helpless in the face of what he explains is a divine plan instantiated by the self-evident – that is, racial – savagery of the Africans, Zurara, again like many Christians after him, absolved himself of complicity in the matter. Indeed, he expressed the hope that the slaves might find salvation through conversion to Christianity. As the captives are sold off, Zurara tells his reader that 'no heed is paid to relations, as fathers are separated from sons, husbands from wives, brothers from sisters and brothers, mothers from children – male and female'.[59] Jesus cried out to his Father in his final agony, Zurara recounts as he draws a parallel with the enslaved crying out to the 'Father of Nature'. Yet despite such a comparison, 'Zurara will not allow himself to see a Jesus-like cry of dereliction in the slaves' cries. That would be to see too much. The Father of Nature will not be fully identified with the Father of Jesus Christ', Jennings explains.[60] Herein lies the crux of the transformations being waged in this Christo-European imaginary; the slaves are defined as belonging to the realm of nature, the Christian to the realm of humanity, that is, the beloved of God, Jennings concludes.

By the fifteenth century, Iberian Christians were enslaving Africans, many of them Muslims, and defining all but royal captives as 'bestial' and 'barbaric'. Muslim as well as non-Muslim Africans were also engaged in the slave trade, they were slavers, traded in slaves, and were themselves enslaved. In 1452, Pope Nicholas V issued *Dum Diversas*, a Papal Bull granting Portugal's King Affonso V (1438–1477) 'the right to reduce to "perpetual slavery" all "Saracens, pagans, and other infidels and enemies of Christ" in West Africa'.[61] Nevertheless, racial distinctions were institutionalized between enslaved Black Muslims and enslaved non-Black Muslims, as noted by Sweet, '[t]hough legally in the same category of enslaved "infidels", Islamic Africans were distinguished from "white" Moors by the term "Negro"'; this term soon became 'essentially synonymous with slave' and with race.[62] As 'infidels', their humanity was theologically – as well as politically – scripted as irredeemable; as 'Black', the theological justifications advanced their dehumanization on the grounds of race.

With the conquest of the Americas and large swaths of coastal Africa, South Asia and the Philippines, European empires expanded these phantasmal, theologically derived concepts sanctioning slavery, conquest, land theft and genocide in 'national' and 'international' law, underwritten initially by Papal sanction and later enshrined in secular juridical institutions. The 'new' world was developed, the 'old' remade, in the materialization of this *religio-racial* logic of power. Over time, as the colonization of the Americas led to the mass conversions of Indigenous peoples and enslaved Africans to Christianity, the benefits of a classificatory system which, although still grounded in religio-racial logics, downplayed the difference of *religion* to accentuate that of *race* had clear advantages. With such conversion, the psychic and politico-economic distance instituted among these various communities could be policed all the more effectively by the idea that such difference was rooted in nature itself, in the materiality of their very biology, in the spirituality of their being. European colonists did not accept the religious conversions of natives and slaves as placing the converts on the same human plane any more than had the Spaniards during the Reconquista, so that race became the implacable barrier that could not be surmounted by religious proximity. In any case, an emphasis on religious identity – Christian as Subject of salvation – would prove a liability in the changed circumstance that had brought 'Indians' and 'Blacks' into much greater proximity with Europeans as co-religionists across the Americas.

The racial dimension, not the religious, held distinct advantage as the means of turning proximity into distance – psychic, corporeal as well as political. Although Christian theology was the overarching paradigm for the classificatory systems organizing these increasingly complex configurations of identities and relations in a globalizing system that directly tied the Atlantic to the Mediterranean, the peculiarities of its religio-racial logic was to unfold differently in different locations.

Islam, however, was not displaced from its (negatively) privileged role in this classificatory system, the racialization of Muslims also racialized Islam. Where Muslims were dominant, Islam was declared exotic, despotic and fanatic; where Islam was found among marginalized and enslaved peoples, as among those Muslims who came to the 'new world' with the Spanish explorers and among the enslaved populations, Islam was suppressed and relegated to a status where it could be 'forgotten'.[63]

With the advance of modernity, Western intellectual traditions attempted to cleanse themselves of the theological world view described above. Politics and philosophy, as well as the natural sciences, developed on the notion that reason, not faith, ordered the universe. Reason hence characterized the modern subject, not the irrationality and superstition that ran through religious dogma. These new intellectual traditions and disciplines, along with the new socio-economic order they were shaping, were thus legitimized as signalling a definitive rupture with the past. Modernity had overturned the old theological paradigm and 'Man' was to now occupy the exalted status previously claimed by the 'Christian' as embodiment of humanity's greatest accomplishment.

In her insightful critique of the production of 'Man', that is, of the Western bourgeois 'conception of the human' which 'overrepresents itself as if it were the human itself', Sylvia Wynter argues this 'overrepresentation' reflects the ongoing 'coloniality of being'.[64] Wynter ties the emergence of Man as the singular model of the human in the 'escape' of 'the world of laity' and the modern state from subordination to the church. This feat was accomplished by 'the Renaissance humanists' epochal redescription of the human outside the terms of the then theocentric, "sinful by nature" conception/"descriptive statement" of the human, on whose basis the hegemony of the Church/clergy over the lay world of Latin

Christian Europe had been supernaturally legitimated'.[65] In other words, the secularization of the Western Subject is identified by Wynter, as by other scholars, including Mignolo and Quijano, as the transformation of the Christian into Man, 'the political subject of the state'; this secularized being 'transumed and reoccupied' the 'earlier matrix of identity Christian' to represent itself as 'the' sole model of humanness, in contrast to 'human Others'.[66]

This new construction of the human in the emergent modality of secularism was accomplished through the 'coloniality of power', Wynter argues, for the mechanism that produced the difference of Man from 'human Others' was 'racial'. Earlier at work within theology and anthropology, the 'racial' was at work now in the discourses of science, natural history, philosophy and economics.[67] Wynter's reading of the constitution of the Western Subject as *the* human Self underscores the point that this Self, re-inscribed as white and secular, simultaneously gives meaning to 'Blackness' as its opposite in the 'new' world. The secularization of Man thus did not herald an end to the underlying logics of the theocentric paradigm. Rather, the secularization of Man was a reworking of this paradigm's core assumptions, for Christian ideas about 'religious' difference – and the discursive markers of such difference (blood, flesh, faith, language, etc.) – that had prevailed during the pre-/early-modern period were now compatible with modern ideas of both racial difference and secularism.

Wynter's essay traces how the 'description' of Man was advanced in two stages: first, in the period from the Renaissance to the eighteenth century, when the natural sciences made possible the conceptualization of nature as shaped by its own autonomous laws ('natural causality'); and second, the period from the nineteenth century into the present wherein the 'emancipatory' physical and biological sciences of Man were advanced. These developments were 'made possible only on the basis of the dynamics of a colonizer/colonized relation' which the West constituted 'discursively' and institutionalized 'empirically' in the 'Americas and the Caribbean', Wynter has argued.[68]

While the analysis of the religio-racial nexus that I am developing here draws on Wynter's reading of the processes that instituted Man as bourgeois, white and European, I am interested in addressing how this 'Man' is produced in relation to Islam, which was the structuring feature of the theologio-secularizing trajectory of such Western self-making. Certainly the expansive plane on which the Western Subject was constituted integrated the Americas, the Caribbean, Africa and Asia with Europe at the centre, it linked the Mediterranean with the Atlantic as well as the Pacific as crucial sites for the production of the racial. But this expansiveness did not do away with Islam as the pivot of the West, for along with the racial makings of the Americas went the shifts in the racial remaking of the Orient, with its Islamic empires. Europeans were hence simultaneously engaged with this 'East', and as Said reminds us, Orientalist structures of representation were also driven by the 'whole impulse to classify nature and man into types'.[69]

Once enslaved and colonized populations were converted to Christianity in the 'new' world, religious difference was eclipsed in this site even as this form of alterity was concurrently being reinvigorated in the 'old' world. For Man's colonization of the 'East' – and the discourse of Orientalism – buttressed his exalted status by his 'discovery' of his own Aryan-Hellenic origins through the 'invention of world religions'. The question of Islam in this reordering of Man, and of his relations with several Others, would become more, not less, integral as religious difference moved to the forefront of the religio-racial nexus in the Orient. Here, the idea of 'religion' became yet again saturated with coloniality, as is demonstrated in the work of Mandair and Masuzawa.

With its this-worldly privileging of reason and philosophy, the Enlightenment is taken to mark the radical rupture of the West with Europe's earlier theologically oriented world view. The dominant trend within the emergent tradition was the exaltation of Man, now himself the embodiment of the 'universal' capacity for reason and perfection, in moral, ethical and aesthetic life, future-oriented in biological, cultural, social and geographical terms despite the ongoing conception of this figure as simultaneously Christian and subject of salvation. Man, soon to be joined by Woman as his 'equal', was thus set apart from his Others who were defined by their lack of these very characteristics and qualities. To be white was to be fully human, to have an unquestioned capacity for the philosophical-secular life, to be Christian was to be at the apex of the hierarchy of religions.

From Christian theology to Western philosophy

A luminary among Enlightenment philosophers, Kant is credited with a 'Copernican-like revolution' in developing the idea that reason and science, not religion and superstition, are the organizing principles of the universal order; his intellectual project became a breakthrough for the Western philosophical tradition. Yet neither 'religion' nor 'race' are absent from Kant's ideas about reason, both are integral – and interlinked – in his understanding of nature and of the principle of reason.

Among the host of concerns that shaped Kant's body of work were the Christian 'arguments for the existence of God, the attributes of God, the immortality of the soul, the problem of evil, and the relationship of moral principles to religious belief and practice', explains Rossi.[70] Although early in his career Kant argued against the idea that God was the 'supreme constitutive element', this critique was somewhat tempered by the philosopher's simultaneous 'affirmation of God' on the basis of 'moral faith' and by his acceptance of religion as a 'regulative' force 'in human efforts to sustain conscientious moral endeavour'.[71] Kant's rejection of Christianity as 'blind' faith was thus moderated by his affirmation of faith as a necessary foundation for the moral life of the modern individual.

Although many scholars make a distinction between Kant's early writings on religion and philosophy and his 'mature' work on reason and rationality, the continuities in this intellectual project when taken as a whole have been noted within critical scholarship, particularly critical race scholarship.[72] Rossi, for example, explains that Kant continued to advance a 'moral argument' in support of the idea of the existence of God and 'the immortality of the soul' in his later career (after publication of *Critique of Pure Reason*).[73] These ideas were controversial. Moreover, the critical scholarship on the philosopher's work demonstrates that even as Kant rejected literalist interpretations of Christianity, he reworked these in the emergent 'practical morality' that he defined as shaped by the principle of reason and grounded in faith. Critics therefore point out that the idea of the divine author as the originating principle was replaced with that of universal reason as the ordering principle to shape the Kantian schema.[74] Where faith in the divine author had earlier legitimized Christian claims to superiority, reason became the distinguishing quality which marked European superiority in Kant's work. More to the point, however, Kant's work advanced the Enlightenment construct of Man as a rational, autonomous and self-determining being, and of the Western European as the model of Man, now the sovereign Subject. The racial logic undergirding the conceptualization of this Man are clear.

Kant's teaching, particularly his courses on race, tend to be discounted by most scholars as irrelevant to his later mature work, and as an ill-informed and unfortunate deviation.[75] Within critical race theory, however, Kant is identified as a key figure in giving shape to the modern idea of race.[76] Reading his work on politics, law and morality in the context of his ideas about race – informed by the natural scientists such as Comte Leclerc de Buffon and Johann Friedrich Blumenbach – demonstrates how deeply the idea of race ran through his conception of reason and modernity, critical race scholars argue. Indeed, Larrimore considers Kant to have 'invented' the concepts of both 'race' and 'whiteness' in his ideas about freedom, nature and diversity. Kant, he argues, 'the Inventor of autonomy, was also the inventor of race', given that race influenced his 'larger understanding of human diversity and destiny' throughout his career.[70]

Kant located reason, sovereignty and universality squarely in the culture of Europe, which he considered civilized.[78] Eze's reading of race in the Enlightenment finds that '"reason" and "civilization" became almost synonymous with "white" people and northern Europe, while unreason and "savagery" were conveniently located outside of light', in the writings of Kant, and also of Hume and Hegel.[79] Despite the differences in their approaches, views and focus, these philosophers nonetheless relied upon, cited and reproduced each other's ideas so that as a corpus, their work 'played a strong role in articulating Europe's sense not only of its cultural but also racial superiority'.[80] In this framework, philosophy itself, as the capacity to reason, became a racializing project.

If Christianity influenced Kant's ideas about 'practical morality', the working of the religio-racial logic in his work can be seen even more clearly in his treatment of Islam and Judaism. Almond has discussed how Kant defined both Islam and Judaism as 'anti-rational' religions, and how he considered Jews and Muslims to be alike in nature – servile and inclined towards submission to authority.[81] In the philosopher's opinion, Jews willingly complied with rigid religious laws whereas Muslims submitted to a faith that was overpowering in its irrationality and sensuality. Islam, characterized as 'Mohammadan fanaticism', was considered by Kant to inspire Qur'anic 'harlotry'.[82] This characterization of Islam as sanctioning sexual excess and violence was hardly novel, the Christocentric world view had already made these tropes a staple of the European imaginary.

Larrimore makes a case for analysing Kant's courses in order to understand the philosopher's ideas about race, for these courses were significant to the development of his intellectual project. In his course on physical geography, for example, Kant defined its two main topics, 'nature' and 'man' as 'appraised *cosmologically*, not in terms of isolated differences but in terms of "their relation in the whole, within which they stand and, wherein each takes its place".'[83] Kant's lectures in the companion course on anthropology (1772), on the other hand, focused on 'difference' among 'peoples of the world', included in this idea of 'difference' were traits such as national character, gender, and moral and aesthetic sensibility; like many of his contemporaries, the philosopher located race in biology, culture as well as geography.[84] Much like the systems developed by Comte de Buffon and Blumenbach, Kant outlined a fourfold classificatory system of 'racial' types: the first is white and 'very blond', Northern European ('of damp cold'); the second is 'copper red', American ('of dry cold'); the third is 'black', Senegambia ('of damp heat'); and the fourth is 'olive-yellow', Indian ('of dry heat').[85] All others he considered sub-types, derivative of the four basic types.

The idea of four basic racial types was tied to the concept of monogenesis, and given that Kant considered the 'Stem Genus' as identifiable within 'whites of brunette colour' and the 'white race', this became its closest proximate. Defined as a 'potential' (carried in 'seeds') that developed in relation to geographical conditions, racial typology, once sparked, became irrevocable: 'A race, when once it has taken root and extinguished the other seeds, resists all further transformation because the character of race at one point became dominant in the generative power.'[86] In other words, although monogenesis conceived of human beings as having a common origin, this was undercut by their racial development in terms of proximity to, or distance from, the 'stem genus'. This 'natural history of humanity' thus 'allowed a special status for Whites as at once a race and the transcendence of race'.[87] The 'transcendence' of its race thus made the white race the universal human type: it represented the perfection of humanity. This is the move described by Wynter as the transmutation of the identity 'Christian' into 'Man' as 'the general order of existence', 'homo politicus', posited as a singular model of human perfection.

The Christian idea of 'all mankind's enslavement to original sin' was thus shifting in the philosophical construction of 'mankind's enslavement to the irrational aspects of its human nature', an irrationality overcome only in the figure of Man as rational being.[88] Likewise, the Christian concept of redemption/salvation was shifting, a matter no longer in the hands of the clergy to decide but determined by Man's ability to live up to what these philosophers defined as the racial potential for human perfection. With Europeans now standing in for the Human, whiteness came to signify a (perfected) quality of the (perfect) human that was unattainable to other races who remained mired in the racial particularities of their environmentally and geographically stunted potential, as these scholars note.

Yet Kant's conceptualization of Man did not only integrate Europe's racial logics into the emergent philosophical tradition he was advancing, incorporated into this tradition was also his reworking of Christianity as a unique religion by its re-interpretation on rationalist grounds. Kant thus 'defended new, morally focused interpretations of a variety of Christian doctrines', Palmquist argues, which both affirmed the divinity of Jesus and also recuperated Christ as exemplary of the human capacity for moral perfection.[89]

Referring to (a non-Jewish) Jesus as the 'truly divinely minded human being, who through his teaching, way of life, and suffering had provided in himself the *example* of a human being pleasing to God', Kant's Jesus was available to secular-Christians for their own moral improvement through emulation of his virtues.[90] Palmquist highlights how Kant redefined Jesus by representing as 'sudden' the coming of Christianity. This 'sudden-ness', Palmquist explains, is described in Jesus having 'announced himself as one sent from heaven', as the 'one worthy of such a mission', and after 'conforming to the only archetype of the only humanity pleasing to God, he is presented as going back again to the heaven from which he had come'.[91] In such a representation of Jesus, Kant does not deny the divinity of Jesus but instead redefines him as a philosopher to argue that the 'true' philosopher 'need not appeal to miracles'; Palquist reads this move as an implicit acceptance of Christ's divinity through substitution of a 'rational' and 'moral' claim in place of the religious one to conclude that 'the revolutionary effect that Jesus had on the moral evolution of the human race could just as well have been accomplished by someone who was completely human'.[92]

Just as significant is Kant's depiction of the coming of Jesus, which he sets up as an epic battle between good and evil; Jesus came as 'a symbol of the good principle affecting a revolution at the very moment when the evil principle appeared to be at its strongest'.[93] Palmquist's argument is that the Christian cosmology invoked in Kant's representation of Christ is unmistakable:

> there appeared all at once a person whose wisdom was purer still than that of the philosophers hitherto, as though it had come down from heaven. And he also proclaimed himself, in regard to his doctrines and example, as indeed a true human being, but yet as an envoy of such an origin that he, in his original innocence, was not also comprised in the compact that the rest of humankind ... had entered into with the evil principle.[94]

The reference here is to the idea of original sin, of which Jesus stands free given his divine origin and nature. Transmuting the divinity of Jesus into the modern register of philosophy, Jesus becomes the 'pure philosopher' come 'down' from 'heaven', whose 'true' wisdom is recognizable only to other philosopher-rational subjects. The key point, however, is that race and religion are deeply enmeshed in Kant's framing of this divine philosopher, and hence of philosophy itself. Here, one sees an early example of the secular exaltation of the divinely sanctioned white subject who also represents a higher order of humanity by virtue of his innate character, determined ontologically as well as epistemologically.[95] For his part, Carter has argued that the occidentalization (i.e. whitening) of Jesus was accomplished by way of his extraction from his 'Jewish flesh'. The racializing imperative within Christianity is traced to the field of Christology, 'that area of the theological curriculum that investigates the person and work of Jesus the Christ', which Carter identifies as the 'genealogical taproot of modern racial reasoning'.[96] By this, Carter means that theology's racial logic arises from the 'abstraction' of Christ from the material figure of Jesus, with his undeniably Jewish body. This 'abstraction' results in 'a religious conversion' of the Jewish body into 'racial flesh', situating it 'within a hierarchy of racial-anthropological essences, and lodged within a now racialized chain of being' which accomplishes the transmutation of Christ into whiteness.[97]

In a later period, another philosopher, Hegel, would rework a different strand of Christo-theological concepts into his philosophical formulations by, for one example, redefining the doctrine of the Trinity as 'a moment in the unfolding of the World-Spirit'.[98] More will be said later about Hegel's reworking of Christianity and the concept of religion, there is one additional point regarding Kant's contribution to this endeavour that requires noting here.

With theology metamorphosizing into philosophy in the Enlightenment tradition, the articulation of its world view to a universalizing 'secular' conception of humanity centred on Man as mandated by nature itself to civilize the lesser human types was a mission that readily carried over into the colonial enterprise. If Kant's philosophy engaged the theological questions Christo-Europeans had been consumed with regarding their place in the universe – the quality of their humanity, the truth of their religion, the place of their God in their social and moral life, and so forth – his philosophical answers exalted their innate intellect and tied this to their capacity for 'freedom', which made it their right to accordingly reshape the world.[99] Presenting reason as the only sound basis for the moral community of Man, Kant named this Europe to-come the 'cosmopolis'. Jesus, the divine-philosopher extricated from the Christian tradition, was thus absorbed as a prototype of the first philosopher-Man, situated at the centre of the Western tradition that would develop secularism as His greatest accomplishment.

It is notable that most studies of the treatment of religion, or even of race, in Kantian philosophy make almost no mention of the place of Islam in the tradition he helped fashion (Almond's essay is significant in this regard). If Kant distinguished Christianity as a revolutionary and rational religion, he did this by contrasting it to the servility he ascribed to Islam and Judaism. Although little travelled himself, the philosopher was hardly unaware of the intellectually and aesthetically rich, thriving cosmopolitan societies that Muslims had built, as Almond points out, given 'an enormous Turkish embassy had established itself in Berlin, invited by Frederick the Great' (1764), and given that such an embassy had also earlier been established in Paris (1721).[100]

German Orientalism, Almond observes, was formed by a contradictory set of ideas in which one finds a 'demonization' of Islam but also notable attempts to 'correct' the depictions of the 'Turks'. Almond characterizes the treatment of Islam by elite German philosophers, including Kant, as 'an anatomy of prejudice'[101] yet he points out that this body of work is informed by a 'filtering' process, so that if an author demonized Islam in one instance, he might also praise the accomplishments of Muslims in another. Nevertheless, the overall effect was that 'German intellectual elites sifted through a variety of Orientalia, taking the nuggets they needed by either overlooking or consciously rejecting anything which conflicted with their requirements'.[102] This 'prejudice', as Almond describes it, ran through the work of Kant. The key point in these representations, however, is the constitution of such alterity; as Said noted, Orientalism as a discourse incorporated negative as well as positive representations, the point is its constitution of absolute alterity in a binding hierarchy.

Let me now turn to a major theme identified by Almond in this encounter of the German intellectual elite with the Islamic world of the Ottomans, which, with its 'superior religious tolerance' of Jews and Christians, including Protestants, often impressed critically minded Europeans. 'It was a tolerance which often attracted the eye of European observers critical of sectarian politics in their own countries; the idea that Christians should feel ashamed at the superior religious tolerance of their Turkish neighbours became a standard and familiar refrain', Almond explains.[103] Massad has also noted the trend among Europeans who compared the 'intolerance of London and Paris', to the situation in Istanbul with 'a church here between a mosque and a synagogue, and a dervish by the side of a Capuchin friar' (1788), yet concluded that

> It must be from degeneracy of Mohammedanism that this happy contrast can be produced. What is still more astonishing is to find that this spirit of toleration is generally prevalent among the people; for here you see Turks, Jews, Catholics, Armenians, Greeks and Protestants converging together on subjects of business or pleasure with as much harmony and goodwill as if they were of the same country and religion.[104]

Certainly this narrative of 'harmony' is a partial record of the period, but it is notable that even what they considered admirable traits within the Muslim world were taken by Europeans as confirmation of the overall 'degeneracy of Mohammedanism'.

Urbane, prosperous and powerful in the early Enlightenment period, these heterogeneous Muslim societies articulated their ethico-moral concerns and ambitions with regard to the Islamic tradition. Across Asia to Africa, from the 'Holy land' to China, Europeans encountered Muslims striving to follow in the Prophet's path – *As-Siraat al-Mustaqim*. This point may be too obvious, but it does need to be made: the highest aspiration of the coming cosmopolis that Kant named as a Western ideal was, no doubt with all its limitations, the living present, even the recent past, of the Islamic societies that Europeans encountered.[105] The splendour of the Muslim courts, with representation of the many communities that made up these empires, the centres of learning they supported, the refined arts and the thriving bazaars found from Baghdad to Damascus, Timbuktu to Istanbul, Delhi to Samarkand, no doubt demonstrated to Europeans a cosmopolitanism they could only imagine achieving at some point in their own future.

After Kant, Hegel's work would significantly advance the absorption of the intertwined concepts of religion and race into the Western philosophical tradition, their nexus is embedded in his ideas about the world historic unfolding of the Spirit. Hegel's contribution to the classification of religions is discussed in some detail by

2. Western Constitutions

Mandair and Masuzawa, for the German philosopher featured among the most influential thinkers in the remaking of the Western tradition as well as European identity. The classificatory system for religion developed by Hegel deepened the correlation between religion, language, race, nation, culture and geography, this system was to solidify further in the 'invention' of 'world religions'.[106]

Blumenbach's racial theories (mentioned earlier in relation to Kant) and his foregrounding of the Caucasoid as the white ideal also influenced Hegel's ideas on the subject, he used a threefold evolutionary classification of race that lined up with religion: African/ Ethiopian (defined as childlike); Mongol (Chinese and Indian, with a beginning awareness of spirituality); and Caucasian (Europeans, Arabs, Persians and Turks, all followers of monotheistic religions).[107] Within the 'Caucasian' category, however, Hegel distinguished between Christians (Europeans) and Muslims (West Asians). Although he claimed 'no colour has any superiority', this did not prevent him from ascribing an 'objective superiority' that was apparently self-evident among Europeans in the spiritual realm.[108] Put differently, the 'inner' spiritual quality (religion) was treated by Hegel as evident in the 'outer' corporeal quality (race) of peoples; this play of interior and exterior qualities fused religion with race.

Hegel's treatment of Islam was complex, for although he defined this religion as inferior to Christianity, he also considered it a positive force for having introduced monotheism into Africa. In his view, 'when the race is inferior and its culture "lower", Islam cleanses and teaches; when the race is superior and its culture "higher", it conquers, floods and swamps'.[109] Islam was thus beneficial to Africans, but a threat to Europeans. Moreover, Turks were declared 'incapable of culture' and Arabs as 'forever prone to fanaticism'.[110] Race and religion thus worked in conjunction to reproduce the global hierarchy among various populations.

The Hegelian 'epistemograph' sought to counter the growing influence of the Orientalists who were increasingly becoming enamoured of Indian civilization, Mandair explains; it 'exerted a theoretical and political influence with important consequences for future intellectual encounters between India and Europe'.[111] The Hegelian schema wrote India out of history and philosophy and located it instead 'within the plurality of world cultures as "religion"'.[112] This framing of India through the lens of antiquity fixated upon what came to be constructed as 'Hinduism', a tradition defined as intrinsic to the society and reflective of its 'glorious past'. The construction of 'Hinduism' as a unitary 'religion' is, however, of fairly recent vintage, for this was codified, Sanskritized and Brahmanized during British rule, as postcolonial scholars have demonstrated.[113]

No less significant, Hegel linked divine revelation to the process of 'historico-spiritual evolution', thus elevating revelation as a marker of the superiority of Western religion, which he considered lacking in non-European Oriental and African cultures. The latter therefore had to be 'excluded from the history of philosophy'.[114] Although in the case of Islam, the tradition was founded in revelation and had developed into a syncretic tradition within Arab, Persian, Turkic and Mughal societies, it was nevertheless treated as monolithic and static in this history of world religions, not dynamic and changing as was the case with Christianity.

It should be remembered that both Kant and Hegel were averse to Catholicism and linked this to idolatry and slavishness, in contrast with Protestantism, which they defended. The Muslim and the Jew represented, to both philosophers, the quintessential outer-determined Others who existed in a state of exteriority, unlike the self-determining Subject, Man, with an internally determined capacity for self-actualization that was sanctioned within Protestantism. In this view, the Jews were servile to their unchanging religious law and constraining rituals; the Muslims submitted to their overwhelming passions, and to the sexual and sensual excess inspired by Islam.[115] Notwithstanding the glories of their past accomplishments, so long as Muslims adhered to Islam they would remain incapable of mastering these irrational passions, was the view of these philosophers.

With the privileged positioning of philosophy in secular modernity as foundational to the production of knowledge, Hegel's contributions to this tradition permeated its political, literary and cultural discourses, including the counter-hegemonic Marxist critique. Hegel's evaluation of Africa and of Africans, as well of other non-European peoples as irrelevant to the unfolding and realization of the Spirit, his equation of the Turks with barbarians, have all been noted by scholars.[116] Buck-Morss has also critiqued Hegel's use of slavery as a 'root metaphor' for 'evil powers' by dehistoricizing the phenomenon during a period in which slavery actually 'came to underwrite the entire economic system of the West, paradoxically facilitating the global spread of the very enlightenment ideals that were in fundamental contradiction to it'; such use of slavery as a metaphor has been read as justification of the racial enslavement of African peoples.[117] Hegel's ideas about religion, philosophy and human progress were certainly complex, for he 'saw his own Protestant Christianity as largely synonymous with a vocabulary of Enlightenment and education ("Our universities and schools are our churches"), he sometimes even seemed to see himself as a Luther figure, teaching philosophy to speak German'.[118] Fanon has written about Hegel's linking of the question of human consciousness to race, but the philosopher's linking of both to religion by defining 'religious consciousness as the most important subjective criterion that differentiated the four races' has not received the same level of scrutiny.[119]

Establishing a strong connection between Protestantism and modernity, Hegel considered 'the doctrine of the Trinity [was] itself a moment of progress in the development of World-Spirit, a "life-process . . . in which the universal places itself over and against itself"'.[120] In this context, Islam's rejection of the divinity of Christ 'as the embodiment of the universal in the particular was both a denial of Christian doctrine and a refusal of this necessary step towards Absolute Knowledge'.[121] With the self-determining subject, Man, defined as actualization of the World-Spirit, his religion - Protestant Christianity - could be no less than the most rational of all religions. Islam, which presented a challenge to Christianity, was hence an obstacle to the unfolding of the World-Spirit, a threat to the ongoing project of human progress and freedom and to the actualization of human self-consciousness. This is not to suggest that Hegel was not critical of Christianity, but such critique was rooted in the philosopher's commitment to locate the meaning of the human in the subjectivity of the sovereign subject.

Steunebrink argues that Islam is 'absent' in Hegel's *Philosophy of Religion* because it 'does not fit' into Hegel's evolutionary schema, wherein 'Christianity is the absolute and therefore final religion that completes and ends the history of religions'.[122] Not a 'true' religion, Islam became 'just a kind of Judaism and specifically denationalized Judaism', argues Steunebrink.[123] Islam 'dominated [Muslims] by abstraction', and as such, was a lesser religion that invoked fanaticism, a religion of terror, Anidjar has also argued with regard to this philosophical tradition.[124]

Yet as Almond argues, Hegel did sometimes express admiration for Islamic art and poetry, its mystical tradition and its military successes.[125] In these instances, Islam appeared to the philosopher to have 'civilized Europe' through a positive impact on the Crusaders. He held the opinion that the 'boundless magnanimity of Oriental prowess' with its 'oriental chivalric spirit' had evoked 'in Occidental hearts a response, which paved the way for their attaining a nobler virtue than they had previously known'.[126] Islam had, in this manner, 'inspire[d] Christians to the realization of their specific, concrete universality', prompted 'the emergence of new ecclesiastical orders ... engaged in works of charity', and in the Arab sciences, a 'moral phenomena tending in the direction of a general principle' had stimulated 'the direction to generality' within Europe. Yet even though Islam was seen to have also influenced European ideas about sovereignty and law, ultimately it was only Christianity that had accomplished the unity of 'generality with particularity', and was hence superior, in Hegel's view.[127] Unlike Christianity, for which 'freedom' was its very condition, Islam was a religion of the 'sublime' and demanded utter subjection from its followers.[128] Muslims were therefore fanatical in their faith and lacked the capacity to reason, they were bereft of autonomy and freedom.[129] Hegel's assessment of the primitivity of Islam and of the fanaticism of the Muslim thus remained intact, although 'In a text such as the *Lectures on the Philosophy of History*, a curious parallel movement seems to take place, a whole variety of different adjectives – "monstrous" (ungeheuer) and noble (edle), "enthusiasm" (Begeisterung) and "fanaticism" (Fanatismus) – seem to pull Hegel in different directions', observes Almond.[130]

Although attraction and revulsion are to be found in Hegel's work on Islam, he did not include Islam in the category of world religions and likewise wrote the Ottoman Empire out of world history.[131] The philosopher had enough access to information for a contrary reading of Islam and Muslims, so 'Hegel's savage Turks, fanatical Arabs and historically defunct Islam were interpretive choices, not "child-of-his-time" consequences of his reading or milieu'.[132] In short, Hegel's hermeneutic choices were strategic to his overall politico-philosophical endeavour.[133] Almond identifies the following sorts of denunciations, dismissals and outright hostility to Islam in Hegel's work: Islam was responsible for the degeneration of 'the East itself, when by degrees enthusiasm has vanished, sank into the grossest vice, the most hideous passions became dominant, and as sensual enjoyment was sanctioned in the first form in which Mahometan doctrine assumed and was exhibited as a reward of the faithful in Paradise, it took the place of fanaticism'; and that 'driven back into its Asiatic and African quarters, and tolerated only in one corner of Europe through the jealousy of Christian Powers, Islam has long vanished from the stage of history at large, and has retreated into Oriental ease and repose'.[134] In contrast to Christianity, Islam's ambitions of 'world domination' threatened terror and fanaticism,[135] its 'purpose is "a universal condition of the world, world dominion, universal monarchy"'[136] such that '[n]o positive right, no political limitation of the individual is available. Property, ownership all individual purposes are null and void' in Islam, concluded Hegel.[137]

Yet one can read in Hegel's dismissal of Islam and Muslims a deep anxiety, for the philosopher was well aware that Islam was a rival to Christianity, so that the former's universalism presented strong competition to that of the latter. Such anxiety is evident in Hegel's misidentification of Europeans as Muslims, as suggested by Almond, who points out that Hegel, 'the Enlightenment thinker [who] shared an equally Kantian desire to police and patrol the boundaries of Europe as place of Reason, Reflection and Freedom' mistook a Greek Prince for 'a Persian or a Turk'.[138] Hegel was aware of other such misreadings by other Europeans, including an incident in which German soldiers mistook Bavarians for Turks, thinking they were in Turkey while they were actually still in Bavaria (Almond). The porosity in the boundaries being drawn around 'Europe' surely caused alarm, for these instances and misreadings demonstrated that the possibility of the erosion of borders was ever present. Almond notes also that 'nothing irritated Hegel more than the blurring of the present-day borders between Europe and Turkey'.[139]

The fixity of such borders was crucial to the fourfold categorization of the racial hierarchy as used by Kant, which was reflected in the fourfold categorization of 'religion' by Hegel, namely, Christianity, Judaism, Islam ('Muhammadanism') and Others. This classificatory system developed into what Masuzawa has called the 'invention' of world religions in the late nineteenth and early twentieth centuries, in which religion overlapped with race, nation, language, culture and so forth. The impetus for the development of this new field (which included approximately a dozen 'major religions' and various minor traditions) was the 'sea change in the European relation to the rest of the world'[140] brought about by European colonial expansion. This required the increased engagement of Europeans with the belief systems, cultures and traditions of the many peoples they colonized, and such prolonged contact eventually led to the development of the discipline of philology, the scientific and comparative study of languages. Developments within this field would reach well beyond the issue of language to reshape the epistemological traditions of the West, for

> [W]ith the discovery of language families or language groups... new possibilities opened for European scholars to reconstruct their ancestral roots, realigning their present more directly with pre-Christian antiquity. This new thought about a specifically European ancestry located its genealogical origin above all in the imagined glory – and allegedly 'timeless' modernity – of Ancient Greece, but also found a root of even greater antiquity, the hitherto unknown past of the so-called Proto-Indo-European progenitors.[141]

Such 'discoveries' led European scholars to make the case for linguistic affinity among these 'Indo-European' peoples and to link specific linguistic practices to Western ideas about race, nation, religion, culture and so on. As Masuzawa points out, coming to terms with the 'antiquity' of 'Eastern' societies, religions and civilizations provoked a crisis for these European scholars as they were in turn compelled to account for, and rethink the overall history of the West, of its spiritual and cultural legacy. In their revised conception of history, 'Christianity alone now appeared to be of Semitic origin, unlike all the other constituents, which were supposedly thoroughly Greco-Aryan'.[142] Hellenizing and Aryanizing Christianity became the way out of this not-so-desired connection to the Semitic/Orient. In the process, Christianity was re-envisioned as a religion 'that genuinely embodied the principle of unity and universality', that is, Christianity was (still) congruent with reason and philosophy as Kant had redefined this religion. In tandem with this reconceptualization of Europe's civilizational roots, Islam was yet again confirmed to be a 'Semitic' religion that was thoroughly Arabized, it was redefined as static, not only highly intolerant but a dead tradition. The invention of the classificatory system for religions thus placed Islam in a particularly disadvantaged position even as it was recognized as a 'world religion'.

Such reworkings and reclassifications of Islam's fanatic nature, deadly ambitions, sexual excess and degeneracy is a story the West continues to retell itself, with the war on terror only the latest version. It is this narrative, deeply embedded within the Western imaginary and reiterated in the works of generations of its most venerated thinkers, that sanctions the terrorizing of Muslims by construing them instead as the origin and the embodiment of terror in the world.

Yet Almond's pointing to the 'standard and familiar refrain' among elite German philosophers regarding the pluralism and tolerance in the Muslim world suggests a certain worry, insecurity even, about the state of the social and political world of these Europeans. The 'refrain' probably speaks to the uncertainty in their conviction of their sense of superiority, in their belief of the perfection of their own humanity that was the dominant theme in the developing philosophical tradition. Indeed, the refrain is more indicative of self-doubt than conviction. The earlier Crusader imagery was, of course, shaped during a moment when Islam was on the rise and Muslims were building dazzlingly urbane societies. The European intellectuals shaping the Western philosophical tradition during the seventeenth and eighteenth centuries were aware of these accomplishments, as they were of the racial, linguistic, religious and cultural intermingling to be found across that Muslim world. Eventually, the 'spirit of toleration' among Muslims that was noted by many European travellers would be radically transformed with the decline of the Islamic empires, most gruesomely in the partitions and genocides that produced the modern nation-state system across the Muslim world.

Nineteenth-century Orientalist scholarship – particularly that concerned with world religions – attributed to Islam 'a new alienness' by defining it as a religion of the Arabs, hence 'rigid and stunted'; Islam's 'essential attributes were said to be defined by the national, racial, and ethnic character of the Arabs, the most bellicose and adversarial of the Semites'.[143] The long-lasting and deadly consequences of such 'alien-ness' can be discerned daily in any newspaper in any part of the world.

I have engaged in this somewhat lengthy discussion of Kant's and Hegel's treatment of Islam to illustrate how interlinked were 'race' and 'religion' in the Western imaginary, how their nexus gave concrete shape and content to the philosophical-political tradition that created the discourses of colonial-modernity. These constructs have shaped how Islam has been, and continues to be, seen, within global politics as well as in the epistemological traditions of the West. If the defeat of the Mughal Empire was to give the British Empire its most prized possession, the famed 'jewel in the crown' that was Mughal India, and the French Empire was utterly invested in the forceful integration of Algeria, the histories, ambitions and desires of these European empires were hardly transcended in their post-independence policies and technologies of governance. These prized colonial acquisitions were to transform the fate and fortunes of not only Islam and Muslims but also of the European empires, indeed, of the now US-led Western enterprise itself. The historical record demonstrates how these European empires allied themselves with one or another Muslim power or ruler to further their own interests and control of particular regions, and how these Muslim rulers in turn used such alliances with different European powers in their rivalries with each other. Such realpolitik, however, sat uneasily with the underlying anti-Islamic antipathy that shaped the Western politico-cultural imaginary. The decline of the Muslim empires would make the internalization of such antipathy towards Islam within the Muslim world itself the most significant of its postcolonial inheritances. These histories of the West and their imbrication in on the emergent political and philosophical traditions allow a glimpse of how the category 'religion', ostensibly the antithesis of 'secularism', re-instantiated the colonial and racial logics of the theologically rooted Westernizing world. Such histories, and their successive reworkings of religio-racial logics at different junctures, were mutually constitutive of the subjectivity and sovereignty of the West.

The organization of the relationships within, between and among the formations of 'Islam', 'Christianity' and the 'West' are complex. Not one of these formations can be taken in isolation as monolithic, unchanging, ossified or unrelated in any meaningful sense, for they have been historically intertwined. Nor can they be adequately accounted for – let alone transformed – if considered in isolation of each other. Moreover, it is not insignificant that the early Christo-European construction of 'Islam', of its alleged values and practices, that was to become dominant within global politics was forged in the registers of religion as well as race. These registers would reshape Christianity itself as its Latin variant moved away from its 'Eastern', 'Semitic' roots to transform the tradition into 'Europe', and subsequently, the secular modern West.

The alignment of this branch of Christianity with the early-modern nation-state enabled the theologically derived concepts of 'race' and 'religion' to be incorporated into the modernizing secular discourses. The violence entailed in a world thus produced incorporated the colonized and enslaved Muslim and Indigenous, Black and other peoples who were subjugated to Western power. The fusing of religion and race thus set in motion the processes of European self-fashioning through the ensuing centuries.

Whether from a position of relative powerlessness in a period when Islamic empires were at the zenith of their power, or later from that of unparalleled strength following its colonization of the Americas, Asia and Africa, the Christo-European political and intellectual traditions' engagement with Islam was shaped by (non) engagement with the latter on its own terms. Instead, with few exceptions, Islam was derided either as irrational incitement to servitude and lasciviousness, indolence and despotism, or as barbarism and fanaticism. The trend that would remain constant within modernity was the construction of Muslims, and Islam, as antithetical to the civilized order, notwithstanding the intermittent positive engagement by individual Western thinkers with particular aspects of Islam and Muslim life.

The growing body of work on the Western philosophico-political tradition's development of the concept 'religion' rarely discusses how this was interconnected with the issue of 'race'. When race is mentioned, this is only done in passing and rarely shapes the analytic frame. The same is true in the case of critical race scholarship, which hardly ever attends to religion. Yet these concepts were mutually constitutive within the Latin Christian tradition, as was the case with the politico-philosophical tradition of modernity. Race and religion were articulated in and through each other in the work of the most influential philosophers credited with the development of modernity's epistemological traditions; Islam was a constant reference point in their intellectual endeavours. Latin Christendom developed through a relation of enmity towards this insurgent tradition; such enmity remained steeped within the ideas that shaped the theocentric paradigm, with the concept of race often eclipsing that of religion in the Americas while religion eclipsed that of race in the Orient.

Latin Christendom had to contend with the wealth, status and magnificence of the Islamic world, which proved attractive to the Crusaders in the pre- and early-modern period. As Sardar explains, 'the powerful civilizations of the East were a lure to the desires of Western civilization; and the civilizations of the East did not immediately collapse at the onset of Western power'.[144] Indeed, it would take Christo-European empires several centuries to assert their power over that world.

During these centuries, Europeans would become aware of Islam's universalist appeal, its 'global' presence, so to speak. Indeed, the extent of the anxieties provoked by this state of affairs are reflected in the powerful theories of racial degeneracy that the early Westerners developed as they produced and protected their own onto-epistemological distance from the Muslims, from the Jews and from all the peoples they enslaved and colonized. The Enlightenment narrative of Europe as racial perfection and futurity was a narrative that countered an Islam that was already powerful, its ideals well entrenched, and more so, with universalist ambitions of its own. The heterogeneity – cultural, linguistic and racial – of the Islamic empires that was common fare in daily Muslim life in the Balkans to the Bengal complex became, when witnessed by Europeans, desired as their (own) highest (promised) goal. Kant, like other Europeans, had a practical, historical model for what he named the coming 'cosmopolis' of the West.

The balance of power between early-modern Europe and Muslim empires would be transformed by the former's colonization of the Americas, Asia and Africa. The ensuing development of capitalist modernity as a global system, institutionalized in Christo-Europe's racializing hierarchies and theories, produced new formations of sovereignty and subjectivity that have endured into the present. Yet despite its derision, the Islamic tradition would continue to shape relations, values and practices among and between Muslims, including a growing tide of resistance to the Western domination of the Muslim world. That the Qur'anic message persisted throughout the centuries of European rule to sustain visions for futures other than Westernity is evident in the global war.

Chapter 3

SEX/UALITY IN THE ISLAMIC ORIENT

Among the most conspicuous aspects of the war on terror is its transformative effect on sexual/gender politics, for sex quickly became an essential component of the political and military arsenal. The experience recounted by a detainee held at Abu Ghraib by US forces provides a graphic illustration of this:

> they put sandbags over our head and kept beating us and called us bad names. After they removed the sandbags they stripped us naked as a newborn baby. Then they ordered us to hold our penises and stroke it and this was only during the night. They started to take photographs as if it was a porn movie. And they treated us like animals and not humans. They kept doing this for a long time.[1]

This detainee was not alone in being traumatized by such treatment, for it quickly emerged that sexual torture was among the key techniques of power to be used against the Muslim detainees. Stripping, nudity, bestialization, masturbation, simulation of gay sex and even rape were apparently among the practices endorsed and/or tolerated by the army leadership.

Sexuality was also integral to the overall ideological waging of the war, as for example, when US president Obama publicly addressed the issue, although his approach was at odds with those of the Bush Administration which sanctioned the use of torture. Obama's concern was that 'no country should deny people their rights because of who they love, which is why we must stand up for the rights of gays and lesbians everywhere'.[2] This statement speaks to a key justification for the war, namely, the right of the United States to intervene 'everywhere' on behalf of, first, the rights of veiled Muslim women, and soon after, 'the rights of gays and lesbians'. This chapter examines why and how sex, sexuality and sexual orientation became so central in the waging of the global war.

The torture of Muslims, documented in the Abu Ghraib photographs as well as the Taguba Report, was apparently calculated to impose sexual degradation on detainees, to teach them of their absolute powerlessness in the face of US might. US officials and the media subsequently downplayed such violence by redefining it as 'detainee abuse' after the Abu Ghraib scandal broke, but the release of official documents following the inquiry into the prison revealed that the CIA had drawn upon decades of research on the efficacy of torture techniques and on the work of experts who identified sexual repression as characteristic of Islamic culture. This is what apparently led them to settle on sadism as the most effective tool to break the will of 'terrorists'. Shaming these sexually backward Muslims and turning the sexuality of the Muslim male against himself was thus among the preferred methods to destroy the 'terrorist' threat. Sexual torture, heterosexual or homosexual in form, was a calculated affair. Moreover, sexual fixation with Muslims is at work in other spheres of social life touched by the war, such as the anti-hijab policies and the political campaigns to unveil Muslim women that proliferate across Western societies. The idea that the 'truth' of Islam is to be found in the realm of sexuality, that this is the terrain in which the full measure of Islamic barbarity can be confirmed, has a strong – and long-standing – hold on the Western imaginary. The originary impetus for such a perspective, however, can be located in the very formation of Western politics and the early desires of its subjects rather than in the 'Islam' that they conjure up.

I begin this discussion of sexual politics with Abu Ghraib for a number of reasons. The Abu Ghraib photographs recorded how state power was to be exerted in the war, but these images also put on display the Western Subject's desire for the Black/brown Muslim body. As significant, they demonstrated that white women were not immune from partaking of the sadistic pleasures of the war. Abundantly evident in the photographs is the pleasure derived by US soldiers from this assertion of sexual power over the Muslim male, this was no less brazen for the women than for their male compatriots. It should be remembered that the Taguba Report documented how these women's participation in the sexual violence – which included the use of 'objects including a truncheon, wire and a phosphorescent tube'; un-muzzled guard dogs; fake menstrual blood; and women's underwear – were no isolated events.[3] The effects of such *monstrous intimacies*, as Christina Sharpe has named them in a different context, are of lasting consequence. The hedonism such violence organizes cannot be delinked from the terror it generates among the communities of the victims, the effects of which are trans-generational.[4] Nor can such violence be taken as having no effect on relations between Muslim women and men, on the treatment of sex and of relationships within Muslim communities.

My reading of such sexualization of Muslims defines this as a 'primal scene' for the constitution of the Western self in the twenty-first century. That the fixation with the sex/uality of 'Islam' is widespread is clear in the range of spheres and sectors – politics, academia, law, social services, community and religious organizations, intelligence services, military, psychoanalytic and health care professions, media, women's organizations, human rights groups and so on – that are engaged in projects to monitor and discipline Muslims on this front. The surveillance and profiling of Muslim men across the spectrum of these institutions of 'everyday' life, like the targeted shaming of veiled Muslim women, encodes this sexual fixation.

The obsessive attention directed toward the 'sex' of Islam and the grotesque nature of the Muslim can be tracked to the very formation of the West, albeit the focus, expression and level of intensity of the fixation have varied over time. The sexualization of Islam began with its early designation as diabolical in Latin Christendom's theologio-cultural imaginary, which projected sexual debauchery as an aspect of Islam and confirmation of the satanic nature of the Muslim. As I show below, this construction of Islam passed into the Orientalizing discourses of the colonial period; it has most recently been recast as 'Islamic' sexual repression and perversion in the discourse of the global war. The Western tendency to isolate and elevate 'sex' to overshadow other aspects of Muslim life has remain unabated through these discursive formations: their incitement of particular kinds of antipathies, desires and forms of revulsion have been fixated on the figure of the Muslim.

Sexuality, terror, imperialism

Upon the publication of the Abu Ghraib photographs, critical race scholars were quick to point out the racial dimension of the sexual torture. Many drew a parallel with the history of lynching of Black men and women in the United States to highlight the similarity in the spectacularized enactment of the violence, and in the generation and circulation of sexual pleasure by the capture of the brutalization in these images.[5] The link between race and sexual sadism was also highlighted by critical commentators, as was the homosexual idiom in which much of the violence was perpetrated. The photographs' direct linking of the fanaticism of the 'terrorist' to the hatred of female sexuality and 'queerness' constructed the Muslim male as simultaneously misogynist and queer-phobic.

In *Terrorist Assemblages*, Jasbir Puar linked the 'queering' of the 'terrorist' to the shifting treatment of homosexuality within US nation-formation. Making the case that homosexuality was incorporated, along with heterosexuality, as normative in US national culture in the war on terror, she argued such gay inclusion was intrinsically tied to the projection of perverse queerness and failed masculinity onto the Muslim. The idea of US exceptionalism was thus expanded, symbolized now by its 'freedom-loving' culture which included the 'sexual freedoms' of gay and queer subjects. In contrast, the terrorist was constructed as sexually repressed, hence the source of a deadly threat that was rooted in his repressive 'Islamic' culture. This sexual exceptionalism of the West, Puar further argued, enfolded queer subjects into patriotic forms of belonging, which she described as homonationalism. With the superiority of Western culture thus redefined, gender as well as sexual egalitarianism confirmed its unique and distinct values. This new alliance between the imperialist state and gay rights activists led to the convergence of their interests in a queer politics that extended the reach of US imperialism. Such homonationalism, however, was saturated with racial politics, for it was mostly white queers that were being integrated into the nation as subjects of life (gay marriage, adoption, families) not death (aids, non-reproductive relationships), while queers of colour were associated with repressive cultures. 'Gay Islamophobia' was the result of such integration of white queers, it targets Muslim communities for punishment for their supposedly queerphobic culture and aims to 'rescue' queer Muslims from these communities. Whiteness thus came to function as the 'queer norm' in the global war, Puar argued, whereas 'straightness' became constructed as the 'racial norm'.[6] Such queer politics advanced '*convivial* relations between queernesses and militarism, securitization, war, terrorism, surveillance technologies, empire, torture' in 'our contemporary war machines', Puar astutely pointed out, gays in the military being an example of this.[7]

While sexual-gender politics and the status of the queer subject were indeed transformed by the global war as Puar has demonstrated, and while novel forms of national belonging were indeed extended to queer communities, what is left unexamined here is the desire of the white subject – queer as well as straight, male as well as female, sexual as well as cultural – for the racialized Muslim body. Such desire is a long-standing feature of Western sexual-gender politics, it has been formative of these and their organization of sexual subjectivity. Indeed, the Western subject's sexual desire for the racial object cannot be isolated from its investment in colonial/imperial relations of power, for it is these relations that underwrite access to the Black/brown Muslim body. Moreover, a number of Puar's conclusions are too hastily drawn. So, for example, as she deliberates on the possibilities of post-9/11 political solidarities, she asks '[w]hat is queer about the terrorist?'. In response, Puar points to how the gay subject was previously marked by a death-oriented 'corroding' masculinity, and how it is now the terrorist who stands as a figure of such deadly masculinity: 'The depictions of masculinity most rapidly disseminated and globalized at this historical juncture are terrorist masculinities: failed and perverse, these emasculated bodies always have femininity as their point of malfunction, and are metonymically tied to all sorts of pathologies of the mind and body – homosexuality, incest, paedophilia, madness and disease.'[8] In other words, the discourse of war has constructed the figure of the terrorist as that of pathological sexuality, whose failed masculinity associates him with femininity. Moreover, as she rightly notes, this failed masculinity is marked as monstrosity, '[w]ith the unfurling, viruslike, explosive mass of the terrorist network, tentacles ever regenerating despite efforts to truncate them, the terrorist is concurrently an unfathomable, unknowable, and hysterical monstrosity' which can only be defeated by patriotic US masculinities, including gay.[9] She therefore identifies queerness, informed by anti-racist/imperialist politics, as the site of a possible kinship.

Puar's treatment of 'queerness' as *the* orientation that defies the politics of heteronormativity goes beyond the issue of sexuality. Such a theoretical move allows for gestures of solidarity that can encompass, under the sign 'queer', radical politics which fail to signify under the white racial politics of hetero-, and now, homo-normativity. This expansive definition of 'queer' may well include all non-white, as well as white non-bourgeois, gendered/sexual subjects.

Yet with regard to the 'queerness' of the terrorist, Puar emphasizes the point that '[i]t is not that we must engage in the practice of excavating the queer terrorist, or queering the terrorist; rather queerness is always already installed in the project of naming the terrorist; the terrorist does not appear as such without the concurrent entrance of perversion, deviance'.[10] This conflation of 'perversion' with 'queerness', and privileging of 'queerness' as the analytic in which the 'terrorist' acquires legibility can be a tricky proposition on at least two counts: first, it is the figure of the Muslim-as-Muslim that is constructed as 'terrorist', Puar's situating of this figure under the sign of 'queerness' disappears Islam; and second, this gesture incorporates this figure of the Muslim under an externally imposed sign, 'queer'. The result is an assertion of a Westernizing discourse of sexual difference/deviance ('queerness') to subsume the (radical) politics of the Muslim ('terrorist') that are self-consciously articulated by said terrorist to Islam. If homonationalism enfolds the normative queer into the nation's sexual-racial-imperial ventures, an all-encompassing definition of 'queerness' as 'the' sign of the non-normative engulfs the politics of resistance emanating from the Islamic – cast in the war as terroristic – in the register of counter-hegemonic, but nevertheless binary, sexual/gender politics. Such a framing implicitly upholds 'queerness' as the privileged site for resistance politics and affiliative kinships to override other possible sites, including in this case, Islam. Obfuscating the rootedness of the Muslim – heterosexual, homosexual and queer – in the tradition of Islam to privilege 'queerness' is thus the condition for political solidarity, one which extends an inclusionary imperative in a gender/sexual regime that is rooted in Westernizing discourses, well meaning though the gesture of solidarity may be. To put it differently, if all such 'perversion' and 'deviance', that is, counter-hegemonic practices, are to be taken as 'queer', what/where is the place for an explicitly anti-colonial, anti-racist, anti-imperialist resistance that is organized invernaculars other than those of 'sex/uality?'

The affinity of the queer (of colour) with the terrorist (Muslim, straight, queer) is here posited on the grounds of 'queerness', not that of 'terrorism' (let alone Islam!) in a moment of great peril for Muslims resisting Westernity. My point here is that the categories 'queer' and 'terrorist' signify 'threats' and 'politics' (that is, 'deviances') whose conflation may well prove counterproductive to those anti-colonial and anti-racist politics that set their horizons beyond the West, including beyond its sexual-gender regimes, that may even be inspired by a tradition long defined as 'enemy' of this West and its sexual politics. For the white gay male subject incorporated into the individualizing sexual freedoms of neoliberalism is now *accompanied by* the upwardly mobile and socially desirable queer of colour, the latter integrated into the post-9/11 cultural-political assemblage as emblematic of the multicultural aesthetic, of cosmopolitan and urbane styles, of 'post-racial' individualism and 'progressive' free choice, to signify transcendence of the colonial histories of the West, as argued by Haritaworn. These 'queer lovers' are now celebrated and distinguished from 'hateful Others', including Muslims, migrants and other Black/brown bodies, to mobilize Islamophobic and racist politics on the basis that it is they who are innately homophobic, argues Haritaworn. The inclusion into Western globality – even if not into any particular Western nationality – acquired by the 'multicultural' queer subject comes at a high cost, that is, incorporation into that most touted of Western-capitalist value, individual choice and personal freedom. The commitment of the resisting Muslim seems to move beyond such Westernizing individualism, critiquing this as a form of religio-racial, even sexual, subjugation.

In contrast to Puar, Joseph Massad argues in his study of transnational queer activism that this advances sexual imperialism into the Arab world in a manner that strengthens the institutionalization of heterosexuality; he defines this transnational activism as 'the Gay International'. The US gay rights movement which emerged during the 1960s had, by the 1990s, become internationalized as sexuality became a matter of keen interest in global human rights discourse.

Here, sexual rights were linked to dominant concepts of 'civilized' and 'uncivilized' sexual cultures and practices, linked to particular communities, such that women and homosexuals became identified as 'prime victims' of human rights violations in the Arab world.[11] Where colonial discourse had identified deviance with all matters sexual as characteristic of the Arab/Muslim world, postmodern constructs now defined these societies as sexually repressive at their core.[12]

Massad's argument is that while same-sex practices were historically pervasive across the Arab/Muslim world, the sexual identity 'gay', that is, an identity tied to a particular form of sexual subjectivity, is not to be found prior to the era of modernization. He therefore poses the question, 'How can one, for example, collect data on whether people's sexuality is "repressed" if the notion of sexuality itself is not first imposed on people as an epistemological and ontological category that is said to constitute identity?'[13] Massad's point is that the emergence of 'gay' as *an identity* was a distinctly Western phenomenon, a reflection of Western sexual politics. Through the activities of the Gay International, the extension of this sexual politics into the Arab world was escalating during the late twentieth century. His reading of same-sex practices in the Arab world finds that these were not necessarily considered fixed or oppositional, but rather as flexible and compatible with, opposite-sex practices. Drawing attention to the fluidity and porosity of such sexual expression, practice and relations, his argument is that these were not bordered or contained within sexual binaries, nor were they connected to sexuality-as-identity. In Massad's view, the rigidity of the hetero- and homosexual binary, like that of the straight and queer binary which shapes the Gay International's sexual politics, has, by constructing sexuality as identity, actually deepened the institutionalization of heterosexuality through globalizing such binary approaches and through the imposition of sexuality-as-subjectivity. Popularly represented as advancing gay rights, these binary constructions of sexuality consolidate heterosexuality as an identity and fix particular forms of sexual expression as 'heterosexual' where these had previously exceeded such boundaries.

Massad's analysis points to the imperialist function of international gay activism, for as he notes, '[T]he categories gay and lesbian are not universal at all and can only be universalized by the epistemic, ethical and political violence unleashed on the rest of the world by the very international human rights advocates whose aim is to defend the very people their intervention is creating.'[14] Such human rights advocacy advances the destruction of those approaches and practices that do not take the binary approach to what is defined as 'the sexual', nor consider this immutable; instead the human rights approach furthers the exclusion and marginalization of those who would eschew sexuality as the sole, or primary marker of identity. Sexual imperialism is thus identified with post/modernity: its link to the human rights agenda illustrates how sexuality functions in the global field as an extension of Western power. Where Puar takes the underlying binary organization of sexuality as stable, albeit in an expansive definition with significant shifts in its modes of expression, address and reception, Massad's study compels a rethinking of this foundational assumption of the now hegemonic sexual politics of the West.

Certainly the reworking of sexual politics as identified by Puar (homonationalism), Haritaworn (racialization of queer lovers vs hateful Others) and Massad (Gay International) is significant to the remaking of Western forms of belonging in the war on terror, yet there are some specific aspects of this reformation of the West that need also to be addressed, namely, the Western Subject's – Man and Woman – desire for the Muslim, male and female; fascination with what is taken as the 'sexual barbarism' of Islam; existential anxieties arising from such violent projections; and intricate cultural rootedness in the sexual-gender binary. In other words, the contemporary sexual-gender politics of the West have long histories and deep roots that extend right back to its formative moment.

Let me return to the case of Abu Ghraib to illustrate the significance of these points. Whereas the trophy photographs sparked public debate and critiques about the use of torture, as well as of its racial/sexual nature, hardly any attention was paid to the white sexual desire – male as well as female, heterosexual as well as queer – for the Muslim male body that was so strikingly on display. Likewise, there was virtually no questioning, let alone rejection, of the construction of 'Islamic culture' as innately sexually repressive that was identified as the impetus for the torture. Finally, the pleasures of the women – as feminized, indeed even feminist subjects – in this brutalization of Muslims led to no rethinking of the concept of patriarchy, the core assumptions of feminist politics, nor of the attribution of the vicious queer-phobia to Islam.

Primal scenes: Subjects of sex, objects of perversion

Attraction and revulsion are integrally linked in the formation of desire, the psychoanalytic tradition has long argued; both are abundantly present in the fusing of race with Islam, torture with sadism, and disgust with pleasure in contemporary racial/sexual politics. Disgust and revulsion rapidly overtook attraction as the modality of Western erotic expression towards the figure of the Muslim in the global war, but it is important to remember this was not always the case. For attraction held the upper hand in erotic overtures towards the Islamic Orient not so very long ago.

On his first visit to Egypt, E. W. Lane, the renowned Orientalist, thus described his feelings, 'As I approached the shore, I felt like an Eastern bridegroom, about to lift the veil of his bride, and to see, for the first time, the features that were to charm, or disappoint, or disgust' him.[15] A century later, Bernard Lewis, the Orientalist-turned Islamophobe, one of the ideological architects of the war on terror, was, like Lane, not immune to the charms of the Islamic Orient. On his first visit to the Middle East, Lewis described feeling 'like a Muslim Bridegroom first seeing his wife, with whom he is to spend the rest of his life'.[16] These 'first' experiences of the Orientalists were not far removed from the excited European reception of the 'Arabian Nights', its decontextualized and phantasmally eroticized renditions titillating generations of Western audiences. Nor was sexual mastery of the Orient confined to heterosexual phantasies of penetrative possession. T. E Lawrence ('of Arabia'), like many before and after him, was drawn by a homoerotic variation of this theme, by the desire to be possessed as well as to possess. The histories of such complex experiences of sexual attraction and enrapture, hatred and disgust, supposedly incited by Muslim perversity (sexual excess, at that moment), signal a dynamic not quite captured by the idea of 'clash of cultures'.

In their expression of the not quite so latent desire fuelling their scholarly ambitions, Lane and Lewis fancied themselves *Eastern* or *Muslim* bridegrooms to phantasize the Islamic Orient as the 'bride' they intended to 'know' and 'own', penetrate and possess, for 'the rest of his life', in Lewis' ambitious words. Of note is how the origin of the Orientalist's desire is here located not in the aspiring Western self, but instead projected onto Islam/Orient as the object that incites such passion, the virgin bride awaiting the momentous (sexual) arrival of these men. The Oriental/Islamic 'groom' is, of course, disappeared in this primal scene.

This Orientalist aspiration to 'husband' Islam/the Orient is curious for another reason, for it suggests a desire for the familial obligations that usually arise from such union. This desire appears to include that of assuming the role of patriarch, not only 'groom', to the Orient. Not surprising, Lewis described women's status as 'probably the most profound single difference between the two civilizations', that is Islam, and his own, the West.[17] But this 'difference' was one that clearly attracted the Man, for it incited excitement at the idea of possessing this female/feminized space. Moreover, if the status of the women was the 'single difference', so too clearly was that of the men, that is Man versus the Oriental/Muslim male.

The consummation of the desire expressed by Lewis relies on the disappearance of the Muslim man; for the desire to possess the Islamic world – the bride – requires elimination of the Oriental 'groom'. The erasure of the Oriental male upon the arrival of the Western Man requires a symbolic castration of the Muslim man, of the Oriental male, the condition for the realization of Orientalist desire. Interestingly enough, Lewis is reported to have kept a photograph of this first experience – in which he wears a *dishdasha* – on his office desk during his lifetime.[18] This desire to be possessed as well as to possess, to go native and retain mastery, no doubt gave rise to the anxiety to dis/prove authenticity, which I think can be read in such a display.

The shift from attraction (Lane, Lewis) to disgust (Abu Ghraib, Guantanamo) as the dominant modality of Western desire reveals the sea change that has taken place in representations of the 'Orient', from its earlier mode of expression in the European age of empire to its articulation to US power as the Western hegemon. Europeans had long-standing, direct and sustained contact with Muslim societies, which had shaped attitudes of attraction as well as disdain (Said defined both as aspects of Orientalism) over many centuries. In contrast, the US experience with the Oriental/Islamic world has been of relatively shorter duration and of an entirely different order.[19] The reasons for this are complex, but they include, in brief, Cold War politics; US covert operations, militarism and backing of authoritarian states; the Islamic revolution in Iran; Palestinian resistance to Israeli settler colonialism; the politics of oil and so on. The US variant of Orientalism was hence shaped by aversion and temptation, which, in the global war, quickly transformed into outright Islamophobia. Given the complexities of this dialectic of desire, it is useful to consider what a religio-racial hermeneutic reveals about the constitution of 'sexuality' itself during the junctures marked by these shifts. Attending to the historical antecedents of contemporary sexual politics yields important insights into the psychosexual pleasures harnessed to the antipathy towards Islam, keeping in mind that the sexualization of this tradition in the Western imaginary has not left gender or sexual practices within Muslim societies untouched.

Studies of the gender/sexual politics of Orientalism have been influenced by Said's work, as discussed in Chapter 2. Said's reading of Orientalism argued this led to the feminization of the Orient as inert and passive, even as the discourse simultaneously constructed the West as masculine and historical agent. The earlier statements by Lane and Lewis certainly confirm Said's argument, but these comments also point to the multifaceted nature of the desire at work: in this quest for knowledge was infused a sexual desire that implicitly recognized the 'masculinity' of the Oriental male but sought to displace this. In the heterosexual register of expression for this desire, the Muslim male is not imagined as feminized (he cannot, after all, be the 'veiled bride'), but instead sought to eliminate his presence in the penetrative desire to possess what was conceived of as his possession. Put differently, this sexualizing-colonizing impulse was driven by the assertion of the mastery of the Western Man through his *displacement* and *replacement* of the Muslim/Oriental man as *male*, that is, by claiming the latter's place as 'groom'. What one sees here is not so much a *feminizing* as a *castrating* of the Oriental male, for this Will to master the Orient refused to 'see' his presence as man. This disappearance – which subjectifies the Orientalist – is closer to what Eng has described as racial castration than it is to Said's notion of Orientalist feminization. In this libidinal economy of exchange, Western masculinity finds its expression in relation to both the Muslim female *and* male, the condition of its affirmation being the elimination of this Muslim Male.

The thrill and anxiety that run through these encounters with Islam, linked as they are to the production of authoritative knowledge about Muslims, also infused the early Christian texts, except these featured the Muslim male as hyper-virile and the Christian subject as hyper-vulnerable to the former's overpowering presence. Latin Christendom's understanding of Islam, such as it was, identified the existential threat emanating from Islam as located in the carnal excesses of the Muslim to imperil the chastity of the Christian. The writings of John of Damascus, described as the 'first outstanding scholar to enter the field of polemic against the Moslem ... known to history as the most honored of the later theologians of the Greek Church', defined Islam as 'heresy' and presented its Prophet as the Anti-Christ.[20] As he explained to his Christian audiences, 'this Mohammed wrote many ridiculous books to each one of which he set a title. For example, there the book, *On Woman* [109] in which he plainly makes legal provision for taking four wives and, if it be possible, a thousand concubines – as many as one can maintain.'[21] Such representation, particularly given the author's knowledge of Arabic and his experience in a Muslim court, mapped the contours of the early Crusader imaginary, orienting subsequent Christian attitudes towards Islam through a lens that privileged sexuality. Presenting the Prophet as 'a man of unbridled sensuality',[22] influential and powerful Christians linked fornication and devilry to his 'falseness' as a Prophet. The 'sexual perversity' projected onto him was then taken as confirmation of his satanic nature, the 'Anti-Christ'.[23] Early Christian ideas about religio-racial alterity were thus expressed in the idiom of *sexual* excess, a threat to Christendom's theologically derived gender ideologies. Unearthing these antiquated Christian attitudes and statements provides a valuable archive of the *sexual* formation of Europe.

While the hyper-potent nature of the Muslim male was, according to John of Damascus, evident in his multiple wives and numerous concubines, medieval Crusaders would also link this Muslim male to sodomy and lechery so that homosexuality – which Christians defined as sin – was also associated with Islam, further proof of its perversity. The continuities in such sexualizing of anti-Islamic discourses can be read in the historical record as documented in a number of studies. For example, one such study found that

> The sin of sodomy indeed was most tenaciously ascribed to Europe's most dreaded enemy. The Crusaders' fear, once captured, of being used to satisfy Arab sexual demands deeply penetrated into the mind of Europeans and intensified as the Mamelukes, a military caste, made up of men of Georgian and Caucasian origin, dominated Egypt from 1249. . . . At home, both Jews and Christians were believed to have 'learned' the practice of sodomy in Egypt or Arab Spain,

although Jews were also associated within the 'biblical narrative of the destruction of Sodom'.[24]

The proclamations linking Islam with sexual depravity would travel through the centuries, the 'perversity' attributed to Muslims was projected onto other 'pagans' likewise identified with racial degeneracy across Asia, Africa, as well as the Americas.[25] In the high age of empire, the threat (pleasure) of (homo)sexuality was encoded in Orientalist desire, for, as Said noted of this period, 'the Orient was a place where one could look for sexual experience unobtainable in Europe'.[26]

This European characterization of Muslim societies from the Middle East to Africa to Asia as sexually degenerate, it should be noted, included heterosexuality, (excessive, debauched and life-sapping) as well as homosexuality (the 'sin against nature'). Muslims were thus construed as failed sexual subjects in heterosexual *as well as* homosexual registers: the failure being taken as reflection of their religious as well as racial degradation.

Foucault's work transformed the study of sexuality and remains foundational in queer studies. His deconstruction of the 'repressive hypothesis' led him to argue that 'sexuality' – as a discursive object – was invented in the nineteenth century, and that the injunction to 'speak' its truth not only incited particular forms of desire but also allowed the permeation of sexuality by disciplinary power.[27] The injunction to 'confess' and thereby present one's sexual self for judgement was traced by Foucault to the Catholic Church, more specifically to the Counter-Reformation. In the nineteenth century, the secular medical and scientific discourses, consolidated the binary organization of sexuality into healthy 'heterosexuality' and deviant 'homosexuality' by centring their ideas about normality and abnormality. Yet Foucault's work on sexuality overlooks how the formulation of this binary as 'Western' and 'universal' was not an internal 'Western' affair, whether in the Christian or scientific-secular worldview. The formulation of the binary as *Western* – which is crucial to its construction as universal – was historically accomplished by Christo-Europeans in relation to the sexual 'perversities' they projected onto Muslims as the antithesis of Euro-Christian chastity. In other words, the Westernization of this sexual binary – no doubt originating within the Christian-Catholic theological frame – entailed distinguishing the chaste sexuality of Christians from the monstrous sexuality of Muslims, which included heterosexual as well as homosexual 'perversity' as the latter's very condition of being. Moreover, Foucault noted that in the earlier Christian period, sexual 'deviance', including sodomy, were considered sins by the Church, not the innate quality of the individual. Yet a quick glance at the Christian statements on Muslim perversity in earlier centuries as well as during this period demonstrates that in this case, these 'sins' were considered a quality innate to Islam, to Muslim being. This view is so firmly fixed in Western gender-sexual politics that even now the sexual barbarism of the Muslim, the male in particular, is considered a matter rooted in his religio-racial condition of being.

The Western binary regime of gender-sexuality would fundamentally reshape the colonial world. In the Muslim world, the binaries were scripted onto Islamic culture as perversions, so that Muslims – males and females – had to contend with their construction as always-already failed sexual/gender subjects within colonial discourses. The violence entailed in such sexualization of Muslim societies was hence not any abstract form, nor a reflection of the supposedly gendered patriarchal global condition. Instead, such sexualizing and gendering formation extended outwards from what were Christo-European fixations and anxieties, desires and phantasies, to subsequently become institutionalized in the colonizing apparatus; the construction of such sexuality, as well as the construction of sexuality as identity, was hence rooted in a *particular* religio-racial configuration.

This binary organization of sexuality was, of course, rooted in the construction of gender as correspondingly binary: both shaped the masculinity and femininity that would be simultaneously produced as Western-universal. I have discussed in Chapter 2 how Man – as the secular Human form – was produced in relation to his non-human others. The masculinity of Man, a civilizing quality that produced him as masterful, disciplined, controlled and controlling, thus set him apart from the failed masculinity of the non-evolved 'males' who were neither disciplined nor masterful. The conventions of feminist theory notwithstanding, this Christo-European regimenting masculinity was constituted not only, not even primarily, in relation to femininity but within the global-colonial field. This was also the case with regard to the constitution of Man's binary other, Woman, cast in the image of the Christo-European female. In the global-colonial field, she stood apart in her femininity from the erotic, over-sexualized Muslim, Oriental African females. Woman, cast as the worthy companion of Man, partook in his civilizational missions, albeit in her gendered condition.

Said's *Orientalism* privileges 'femininization' as the gendered referent in constituting the relation between the West and the Orient, but closer interrogation of the making of Latin-Christian gender/sexual norms as 'Western' demonstrates that these norms were considered the properties natural to Christian subjects. The femininity of Woman was hence ordained from her very nature that is, Christian and female. To equate this femininity with the condition of enslavement and colonization of Black/brown fe/males , that is, to describe the latter as 'feminized', elevates and privileges gender as a category shorn of, and isolated from, race, religion and coloniality. Western feminists have long equated the status of white women with that of enslaved, colonized and even occupied peoples, appropriating their experience to claim the power to speak for these peoples. The privileging of this feminist discourse, as one sees in Said's rendering of the process of colonization, has been contested by anti-colonial feminists who argue that this practice obscures the active participation of Western women in the institutions of slavery, genocide and colonial subjugation, and in the extension of the gender/sexual binary over the colonized world.

Access to the status Man and Woman was thus already foreclosed to the Muslim, to colonized men and women, as was access to the 'masculinity' and 'femininity' proper to the civilized being. Defined as the gendered qualities of 'normal' humanity, masculinity and femininity were inherently racialized formations. The Muslim could not, by definition, attain these religio-racial, gender/sexual qualities. Instead, perversity, lack and diabolic excess, were the lot of this Muslim. The conjoining of sexuality and gender with religion and race was such that, to be properly human, that is, to be Man and Woman, and to be properly gendered, that is, masculine and feminine, was to be white. Put differently, 'masculinity' and 'femininity' were the exalted characteristics of the self-determining Christo-modern subject – masculinity and femininity were the gendered properties of their whiteness.

The religion of sex

Pre- and early-modern Christian depictions of the East – the 'home' of Islam – pivoted on two key themes, namely, 'the designation of the "East" as the site of a "lascivious sensuality"' and an 'inherent violence'.[28] These twin thematics, sex and violence, were to remain surprisingly constant in Western depictions, crystallizing as they later did in the forms of colonial knowledge that produced the Orient. In order to account for the sexual politics of Orientalism, however, it is useful to contextualize these in the earlier histories of the Latin Christian treatment of Islam as viewed through the theological concepts of 'sex' and 'sin' (that is, the 'original' sin against God, i.e. heterosexuality, as well as the sin against 'nature', homosexuality).

The theological concept of original sin linked this to sex, sex to woman, woman to temptation, and all three to the fall from grace that had led to the expulsion of the first couple from Eden. Sex – embodied in Woman, the debased gender – signifies the end of innocence, the 'fall' of humanity and the beginning of sinfulness in the world, a condition that demanded atonement. Sodomy, on the other hand, was a perversity that went against divinely ordained 'nature'. The Christian subject of salvation was hence one given to chastity by freeing himself of the temptation to sin. This particular chain of associations that shaped Latin-Christian approaches to sex, sexuality and gender, was transmuted into Western ideologies, well into the twentieth century. Although significant shifts in attitudes towards sex and gender occurred over time (as, for example, in the Reformation, racial-sexual slavery, the Victorian age, the emergence of feminism, and the twentieth century sexual revolution, etc.), the guilt-inducing idea of original sin remained a powerful force.[29]

This linking of sex with sin shaped Christian-Europe's political as well as cultural formation and was given shape in relation to the Jews as well as the Muslims. So, for example, in his study of Europe's making of the Jew as an enemy, Anidjar has discussed how Paul distinguished Christianity from Judaism in Romans by defining the former as offering the gift of salvation to the Christian, including, most particularly, release from the sin of sex.[30] Anidjar's reading of Romans highlights Paul's counsel to the early Christians to 'No longer present your members to sin as weapons of wickedness, but present your members to God as weapons of righteousness'.[31] Paul thus conceived of the Christian's 'member', his penis, as a 'weapon' of righteousness when put to the proper service of God. With the body itself transformed into the site of sin and war, equipped with a 'weapon' of wickedness and (potential) redemption, sexual desires and passions were to be kept under tight rein. As Anidjar reads this letter, Paul's advice to Christians to 'let us lay aside the works of darkness, but let us put on the weapons of light' refers also to his own struggles, 'I see in my members another law at war . . . with the law of my mind, making me captive to the law of sin that dwells in my members.'[32] The sexually unruly male body was thus the site of a furious conflict fuelled by desire, its wickedness located in a genitally oriented sense of having been born in sin. As Anidjar argues, 'The permanent possibility of war in which body parts can always become weapons and in which they can be put on like armor proclaims that being is being at war', that the mind when 'set on flesh' is 'hostile to God'.[33] Part of the New Testament and considered among the most influential of Paul's epistles, Romans was written to impart a 'spiritual gift' to the righteous by warning them of the 'vile' passions and 'unnatural' functions of those upon whom God had turned his back. Certainly this treatment of sex and sexuality were contested in the making of early Christianity, but Paul's influence on the Latin Church, like his followers' counselling of celibacy, was to prove highly influential as it shaped the gaze that would be directed at Muslims.

Islam, emerging a number of centuries later (670–732), had no concept of original sin, nor was it fixated on sex. Instead, sex and sexual pleasure were considered integral aspects of human life, a gift to humanity. In this tradition, men were allowed four wives, and marriage was a contract to be entered by consent, the *mahr* was to be paid to the bride (not her family), sexual pleasure was not tied to reproduction, contraception was acceptable, the enjoyment of sex was defined to be as important for women as for men, and men were advised to attend to women's desire. In her study of Islamic sexual ethics, Kecia Ali explains that although '[S]ignificant texts in the Qur'an and hadith allude to the importance of female gratification and satisfaction in the sexual act', the practice of slavery and concubinage impacted on the treatment of women.[34] Although classical texts often focused on the 'discord-producing effects of female dissatisfaction (the potential for *fitna*)' and treated marriage as a condition that ensured women's sexual availability to their husbands, Ali argues that providing sexual pleasure to a wife was identified as a husband's duty and women could file for divorce on the basis of a husband's impotence. Although women's consent to marriage and sexual pleasure were thus significant in the classical Islamic tradition, this consent was corrupted by slavery and concubinage.

Strong disagreement regarding the issue of women's consent to sex after marriage emerged as the Islamic tradition evolved. The Hanafi school took the view 'that husbands were entitled to have sex forcibly with their wives when the latter did not have a legitimate reason to refuse sex', but this position was not 'shared outside this school': indeed, even within this school, the majority of the Hanafi thinkers 'recognized a distinction between forced intercourse and more usual sexual relations between spouses'.[35] The continuing practice of slave concubinage also complicated the structure of marriage, Ali argues, and while the 'Qur'an accepts the notion of men's sexual access to some free women . . . it does not explore the possibility of large-scale concubinage, nor was such practiced in the first Muslim community'.[36] It is notable here that in the early Islamic tradition, the Prophet rejected the Christian ideal of celibacy and 'gender' was defined as not a factor in shaping the believer's relation to the divine.

Yet early Christian depictions of Islam fixated in explicitly sexual terms on the Prophet Muhammad himself, on his body, as well as his relation to the tradition he founded. John of Damascus defined the Prophet, the prototype of the ideal Muslim man for his community, as sensual/sexual 'debauch' and described him as 'an arch-seducer, who wore purple, coloured his lips, and delighted in scented things and cotton'; moreover, the Prophet was also 'accused of having conjured up a false God to warrant his sexual indulgences'.[37] Islam was thus linked with the perversion of gender as well as sexuality, it became here an alibi for devilry and sexual temptation embodied by the Muslim male as hyper-virile ('arch-seducer') *and* effeminate object of ridicule ('wore purple', 'coloured his lips', 'delighted in scented things', etc.), a practitioner of deception (seduces) who had lurid desires (colours the lips). Such depictions of the Prophet as the 'Anti-Christ in alliance with the Devil' and an 'evil sensualist'[38] were to imbue the Christian imaginary. So, for example, Petrus Alfonsi, 'the early prototype of the Islam expert', claimed in his text (1109) that 'Muhammad loved women a great deal and was too much the voluptuary, and, just as he claimed, the power of the lust of forty men dwelled in him.'[39] Indeed, so insatiable was this Muslim male sexual appetite believed to be that it extended into the afterlife; as Kabbani noted, 'To support the idea of a voluptuous East, the West inflated the Qur'anic idea of Paradise, arguing that Muslims were not only lewd in everyday life, but had conceived of a heaven that would permit endless sensual gratification.'[40]

This privileging of 'sex', and the obsession with the virility of the Muslim male, in the derision of Islam speak to the sexual anxieties that were entangled with the lures of the material wealth and learned power of the Muslim empires in Latin Christendom's wars with Islam. Such casting of the Prophet – whose moral universe, critical scholars generally agree, was shaped by an overriding concern with the well-being of widows and orphans, that is, women and children; who remained loyal to his first, considerably older, wife, during whose lifetime he was married only to her; and who was reported to prepare his own food and mend his own clothes[41] – points to the fixation with sexual perversity as being more about *Christian* insecurities than Muslim excesses. Such early anxieties regarding male sexual prowess are to be found at a later date in the twelfth-century texts such as the *Liber denudationis*, which claimed that 'Muslims believe that in the next life each Muslim in paradise will be awarded for his virtue by an elongation of his penis: it will be so long, in fact, that he will need seventy Christians and seventy Jews to carry it before him'.[42] Such phantasmic writings – influential in the Christian world over a number of centuries, as Talon notes – invariably construed the Muslim male as monstrously endowed, the 'truth' of his being located in his 'sex', or more accurately, in its, and his, perversion.

The charged construct of the Muslim male as a distinct threat to Christian men and women, and its projection outwards onto the 'East', that nebulous zone of monstrous beings, illustrates how sexuality shaped the theologio-racializing logic of war. The Crusader constructs were soon followed by the sexualization of the archetypal Muslim figures that peppered the Middle English Romances, including the 'lewd Saracen' and the pining 'princess' whose desire for the Christian knight would lead her to betray her family and community.[43] Rabbani describes these figures as 'wish-fulfilling embodiments', for the tropes of 'the Saracen giant killed by a Christian hero, the defeated emir, the converted Saracen', along with the languishing princesses, were associated with the victory of Christianity over Islam in the Romances. Such tropes were 'essentially vehicles of propaganda in which the ideal of chivalry became subservient to the requirements of religion and politics'.[44] These iconic figures remained staples of the Renaissance: they are also to be found in the corpus of the Romantics. Tales of sensual 'Arabian Nights', of harems filled with 'doe-eyed women in abundance, languishing with love and expiring of desire, wicked men who kept them in captivity, gorgeous brocades and cashmeres, jewels, perfumes, music, dance and poetry', became standard tropes and motifs in the eroticized Western imaginary, in the hungering for sexual mastery over the phantasmal Orientals whose sex lives were animated by a violence that was primal.[45]

If the Muslim male was to be feared for his potency, the Muslim/Oriental 'woman' was recipient equally of condescension and commiseration as of revulsion and suspicion. Her abnormal sexuality was 'hidden' by the veil and in the harem, both conceived of, at sometimes as enslavement and sexual imprisonment and at other as excessive eroticism and sexual savagery. This female could hardly attain the respectable 'femininity' that characterized the Christo-European woman. Exotic and seductive but ultimately treacherous, this Oriental female figure is even now represented in the political phantasies and governance systems of the West as pitiable object (forced to veil) and threat to modern femininity and liberated feminism (suicide bomber).

The projection of sexual envy and anxiety onto Islam transformed this into a phantasmal site for the production of 'sexuality' in the early processes of Western self-making. Europe soon also 'discovered' the perversions which it identified with the Moor and Saracen among other 'pagans' and 'savages' around the world, from the Americas to Africa.[46] So long as Latin Christendom remained unable to defeat the Islamic empires, the former's obsession with the 'sex' of Islam would probably have been little more than idiosyncratic peculiarity. However, once Christo-European states began to crystallize their power through the expulsion of Islam and Muslims from *al-Andalus*, and to extend this into the Americas and Africa, Muslims would be compelled to engage with the violence of these constructs of 'Islamic' perversity.

The Christian male anxiety regarding the sexual potency of the virile masculinity projected onto the Muslim male was exacerbated by the apocalyptic vision of an Islamic future. Such constructs of the Muslim male betray an attraction that exceeds heterosexual boundaries, for the genitally focused fixation with this figure (his 'elongated' penis) speaks to a homoerotic/sexual tenor that runs through the public statements. These texts provide some of the historical context for why and how the issue of 'sexuality', as a particular 'cultural formation',[47] was to emerge as such a crucial aspect of the war on terror. The authoritative and enduring power of the early Christian statements can be seen in instances such as the depiction of the Prophet Muhammad in the Danish cartoons.

The link between the satanic and sexual is explicitly evident in the depiction of Osama bin Laden as monstrous and gay. Here is a wording on the poster (discussed by Puar) that appeared in Manhattan following the 9/11 attacks: 'The Empire Strikes Back. . . . So you like skyscrapers, huh, bitch?' Puar describes the poster as depicting 'a turbaned caricature of Osama bin Laden being anally penetrated by the Empire State building'.[48] This representation of the Muslim male is also discernible in a drawing posted on Facebook by a young man, describing himself as a member of the Israeli Defence Forces, which shows a pig in a Palestinian *kaffiya* with his feet on the pages of the Qur'an. The image is accompanied with the statement, 'Arab is fucking pig!!! Muhammad is fucking gay.'[49]

It is notable that Christian women were actively involved in the historical production and dissemination of such phantasms of the sexual monstrosity of the Muslim male. As was the case with the Christian men, the images conjured up by the women reveal their sexual desires and anxieties as they set about constituting and universalizing their own identities as women.

The statements made by these women demonstrate that as Christians, they were not hesitant in denouncing Islam, and as women, they too gendered and sexualized Islam as a threat to their feminized chastity. In other words, the labour these women expended on constructing, and fighting, the Islamic threat as one embodied by the sexually potent Muslim male gave expression to their sense of their own femininity as vulnerable, centered on their fear-phantasy of being sexually overpowered by Muslim men. So, for example, the situating of the threat of Islam in the Muslim male's genitalia is also to be found in the tenth-century writings of the Christian nun, Hrotsvitha of Gandersheim, identified as a feminist foremother. In a poem glorifying the martyrdom of a Christian boy, she presents a graphic, if phantasmal, image of King 'Abd ar-Rahman (defined in the parlance of the time as a 'Saracen', a 'Moor') as 'stained with bodily lust', his sword 'aflame' as he sets out in hot sexual pursuit of the boy-martyr, Pelagius.[50]

Depicting the boy's death as heroic resistance to the Moor's sexual advances, the nun described in some detail the Muslim king's attempts to possess the boy:

> Pelagius hits him in the face; blood stains the king's beard. Furious, the king has his men hurl the boy over the city wall to the banks of the river below;

miraculously the boy falls gently and is unharmed. The king's men then find they are unable to harm the boy's body with their weapons. Finally, Christ allows his head to be cut off, so that the angels may bring the new martyr to heaven.[51]

As the erstwhile nun celebrates the boy's sexual purity, she equates this with his love of God; in contrast, the wicked king's (homo)sexual desire is presented as 'inspired by the demons whose idols he worships'.

Talon's study of European representations of 'Saracens' identifies Hrotsvitha's poem as especially notable for her use of an (alleged) rape of the Christian boy in a manner that 'evokes armed struggle to resist the evil forces of paganism'.[52] The nun's mixing of demonic sex, violence and death in 'a potent ideological cocktail' to spur Christian 'resistance' to Muslim rule in Europe is such that although she herself

> makes no call to war, does not urge Christian knights to aid their oppressed Spanish brethren . . . it is easy to see how this view of the pagan other could (and would) subsequently be used to justify war against the Saracen 'pagans'. . . This strategy will become common to centuries later, as the writers on the first Crusade glorify and justify the killing of Saracens by Christian knights.[53]

Muslim despotism, their worship of a false god, the sexual perversity of their faith, and the innocence and overpowering beauty of Christian whiteness, these tropes advanced in the poem would fashion Western representations of Islam, and Muslim men, for centuries to come.

The rape phantasy that drives the violent imagery of the poem bespeaks a *female* desire that is expressed here *as* Christian in nature. Moreover, this desire is doubled in its erotic expression. While the poem seemingly mourns the Christian boy-martyr as victim of a diabolical paganism-as-sexual-violation, it simultaneously displaces the boy as the Muslim king's object of desire, for the nun who pens the poem presents herself as akin to the boy-martyr, that is, like him, she is also Christian and sexually chaste. Such identification with the boy allows the nun to be represented as just as likely a victim of the Muslim's violent desire, for it is *the* Christian that this king desires. The ostensibly 'homo' sexual desire attributed to the king can hence also be read as the nun's 'hetero' sexual attraction to the Muslim male, whose story she recounts (conjures up?) in such detail, including her fanciful imagining of his 'flaming sword'.

In his reading of the episode as presented by Hrotsvitha, Wolf notes the nun's misreadings to point out that the poem reveals more about the author's world than it does about the boy-martyr's world. The poem, he finds, recounts a 'Romanized' account of persecution (the Christian boy is presented as 'dressed in a toga' and Caesar's 'proud command' is referenced) and misidentifies the Muslim king as an idol worshipper. The poem was also likely written for Hrotsvitha's sister nuns, Wolf surmises, drawing attention to the nun's larger corpus, where 'among her heroines were chaste virgins from the Roman period whose vows of chastity were threatened by aggressive pagan suitors'.[54] If this was indeed Hrotsvitha's intended audience, the Christian boy-martyr can be read as standing in for this community of nuns anxiously guarding their own chastity and fearing ravishment by pagan-Muslims with their 'flaming swords'.

Hrotsvitha's formulation of the 'pagan' perversions of the Muslims as sexual in nature provides a glimpse into the rape-phantasy of Christian female desire (to be saved from? or be possessed by?) for this sexually aggressive Muslim figure. Indeed, the poem's sensationalistic use of the trope of the 'Muslim sword' – flaming or not – has endured into the present. Contemporary accounts of 'radical Islamic terrorists' routinely link sexual frustration to the 'terror' threat. The anxieties embedded in such projections of sexual violence onto the Muslim male demonstrate how complex is the psychosexual dynamic of Western subjectivity, and in particular, its gendered formation.

Additional examples from different historical junctures point to how the fascination with the Black/Muslim male body repeatedly sexualized this as an overpowering threat. Shakespeare's cautionary tale, *Othello*, provides a classic, richly layered example of this mingling of sex, religion and race in its presentation of the Black/Moor/Turk. At a later date, English men and women who travelled to India during the British Raj offered similarly sexualizing accounts, images, even tributes to Muslim/Oriental maleness: 'William Hodges, a professional artist under the patronage of Warren Hastings, records his first impression of "delicately framed" men with feminine hands and "mild, tranquil, and sedulously attentive" manners. Some of the men, Hodges observes, are "wholly naked", while others wear "long muslin dresses", their "black faces adorned with large gold ear-rings and white turbans".'[55] Flora Annie Steel, who went to India in 1867, had this to say about her 'first' experience,

> My first entry into India was in a masulah boat through the surf at Madras. It was exhilarating. Something quite new; something that held all possibilities. A boat that had not a nail in it; dark-skinned men with no clothes on, who did not look naked, a surf such as I had never seen before, thundering on the yellow sands.[56]

Steel's account assumes a penetrative position for its author, what might be referred to in contemporary feminist politics as a masculine subject position; the desire for 'all possibilities' in the context of the naked male bodies and the 'thundering' surf around her clearly does not preclude the possibility of sex. As for E. M. Forester, 'his entry into India focuses quite explicitly on the ambiguous beauty of the racial male body: "The last horrid meal on the horrid ship ended as we reached Bombay, and we went ashore in style in a native boat, an ugly crew but beautiful skins".'[57]

St. John of Damascus' focus on the Prophet's lips and his seductive virility, Hrotsvitha's poetic alarm warning against the dangers of Muslim lust/power in medieval 'Europe', Shakespeare's imagining of the murderous sexual attraction and brute power of the Muslim/Moor, Othello, who seduces/kills Desdemona/Europe and E. M. Forester's fascination with Muslim male sexuality in India (Dr. Aziz in *A Passage to India*) and the Abu Ghraib photographs are very different kinds of texts, wide-ranging in their approach to gender and produced at different junctures in the formation of the West. These texts were also produced in conjunction with the different political moments in which the socio-economic fortunes of Europe/the West were in flux as the balance of power with Muslim empires was shifting. Yet the fascination with the Muslim male body, its association with sexual power, virile physicality and overpowering violence runs through this archive of Western desire.

The religion of gender

As Christendom coveted the power of the then fabulously wealthy, urbane and sophisticated Muslim empires, access to material wealth as well as sexual/sensual pleasure were intermingled in the desires of these early Europeans. Yet such attractions also provoked insecurity: the projection of perversity onto Muslims required the policing of Christo-European sexual and moral chastity. Attraction, of course, threatened to undo this border.

With European nations expanding outwards in the following centuries, their influence and power increased, and their increased mobility meant the figure of the Muslim was no longer abstract. Closer proximity to this figure increased the possibilities of intercourse, social or other. I have read in Hrotsvitha's poem, as discussed above, the expression of white female desire for the Muslim male, of the dangers raised by such desire. The threat this desire posed to the European male and the fortunes of Europe-in-the-making can be found pulsating in Shakespeare's popular sixteenth-century play, *Othello: The Moor of Venice*, a cultural text that continues to fascinate and attract audiences around the world.

In his brilliant reading of *Othello*, Daniel Boyarin points to the European male obsession with Muslim male sexuality that runs through the play. Boyarin's argument is that although Othello is a Moor, a Muslim who has converted to Christianity, his nature is nevertheless conceived of as savage in an explicitly *sexual* register; Othello's circumcised penis marks his nature and fixes his sexuality to his racial and religious difference.[58] More than his dark skin and thick lips, the Moor's penis is the 'marker of his indelible identity', Boyarin notes, so that it is his religio-racial identity that makes his sexuality more bestial than human.[59]

Boyarin explains that the nature of the sexuality attributed to Othello ('an old black ram', 'a Barbary horse', as Iago describes him) is a complex matter, that '[i]f for the rampant male sexuality of the ram we have to go to Greece and satyrs (cum devils), for the horses we need go no further than Ezekiel 23:20: "There she lusted after her lovers, whose genitals were like those of donkeys and whose emission was like that of horses"'.[60] Delineating the Christian imagery at work in Shakespeare's projection of this bestial masculinity onto the Black-brown Moor, Boyarin identifies the 'biblical allusion' as 'a rich and important clue for the reading of Othello': this is a 'hermeneutic key' to the entire text.[61] The reference to Ezekiel clarifies that the transgression that animates the play is not only that of illicit or inter-racial sex, but that 'religious infidelity' is the issue that is at stake.[62]

Desdemona's death at Othello's hands is not much different from that of other tragic Shakespearean heroes, observes Boyarin.[63] However, Othello's end is another matter, for his 'penis marks the site of the knotting and unravelling of a complex that is intimately bound up with . . . a political theology of race'.[64] It is worth taking the time here to follow the associations that Boyarin establishes between race, religion and sexuality.[65] Described as a Barbary stallion, Othello is associated with the 'Corsairs', that is, the Barbary pirates. Although this Muslim identity is precisely what Othello gives up in his conversion to Christianity, he remains trapped in this identity in the play's Christo-European imaginary. It is this *Muslim* identity that Othello invokes as he condemns himself to die in the same manner as the 'malignant and unturban'd Turk', a 'circumcised dog', who he had earlier slain in Aleppo while fighting to defend Venice.[66] In short, Boyarin's reading of the play is that Othello-the-Muslim has penetrated Europe (Desdemona) and the penetration reveals Europe's sexual attraction to him; Desdemona is killed and the Moor pays with his life for such attraction.[67] Read in the context of the reference to Ezekiel, Desdemona's desire for the Moor presents her sexual desire as 'religious infidelity' not just racial transgression, and as Boyarin puts it, the play is an implicit 'representation of the nearly sexual attractiveness of Islam as well'.[68]

Although Othello converts to Christianity, kills Turks to defend Venice-Europe, his loyalty remains suspect in the eyes of this Europe. In the end, Othello does turn Turk, so to speak, so that he 'is his own worst enemy' and is 'split between the turban that can be removed and the mark on his penis that cannot'.[69] The Muslim man is here, as elsewhere in the European imaginary, always already the enemy; violence and betrayal are never far away from even his most ardent expression of loyalty to Europe.

Boyarin goes on to identify the homosexual undertones to the heterosexual threat posed by Othello, as 'Desdemona's vagina is, in a powerful sense, a displacement of the male Christian's (Brabantio's) anus', and being sodomized was 'of course, the *historically* classic sign of political/military defeat for a man'.[70] Othello's Black Muslim penis, with its power to attract and conquer both Desdemona and Brabantio, is therefore as dangerous to white heterosexuality as it is attractive to white homosexuality.[71]

Boyarin's close reading of the sexual/racial politics of Shakespeare's Europe illustrates that what is at stake in the Muslim penetration of Europe in such sexually murderous terms is not only the Christo-European male control of the European woman attracted to the Moor's (bigger) penis but also the European male's desire for Othello's penis, 'the thing' that animates the entire plot. Othello's potency – sexual and military, that is, military as sexual – elicits the desire of both the white man and woman and transforms them into sexual rivals. Indeed, their common desire for Othello threatens to reduce the (homo/heterosexual) distance between the white man and woman *and* paradoxically enhance this distance (their gendered rivalry) as they each vie to win the Moor.[72] Othello's death, as ordained by Shakespeare, can therefore be read also as an act of castration, the elimination by the white man of the monstrous penis that attracts yet also threatens white fe/male desire. If the death of Desdemona is to be taken as the white man's retribution for the white woman's desire for the Moor, and for Islam, this desire is shared also by the white man. As such, Othello's death symbolizes also the white man's destruction of his enemy/sexual rival, whom he can neither possess nor replace.

If this figure of the Muslim male was threatening to a Europe facing the power of as-yet undefeated Muslim empires, its allure only deepened with Europe's conquest of these empires. The fixation with the sex of 'Islam' and the 'potency' of the Muslim body grew in magnitude during the colonial period with 'issues of Muslim sexuality and Islamic marriage practices, customs, and laws' placed 'at the forefront of the imperial agenda'.[73] The challenge to 'civilize' and 'modernize' Muslim societies once these came under direct rule also targeted Muslim women as the key to accessing, and maintaining control over, the Muslim male and family, and through them, the larger community of Islam.

European rule took on increasingly secularizing tendencies in the eighteenth and nineteenth centuries, the fixation with controlling the Muslim/Black body was now taken up in the emerging scientific and anthropological discourses that employed empirical, biological and ethnographic methodologies and technologies. Richard Burton, the famous explorer, explained to European audiences that

> debauched women prefer negroes on account of their parts. I measured one man in Somaliland who, when quiescent, numbered nearly six inches. This is characteristic of the negro race and of African animals; e.g. the horse; whereas the pure Arab, man and beast, is below the average of Europe; one of the best proofs by the by, that the Egyptian is not Asiatic, but a negro partially whitewashed . . .[74]

The compulsive measuring of the 'manhood' of native males in the service of racial-imperial sciences was formalized as 'phalloplethys-mography'.[75] The bigger the penis being described, the more impotent became the actual male-turned-object thus described, for the power to define, probe, feel, measure, fondle lay in the hands of the white male expert. Using the power to expose and classify the Arab, African, Asiatic male, the labours of these Western experts fetishized this organ even as they made it available to white public gaze, sexualizing these emergent onto-epistemological traditions.

The desire to possess *this* manhood was accompanied, in the case of Burton, with an overt desire to replace it. Hence Burton was not averse to dressing as an Arab, to pass himself off now as Muslim, now as Indian. Deceiving the communities who offered him hospitality, he collected 'ethnographic' data to reveal their peculiarities to Europeans. Like other Westerners before and after him, Burton claimed to understand Islam better than the Muslims themselves, to know the Orient more deeply than it could be known by Orientals themselves. Not altogether surprising then, Burton claimed expertise in the sexual perversities of these worlds. The interweaving of various epistemological traditions with these sexual phantasms which informed his claims of mastering the 'Orient/al' no doubt came with its own pleasures, some proudly acknowledged in Burton's works, others hidden in the apprehensions attached to the establishment of such mastery.

Nor was Burton alone in publicly explicating his preoccupations and pleasures, many such examples abound in the colonial archive. Homoerotic and homosexual desire fuelled the 'public' and 'hidden' practices and politics of some of the most respected and influential – British and French – imperialists (Cecil Rhodes, Lawrence of Arabia, E. M. Forster, Henry Morgan Stanley, etc.)

according to Aldrich, who argues that to these men, the colonial environment was seen to invite sexual adventure and transgression, unlike the staid norms and stigmas attached to these matters in their domestic environment. As 'Europeans fantasised about "vice" in the Islamic world, and writers from Gustave Flaubert to Paul Bowes were seduced by the hammam, the Kasbah and the desert', the Orient offered escape from the confines of Christian marriage into a world conceived of as sexually untamed.[76] Seeking relief from the stifling regimentation of their own cultural, educational and class milieu, these European men approached the colony as a site for sexual gratification as well as material progress, an avenue of escape from Evangelical revivalism and the Victorian era.[77] Sex and violence were thus entwined with material and political advancement in the architecture of colonial desire.

Aldrich has found that almost all the Europeans whose lives he studied subscribed to racist views and considered it their right to avail themselves of the native bodies that caught their fancy, so that racial '[r]elations of power permeated colonial sexual culture'.[78] One French text on sex in the colonies, *L'Art d'aimer aux colonies*, is identified as especially significant. Penned by an anonymous writer (1893), the author's views on 'Arab homosexuality' are notable: 'The Arab is an inveterate pederast, even in his own country, where women are not lacking.... All the travellers writing about morals in Arabia and Turkey have commented on this fact.'[79] Like others before him, this author paid the obligatory attention to the penis in his discussion of sub-Saharan Africans, attributing its (large) size to circumcision. Pronouncing 'heterosexual sodomy' uncommon to the region, the author explained that 'The reason is perhaps the practice of anal coition, because of the size of the Negro's penis, would be a real torture, a sort of empaling'.[80]

The angst provoked by such an idea, by the 'empaling' power of the Arab/African penis was perhaps counterbalanced by the figure of the indolent and impotent 'Sultan', much despised in the eighteenth-century narratives of British officials and travellers in India. These narratives, 'while disapproving, also betray a deep rooted envy for the excesses of courtly and quotidian life in Mughal India'.[81] British officials often expressed jealous views of the excessive pleasures they imagined to be rampant in the Mughal courts; 'Travel journals thus expose the "envy complex" which was to become a factor in colonial mastery; what the Western subject wants is access to the excessive, feral and carnal energy long removed from Western modes of subjective existence and now fantasized as being in the Orient'.[82] The British obsession with such excessive pleasure led the more intrepid among them to acquire these delights for themselves through literal emulation of the courtly lifestyle, including copying its dress and culinary style.[83] Yet these upright British officials also declared themselves repelled at what they described as the flaccidity and sensory overindulgences of the 'Sultan', caricatured often as a grotesquely obese and carnal figure. With regard to the Arab world, Massad explains the 'shaming of non-Europeans on the basis of sexual desires and practices begins at the dawn of the colonial encounter, inciting a negative discourse of assimilation into (and at time difference from) European norms'.[84]

Muslim/Oriental women were not spared from the sexualizing power of the Western gaze, that of Man or Woman. Veiled and unattainable to European travellers and administrators, revealing the 'truth' of the 'Oriental' woman became a frustration of European men and fed the ambition of European women. Malek Alloula's study of the nineteenth-century voyeuristic postcards of Algerian women that were produced by French photographers studies how these photographs, carefully choreographed by the photographers, featured the women in semi-naked and sexualized poses that were passed off as daily life in the Orient. Some photographs display more than one semi-clad woman, catering also to homosexual desire. As featured in the postcards, the veil was a shielding of the gross sexuality of the Muslim woman, masking her insatiable appetite and seductive power. Alloula argues that these photographs are a site for the transformation of the impotence of the French photographer – his 'initial experience of disappointment and rejection' at failing to penetrate the veil – into a 'double violation' of the women, that is, 'unveil the veiled and give figural representation to the forbidden' by staging these scenes.[85] Using paid models and studio props, the photographer created the phantasm that became the 'Algerienne', the Muslim, Moorish, Oriental 'woman' of the French colonial imaginary. Bare breasted and sexually available, yet veiled and imprisoned in the harem, this woman lived in a state of unfulfilled desire as well as sexual degeneracy from which the French man (and woman) were to liberate her. The unveiling of this woman, the imposition on her body and life of the Westernizing heterosexual patriarchal family structure, with its processes of domestication and housewifization, was a key objective of the French colonial mission. This was no less the case with the British in India, or most recently, the Western alliance in Afghanistan.

Imagined as 'an erotic universe', the harem was characterized by the absence of men, and as Alloula notes: 'This lack of the phallus is eloquently symbolized by the two figures of the High Lord, who can neither enjoy all the women in his seraglio nor satisfy them, and of the eunuchs, who are the absolute negation of the male principle.'[86] The Muslim male and female body thus bore the burden of the psychosexual preoccupations of the white man and woman, making the former prime target-beneficiaries of the violence that stabilized white masculinity's and femininity's assertion of phallic power through the domestication of these bodies.

Seen to lack the phallus (despite being endowed with the monstrous penis), Oriental male impotence was here defined as evident in the abundant promiscuity of the Oriental female. Her sexual appetites spoke to the sexual inadequacy of the Muslim male, the frustrations of both finding release in the fanaticism and hatred they would unleash upon the world. This idea of male impotence dovetailed with the notion that the Muslim male could acquire access to female bodies only through imprisoning these in the harem and punishing female sexual desire (genital mutilation, honour killings, acid-throwing, etc.). This innate 'cultural' misogyny, the result of the curious fusing of insatiable male virility with pitiable impotence, is read into the racial-cultural fabric of 'Islam' in the discourse of the global terror.

The effects of such ongoing stagings of the monstrosities of 'Islamic culture', through the projection of sexual depravity onto the figure of the Muslim fe/male on Muslim societies have yet to be studied. It is, of course, inconceivable that these phantasmic creations would have no effect on ideas, interactions and relationships within Muslim communities. Muslims – male, female, queer – all have been schooled now for several generations in the sexualizing ideologies of Western political-epistemological traditions, how might these communities have remained immune to the castrating impulse that runs through these traditions?

There is one final example of the meshing of hetero- and homosexual desire in the phantasmic potency projected onto the Muslim male to consider here, even if only very briefly. For this incident is highly instructive in how deep runs the association of sexuality with race, religion and violence in the Western imaginary, not the least for the identity of the protagonist. Hegel was familiar with *The Thousand and One Nights*, a text that fuelled many a European phantasy about the Islamic world. The trope of the Oriental despot that runs through this text is reproduced in Hegel's description of Turkish Emperors, they were 'of the kind who saw and fell in love with Christian maidens, spent four weeks of infatuation with them and then had them killed before moving on'.[87] The 'baggy trousers' of the Turk are reported to have irked Hegel; he considered this clothing completely unsuitable for the 'lively and busy' lifestyle of Europeans.[88] But is it the 'baggy trousers' that irritated the philosopher, or is it what lay underneath that unsettled his sensibility?

The question comes to mind upon reading Almond's study of Orientalism in German philosophy which mentions a 'dream' recounted by Hegel in a letter to a friend. Apparently, it was Hegel's wife who had the dream while the two were in Nuremburg at a time when Bashkiri Muslims were in the city as part of the Russian forces. Their presence left Hegel, who considered them akin to 'animals', and his wife 'filled with fear and dismay'.[89] This was the context in which Hegel reported to his friend that his wife

> dreamt she found herself in a huge camp just outside Paris, full of wild soldiers, Cossacks, Prussians, all mixed together. She was terrified – but you [Hegel's friend and recipient of the letter] rode through the turmoil on a horse next to her and made a way through; whenever they hemmed close around her, you reached down from your horse and gestured, that she was under your protection.

Hegel went on to complain to the friend, 'I was a bit concerned in this story about the fact that I didn't appear in it at all. My wife excused herself by saying that I was part of her in the dream; and it certainly pleases me to think that under your protection you brought us home to safety through all those Chuvashes and Bashkiris.'[90]

Almond refrains from 'plunging too deep into a psychoanalytical reading' of the dream, but he does note 'the emasculating consequence this has for Hegel himself', for the dream 'reveals a telling anxiety about Hegel's own inability to control events'.[91] This dream is most certainly worth a deeper psychoanalytic reading, for it reveals rather more about the 'emasculating consequence' than just the inability of the philosopher 'to control events'. My reading of the snippet of the incident provided by Almond suggests the workings of a rape fantasy, not to mention an intermingling of hetero-homoerotic desire in the dream, and in Hegel's recounting of this.

The dream can be read as revealing anxieties regarding inter-racial and inter-religious sexual transgression (the presence of the Muslim soldiers in the city, the wife surrounded by the 'wild' soldiers in the dream) as well as intra-racial adulterous desire (for the philosopher's friend). One might read also a fear of being overpowered by sexual bestiality at work (the appearance of the horse, a stud, and of a 'horde' of Muslim males already considered akin to 'animals'). The anxiety regarding infidelity is belied by Hegel's insertion of himself into the dream (by way of his wife's alibi), for as he recounts its details, he *consciously* mentions his dismay to this friend about his own absence from the scene. The philosopher's repetition to his friend of his wife's explanation that Hegel is 'part of her' is not an insignificant detail. Finally, the friend on a horse (signifying a doubled masculinity, a doubling of the power of the penis) suggests the wife's (unconscious) desire, but also Hegel's (homoerotic) desire as he expresses his own relief at being 'protected' (possessed?) by the friend.

As Almond does note about this telling dream, '[t]he "turmoil" of the chaotic, pressing mob of Russians and Muslims, jostling around his innocent wife, encapsulates the kind of feelings Hegel had about a modern, democratic Europe which had to emerge against a whole series of feudal despotisms, both internal as well as Oriental.'[92] The wife's innocence is clearly reliant on repression of the desire for the 'chaotic, pressing mobs', mostly Muslim men, about her, as well as repression of desire for the more masterful masculinity (sexuality?) of her husband's friend, who will 'save' her – along with her (in the dream at least, impotent) husband – from these mobs. Much like Boyarin finds to be the case with Shakespeare's *Othello*, the 'innocence' of Europe is here reliant on disavowal of its desire for the Orient/Islam, with its 'chaotic, pressing' terrorizing mobs in their 'baggy trousers' that conceal only God knows what dangers. The circumcised penis?

Feminist desire in the Orient

The harem featured large in European constructs of the Islamic Orient, scholars have found, many of whom concur with the view that

> the harem as the locus of an exotic and abnormal sexuality fascinated Westerners. It came to be regarded as a microscopic Middle East, apotheosizing the two characteristics perceived as essentially Oriental: sensuality and violence... From the enlightenment onwards, the harem came to be not merely a psychosexual symbol, but a metaphor for injustice in civil society and the state and arbitrary government.[93]

The lure of this Orient was too powerful for European men to resist, Kabbani argues, many of whom were 'led into the East by sexuality', by their 'inexpressible longings' for entering the harem, given that the European woman, constructed in the ideal of middle-class wifehood was 'supposedly dormant sexually', the domestic servant was 'unsexed' by labour, and the prostitute was 'burdened with all that the wife was protected from'.[94] What then of this European Woman? What was her relation to the 'Orient/al'?

Entering the space of the harem, literally and metaphorically, was a desire that excited more than intellectual curiosity among Western women. For example, European women travellers to Turkey in the eighteenth and nineteenth centuries wrote extensively about the 'reality' of harem life and mapped out their own subjectivity in the process, as has been analysed so insightfully by Yeğenoğlu. These women were able to enter into the harem *as women*, and in the process, they 'supplemented', that is, completed, the white male penetration of the interior spaces of the Orient that remained inaccessible to the men.

Rendering the Orient/Woman legible as object of a precise and deeper knowledge in this manner, the women writers reproduced 'the imperialist and masculinist act'.[95] Substituting for the white man's phallus inside the harem by deploying their own gender identity, these feminists extended the white fe/male gaze into the most 'intimate' spaces of Muslim life, enabling the Westerner to enter the 'interiority', or so they assumed, of the Muslim woman. As the lens sharpening and refining the male gaze, these white women fulfilled their own ambition to penetrate the interiority and possess the 'truth' of the Muslim woman, of her sex/uality, of her being. Inhabiting the masculine subject position in their writings on the harem, Yeğenoğlu argues, European women were able to participate in the 'phallocentrism' that trades in the economy of sameness, that is, an economy wherein 'the self always knows and represents the other through himself'.

In these adventures, the Western women acquired power – *as Woman* – over the Muslim/Oriental male, not only the female. Their discoveries of the 'truth' of the harem, inaccessible to their male compatriots, and their public assertion of this 'truth', allowed the women to extend their own authority over the representation of the Muslim male as well as the female. These European women's writings encode also their desire for 'knowing' the truth of the Muslim male; by 'knowing' the 'truth' of the harem, of the Muslim female, these women writers gained access to the 'truth' of the Muslim male, particularly with regard to his 'sex'.

In entering the harem, Western women placed themselves literally, even if only temporarily, in what they conceived to be the 'authentic' Orient/Islam. Much like their present-day feminist daughters who travel undercover to Afghanistan and the Middle East to reveal the 'truth' of Islam to the Western world, these earlier women writers acted on their desire to *know* and *possess* Islam/the Orient as it *really* is, to penetrate the hidden world of its dark interior, to seek out the experience of being possessed by, and in turn possess, the 'secret' of the Orient/Islam. In short, these feminists fancied themselves experts on this inner world of the Orient, conceived of as female, yet apparently entirely alien to them as women. Their forays were depicted as taking them deep into the Orient, yet these led them not only into the living quarters of Muslim women but also into their own phantasies, shaped by centuries of Western propaganda, lured on by the figure of the dark, handsome and violent Sheikh who was easily besotted by their fair skin and blond hair.

One site in which this Woman's desire for the Muslim male can be tracked is the highly popular genre of the 'Sheikh' romance. As Jarmakani's study of the genre demonstrates, these fantasy romances present their female readers with the figure of the (Muslim) Sheikh as 'a noble desert leader, as a savage and potentially dangerous figure, and as an oil-rich, powerful man' who functions as a 'bridge' between the traditional and the modern.[96] This heroic figure, 'particularly desirous of white women', offers the white heroine (usually British, American, Canadian or Australian) the opportunity to become a 'princess bride'.[97] The Sheikh is invariably supportive of (white) women's equality, for much of the literature deploys the language of liberal (equality rights) feminism. The native Arab woman serves as a 'foil', oppressed and obedient, unable to 'ignite the sheikh's passions as can the white heroine' who is 'proud' and 'independent', hence his *true* match and soulmate.[98] The white woman's love saves the Sheikh from his own 'monstrosities' as she becomes the 'link' that enables the traditionally chivalrous hero to move into modernity. As Jarmakani explains, 'the fantasy of the white heroine as a model of liberation achieves a double valence' for not only is the white woman loved by the Sheikh for her more desirable feminine qualities, it is also her support that allows him to become a modern (manly) leader.

Engaging 'imaginatively' with discourses of global feminism and neoliberal globalization, the more recent Sheikh literature pivots on the 'theme of freedom and progress through global (free) trade and investment with the theme of rapprochement between East and West through heterosexual nuclear union'. As such, it articulates to global feminism with its central trope of 'rescue', except this time, it is the Muslim male who is to be rescued. The Sheikh, depicted by ethnic and religious markers that tend to get racialized and conflated as 'Arabian', Jarmakani argues, now also 'echoes the fluidity and conflation' of the discourse of the war on terror so that he becomes the 'racialized figure of the Arab/Muslim/sheikh/terrorist'.[99]

Put differently, key tropes of the Crusader ideology, reworked into the Orientalist frame and later still in the Islamophobic discourse of the global war, are the cultural terrain in which white women have claimed gendered access to the phallic power of the West over the Islamic world. In so doing, their subjectivity and identity are transformed through their gendered contribution to these discursive regimes, whether from the 'feminine' position of 'being the phallus' or the masculine position of 'having the phallus'. It is in the constitution of these women's own identity as 'Western' that such feminist labour captures the 'inner' truths of Muslim 'man' and 'woman' for the pornographic white fe/male gaze. In the global war, such feminist investments fixate on unveiling of the Muslim woman, a project that feeds Western women's investment in their own gender and sexual 'freedoms' to ally them more closely to their male compatriots.

If, as I have suggested earlier, relations between Muslim men and women would not go unaffected by the reworking of Orientalist tropes, relationships between white women and men would also be mediated by these. For Western women had to contend with the Western Man's fascination with the Muslim/Oriental fe/male, a figure for which his desire has been publicly expressed and saturates Western culture. Take the iconic image of 'Cleopatra', for instance, who held reign as the epitome of 'the indulgence of the senses, oblivion to the world's affairs, and overwhelming sexual desire . . . she is the sexual urge itself, unappeasable and intransigent' in the Western imaginary.[100] This is only one such 'Oriental' femme fatale. Kabbani describes a host of other such 'Oriental' women who personified for the West the essence of the sensuality and sexuality of the Orient: 'Balquis of Yemen is the Arab beauty to whom King Solomon addresses his most passionate words. . . . Salome's dance arouses as it horrifies. In 1704, yet another prototype of Eastern sensuality perceived the day, and she took Europe by storm. Her name was Scheherazade.'[101] The representation of these Oriental women's attractions as associated with death did little to quell the Western desire for them:

> The eroticism that the East promised was mysterious and tinged with violence. The oriental woman was linked, like a primitive goddess, with cycles of the supernatural. Cleopatra possesses knowledge of magic and poisonous prescriptions long before the need for death arises. Scheherazade lives on the edge of the sword, its blade is what her narrative must defeat, its shadow what makes her tale so captivating. Salome's dance is sexual and macabre at once. Her beauty is linked to the darker elements, complicit with the corruption that John the Baptist's words uncover. Her dance is delirium inspiring, and causes the unleashing of evil.[102]

Indeed, the deadly mix of beauty, sex and violence embodied by such cultural archetypes only magnifies the desire to possess them. Western women have lived with these Orientalized figures and phantasies; they are witness to the violent passions invoked by this sexualized female figure for whom Western men have expressed their passion in art, painting, literature, music, opera, photographic image, play, pantomime, film and other popular culture over the centuries. Western women are hence well aware of the place occupied by the Oriental woman in the phantasy-desire of the white Man.

These histories of attraction and revulsion, of desire and horror, are the context for the contemporary mobilization of the not insignificant feminist and queer resources that depict the Muslim woman as pitiable object beneath the veil, or as the death-dealing 'Black widow' and the sexually vengeful 'female suicide bomber'. The campaign to unveil the Muslim woman may well be one strategy in Western feminist responses to the obsession of the white Man with the Oriental fe/male. The politics of the veil are certainly far more complex than can be done justice here, nevertheless, it is necessary to point to these complexities in order to understand how they play out in the formation of contemporary gender/sexual politics.

The reconfiguration of Western sexual/gender politics as uniquely attuned to freedom and choice in contrast to a repressive and intolerant Islamic culture is now the driving factor in the extension of sexual-cultural practices over the Muslim world. This 'sexuality' has now become globally hegemonic, as have the forms of masculinity, femininity, queerness in which it is manifested. Such a sexualizing hermeneutic distinguishes the West as exceptional in its *enlightened* sexual values even as the ideologies of terror incite the desires that keep the Western Subject fascinated with the Muslim body, with its sexual valences and proclivities. The valorization of such sexual 'freedom' – with its contempt for the Muslim body – trumps any disquiet provoked by the violence of the war. Take, for example, the killing of Bin Laden. The Navy Seal who claimed in a tell-all account to have killed the al-Qaeda leader described how his body 'flopped on the cement floor like a dead fish'.[103] Highlighting Bin Laden's 'lack of defence' during the attack, the Navy Seal went on to characterize the Jihadi leader as a 'pussy'.[104] Bin Laden's wife and children were present when the *Kill Team* burst in on them that fateful night, but like many Muslim men before him, the 'terrorist' could only be seen as castrated. This act of not 'seeing' the Oriental/ Muslim male as 'man' and 'seeing' him only in bestializing terms, in spite of the actual circumstances, is a cultural practice Eng referred to as *racial castration*.[105]

It is indeed striking how much of the violence of the global war speaks to the sexualizing impetus of the religio-racial logic; the sexual caricatures of Islamists – and other Muslims – remain common fare in public-political discourse. In a recent illustration of this, *The New York Times* reports that 'Homosexuality, cloaked in the traditions of strong masculine bonds that are a hallmark of Islamic culture and are even more pronounced in southern Afghanistan's strict, sexually segregated society, has long been a clandestine feature of life here. But pedophilia has been its curse.'[106] The violence of the Jihadi, Western experts warn, arises from such sexual perversity: 'The terrorism of Bin Laden harnesses the chaos of young men, uniting the energies of political ardour and sex in a turbulent fuel.'[107] Islamic culture is sexually repressive, goes the thesis, Muslim men are sexually frustrated hence they want to blow up the West, which is sexually liberated and hence intolerable to them. These Muslim men dress like women; they are impotent yet they keep armies of sexual slaves; Muslim women are sexually frustrated, they are hated by their men, so they blow themselves up; Muslim women are hated by Muslim men, yet they line up to join Muslim men to kill Westerners and to become sexual slaves, and so on and so forth go the narratives of the experts on terrorism, on security, on radicalization. This strange fusing of the sexual with the religious and the racial elides the political and the economic; such fusing runs through the dominant characterization of Muslims. To return to the example of Bin Laden, this is how he is described: Evil; Monster; Pussy; Dead fish. The figure of this monstrous Muslim fe/male (Bin Laden was repeatedly reported to pass as a veiled woman) is here catalogued in the register of the grotesque. These are certainly not qualities - or names - attributable to the human, to Man or to Woman. They all, however, carry a potent sexual charge.

This chapter presents the case that the organization of 'sexuality' and 'gender' in their binary formulations have been indelibly shaped by early Christo-Europe's sexual obsession with what it deemed 'Islamic' perversities. The early Latin-Christian response to an ascendant Islam elevated sex, gender and sexuality in its perception and in the treatment of this tradition. This lens confirmed the Christian identification of Islam as diabolical, it has shaped the cultural, political and sexual landscape of the Westerners who constituted their own sexuality in relation to the gross appetites of monstrous Muslim maleness. With sexuality thus isolated and privileged in the distinguishing of Islam from a Christian-Europe in the making, the Muslim male and female emerged as objects of desire and embodiment of the threat of Islam in authoritative Christian statements that have echoed through the ensuing centuries.

As European empires began to assert their dominance over the Islamic world, the perverse sexuality earlier attributed to the Muslim male and increasingly to the Muslim female, drew the attractions of the desiring Western Subject, Man and Woman. Such desire lay in uneasy tension with the subsequent inscription of impotence onto the Muslim male as his presence was both magnified and elided in the imagining of the Orient as a site awaiting penetration, possession and mastery. Conceived of as the space of deviant sexual excess, a colossal harem where all manner of perversity flourished, the idea of the Islamic Orient was shaped by a religio-racial symbolic castration of the Muslim male along with the hyper-sexualization of the Muslim female through the fixation on the veil and the harem.

Over time, the binary formulation of hetero/homosexuality peculiar to the Christocentric tradition of the West came to be imposed as universal across the colonized world and, with its underlying gender binary, became hegemonic in mapping out the range of practices and identities integrated into 'gender' and 'sexuality'. Hence, the very constitution of hetero- and homosexuality, like masculinity and femininity, can be defined as colonizing technologies imposed on the Muslim world. Nevertheless, their systematization within modernizing discourses as properties of the self-determining agentic Subject foreclosed access to these 'civilized' sexual-gender norms to Muslims, who were thus transformed into 'failed' sexual and gender objects of reform.

The historical fascination with the gender-sexual practices of Muslims I have outlined above clearly remains unabated; indeed, such fixation came to the fore to shape the waging of the global war. The political motivations and economic conditions that give rise to Muslim resistance get scarcely a mention, but public deliberations abound about Muslim sexual frustration and savagery.[108] Reading groups and book clubs debate the 'right' of Iranians to *Read Lolita in Tehran*, scintillating conversations are held about *The Caged Virgin*, *Lipstick Jihad* is lauded as heroic feminist revolt, and the opening of beauty parlours in Kabul is pronounced to confirm the victory of 'freedom' for Muslim women over Islamic sexual barbarism. Does the water in Kandahar city really work as an aphrodisiac, wonders a Western reporter in his coverage of the Afghan war.[109]

The onslaught of colonial power and its Westernizing technologies escalated the sexualization of the Islamic world with the imposition of its binary undertaken by the white Man *and* Woman. The Muslim male, like the female, was thus made available as sexual fetish, object of desire and loathing – by the *gendered* labour of Western men as well as women. The sexual dynamic that fuelled such labour extended the Western phallic order over the intimate and erotic spaces, expressions and practices within the Muslim world – unveiling the 'truth' of 'Islamic sexuality' informed the classification, measurement, display, institutionalization necessary to colonial governance, it was systematized in Orientalizing discourses in the arts, literature, sciences, politics and statecraft. In the process, civilized bourgeois heterosexuality became tethered to lascivious Oriental hetero/homosexuality, a product of colonial violence in at least two ways: sexuality as cartography of the religio/racial divide, and sexual control of the Muslim as a measure of modernization.

It is thus important to note, particularly in a juncture wherein neoconservatives, liberals, white supremacists as well as feminists are decrying the hateful misogyny of Islam and the Muslim male, that it is not just any phallus that reigns over the Islamic world. It is a very particular kind of phallus – the Westernizing order – which now dominates this world. The phallus, critical scholars and feminists have argued, is a politico-cultural construct, not just the physical organ that is the penis. The phallus symbolizes power, such that 'those who gaze upon it immediately feel themselves to be its subjects. . . . Like the penis, the phallus must be able to rise to the occasion – but in the conscious service of history, not in blind animal instinct.'[110] Even now constructed as living outside history and politics, in the timeless state of fanaticism, the Islamic world 'has' no such 'phallus' of its own, so to speak. Indeed, as objects of the globally sexualized politico-cultural space, Muslims live in a world with little power at present to shape their historical being-for-themselves. The Abu Ghraib photographs are but the most recent instance of such historical sexualization of 'Islamic culture': these stark images reveal the 'lack' of an Islamic/Oriental 'phallus' as defined in Westernizing sexual-political culture.

Chapter 4

FEMINISM AT WAR

The Abu Ghraib photographs discussed in the previous chapter captured more than the willing participation of US servicewomen in the sexual torture and killing of Iraqi men. This documentary record was met with expressions of shock, horror and grief by some of the most influential feminists in the United States. Even now, as one reads their public reactions, it is difficult to overlook the depth of the sense of betrayal that runs through what became a collective feminist lament:

> Even those people we might have thought impervious to shame, like the secretary of defense, admit that the photos of abuse in Iraq's Abu Ghraib prison turned their stomachs. The photos did something else to me as a feminist: They broke my heart. . . . If you were doing PR for Al Qaeda, you couldn't have staged a better picture to galvanize misogynistic Islamic fundamentalists around the world.[1]

Why would the murderous violence of the US military and the armies of its allied nation-states be met with the language of 'heartbreak', 'shame' and 'betrayal' by feminists? After all, it was the armed forces of the world's most powerful state – overseen by a right-wing neoconservative party – that had perpetrated the torture, for it was the Pentagon and the CIA that were allegedly responsible for the violence. Yet for these feminists, 'Women soldier's participation in the brutal acts of torture stands as the single most shocking revelation to emerge from Abu Ghraib.'[2] Might such torture and killing have been rendered less heart-wrenching, understandable perhaps, were it perpetrated *only* by male US soldiers, intelligence officers, contractors and guards? Why would the instinctive affiliation of feminists – including those on the left, who would presumably be critics of state violence – be with the perpetrators of state violence and not with the brutalized victims, who also included Iraqi women and children? Why the collective pronouncement of shame? Perhaps the use of the occasion by feminists to take yet another swipe at 'misogynistic Islamic fundamentalists' to denounce the very Muslims in US custody who were being terrorized provides a clue. It should be recalled that some of these same feminists had earlier rejoiced at the stationing of US servicewomen in Saudi Arabia during the first Gulf War, congratulating the women soldiers for 'irking' the Saudis by their very presence.[3]

The substance of the above feminist response to Abu Ghraib, the specific issues on which it was focused and those that it pushed out of view, is instructive.[4] The question feminists repeatedly asked was the following: Where had feminism gone wrong? This problem was apparently particularly vexing as many of these feminists had championed the opening up of military service to women, defining this as a major advance in the state's recognition of the equal citizenship of women.

The explanations feminists offered to the question of why/where feminism had 'gone' astray were variations on a number of main themes. The US servicewomen who had participated in the torture must themselves be victims of sexual abuse; poor and uneducated; manipulated by the military leadership; young and unable to fully comprehend the consequences of their actions; scapegoats for the military establishment; seeking to impress their male comrades; confused, poorly trained or given conflicting orders; vying for the romantic and sexual attention of male soldiers; under pressure to prove they were as tough as the guys; stressed by men's resentment of women's presence in the army; held to higher moral standards by the public, the media and military courts and so on.[5] As these feminists mourned the death of their own naïveté at Abu Ghraib, that is, their conviction that women's advancement in political institutions would lead to more humane politics (wars?), many came to the conclusion that it was time for feminism to grow up, to toughen up. A mature feminism would emerge from the trauma of this wanton display of women's willingness to inflict torture, these feminists comforted themselves.

In the few instances where feminists did recognize the presence of the actual victims of the torture, they did so in the most cursory and dispassionate of ways. Notably incurious, such acknowledgement was often swiftly followed by a denunciation of 'Islamic fundamentalists' and 'misogynists'; this gesture only served to deepen the state's linking of these men's (presumed) religio-cultural values with terrorism to pin the responsibility for the torture on the Muslims' own supposedly retrograde attitude towards women, sex and homosexuality.[6] The actual violence and terrorizing of Muslims – men, women and children – at Abu Ghraib *in itself* did not seem to elicit this feminist outrage.[7]

As the Black/brown Muslims who had been brutalized disappeared from their commentary, feminists declared themselves guilty of a well-intentioned faith in the power of feminism. The feminist subject thus moved to the centre to assume the position of the *real* victim in the sordid saga. Such a representation of the feminist subject as bruised by this tarnishing of her cherished ideals was, of course, sustainable only on the condition that the long-standing feminist relation of conviviality with the imperialist-colonial state remain un-interrogated.

This chapter revisits my reading of key feminist texts, political statements and cultural production which directly engaged the early phase of the global war. The particular texts (discussed below) were selected at the time not because I considered them any better or worse than others in this particular genre of feminist political activism, but because they were representative of the sorts of authoritative claims and perspectives feminists were developing as they negotiated their own positionality, political allegiances and epistemological investments in the idea of the West at a moment of intense geopolitical turmoil.

My earlier opening up of the question of the relation of feminism to the global war problematized the emerging feminist narratives of innocent Western women and misogynist Muslim men, of abject Muslim womanhood and barbaric Islamic culture. Challenging the popular feminist claim that Muslim women were passive objects of Islamic misogyny and that the global war was fought in their interest, I drew attention to the feminist investment in the discourse of Islamic terror which was opening up fields for feminist advancement, including in the military, politics, media, academia, cultural production, fashion and advertising and so on.

Moreover, I noted how the equally simplistic formulation by feminists on the left of women being 'duped' into extending the politics of the imperialist state had been thoroughly debunked by critical race, postcolonial and Indigenous feminists in the decades preceding the war. Why these formulations gained such traction among feminists – academics and activists – in the global war therefore required attention. The revival of the above brand of feminist politics in the global war, I then argued, elevated gender to a position of primacy and, in this manner, derailed the Black, Indigenous and other feminist of colour critiques of the racial-colonial politics of Western feminism. I also pointed to how the enthusiastic mainstream reception of these developments in feminist politics – in political, media and public debates – was facilitating a renewed alliance between feminists and the Western nation-state, such that feminists were directly contributing to the re-stabilization of Western claims of cultural superiority on account of its gender norms and practices. My revisiting here of this critique of feminist interventions in the global war is informed by a number of recent developments within feminist politics as the global war has shifted into a new phase.

The first of these is the feminist support for the global war, which retreated into more limited projects upon the defeats experienced by the US-led alliance in Afghanistan and Iraq; campaigns to ban the burqa and promote feminist foreign policy replaced the championing of occupations, invasions and war, for example. Moreover, feminist politics came under attack on the domestic front with the election of right-wing populists across the West, including the Trump Presidency in the United States. The feminist contribution to the global war therefore shifted – in form and intensity –within the West but remained a key factor in the remaking of global politics and international institutions. Second, the resonance between the feminist construction of the West as threatened by the 'cultural barbarism' of Islam and Muslims in the war's early phase and the contemporary white supremacist claim that whites are under siege by people of colour, especially in the United States, cannot be overlooked. Although feminists are now under attack in the white supremacist takeover of the political mainstream, this has yet to prompt a rethinking of the liberal-feminist castings of whiteness and the larger racial-imperial dimensions of Western feminist politics, or the feminist gendering of Islamophobia. Third, among the long-term effects of the transformation of feminist politics in the global war is the ongoing projection of gendered Westernity – in its gender-sexual 'egalitarian' variant – as the desired feminist future. This allows the white feminist-queer to be situated at the forefront of critical Western onto-epistemological traditions, embattled though this Subject is by the white supremacist onslaught on liberal egalitarianism. The reformation of feminist politics in the ongoing global war is no doubt even more complex than suggested here. My contention, however, is that so long as feminists gender the Islamophobic discourse of the war and refuse to interrogate the religio-racial foundations of the feminist tradition itself, the affiliative relation between feminism, the colonial-imperial state and the formation of the West will continue to shape the global field.

I discussed in Chapter 3 how the self-constitution of Christian women as 'European', 'Western' and 'white', and later still as 'feminist', was an intrinsic aspect of the religio-racial and sexual-gender logics that founded and extended Western power in a relation of animosity with Islam. These logics were later materialized through, among other events, the Orientalization and subjugation of Muslims to the colonial powers over several centuries following the Reconquista. In the post-independence world, these politics were articulated to the project of modernization and secularization. The identities and subjectivity that were integrally connected to these advances in Western power included that of the feminist subject, who, I have argued, acquired her right to global mobility as an integral aspect of her Westernization. These historical dynamics, processes and relations of power came to the fore in the global war in a particularly explosive manner as its imperialist-colonial ideologies found their most potent expression in gender-sexual politics.

This chapter maps out the shifts in feminist politics and subjectivity as these now reconstitute the Western political imaginary, my reading reveals that they pivot on the long-standing phantasmic construct of the Muslim male as hyper-misogynist and the Muslim woman as abject object. It is these constructs that incite the Westernizing feminist desire to serve as the benefactor of the Muslim woman: 'As a feminist, I have long dreamed of rescuing women who are trapped in domestic and sexual slavery against their will with no chance of escape', explained a feminist who rallied support for the global war.[8] The same desire was evident in the work of another feminist, a human rights advocate, to save the 'daughters' of Afghanistan: 'They [Afghan women] have been playing on the back of my eyelids like old movies, the images of these women and girls I met during the last 11 years in Afghanistan. It has at times felt as much like a crusade as a journalistic assignment.'[9] The Crusades, as I have discussed in the preceding chapter, were fought by Christian women alongside the men; that the feminist project of 'saving' Muslim women would presently be described as a crusade should come as no surprise. Not surprising either should be the conviction of Western feminists, after years of the occupation of Afghanistan that this was 'to do good', to 'beat back the Taliban so Afghans can build a secure and peaceful state where little girls can go to school and their mothers have the right to go to the market without having acid thrown in their faces'.[10]

There is, no doubt, a significant difference between the feminist who champions the wars of the imperialist state and one who wants to 'save' the Muslim woman, between the woman intelligence officer or prison guard who brutalizes the Muslim male for his 'perverse' masculinity and the human rights activist engaged in a reconstruction project in Afghanistan. Yet what they share in common is the sense of *their right* (responsibility even?) to intervene in the lives and communities of Muslims, especially the women. This right/entitlement is conceivable *only* in the context of the religio-racial logics of colonial power, this right/entitlement has remained unshaken within feminist politics in the various phases of the war.

In the following sections, I analyse key representational strategies deployed by a number of feminists that remain vital to the constitution of what I refer to as the Westernizing feminist subject. This subject identifies 'woman' as the *real* target of the hatred she imputes onto Islam and Muslims, with very little actual engagement with either Islam and/or the historical experiences or contemporary political claims of Muslim communities, including the women. Normalizing the politics of her own location within Western imperialism to represent Islam and Muslims as self-evident threats to 'Woman', I show how this subject advances the feminist regime of truth through the development of novel feminist concepts, including 'gender apartheid', 'new anti-Semitism', 'precarious life', 'disposable life', 'grievable life' and so forth. These concepts now dominate the feminist analytic field to gender the cultural-political landscape of the West. The work done by these now authoritative and disciplining concepts eject and/or override the anti-racist and anti-colonial politics of Muslim, Black, Indigenous and other women of colour.

Moreover, such feminist engagement with the global has enabled Western feminists to regain the ground they lost to the anti-colonial and anti-racist politics of Indigenous, Black, Muslim and other women of colour who challenged the right of white women to represent the interests of all women. One argument presented here is that the power of representation was recuperated in the Western feminist gendering of the Islamophobic discourse and reassertion of the superiority of their own politics – gendered Western exceptionalism – in a direct relation of antagonism with Islam and Muslims.

This gendering of Islamophobia countered – *on the grounds of feminism* – the destabilizing effects of Islamist and anti-colonial Muslim resistance, including that of Muslim women, to Western power. In the process, feminism was re-aligned with hegemonic masculinity, which became the means to reassert the privileged position of Western feminists over Muslims in national and global politics, networks and institutions. Consequently, the feminist reconstitution of the sign 'Woman' as vulnerable to the threat of Islam simultaneously reconstituted feminist subjectivity as essentially Western in orientation. Even when the devastating brutality of the global war could not be entirely hidden from public scrutiny, as was the case at Abu Ghraib, feminists undermined its significance by attributing an even greater violence – misogyny – as intrinsic to these Muslims.

Feminists fight the global terror

One political trend to emerge early in feminist responses to the global war was support for the invasion of Afghanistan.[11] Defining the occupation as the means to 'rescue' Afghan women from the 'terrorists', a nebulous category that began with al-Qaeda, included the Taliban, then 'war-lords' and Afghan men, and finally all Muslim men.

> Peace and security must be established across Afghanistan to enable the restoration of women's rights, the reconstruction of the country, and the

establishment of democracy. . . . In addition, we must not fool ourselves that women's safety in Afghanistan is secure when women continue to fear violence and the imposition of Taliban like restrictions by regional warlords. . . . Without expanded international security forces and without adequate funding, women's rights and an end to terrorism will be unobtainable goals,

proclaimed the president of the US Feminist Majority Foundation.[12] Such conflation of Afghan women's rights with ending terrorism; identification of international security forces with protection of women; and linking of peace and women's security with the US state and military became highly effective in mobilizing public support for the war. It also forwarded some of the key ideological elements for the restabilization of the West as a benevolent force for the protection of Muslim women.

This feminist advocacy for the war on terror was not restricted to Afghanistan, it soon extended, despite initial reservation, to include Iraq long after the invasion:

The ongoing conflict, high levels of insecurity, widespread impunity, collapsing economic conditions and rising social conservatism are impacting directly on the daily lives of Iraqi women and placing them under increased vulnerability to all forms of violence within and outside their home. . . . Violence against Iraqi women is committed by numerous actors, such as militia groups, insurgents, Islamic extremists, law enforcement personnel, members of the family as well as the community',

argued the UN Special Rapporteur on Violence Against Women.[13] The equivalence drawn here between violence 'within' the home and the violence of invasion and occupation, between representatives of the state and its armies and family members, constructed them as equally responsible for the violence women lived with in the 'ongoing conflict'. The feminists who advanced these politics were among those most closely associated with the state and other international institutions of governance, but their message carried the day in terms of public awareness and support. As they linked Muslim men with 'terrorism', and both with misogyny, the feminist argument was that violence against Muslim women was part of the social fabric of Muslim societies, such that this minimized, or even shielded from view, imperialist and state violence.[14] This perspective became dominant in political and public discussion, it dominated the media in particular. With images of burqa-clad and hijab-wearing women flooding news reports, the idea that the war would 'save' the women shaped much of the public perception of 'terrorism', the 'problem' of Islam and the exceptionalism of the West.

Such feminist construction of Islam and Muslims was hardly novel, as demonstrated in earlier chapters. What was new was the network of well-established transnational feminist organizations with the capacity and resources to disseminate and mobilize these politics rapidly at the international level. Not surprising, as feminist organizations amplified the US Administration's denunciation of Muslim men and redefined 'terrorism' as rooted in misogynist hatred, the elevation of feminists as the experts on Islamic patriarchy and Muslim culture soon followed.

Feminists claimed – and were granted – such recognition largely on the basis of their gender. As 'women', feminists came to be seen as not only understanding the 'real' cause of 'Islamic terror' but also the experts best suited to understand and represent the interests of Muslim women.[15] The feminist access to the institutions of the state and media that had been acquired over the previous decades was now put to use to consolidate the authority of these Western feminists on the 'problem' with Islam. Leading feminist organizations, including the US National Organization of Women, also used the war as an opportunity to strengthen the alliance between feminist and gay activism. NOW, it was reported, 'use[d] the terrorist attacks to flak its own domestic agenda, declaring that "in this time of national and global turmoil, the reasons we celebrate 'Coming Out Day' are more visible and important than ever and proceeded to call for a permanent lifting of the ban on gays in the military"'.[16]

Some feminists also linked the war on terror directly to Western support for the Israeli state. An early example of this trend in the remaking of feminist politics and alliances came from Phyllis Chesler, a founding figure of second-wave feminism. Her book, *The New Anti-Semitism: The Current Crisis and What We Must Do About It*, advocated expansion of the war on terror across the entire Middle East. Chesler identified the United States and Israel as the twin targets of a deadly 'new' anti-Semitism directed at them from an 'old' enemy of this (new) West: Islam and Muslims. Chesler called for a US–Israel alliance to defeat the Islamic threat to their respective populations; she was joined in this view by a number of Muslim feminists including, for one much celebrated example, Irshad Manji.[17]

Chesler's argument that the West is hated by an irrational Islamic enemy which seeks to destroy the societies founded on superior Judeo-Christian values tethered Judaism to Christianity, it also linked Jews to the historical Christian antipathy towards Islam. This reconfiguration of the West as Judeo-Christian in the discourse of the global war is taken up more fully in the next chapter, what is notable in Chesler's representation of a united US–Israeli front against Islam and Muslims is her identification of Christian-Jewish unity as rooted in a common racial identity (white), shared gender values (feminist) and political–economic interests (globalization) in addition to their religious affinity. In contrast, Muslims and Palestinians are the racial Enemy, religiously fanatic and murderously anti-woman.

This presentation dehistoricized and depoliticized the Palestinian resistance and larger Arab and Muslim opposition to Israeli colonization to redefine it as rooted in Muslim racial envy and Islamic cultural barbarism. Chesler went on to reframe the 9/11 attacks as primarily directed against Israelis and all Jewish people, who were its real target: '[t]his fight against the Jews is as old as the Jews', she argued as she redefined the attacks as a 'new' anti-Semitism of the Muslims.[18] The main argument in Chesler's book was that the United States had become a target of 'Islamofascists' as a result of its support for Israel.[19]

The 'old' anti-Semitism was based on biologically determinist ideas about Jewish inferiority, but its 'new' form was defined by Chesler as particularly pernicious because its 'acts of violence against Jews and anti-Semitic words and deeds are being uttered and performed by politically correct people in the name of anticolonialism, anti-imperialism, antiracism and pacifism'.[20] In other words, anti-colonial and anti-racist politics were identified as inherently anti-Semitic and anti-feminist. Defining support for the Palestinian cause as particularly noxious, Chesler accused supporters of Palestinian resistance with 'betrayal of the Jews'.[21] Judaism was seamlessly conflated with Zionism and Israeli settler colonialism with US interests, Palestinian resistance was denounced as 'terrorism' and 'anti-Semitism'.

The framing of the global war as a primal battle between Jews – now existentially allied with a Christian West – and an Islam that hated both gained traction among liberal, as well as some Muslim, feminists.[22] These ideas were given added force as the construct of a 'new' anti-Semitism was adopted by Western states (from the right-wing US Administration to the Liberal Canadian government) and by academic institutions who banned public campaigns and political support for the Boycott, Divestment and Sanctions non-violent movement against the Israeli occupation. Chesler's arguments may have been regarded as somewhat extreme within some left feminist circles, but their political consequences have not been insignificant. Accusations of the new 'anti-Semitism' now abound against anti-racist and anti-colonial feminists, particularly Muslims, within the women's movement, including in the recent Women's March in the United States; many university administrations across North America have specifically targeted pro-Palestinian activism on campuses to shut this down.

With regard to gender politics, Chesler described Afghanistan in the Orientalist tropes of a 'beautiful and treacherous country', its women locked in 'gender apartheid', contrasting them to the American and Jewish women who enjoy 'freedom' and are 'privileged'.[23] In a subsequent discussion, Chesler identified this 'gender apartheid' as the biggest threat to 'freedom' and warned that feminist support for anti-racist and anti-colonial politics would lead to the 'death of feminism' itself.[24] Excoriating multicultural and anti-racist feminist activism, she raised the white supremacist spectre of the West being invaded by 'Islamikaze terrorists': 'To my horror', she declared,

> most western academic and mainstream feminists have not focused on what I call gender apartheid in the Islamic world or on its steady penetration of Europe. . . . Islamic terrorists have declared jihad against the 'infidel west' and against all those who yearn for freedom. Women in the Islamic world are treated as subhumans. Although some feminists have sounded the alarm about this, a much larger number have remained silent.[25]

If the 'threat' of Islam was clear to the feminists who shared Chesler's perspective, so too was the remedy. Among other strategies, Chesler urged her readers to 'Form Jewish-Christian Alliances' to fight the global menace of Islam.[26]

These developments within feminist praxis pointed to the ongoing explicit compatibility of a brand of feminist politics with older colonial ideologies and the new imperialist wars of the early twenty-first century, with the underlying religio-racial genocidal logic upon which the settler societies of the United States, Canada and Israel are founded. Western women's participation was historically vital to the establishment and reproduction of these societies, and Chesler's work reveals the powerful hold of these ideologies and alliances over the Western feminist imaginary.

Chesler's work on the 'new' anti-Semitism contributed to a major development in the ideology of the global war, the iteration of a 'new' West defined as Judeo-Christian and secular-feminist in essence, centred on the identification of the Israeli nation-state as Western. This 'new' anti-Semitism was mapped out in a relation of murderous animosity with Islam and Muslims, particularly the women; it was also a recasting of the old Christo-European and larger Western antipathy towards Jews (Chesler argued the Church had 'evolved' and 'begun to rethink and regret some of its earlier positions').[27] Locating Zionism at the centre of the political and cultural reconfiguration of the new West, Chesler's analysis demonized in the feminist analytical field the resistance of Palestinian and other Muslim women to colonial occupation, Western imperialism and Islamophobia.

No doubt many feminists consider Chesler's views to be beyond the pale, but this has not stopped such ideas from being enthusiastically received within neoconservative and neoliberal political circles, or being used to deepen the relationship between feminism, Christian women and the ultra-right. These views have also shaped mainstream liberal anti-Palestinian campaigns, particularly BDS, as well as anti-Muslim sentiments more generally by giving these an acceptable feminist political language. The rise of white nationalist politics across the West point to the necessity of understanding the links between white supremacy, Zionism and Islamophobia, especially given the considerably less scrutiny these receive when expressed in a feminist idiom. The reception of such constructs within elite feminist circles has been accompanied by their adoption in the feminist and women's studies curriculum. Closely aligned with the politics of the ultra-right, this brand of feminism garners powerful institutional support.

Imperialism as precariousness

In sharp contrast to the feminists who supported the expansion of the war on terror, many voiced their opposition to US imperialism, which they linked specifically to the invasion of Iraq.[28] Prominent among these was Judith Butler, who argued in *Precarious Life: The Powers of Mourning and Violence* that the distinction between anti-Semitism and opposition to Israeli state policies was vital to recognize and preserve, and that the resort to violence by the United States in the Iraq war was a dangerous escalation. Condemning both anti-Semitism and the US war in Iraq, Butler noted that the charge of anti-Semitism was increasingly being used to silence dissent in the United States and to quash opposition to Israeli state policies.[29] Arguing that the 'root causes' of the 9/11 attacks needed to be addressed, Butler's book sought also to identify the conditions necessary for building community in the face of violence and mourning. Pointing to the dangers of the suspension of the law by the Bush Administration in the name of national security, Butler advocated instead for ethical and moral responses to the 9/11 attacks, which she defined as a demand from the 'Other'.

Butler's main concern in this text was with 'the conditions of heightened vulnerability and aggression'[30] that had been revealed by the 9/11 attacks. Criticizing the Bush Administration's decision to launch the war abroad and undermine civil rights within the United States, Butler also took the media to task for its dehumanization of the Other. The lack of reporting of the violence done to this Other, that is, to the Iraqis, rendered their lives 'unknowable', their deaths 'ungrievable'. As a feminist intellectual and a founding figure of poststructural/postmodern feminism, Butler's intervention was politically significant. Yet it was not without its problems.

Butler's analytic frame centred the injury done to the United States in the 9/11 attacks: 'That US boundaries were breached, that an unbearable vulnerability was exposed, that a terrible toll on human life was taken, were, and are, cause for fear and mourning; they are also instigations for patient political reflection.'[31] Despite this call for 'patient political reflection', the countless breaches by the United States of the boundaries of other countries in the decades preceding 9/11, like its rendering of millions of people in the United States and around the world 'unbearably vulnerable' (most pertinent to her concern about the invasion of Iraq were the first Gulf War and the sanctions that followed to kill over half a million children) did not enter, let alone shape, her analytic frame. When mention was made of US atrocity, this was done only in passing, its consequences overlooked. For Butler did acknowledge that 'others have suffered arbitrary violence at the hands of the US'[32], yet this suffering, which was concretized most pertinently in Afghanistan as well as Palestine *prior to the 9/11 attacks* and explicitly addressed in the public statements released by al-Qaeda, was rendered irrelevant in her treatment of 9/11 as the moment of revelation of the 'unbearable vulnerability' of the (US) Subject. This Subject's experience, then, informed Butler's reflections on the war and her conceptualization of 'vulnerability' as a generic condition of a generic humanity. 'Fear and mourning' were likewise defined from the perspective of the post-9/11 Western Subject – the prototype of the injured subject – in her politico-philosophical deliberations on violence, grief and mourning.

In foregrounding – perhaps unintentionally – the imperial Subject who had suddenly and graphically discovered its own vulnerability, Butler implicitly reproduced the US Administration's narrative of US innocence and the exceptionalism of its Subject. That this subject was unsettled by the war, that she did not deny the obvious violence being done to the 'Other', made her no less imperial/ist. More to the point, this subject was unsettled by the war on terror because of the violent *response* it was likely to engender in the future, not from any unconditional opposition to the imperialist violence of the US state, a violence done and justified in her name.

Butler's attempt to come to grips with the injury done to the Self by the Other, and by the Self to the Other, identified vulnerability to violence as central to the human condition: 'To be injured means that one has the chance to reflect upon injury, to find out the mechanisms of its distribution, to find out who else suffers from permeable borders, unexpected violence, dispossession, and fear, and in what ways.'[33] Although Butler acknowledged that such vulnerability was not equally distributed, her analysis nevertheless proceeded on the assumption that this was the case as she reflected upon the possibility of building a political community on the basis of this condition as a shared one. Such a condition of 'shared' vulnerability, determined from a US-centred experience and perspective, produced the community of the 'we' of her text. 'Despite our differences in location and history', Butler argued,

> my guess is that it is possible to appeal to a 'we,' for all of us have some notion of what it is to have lost somebody. Loss has made a tenuous 'we' of us all. And if we have lost, then it follows that we have had, that we have desired and loved, that we have struggled to find the conditions for our desire.[34]

The relation of violence between Western-imperialist societies and colonized peoples, and their conflicting interests have disappeared in such an abstract, liberal framing of vulnerable individuals.

This de-historicization of the causes identified by the Other, al-Qaeda in the case of 9/11, and the relocation of the Self and Other into such a zone of abstraction led to the universalization of the equally abstract condition of vulnerability in this text. Despite Butler's explicit caution against assuming a universally shared human condition, she nonetheless invoked this very condition: 'I do not even mean to presume upon a common notion of the human, although to speak in its "name" is already (and perhaps only) to fathom its possibility.'[35] This 'common notion of the human' – de-racialized and de-gendered – was the subject of her concern.

The condition of vulnerability she was thinking through, Butler explained, was a primal condition:

> I am referring to violence, vulnerability, and mourning, but there is a more general conception of the human with which I am trying to work here, one in which we are, from the start, even prior to individuation itself, and by virtue of bodily requirements, given over to some set of primary others: this conception means that we are vulnerable to those we are too young to know and to judge, and hence, vulnerable to violence; but also vulnerable to another range of touch, a range that includes the eradication of our being at the one end, and the physical support for our lives at the other.[36]

Such a framing of the violence that was then unfolding in the US invasion of Iraq's national borders and the destruction of its sovereignty through a lens that privileged a biological infancy and a psychic condition of pre-individuation can be read as the narcissistic reflections of the imperial Self. The specific forms of power that have sustained US imperialism are here rendered invisible as the condition of human infancy moves to delimit the discursive frame. These theoretical moves elided how the Self's materialization of its alterity has been historically constituted through colonial-racial modernity in a murderous relation to the Other; more pertinent, this gesture obscured the Self's relation of antagonism with the Other who dared engage in resistance.

The commonality of the human condition as posited here functions first, to domesticate the Other into the position of the Self-same, and second, to subjugate the Other by erasing the specificity and historicity of its experience. As the Self moves into the position of centrality, it enacts the epistemic violence necessary to determine what constitutes *the* experience of the Other in the name of this shared 'human' condition. Put differently, Butler's elevation of the Self's experience of its 'vulnerability' – a 'primal' state – as the very condition of being human reproduces the appropriative gesture that has shaped the Western tradition. Consequently, the imposition of the collective 'we' in prioritizing this condition which originated in the Western Self grasped its colonized Other to subsume it to the power of the Self (if this Other is to be included in Butler's conception of the human). The move foreclosed recognition of the injuries and losses, that is, the injustice inflicted upon this occupied Other. These injuries are, of course, of an entirely different order than those experienced by the Western Subject.

Upholding the primacy of the condition of infancy to anchor her theorization of the 'vulnerability' of Western subjects, and defining this as also the point of departure for the Other's ontological (non)being, makes the Other's experience of loss and injury illegible except as a replication of the experience of the Self. In this manner, Butler could approach the invaded and occupied Other as being essentially the same as the imperial, self-defining Subject. Such a commonality of experience is, of course, made impossible by the violence of US imperialism. However, positing such a shared status does allow the imperial Subject to fashion a position of innocence for herself even as this Subject speaks of – and for – the occupied Object. Butler's 'patient reflection' leads only to a classic colonizing gesture, the Self's engulfment of its Other.

My critique of Butler's approach is not so much that the psychoanalytic and philosophical approaches she draws upon cannot be useful in shedding light on the war on terror. After all, many critical race theorists, Fanon onwards, have drawn on both quite fruitfully for their work on violence, suffering and pain in the colonial/racial context.[37] What is problematic about Butler's use of these approaches is her reproduction of the universalist pretensions of Western philosophical and psychoanalytic traditions, and of the individualistic Western Self as the 'human' subject. Commenting on Freud's insistence that the 'individual factor' demanded attention, Fanon cautioned that 'the Black man's alienation is not an individual question. . . . Beside phylogeny and ontogeny stand sociogeny.'[38] Butler, following the conventions of the Western tradition, avoids engagement with the rich and fruitful theorization of 'sociogeny' developed within critical race and anti-colonial traditions, including their feminist variants.

Butler's analysis thus reinforced the Western denial of the scale and scope of the violence done to the Other by the Western Self, even as her text reworked the representation of this Self as a vulnerable, hence essentially innocent. This failure to address the settler colonialism, racial hierarchy and global imperialism that structure the US nation-state, to attend to its foundational genocidal violence as well as its ongoing dispossession of Indigenous peoples and reproduction of racial violence in its prison-industrial complex and immigration policies, allowed Butler to present the 9/11 attacks as somehow an originary violence against the white Self. Representing the world's most powerful militarized power and its subjects as equally vulnerable to violence as the impoverished communities that are the victims of invasions and occupations in Afghanistan and Iraq in this instance was an astonishing move, Butler's criticism of the Bush Administration notwithstanding.

Reiterating many of the very practices she criticized in the US Administration, Butler recentred and thus re-stabilized the Western Subject. A frame that might have taken as its starting point the injury done to the Other by the Western Self would have not only been historically more accurate, it might have even revealed that the violence done by the Other is not the originary violence within US empire. Unfortunately, Butler's ahistorical and decontextualized references to 'state terror' were no substitute for such engagement. Instead, her problematic framing led to a strange conclusion wherein the violence of the United States came to be represented as 'tragic' and defensive in nature:

> Tragically, it seems that the US seeks to preempt violence by waging violence first, but the violence it fears is the violence it engenders. I do not mean to suggest by this that the US is responsible in some causal way for the attacks on its citizens. And I do not exonerate Palestinian suicide bombers, regardless of the terrible conditions that animate their murderous activities. There is, however, some distance to be travelled between living in terrible conditions and suffering serious, even unbearable injuries, and resolving on murderous acts. President Bush travelled that distance quickly, calling for 'an end to grief' after a mere ten days of flamboyant mourning. Suffering can yield an experience of humility, of vulnerability, of impressionability and dependence, and these can become resources, if we do not 'resolve' them too quickly; they can move us beyond and against the vocation of the paranoid victim who regenerates infinitely the justifications for war. It is as much a matter of wrestling ethically with one's own murderous impulses, impulses that seek to quell an overwhelming fear, as it is a matter of apprehending the suffering of others and taking stock of the suffering one has inflicted.[39]

Apart from such an unwarranted linking of Palestinian 'suicide bombers' to the 9/11 attack on US 'citizens', it was a curious logic indeed that drew an equivalence between the 'murderous acts' of colonized Palestinians and those of the US president, who mobilized the largest military machine amassed in human history to carry out his 'impulses'. Did Butler really mean to suggest such a moral equivalence? The logic became even more curious in the suggestion that it was a similar experience of 'suffering' that gave rise to the 'murderous impulses' of Palestinian suicide bombers and of the US president!

Butler's implicit demand that Palestinians renounce violence even when living with 'unbearable injuries' if they are to be considered 'ethical' subjects so completely subjugates this Other's epistemic and ontological experience and priorities that it renders impossible consideration of this Other's actions as *also* shaped by ethical foundations within a contesting (anti-colonial) paradigm and system of moral (anti-occupation) values. Perhaps Butler's criticism of the media for not covering the deaths of Iraqis in its reportage was most revealing of her ethical preoccupations. Arguing that the media ought to grant greater visibility to those Iraqis killed in the war, and thereby make their deaths 'grievable', Butler explained that such recognition of the war dead as having been worthy of life would invoke a cathartic mourning within the Western Self. In other words, viewing the war dead would not only allow her community of the 'we' to 'see' the suffering of the annihilated Other, but through the granting of such visibility (in death) to this Other, the mourning of the viewing community would *render* 'grievable' the lives lost. The power to grant the Other (in death) such recognition – worthy of human *life* – thus rests in the hands of the witnessing Self. This call to make visible the dead victims of the war thus reinscribes the power of the Self. The act of 'seeing' is here considered the key to humanizing not only the war dead, but the Western Self. For it is this act of 'witnessing' that moves this Self to grief; that is, it is through the mourning that ensues from witnessing that this Self experiences its own humanity as in common with its (now dead) Other. What might the (living) Other have to say about this act of being 'seen' in the moment of its annihilation, about a grief and mourning that is instantiated in the witnessing Subject only upon in the death of the Other? Is the death of the Other to be taken as the condition for the humanizing of the Self? Is the witnessing of the death of the Other a life-enhancing resource for the Self?

Palestine is an important counter-lesson to these politics of deathly grief and life-enhancing mourning, for if there is a people whose lives have been rendered utterly ungrievable by/in Western media, it is the Palestinians. Yet even as Western media has contributed to the dehumanization of this people, Palestinian cinema has been a critical site for contesting such dehumanization, for countering the erasure of Palestinians in life and in death. Consider in this regard what Hamid Dabashi has to say about the politics of visibility in his study of the accomplishments of Palestinian cinema. This cinema is driven by 'the mutation of [that] repressed anger into an aestheticized violence – the aesthetic presence of a political absence'.[40] In the face of the overwhelming violence of the Israeli state, the documentaries made by Palestinians, Dabashi argues, are a visual '"J'accuse" – animated by a tireless frenzy to create an alternative record of a silenced crime, to be lodged in a place that escapes the reach of the colonizer as occupier'.[41] This cinema, testament to the humanity of the quintessential Other of the Judeo-Christian West, the Palestinian, is unconcerned with making Palestinian lives 'grievable' to their oppressors. Instead, its raison d'etre is 'accusation' of those who have committed crimes against its people, who have dispossessed this people and are everyday witness to their ongoing genocide. This politics of visibility seeks life, not death, for those in whose lives and struggles it is invested.

What would Butler have to say about such a media, with its accusation against the colonizing subject, whom she would have 'grieve' over the display of the death of the colonized Other? Where in this frame is the room for the Iraqis, the Afghans, who mourn and grieve the deaths of their loved ones, whether broadcast on the media or not, whether seen or unseen in the West? Do they not themselves 'see' and live with these deaths on a daily basis, does their grieving over these lost lives and broken bodies count? Does the grieving of the Other carry any weight? Do these Others not value the lives of their loved ones, do they not have the conviction that their lives matter, whether or not they are put on display for vindication –

consumption? – by the Self? Do these Others not believe their own lives matter in their own terms? So utterly (self)centred is the Western Subject in Butler's text that such questions do not give her pause for concern, let alone give rise to the desire to learn how the Other has sought to re/define the Self.

The 'vulnerability' of the United States and the Western subject that so concerns Butler can only be 'produced' at the cost of making invisible the racial violence that is the bedrock of US society and its sovereignty. That this racial violence is the condition of possibility for the Western Subject's universalizing of herself is also rendered invisible. Butler's concepts of 'precarious' and 'vulnerable' life were, however, quickly taken up within the feminist field. I return to Butler's work in the final section of this chapter, let me move now to the third set of strategies deployed by Western feminists in the war on terror.

Sexual terrorism and gender apartheid

If Butler's positing of a shared vulnerability displaces the specific claims of the Other to re-centre the imperialist subject as innocent, the concept of 'gender apartheid' as developed by other feminists reworked the victim status of white women in similar manner. I briefly mentioned above Chesler's Orientalizing description of 'gender apartheid' in Afghanistan. A more complex, and critically informed development of this concept can be found in Zillah Eisenstein's *Against Empire*. Setting out 'to uncover the relations and histories of power more fully . . . to move towards a more inclusive viewing of humanity by looking for absences, listening for silences, and imagining beyond my own limits', Eisenstein makes very clear her opposition to US imperialism. The US Empire, she notes, has a long history of violence and exploitation, from the conquest of Native/Indigenous peoples and slavery to its present racial politics.[42]

Eisenstein begins by linking the war on terror to a 'class war [that] is being waged in the US while all eyes look abroad'.[43] This class war is evident in the neoliberal assault on the gains of the civil rights and women's movements, tax cuts for the rich, corporate corruption, and dangerous remilitarization.[44] Tying the war on terror to the policies of previous US Administrations, Eisenstein rejects the East/West binary that shapes the war ideology by pointing out that flows have always existed between the two.[45] Contextualizing her analysis of contemporary US imperialism in the long history of the colonization of the Americas and slavery, Eisenstein associates this violence to the development of capitalism, patriarchy and racism. However, after outlining this larger context, as Eisenstein turns to focus on the impact of the war on terror on women, the politics of race, racialization and colonization are relegated to the historical background and fall out of her analysis. Race, colonialism and class do not inform her discussion of 'women' in the US or in Afghanistan.

Contesting the dominant framing of the war as an intervention to 'save' Afghan women, Eisenstein argued that the Bush Administration had 'hijacked' feminism to serve its own interests.[46] This pre-emptive exoneration of feminism from implication in the war revealed how little Eisenstein's outlining of the history of genocide, slavery and colonialism actually informed her treatment of feminism, or indeed even of the status of white women in US history or contemporary politics. Falling back on the classic feminist strategy of directing attention away from the racist/imperialist practices of white women by elevating gender to focus on patriarchy, male dominance and violence against women, Eisenstein's text obfuscated these women's role in US colonial-racial politics.

Not surprising then, the causes of the war on terror were thus defined in the text:

> A masculinist-military mentality dominates on both sides of the ill-named East/West divide. The opposition implied by this divide is not simple or complete... Flows between these locations have always existed, and they occur today more than ever. Furthermore, the two sides of the divide share foundational relations, even if differently expressed, especially in terms of male privilege. Neither side embraces women's full economic and political equality or sexual freedom. In this sense fluidity has always existed between the two in the arena of women's rights and obligations. The Taliban's insistence on the burqa and the US military's deployment of women fighter pilots are used to overdraw and misrepresent the oppositional stance.[47]

This framing moves away from the materialist analysis used to discuss the US past into a liberal representation of the present; the United States and the Taliban become 'both' sides, equally patriarchal, equally militaristic, equally masculinist. This equivalence obscures the immense power differential between the US and Afghan states, an inequality shaped by the histories of colonization and underdevelopment, US strategic interests, the North/South divide and so forth.

In Eisenstein's formulation, 'gender apartheid' shapes the lives of women in Afghanistan, 'sexual terrorism' is the threat to women in the United States. The conflation of these forms of violence construct women in these sites as equally victim to male violence, such that the status and power of men in the United States is equated to that of Afghan men. Not only are 'patriarchy' and the 'masculinist-military mentality' of both defined as essentially of the same order, so too is the experience of women in the United States and Afghanistan, despite the latter being a war zone. The violence of 'patriarchy' and its consequences for women is presented as the same in the United States as in Afghanistan, then under a US-led occupation.

In this 'patriarchy' that is 'global', Eisenstein identifies control of women's sexuality as the 'real' cause for the 9/11 attacks:

> I do not agree with columnists who attributed September 11 solely to the anger of bin Laden and his followers toward the excessive greed and irresponsibility of global capitalism and its white supremacist ways. Nor did September 11 happen simply because the global economy is displacing men from their earlier livelihoods. These explanations are valid, but September 11 must also be viewed

in relation to the way that male patriarchal privilege orchestrates its hierarchical system of domination. The age-old fear and hatred of women's sexuality and their forced domestication into womanly and wifely roles informs all economies. Global capitalism unsettles the pre-existing sexual hierarchical order and tries to mould women's lives to its newest needs across the East/West divide.[48]

Imputing a phantasmic 'age-old' male sexual motive and gender divide to the 9/11 attacks, Eisenstein's analysis actually furthers the Islamophobic view that Muslim men are motivated by an 'ancient' hatred of women and their sexuality; moreover, there is no attempt at engagement with the specific political demands made by the Taliban or al-Qaeda, there is also no analysis of US strategic interests in Afghanistan.

Drawing attention to male sexual violence within the United States was certainly a welcome departure in Eisenstien's text, for this violence disappeared from the concerns of many other feminists who focused squarely on Islamic culture and Muslim men as the source of misogynist violence. Unfortunately Eisenstien's highlighting of sexual violence in the United States did not undermine the text's reproduction of the racialized and gendered construct of Third-World men, Muslim men in particular, as hyper-misogynist.[49] The construct of 'sexual terrorism' does not 'stick', to use Sara Ahmed's words, to white male bodies in the ways that it does to Black/brown male bodies.

More problematic, however, was Eisenstein's presentation of an age-old 'global misogyny'[50] as the root cause of the war on terror. Her treatment of gender oppression as shared by Western and Afghan/Muslim women alike meant that the specificities of 'gender' and 'oppression' in these sites were lost as an abstract 'patriarchy' was identified as the cause of the violence. Eisenstein thus rejected the East/West binary only to replace it with a gender binary, the East/West divide was disavowed only to insert the man/woman divide. The text thus follows in the classic Western feminist tradition of elevating 'gender' as the primary socio-economic relation, even though it explicitly began by addressing the US as an empire. Consequently, the text serves to reinforce gender as the central factor shaping global politics.

There can be little disagreement with Eisenstein's contention that sexual economics underpin the global economy, nor can the realities of the violence that women experience and live with in the 'East' and the 'West' be ignored. However, in the absence of a substantive analysis of how Western power and white racial supremacy shape global politics, including gender politics and violence against women, Eisenstein's analysis dovetailed with the imperialist worldview– in a feminist casting – that her text attempted to challenge. The claiming of a shared experience of gender oppression between Western and Afghan/Muslim women at the hands of 'patriarchy', and the dispensing with the racialization of Muslim women/men underway in the United States and in the global field allowed Eisenstein to present white women/feminists in the United States as the 'natural' gender allies of Afghan/Muslim women in a 'global sisterhood'. The key point here is that Eisenstein's feminism concealed the global power imbalance that structures the unequal relations between white women and Muslim women, whether in the United States or in Afghanistan.

In short, Eisenstein's discussion of race and racism early in the text served only to relegate these to the past; attribute these to capitalist and imperialist structures; or define these as serving the interests of white men, particularly elite men. While Eisenstein was certainly right to note that race and racialization are integral aspects of capitalism, these relations have also garnered very tangible benefits and privileges for Western women, even for the feminists among them. Indeed, race is as constitutive of white women's identity and experience, as it is of Afghan women's 'gender'. Certainly white feminists have long desired a 'global sisterhood' in the name of their feminism, but as women of colour have also long noted, this comes at the cost of naturalizing the racial power of white feminists and of their dominant position at the forefront of such a 'sisterhood'.[51]

Neglecting to interrogate the racial power invested in the concept of 'global feminism', Eisenstein emphasized the violence done to Afghan women by Afghan men. This approach downplayed the violence done to these women by the US nation-state, and by the Western men *and women* who had then invaded and occupied Afghanistan. It was thus less than persuasive for Eisenstein to make the case that it was the Bush Administration's hijacking of 'the language of women's rights' that was the main issue of concern in the relation of feminism to imperialism, or that the women in the Bush Administration – whom she described as 'masquerad[ing] as a masculinity in drag'[52] – were the only women beneficiaries of US imperialism.

Consequently, this feminist perspective allowed the gendered imperial subject to claim proximity to the Third-World Muslim woman, and from this vantage point, contribute to the demonization of Muslim men. Although violence against women is certainly pervasive in the United States, the notion of 'sexual terrorism' has not demonized white men in the racial discourse of US nationalism or the Islamophobic discourse of the global war. In contrast, the concept of 'gender apartheid' was incorporated into global political discourse to legitimize the war on terror. Predictably enough, Eisenstein criticized Black and Third-World anti-racist and anti-colonial male leaders for their sexism, but little criticism was to be found of white women's reproduction of their racial superiority within 'global' gender/sexual politics, which included here appropriation of the language of 'apartheid' only to make the term's critique of anti-Black violence in its originary context disappear.[53]

Secular critique: Feminist derailment of dissent

The texts on which I have focused so far in this chapter have been influential in mapping out a number of different trajectories within feminist engagement with the global war, texts that I have, for the main, read as white feminist monologues for they speak from, and to, the experience and perspectives of Western women, mostly in the United States. The concepts these feminists advanced in these interventions have become authoritative in the field of gender/sexual theory and the activism of the present.

Yet these texts also betray an anxiety which I take as arising from the destabilization of the power of the West that has taken place in the global war. I therefore read the collective turning away in these texts from the critical histories of the Muslim world, and from the resistance, struggles and perspectives of Muslim women, as a desire to re-inscribe the 'innocence' of gendered whiteness by asserting mastery over, or even the suppression of, such challenges to Western power. The reinstatement of a universalizing feminist politics – thoroughly debunked by anti-colonial and anti-racist feminist traditions during the 1990s – rests on the re-stabilization of the idea of the West to which these texts remain firmly attached. One can glimpse also in these texts a certain compulsion to address, even if this is implicit, the mounting critiques of the racial-colonial violence of this West. For this violence cannot be glossed over at a moment when Western nation-states are engaged in wars, invasions and occupations, nor can opposition to this violence be summarily dismissed. The movements against colonial dispossession of Indigenous peoples, against anti-Black and anti-people of colour racism, Islamophobia, BDS, anti-immigrant and refugee politics have to be reckoned with by Western feminists, in some form or other.

In the final section of this chapter, I present a close reading of an exchange among a number of prominent critical scholars/public intellectuals regarding key issues related to the global war. The text in question, *Is Critique Secular? Blasphemy, Injury and Free Speech*, is a rare instance of direct engagement by Western feminists with issues of race, war and Islamophobia as experienced by Muslim communities. It therefore provides a valuable opportunity to study how such engagement unfolds and to what end.[54] As mentioned earlier, white feminists cannot avoid the growing contestation of the hegemony of the West by critical scholars, activists and movements who draw attention to its racism, imperialism and demonization of Islam and Muslims. These contestations were amplified by the revelations of the Abu Ghraib torture as well as the escalation in hate crimes and racial violence across North America and Europe; they require some response.

As evident in its title, the text addresses key topics that became highly contentious in the global war, including free speech, blasphemy and secularism; the occasion for its production was a symposium following the controversy sparked by the publication of the Danish cartoons (originally published in 2005).[55] As I demonstrate in my reading of this text, the critiques of the religio-racial attacks on Muslims in Europe that were presented at the symposium were met by feminists with a gendered deployment of the authority of the Western epistemic tradition to derail them. In the process, the explicit concerns raised about racial violence and the deteriorating status of Muslims in Europe were displaced as whiteness was recentred in a gender-sexual politics that drew upon and reasserted, the power of the Western tradition.

In the Introduction, Wendy Brown provides a 'brief orientation' to the essays by Talal Asad, Saba Mahmood and Judith Butler that make up the text.[56] The essays by the first two authors, the reader is informed, are particularly 'useful' for raising 'a nest of (often unasked) questions about conventional ordinances of secularity, religion, insult, injury, blasphemy, free speech, dissent, and criticism' in their discussion of the Danish cartoons; these essays, Brown noted, provide 'an extraordinary platform for rethinking the putatively secular foundations and premises of critique.'[57] Let me note for the moment that the cartoon controversy raised for Muslims, as discussed by Asad and Mahmood, the above mentioned issues along with a host of other questions, including Islamophobia, racist provocation, hate speech, anti-immigrant sentiments, Western imperialism, the power of the corporatized media and so on. These latter issues, however, are set aside in the Introduction's 'orientation'.

The 'orientation' Brown provides to the essays to follow thus raises an obvious question: What is it that the reader is being 'oriented' towards? In order to be 'oriented', as Sara Ahmed has explained, one first needs to experience 'disorientation'. An orientation helps one register the familiar, Ahmed argues, it tells one where they are, where they are headed, and how to get there; an orientation is also about the 'familiarity of the world', about how one 'feel[s] at home'.[58] Orientations are therefore about where one begins, how one proceeds, and in this manner, orientations are 'homing devices', as Ahmed puts it.[59] Brown's orientation then, presumably, is to help set the reader right, to identify a point of beginning, find the familiar and get a sense of where the text is headed.

This understanding of orientations, however, raises a larger question: What is the disorientation – that which precedes orientation – that Brown's introduction intends to help set right? In other words, what disorientations have been brought about that the essays – by Asad and Mahmood, and the response to them by Butler – set out to re-orientate?[60] I bracket this question for the moment, the answer will emerge in the following discussion.

Brown's introductory remarks problematize the terms of the question that animate the text, 'Is Critique Secular?' Pointing out the question's 'unfixed quality', she explains that the word 'is' has been made problematic following Bill Clinton's questioning of its meaning (in the Lewinsky affair); 'critique' assumes an interrogative stance; and 'secular' presents itself as transparent in its meaning. The term 'critique', she explains, initially emerged in ancient Athens as 'krisis' (sorting, judging, rupture in politics, etc.), it had juridical implications; she then distinguishes the word from 'criticism', which connotes 'a tacit assumption of reason's capacity to unveil error'.[61] The term 'secular' has a temporal association, it references 'post-Reformation practices and institutions in the West', although its common-sense use refers to 'religiously tolerant, humanist, Christian, modern or simply Western'.[62] Increasingly used in opposition to Islam, 'secular', Brown explained 'veils the religious shape and content of Western public life and its imperial designs'.[63] Secularism is also associated with critique, especially by the 'enlightenment conceits' that claim the practice of critique opened up a site of interrogation beyond religion and faith; a space defined by rationality, science and truth.[64]

Brown then discusses the distinction between critique and criticism by turning to the Young Hegelians who criticized religion as 'illusionary consciousness' and believed that its replacement by 'rational consciousness' would 'free' man. Marx, however, took a position against this view by arguing that religious consciousness exists for a reason, which he famously read as a symptom of the misery of human servitude. In contrast to the Young Hegelians, Marx was interested in the actual conditions that give rise to such religious consciousness, a project which he defined as 'critique'. In other words, Marx developed the concept of 'critique' to counter the mystification of reality within religion, and to decode such mystification in scientific terms. This Marxist approach 'secures the conviction that critique is secular in the Western critical theory tradition' and has been central to the tradition of German critical theory.[65] The question, Is Critique Secular?, therefore 'upends' this tradition, Brown explains, but it does so 'in a spirit that allows for the possibility of other formulations of critique, secularism, and their relation'.[66]

What is this 'spirit' that Brown considers as animating the upending of this tradition? What other 'formulations' of the relation of critique to secularism might be possible within this 'spirit'? To understand the working of this 'spirit', let me proceed to the essays that Brown thus introduces to the reader.

In his essay, Asad defines secularism, as he has elsewhere in his larger body of work, as a doctrine of governance, one that presently underpins the self-presentation of the 'West' as democratic and 'Islam' as repressive. His study of the historical convergence and divergence within Christian and Islamic practices, as well as those of the secular West, have led him to reassess the latter's civilizational claims and, not insignificant, of how 'Westerners' think of themselves. His essay in this volume, *Free Speech, Blasphemy, and Secular Criticism*, points out that the problem of 'blasphemy' with regard to the Danish cartoons is not really a question about the intolerance of Islam, for critics of Muslim opposition to the publication of the cartoons linked these Muslims to 'the "global menace" of the Islamists'.[67] Moreover, the controversy that ensued upon the publication of the cartoons questioned whether Muslims could be integrated into Europe, a question that reflects the anti-immigrant politics of Europe as well as the treatment of Muslims as a threat to national security. Asad thus redefines the context for the cartoon controversy as that of war, geopolitics and the exercise of Western power, not a clash of cultural traditions or of inadequate Muslim comprehension of the practice of 'critique'. The task at hand is therefore 'an attempt to think about the place of blasphemy – a religious concept – in secular liberal society', for he considers the issue of 'blasphemy' to be a 'crystallization of some moral and political problems in liberal Europe'.[68] Asad thus reframes 'blasphemy' in the cartoon controversy as arising from the conundrums of secular liberal Europe, not the 'difference', that is, 'intolerance', of Islam and Muslims.

'Free speech' and democracy were defined by Westerners as the key principles at stake in the Danish cartoon controversy, their claim being that the West respects these while Islam does not. Asad debunks this position by pointing to how the secularism of the West emerged from the historical remaking of Christianity. He also reminds the reader that the idea of 'free speech' was historically tied to class conflicts within Europe; that radical political opinions and traditions are routinely censored in the West; and that colonialism and imperialism have shaped the relations of this West with the rest of the world. In so doing, Asad observes that '[i]t is not easy, therefore, to understand exactly what is being claimed when "democracy" and "free speech" are said to be intrinsic to "European civilization", and inequality and repression are attributed to "Islamic civilization"'.[69]

Moreover, liberal ideals of 'individual dignity', Asad continues, are everywhere undermined by the substitutability of one citizen-voter for another, bureaucratized control, market manipulation and 'statistical modes of thinking and representation' that are crucial to capitalist relations.[70] Copyright laws, patents, trademarks are offered as examples that demonstrate how the 'free circulation of expressions and ideas' are curtailed, as is the case with property rights, indecency and child pornography laws, and prohibitions on trespassing.[71] Indeed slavery, the buying and selling of organs and the treatment of suicide all undercut the idea of the 'self-owning' human subject that undergirds liberal democracy. The range and complexity of these issues suggest that it is not the curtailment of free speech which may be of issue here, Asad argues, the resort to 'theological language' and the issue of 'transcendental power' may be more to the point.[72]

Although Asad briefly discusses Islamic approaches to free speech, faithfulness, manners and belief, the focus of his essay remains on the contradictory practices that have shaped 'secular critique' and 'democracy-freedom' within Euro-American capitalist societies. Despite these contradictions, 'free speech' and the 'critical attitude' – as signifiers of modernity – have come to be accepted as delineating what it means to be human. This is a standard against which Muslims invariably come up short as moderners consider Muslims 'not yet morally autonomous and politically disciplined'.[73] What is at stake here, Asad argues, is the humanity of Muslims.

Turning to the issue of secular criticism, Asad questions the idea that criticism is 'always' sceptical and secular by pointing to its relation to authority and power. Foucault too sought 'to equate critique with the Kantian notion of Enlightenment and thus to present critique as the singular characteristic of the modern West', he argues, where this becomes a 'critical attitude' that enables the subject to live 'heroically'.[74] That is, possessing a critical attitude is treated in the Western tradition as 'equivalent to living in Enlightenment'.[75] Against this view, Asad argues that a survey of the different historical usage and understandings of 'critique' – including within the theological tradition – demonstrates that 'Neither the concept nor the practice of critique has a simple history, and that genealogy has yet to be written', notwithstanding Foucault.[76] Critique and criticism are here shown to be deeply interconnected. Returning to the treatment of Muslims in Europe, Asad links the idea of critique as secular heroism to the violence visited upon Muslims. The essay is a powerful invitation to rethink the idea of secular criticism, its relation to 'freedom' and the 'self-owning' individual who stands at the heart of capitalism and liberalism.

Asad's essay is followed by Saba Mahmood's *Religious Reason and Secular Affect: An Incommensurable Divide?*, which likewise unpacks the religion/secular binary. Mahmood notes that these concepts are interlinked in modern social formations, wherein secular practices have redefined the meaning of religion. Situating the cartoon controversy within an Islamic hermeneutics of iconography, she argues this cannot be captured by the Christian concept of 'blasphemy'. Where the Protestant hermeneutic that infuses Western secular modernity considers religious icons to be representation – not embodiment – of the divine, Muslim piety seeks to emulate the actions of the Prophet Muhammad in a relation of 'cohabitation' and 'similitude'. By this, Mahmood means the Muslim reverence for the Prophet leads them to consider it highly virtuous to assimilate his behaviour into their self-making practices. As a result, the attack on the Prophet, as in the Danish cartoons, was experienced as an attack on the pious believing self. Given that Muslims emulate the Prophet's behaviour in order to follow his example as exemplary human being, the denigration of the Prophet is experienced by Muslims as an attack on themselves, on their relation to the transcendent. This different understanding of – and relationship to – icons was shared in ancient Greek as well as in non-Protestant Christian traditions, Mahmood points out as she rejects the oppositional binary that sets Islam apart.

Mahmood goes on to argue that in the West, the Protestant approach to iconography is considered mature – unlike that of Muslims – for its treatment of religious symbols as not literal embodiments but as standing in for the divine, and of their power as icons as invested in them by human action. The Protestant approach informs most liberal and other well-meaning responses to the cartoons, so that their different reaction to the cartoons was shaped by signifiers and concepts whose meaning is shared among these communities. Mahmood argues for a denaturalization of these shared references, stating that her intention is not to 'provide a more authoritative model for understanding Muslim anger' but to ask 'what constitutes moral injury in our secular world today?'[77]

The Muslim sensibility she is describing, Mahmood goes on to explain, was injured but cannot be assuaged by a juridical response, nor was it expressed in the demonstrations that followed the publication of the cartoons. Moreover, the cartoon controversy revealed how Muslims in Europe are racialized, she argues, but as public attention was focused on the religious dimension of the conflict, the issue of race could be denied as a relevant factor. Had race been the framework for addressing the injury done to Muslims, Mahmood argues, European hate laws would have come into effect against the publication of the cartoons. The denial of racism hence allowed the issues of blasphemy and Muslim intolerance to dominate the ensuing controversy.

Expressing misgivings about the attempts by some Muslims to seek redress from the law, Mahmood considers these to be invested in 'identity politics'. Moreover, this resort to the law 'privileges the state and the law as the ultimate adjudicator of religious difference',[78] whereas Mahmood defines the injury done to Muslims to be 'moral'. In any case, given that European jurisprudential assumptions and the status of Muslims as minorities set limits on the law as the avenue for appropriate redress, she argues what is required is 'a larger transformation of the cultural and ethical sensibilities of the Judeo-Christian population that undergird the cultural practices of secular-liberal law'.[79]

In their different ways, both Asad's and Mahmood's essays unsettle the binary formulation of the 'West' and 'Islam'; they also point to the congruence between 'modernity', 'secularity' and contemporary imperialist discourses. Asad's essay, for the main, focuses on the internal inconsistencies and incoherence of the dominant narrative of the West that Westerners tell about, and to, themselves. Highlighting the contradictions inherent in the Western Self's claim of autonomy, Asad points to the numerous coercions that run deep throughout the liberal–democratic order. Mahmood highlights the centrality of racism in the treatment of Muslims in Europe, but she remained hopeful that despite the virulent polemics that shape the present moment, the academy 'remains one of the few places where such tensions can still be explored'.[80] The extent to which this may (not) be the case is revealed in Butler's essay, *The Sensibility of Critique: Response to Asad and Mahmood*, to which I now turn.

Refusal to learn about the perspectives of Muslims on the impact of the cartoon controversy would be an 'anti-intellectualism that characterizes forms of moral dogmatism, whether secular or religious', Butler begins in her response to Asad's and Mahmood's essays.[81] These two essays, she states, 'petition us to approach the question of blasphemy and injury in another way'.[82] Her response thus positions Asad and Mahmood as supplicants: after all, it is supplicants who generally tend to 'petition' those who stand in a relation of power to them. Locating herself on the side of the 'us', those supposedly being petitioned, Butler stands firmly on the ground of authority, on the side of those who do not need to petition but to whom petitions are made.

Different frameworks are at work in the issues at hand, Butler then explains as she notes that comparative approaches are useful to advance a 'critical perspective'.[83] Asad and Mahmood draw attention to a different 'meaning' of the events, she acknowledges, but she questions them for 'suspending judgment' on the events they describe. It is not enough to provide a different framework for the phenomenon in question, she chides them, because to her, 'it seems most important to ask, what would judgment look like that took place not "within" one framework or another but which emerged at the very site of conflict, clash, divergence, overlapping'.[84] Cultural translation is certainly required here and she credits Asad and Mahmood for their contribution. But the descriptive is tied to the evaluative, and so 'In my view, the point is to achieve a complex and comparative understanding of various moral discourses, not only to see why we evaluate (and value) certain norms as we do, but also to evaluate those very modes of evaluation', she argues.[85]

Butler then points out that Asad does have 'normative commitments', although to her, he seems not to own up to them ('despite his very interesting and confounding protestations to the contrary').[86] In questioning Asad's 'normative commitments', the question Butler seems to want him to clarify is this: On which side does he stand? Certainly she is clear about her side, so to speak, as amply demonstrated in the many references to the community of the 'we' that peppers her essay.

Butler then proceeds to expand on her assessment of the two essays, making a somewhat surprising comment:

> These two anthropologists are trying to get us to expand our understanding of what was at stake, but I gather they are doing this because they think not just that we should all become more knowledgeable (and that broader knowledge of our world is a moral good) but also that the secular terms should not have the power to define the meaning or effect of religious concepts.[87]

Two interesting things are happening here in my view: first is the relegation of Asad and Mahmood to the disciplinary function of the anthropologist; and second is the reintroduction of the dichotomy between the secular and the religious that both

Asad's and Mahmood's essays dislodge. With regard to the first point, it should be noted that Brown's disciplinary affiliation goes unmentioned, as does Butler's, albeit both implicitly occupy in the text the *unstated* position – as the assessors of 'anthropological' work – of the critical theorist-philosopher. Later in the essay, Butler identifies herself as a member of a progressive – but vulnerable – sexual minority community. I will have more to say on this point below, for now, let me return to Butler's somewhat startling designation of Asad and Mahmood as 'anthropologists' who are questioning the power of the secular to define the religious.

Asad has demonstrated, here as elsewhere, his superb command of history, philosophy, political theory, postcolonial and Islamic studies, along with his expertise as an anthropologist; Mahmood likewise displays her expertise here in Islamic hermeneutics, immigration, race and the law, in addition to her ethnographic work within Muslim communities. Certainly both are 'professional' anthropologists, but what is one to make of this jarring reference to their (narrowly defined) disciplinary affiliation by Butler? What does *this* gesture accomplish *here*?

Let me offer a reading of this move, one that speaks to the organization and hierarchies within the disciplines and has been much discussed, including by Asad himself. In his earlier groundbreaking work, Asad interrogated the emergence of anthropology as a colonial discipline that was heavily reliant on the native informant to provide valuable information about her 'culture' to the European expert; such information was indispensable to the colonial administration of native societies. There has also been a long-standing debate about anthropology as the study of culture, a discipline with a focus on the descriptive, in contrast to philosophy, a discipline that studies the nature of knowledge itself. Can Butler's labelling of the two scholars in this manner be read as the critical theorist asserting her (philosopher's) authority over the (merely cultural) work of the anthropologist? Surely this move cannot have been meant to put Asad and Mahmood in the place of native informants in the now supposedly transformed, yet fraught interstices of post/colonial racial/anthropological disciplinary relations of power?

Butler then draws the reader's attention to Asad's earlier work on suicide bombers where he has asked – what are to her, 'shocking' – questions, such as: Why is horror felt in the West at death dealing by non-state actors, but not at death dealing by the state?; Why is killing in the name of religion deplorable to modern subjects, but not killing in the name of the nation-state? Such questions, Butler states, point to a '"tension" at the heart of the modern subject'.[88] But, she goes on to stress, 'we', that is, Westerners, 'would not feel the shock' of Asad's questions unless 'we do, in fact, oppose violence and the differential ways it is justified'.[89] Reading this Western Subject as inherently opposed to violence thus pre-empts the effects of the asking of the disturbing questions by 'them'; Asad's 'shocking' questions therefore do not so much have a transformative effect on this Western Subject as bring it to the realization of her own real inclination, which is already that of opposition to the violence being criticized. In other words, the authority, like the morality and the knowledge, of this Subject is unshakable, always already turning towards innocence ('we do, in fact, oppose violence', which I read as 'we' are, always already, not implicated in it).

A major criticism that emerges in Butler's response to Asad's essay is what she seems to believe is his inadequate comprehension of the distinction between 'critique' and 'criticism', that there is a judgemental element to (either and/or both) these concepts. Although critique 'seems like a Kantian definition', Butler argues, 'this distinction has been "rewrought" several times in the last few centuries with consequences for global politics within and outside the Euro-Atlantic'.[90] Asad has defined 'critique' as having a longer and complex history which defies the enlightenment claim that 'critique' is a unique feature of the modern-secular West. He has also defined 'critique' as Kantian even in its subsequent reformulations, including by Foucault. Butler's argument that this Kantian formulation has been 'rewrought' reinstates the Kantian formulation (without explicitly engaging the substance of Asad's critique), she also extends its relevance to the world 'outside the Euro-Atlantic', a move that undercuts Asad's rejection of the Western formulation of 'critique' as self-serving.

What is at stake here, I think, is a restabilization of the Enlightenment tradition, of its Eurocentric claim of the singularity of the West (Asad demolishes this claim even more forcefully in his very gracious – and restrained – response to Butler's reading of his essay). Butler, however, goes on to defend Foucault by arguing that he advanced the idea of 'critique' beyond the Kantian formulation of Enlightenment as progress. In her reading, Foucault redefined critique as an 'attitude' of the modern subject, rather than as tied to the 'regime of reason'.[91] Butler's defence of the exceptionalism of the Western politico-philosophical cannon (Kant, Williams, Adorno, Arendt, Benjamin, Foucault – via a detour through Spivak – 'inclusion' of the world 'outside' the Euro-Atlantic?) not only attempts to redeem this tradition as 'inclusive' but also to distance it from what she seems to acknowledge are other more lethal traditions of the West.

With regard to Mahmood's insightful discussion of iconography and Muslim piety centred on emulation of the Prophet, Butler's response is to treat this analysis as largely culturalist, and to dismiss Mahmood's view that Muslims should seek redress beyond the law as untenable. Mahmood questions the presumed neutrality of secular law by pointing to its commitment to protect the rights of majorities against the claims of minorities as loaded against the latter. The juridical status of Muslims as religious and racial minorities makes them vulnerable to the demands of the majority, Mahmood has argued. It is for this reason that she advocates instead a far-reaching transformative approach to European cultural sensibilities, rather than reliance on the law. Asking whether such change is feasible, Butler questions whether culture and ethics can ever be separated from the law. She then faults Mahmood for not specifying how the change she recommends is to take place, and for not identifying the institutional avenues to bring this about. Refraining from taking up Mahmood's concerns about the limitations of the law, its relation to race and treatment of minorities, Butler questions whether Mahmood's suggestion for 'comparative dialogue' and new ways of 'thinking' should not also be considered political strategies?

Summing up her reading of the two essays, Butler concludes, 'In reading both Mahmood and Asad, one sometimes wonders whether the problem is not the "reputation" of critique as negative, suspicious, taking religion as its object, differentiating itself from dogma, where dogma is understood to be the presumptive characteristic of religion but not of secularism.'[92] If this is indeed the case, then Butler clarifies the matter: 'let us be clear that critique is not the same as judgment.'[93] Asad mistakes critique for criticism/judgement, is Butler's argument, while Mahmood criticizes the taken-for-granted assumptions of secularism on a culturalist basis.

Having thus dealt with Asad's and Mahmood's contestation of the religion-secular binary as well as the Islam-West binary through her reiteration of both, and of her restabilization of the tradition of critique as free from the judgemental aspects of the modern-secular, Butler engages in a most interesting defence of 'freedom of speech' in her 'Coda on Dutch politics' (the dictionary definition of Coda is 'a concluding musical section that is formally different from the main structure; a concluding part of a literary or dramatic work; something that serves to round out, conclude, or summarize and usually has its own interest', she explains[94]). This defence of freedom of speech is made with regard to the rights of sexual minorities, it is instructive to unpack. As I show below, I read this as displacing the discussion on the violence done to Muslims in Europe by shifting the focus to the vulnerability of the queer subject, represented as Western, Modern, and certainly not Muslim.

This section in Butler's essay begins by pointing out that the issue of freedom of speech has divided the left, and that for her, it is particularly painful how gays and lesbians 'have found themselves in a quandary' over this as 'freedom of expression and opposition to censorship have clearly been cornerstones of the movement for decades'.[95] In light of this development, she explains that

> it is quite understandable that there might be a strong group of sexual progressives who maintain that freedom of expression is essential to the movement, that the lesbian, gay, bi, trans, queer, intersex movement is not possible without freedom of expression and without recourse to freedom itself as a guiding value and norm. Of course, to posit such a principle of freedom does not answer the questions of whether and how that norm is to be reconciled with other norms, nor does it tell us precisely what is meant by 'freedom'.[96]

In other words, 'freedom of speech' is to be defended, presumably (or especially?) against critiques such as those presented by Asad and Mahmood ('other norms'?). It is here that the political ramifications of the Eurocentric leanings of Butler's essay become clear.

'Freedom' is 'socially conditioned and socially shared', Butler notes, as she calls for a coming together of 'progressive' forces to defend freedom of speech.[97] 'The queer movement', she states, 'conceived transnationally, has also sought to fight homophobia, misogyny and racism, and it has operated as part of an alliance with struggles against discrimination of all kinds'.[98] Transnational queer politics centred on 'freedom of speech' are here defined as the overarching frame for struggles against 'homophobia, misogyny, racism', such that 'good' anti-racism struggles are made the purview of these queer politics, in spite of the mounting critiques by queers of colour of the whiteness that dominates queer politics and activism. Anti-Islamophobia struggles do not appear here, presumably the 'sexual progressives' do not include the queer Muslims contesting homophobia and anti-Islam antipathy. A whitewashing of queer politics is therefore implicitly advanced as Butler distinguishes a number of approaches within these politics, 'Of course there is also a now entrenched tension between identity-based and alliance-based sexual minority politics, and my affiliation with "queer" is meant to affirm the politics of alliance across difference.'[99] It is not immediately clear if the reference to 'identity-based' queer politics refers to the 'identity politics' that anti-racist activists are most often accused of bringing into queer, and other, social movements and thereby 'disrupting' them, or whether the reference is to the identities 'gay', 'lesbian', 'transgender', and so on. Whatever the exact reference, Butler declares herself above the fray of such 'identity' politics even as she underscores her own (identity-based) affiliation with (white) queer politics.

Engaging in a robust defence of 'freedom of speech' within the framework of liberal egalitarianism, Butler argues that

> Some crucial part of freedom of speech involves 'speaking out', which means, invariably, speaking out within specific scenes of address: speaking with and from and to one another. This implicit sociality in all address demands the recognition of freedom as a condition of social life, one that depends upon equality for its actualization. At stake is a rethinking of the processes of minoritization.[100]

Here, the asymmetrical power relations among different minorities are not interrogated, likewise there is no critique of the nation-state's inclusionary approach towards white gays, lesbians and queers in opposition to 'homophobic' Muslims in the global war. There is, however, an implicit 'silencing', for lack of a better word, of the Muslims in Euro-America who are identified by both Asad and Mahmood as denied the right to 'speak out'.

In contrast to these Muslims, Butler elevates the rights-oriented white queer subject as the model of 'good' resistance; here is the subject worthy of freedom, the one who 'speaks out' despite her 'vulnerability', that is, who lives heroically. That it is this very subject's 'vulnerability' that is being mobilized by the state to condemn Muslims as 'homophobic', and as such, enemies of civilized humanity escape her notice. Butler's defence of freedom of speech thus begs the question: What are the 'specific scenes of address' in which the demonized and disenfranchised Muslim can 'speak out'?

Indeed, Butler is not above Muslim baiting herself: 'When the acts of one member of a group or some small number of members of a group are taken to be the defining actions and beliefs of the group itself, then that is not only an unjustified generalization but also racism and it must be opposed.'[101] The reference here is to the dominant construction of 'bad' Muslims, the 'few' whose actions (homophobic? terrorist? misogynist?) are equated with those of all (good?) Muslims. Even as she considers the equation of the 'bad' (Muslim) with the 'good' one to be racism, Butler's generalized reference to 'a group' comes in a climate in which the very real

Islamophobic targeting is not of just of any 'group' in the battles over 'freedom of speech', but specifically of Muslim communities, and has reached crisis proportions.

To sum up, Asad and Mahmood are defined as cultural comparativists (anthropologists) by Butler, that is, as providing valuable 'cultural' data for the critical appraisal of the philosopher-theorist who evaluates (judges?) such difference. In the process, the reiteration of the dominant Eurocentric philosophico-political tradition (the exceptionalism of critique as a distinguishing feature of modern Westerners) advances the politics of the (white) sexual minority (the vulnerable subject) as *really* understanding the value of (liberal) 'freedom'. As such, this Subject is in a position to teach Muslims a thing or two about 'freedom', and how this is to be defended in the right, that is, progressive, manner.

Yet this advancement of the interpretive authority of the Western sexual subject remains unstable, as demonstrated by Asad's response to Butler's reading of his essay in which he points (again) to the cruel and subjugating function of the concept of 'critique', particularly its assertion of the exceptionalism of critique as the singular means to get to the 'truth'. Mahmood's response to Butler is also destabilizing, for she notes that Butler's reading of her work is a 'misreading', given that the language of 'culturalism' is 'alien' to her own vocabulary.

Contemporary challenges to Euro-American imperialism by scholars critical of the Western tradition are destabilizing the onto-epistemological claims upon which this tradition relies, in the academy as in other sites. My reading of the exchange in *Is Critique Secular?* illustrates how feminist responses to such critiques of the violence of the West enact the very relations of power these feminists ostensibly seek to 'upend'. Brown opens up this discussion, orients the reader on how to navigate Asad's and Mahmood's essays, all the while reordering the disorientation wrought by the two essays for those subjects invested in the Western tradition.

Although Brown's introduction to Asad's essay recognizes that he 'interrupts at every turn a set of discursive oppositions between Islam and secular Christianity on issues of freedom, speech, and blasphemy, and between a political Islam identified with aggression and death and a secular West identified with rationality and life',[102] she nevertheless sets up 'critique' as a property of the Western tradition and treats the 'West' as a self-contained entity. Brown's introduction itself demonstrates that Asad's work is not to result in a reassessment of the meaning and status of this 'West', particularly of its secular tradition of critique as the fount of all critical thought. Asad 'leaves us with a devastating open-ended reflection on the investments and affect of (Western) paranoia', Brown acknowledges,[103] but Butler, she reassures the reader, 'returns to the notion of critique itself, not only to reestablish its distinction from criticism, but also to formulate it as a rich, embodied practice – one that draws the subject and object of critique into a new relation while avoiding the conceits of objectivity'.[104] In other words, Butler will re-establish the distinction between critique and criticism that is treated as the mark of the superiority of Western critical thought in response to Asad's deconstruction of this.

In her response, Butler rescues the secularity of critique following Asad's 'devastating' *critique* of such equation of critique with the secular. The disorientations brought about by Asad's and Mahmood's essays are thus re-oriented towards

Western exceptionalism. In her coup de grace, white queer activism is forwarded by Butler as 'transnational' and *the* model of liberatory political activism. So much for the 'spirit' upending the critical tradition of the West.

The political projects of feminism have historically been articulated in interaction with different Western theoretical traditions. Despite the varied sets of issues, perspectives and visions to be found in the feminist texts discussed in this chapter, there is significant overlap in their foundational assumptions regarding the relation of gender-sexual politics to the global war, and regarding the West, Islam and Muslims. I have drawn attention to these convergences, namely, the universalization of the West and its traditions in a gendered-sexual register; the redemption and elevation of gendered whiteness in relation to the figure of the Muslim; and the advancement of the Western tradition by positing the gendered-sexual white subject as embodiment of its highest values. Rather than interrogate feminism's relationship to the colonizing tendencies of the West in the global war at the level of epistemology, politics and subjectivity, the texts I have discussed here re-enact the West's imperialist perspectives and colonizing practices.

The key assumptions and representational strategies deployed by these feminist texts, particularly with regard to Islam and Muslims, are compatible with the politics and practices of the neoconservative and other state elites in the global war. One finds in these texts little engagement with the inequalities between the West and the Muslim world; the coloniality that shapes the actual material and discursive conditions in which Muslims are constituted as the enemy; or the political perspective and demands of Islamist – including Muslim women's – movements that are confronting the US-led domination of the global economy. Another important strategy I have discussed is the feminist equation of the reach and power of the US state (with its immense military might) with that of al-Qaeda, the Taliban, Saddam Hussein and in the case of Chesler and Butler, Palestinian suicide bombers. This equation, perhaps more than any other, reveals the paranoid fantasies and destabilized subjectivity of the white feminists who have historically imaged themselves to be imperilled by the very populations in whose exploitation they partake as they claim sovereign status for themselves within the power relations that organize the West.

Refusing to engage the struggles of the Muslim/Islamic 'enemy' as *political* makes it all the easier for the figure of the Muslim to be phantasized as the *existential* enemy of Woman, or the queer Subject. In other words, the Enemy/Other remains mythic, the looming face of death and destruction in this feminist imaginary.

The range of responses to the expanding global war by these white feminists demonstrate that although they are divided in their political responses to different aspects of the global war, their foundational assumptions do not differ much. More to the point, their reiteration of the idea of the West in turn Westernizes these feminists, allowing them access to the power that extends their perspectives of the desirable future over other women and men, including Muslims. In this process Western feminists also revitalize the idea of the West by their treatment of the global as *primarily* gendered terrain in which Western superiority is symbolized by Woman and 'Islam' is the mark of violence, homophobia and misogyny.

Chapter 5

REMAKING THE WEST

SOVEREIGNTY, WHITENESS AND THE JUDEO-CHRISTIAN

Even with the passage of time, President Bush's address in the aftermath of the 9/11 attacks is notable for its casting of the global war in starkly biblical terms:

> Today our Nation saw evil, the very worst of human nature. . . . We will make no distinction between the terrorists who committed these acts and those who harbour them.
>
> Tonight I ask for your prayers for all those who grieve. . . . I pray they will be comforted by a power greater than any of us, spoken through the ages in Psalm 23: 'Even though I walk through the valley of the shadow of death, I fear no evil, for You are with me.'. . . we go forward to defend freedom and all that is good and just in our world. . . . God bless America.[1]

This fixing of the 'terrorist' as 'the very worst of human nature' and exaltation of the US nation as Christian, along with the conflation of 'freedom' with the Christian injunction to fight 'evil', demonstrated how the religio-racial logic of power infused the ideological frame of the war on terror. As such, imperial sovereignty was seamlessly sutured to the subjectivity of nationals-as-Christians: the Christian concept of redemption was translated into the modern discourse of freedom and justice. In this theological-political imaginary, a divinely ordained Christian mission is imbricated with the secular-colonial mission that was the White Man's burden in the nineteenth century, back now with a vengeance in the twenty-first. Western nation-states, of course, have a long history of defining their ambitions in 'apocalyptic', 'expansive' and 'redemptive' terminology.[2] In the global war, these ambitions were being redefined in relation to the Muslims who were challenging the Western domination of the global order. The extent of the Islamophobia that was encoded in the apocalyptic language of terrorism was soon made visible equally starkly in the torture revelations, which demonstrated exactly the manner in which the 'divinely ordained' mission was unfolding on the ground. The exposure of the sexual violence was part of the ensemble of factors that led to the election of President Obama, whose Administration toned down some of the apocalyptic language used by the Bush Administration. Yet neither the religious nor the racial politics of the war were dislodged during the Obama Presidency.

Indeed, President Obama's comments on the ongoing resistance to US violence demonstrated just how intertwined race and religion were in his Administration's foreign policy as he attacked the critique of US power as

> a profoundly distorted view of this country – a view that sees white racism as endemic, and that elevates what is wrong with America above all that we know is right with America; a view that sees the conflicts in the Middle East as primarily rooted in the actions of stalwart allies like Israel, instead of emanating from the perverse and hateful ideologies of radical Islam.[3]

These comments do not of course capture the complexities and contradictions in the Obama Administration's reworking of the war on terror, but the naming of 'radical' Islam as the source of 'hateful ideologies' and Israel as a 'stalwart ally' extended the religio-racial enmities and alliances that were reconsolidated by the Bush Administration. The white supremacist Trump Administration that followed the Obama presidency did not mince words in outlining its position on the global war, 'We are stopping cold the attacks on Judeo-Christian values' was the blunt pronouncement from Trump.[4]

Well into the twentieth century, the dominant construction of the West was that of a Christian, Aryan, white *and* secular modern entity, while its oppositional categories, 'Semite' and 'Oriental' encapsulated both Muslims and Jews. The historical entanglement of race and religion in these identifications and affiliations is discussed in the preceding chapters, here I study their reiteration in the formation 'Judeo-Christian' that is now reshaping the politics of Western nation-states, the formation of its sovereignty and subjects, as well as the international order.

In his study of the history of European anti-Semitism, Sander Gilman found that Jews were often defined as 'Black' and sometimes even conflated with Muslims. So, for example, in 'the German racist tractates of the late 19th century', the 'overlapping of images of Otherness – the Moor, the Jew, the Gypsy' informed dominant constructions of 'good' and 'bad'; the image of the Black Jew led to the denigration of Jews as a hybrid or 'mongrel' race, or 'white Negroes', seen as the 'least pure race'.[5] Gilman traced this association of Jews and Blackness back to the early Christian tradition where, he explains, 'Medieval iconography always juxtaposed the black image of the synagogue, of the Old Law, with the white of the church. The association is an artefact of the Christian perception of the Jews which has been simply incorporated into the rhetoric of race'.[6] This view is echoed in Carter's study of the transformation of Christianity into a 'white' supremacist religion through the severance of its roots within the Jewish tradition. The construction of the whiteness of the Church, and of divinity itself, entailed the 'abstraction' of the figure of Christ from the Jewish body of Jesus, Carter argues, such that 'Jewish flesh' itself underwent a 'religious conversion'. These ruptures led to the 'Occidentalization' of Christ in tandem with the construction of Jews as a 'race' apart from Christians, who came to identify themselves as 'European'. The tying of Judaism to the racially degraded zone that was the 'East' cemented the extrication of Christianity from Judaism over the centuries. Carter argues that the first move led to Christians identifying themselves as European through a 'racial imagination', and with the second move, this 'racial imagination became a white supremacist one'.[7] Hence, argues Carter, race and white supremacy have long been co-constitutive within the Christian tradition, well before the advent of modernity. This 'inner architecture' of race was integrated into the Enlightenment tradition, with the consequence that whiteness 'came to function as a substitute for the Christian doctrine of creation, making "modernity's racial imagination [is] religious in nature"'.[8] The 'Christian thought forms' that were to become the 'cultural reflex' of the Western tradition thus helped fashion modernity.[9]

These racial and religious transformations have been dealt with in some detail earlier in this book, particularly Chapter 3; the point I want to highlight here is that the interpellation of the Western Subject in the Christo-racial discourse of the global war did not consider Jews to be *constitutionally* alien, that is, in racial, theological, cultural terms. Or indeed, even political terms. Instead, the idea of the civilizational clash between Islam and the West located Jews, Judaism and Zionism firmly within the collective ambit of the Western community of the 'us', not 'them'. This is not to say that anti-Jewish prejudice or anti-Semitic violence against Jews has been eradicated in Western nation-states during this juncture, but to note that the earlier political and institutional sanction of such hatred of Jewish communities had been greatly mitigated, even if not entirely uprooted. Consequently, along with Christianity and secularism, Judaism was taken to be commensurable with the reformation of the West in the global war, the integrating term 'Judeo-Christian' redefined the idea of the West on the basis of the now shared and compatible cultural and philosophical heritage and politico-cultural values between the two sides of its hyphenated identity. This then is the 'West' to be 'defended' in the global war.

What do these new filiations – 'Christian' with 'Judeo' – reveal about the actual conditions that led to this momentous shift in the religio-racial politics of the West? What does the change reveal about the working of the religio-racial logics that have historically shaped Western sovereignty and subject/ivity? Where, why and how did this transformation occur? These questions are taken up in this final chapter of the book.

Sander Gilman traces the term 'Judeo-Christian' to the late nineteenth century, when he finds it was used to refer to the European Jews who were converting to Christianity. The earlier attempts by the Church to convert Jews during the late eighteenth century had led to this development. However, such conversion also gave rise to a phenomenon that Gilman termed 'Jewish self-hatred', by which he meant that this conversion came with an internalization of the negative anti-Jewish European stereotypes among the newly converted Christians. This situation led many of the converts to attempt to distance themselves from such negativity, which they did by projecting the anti-Semitic stereotypes onto 'Eastern' Jews and those who spoke Yiddish. Although the term 'Judeo-Christian', in this context, spoke specifically to the process of assimilation of European Jews into Christianity, Gilman argues, the term also implicitly spoke of the suspicions Christians continued to harbour about the loyalties of these Jewish converts.

Masuzawa's study of 'world religions', however, finds that it was not primarily Jewish converts who were referenced by the term in the early twentieth century.

Rather, by this period, the term reflected the changes that were then underway in the representation of the Christian self. The idea of the West as shaped by the 'Judeo-Christian' tradition 'eclipsed' the idea of Europe as Christian during the 1930s, as the now 'hyphenated identity of the West' represented in the term became popular within the United States.[10] Prior to this redefinition, Masuzawa explains, the category 'Semitic' – the opposite of 'Aryan' – was used widely in the Western classification of Judaism not only as 'religion' but also as language (Hebrew), race (Semitic) and nation (Jewish); this was also the case with Islam, which then referenced language (Arabic), race (Semitic) and nation (Arab).[11]

As discussed in Chapter 2, the discoveries in the new sciences of the common grammatical and inflectional structures in the European and Indic languages during the mid-nineteenth century led to their reclassification as Indo-Aryan. The category 'Aryan' now distinguished Europe/ans from the 'Semitic' on the basis of language, the latter, still including Jews and Muslims, was considered linguistically inferior and racially/nationally incompatible with the former.[12] The development of the field of 'world religions' took place on the basis of such 'discoveries', the new classificatory system's conflation of religion with race, nation, language and culture now situated them under the category 'religion' in a global hierarchy. In this systemitization, Christianity remained elevated at the top of the hierarchy and Islam continued to be singled out as 'narrow, rigid, and stunted, and its essential attributes were said to be defined by the national, racial and ethnic character of the Arabs, the most bellicose and adversarial of the Semites'.[13] Indeed, whether Islam should even be considered a 'world religion' was hotly debated, given its 'rigidity' and 'particularism' in the estimation of the European scholars.

Judaism however, although initially derided as 'rigid' and 'stunted' like Islam, was soon met with a very different view. By the early twentieth century, this was identified as the 'ancient faith of the Hebrews' and Judaism became 'co-opted into a dominant universalist scheme of Christianity, particularly of Protestant Christianity, which appropriated the austere Hebraism of the prophetic tradition for itself, in part against Catholicism, but also against various forms of secularism then on the rise'.[14] The reasons for this redemption of Hebraism-Judaism as a heritage of the West – along with Hellenic secularity – included the rise of fascism in Europe and the US decision to become involved in the war against Nazi Germany, as well as the demographic shifts in the United States that were being brought about with increased Asian migration, argues Masuzawa.

Other scholars have also linked the term's increasing popularity during the twentieth century to the growing political opposition within the United States to the rise of fascism in Europe.[15] According to Silk, 'fascist fellow-travellers and anti-Semites had appropriated "Christian" as an identifying mark.... "Judeo-Christian" thus became a catchword for the other side' and was associated in Protestant literature with 'the democratic ideal which is implicit in the Judeo-Christian tradition'.[16] In a reflection of this development, the French Catholic philosopher, Jacques Maritian, made the argument that anti-Semites were also attacking Christ and Christianity in their attacks on the Jews. Maritian, whose wife was of Russian-Jewish origin, wrote an essay while in the United States (1942) praising '"la tradition judeo-chretienne" as a source of the West's enduring values'.[17] Such 'affirmation of a shared religious basis for Western values' had become popular among US liberal academic and intellectual circles by the 1940s.[18] Despite the opposition of some intellectuals, including Jewish, to the term's conflation of religious and political values, in the context of the Holocaust 'Judeo-Christian' became indispensable to the demarcation of 'inclusive' democracies from 'exclusive' fascisms; for '[a]fter the revelations of the Nazi death camps, a phrase like "our Christian civilization" seemed ominously exclusive; greater comprehensiveness was needed for proclaiming the spirituality of the American way', argues Silk.[19]

The term 'Judeo-Christian' also served the handy purpose of distinguishing the Allied powers from the Soviet Union, conferring on the former lofty motivations of superior spiritual and moral values in contrast to the latter's ambitions defined as driven by a 'godless' materialism. By the 1970s however, the inclusionary sentiment towards Jewish communities served yet another useful purpose: 'America experienced a new enthusiasm for ethnic particularism; Jews, accepted as never before in American society, were expected to cultivate some distinctiveness.'[20] Yet Judeo-Christian, a designation that had emerged in 'the search for consensus', was also seen by some as an 'affront to Jewry', according to Silk.[21]

The political rise of the US Christian Right during the 1990s, and the development of Christian-Zionism, paved the way for yet another resurgence in the use of the term. A decade later, and with a global war in rapid escalation, Peter Berger identified this term as attesting to the growing tendency towards tolerance within the United States. Pointing to the Second World War as an 'important turning point in the unfolding drama of American pluralism', Berger noted that

> The concept 'Judeo-Christian' has been immensely useful in the integration of Jews as an ethnic group and Judaism as a religion in America. I think it is fair to say that in no other country in modern history have Jews become as much part of the taken-for-granted *landscape* of the society as in America. Jews are not only accepted; they are esteemed.[22]

The various developments discussed above which contributed to the remaking of Western identity and culture as Judeo-Christian point to the range of factors involved, and the different interests served, by the shift. However, the shift was shaped also by a larger configuration of forces, movements and struggles within the global order that were bringing about a far deeper level of change in which these 'internal' religio-ethnic politics of Euro-America were embroiled. The (partial) genealogy referenced above speaks mainly of the 'internal' factors at work within the West: what this does not adequately address (with the exception of Masuzawa's work) are the colonial dimensions of this change, in which Islam and Muslims featured quite centrally.

The war on terror, as I demonstrate here, reveals the depth of the integration of Jewish communities into the present formation of the West. The political charge of anti-Semitism now associated with the term 'Judeo-Christian' goes hand in hand with Islamophobia and has global ramifications that go well beyond the question of Jewish-Christian relations within Euro-America. These relations have been cemented to an unprecedented degree in the global war, the term 'Judeo-Christian' now signals, among other things, an intractable alliance of Euro-America with Israel in their collective battle against what both define as the forces of 'evil', that is, the Palestinian as well as the resurgent anti-colonial Islamist movements. Consequently, Islam has an internal and structuring role in the formation of *this* West, for this new self-making pivots on the construction of Islam as the existential 'enemy' of both Judaism and Christianity, and of their secular-modernity. This reiteration of the West was certainly decades in the making, as the scholarship cited above illustrates. So too, however, was the structuring role of Islam and the figure of the Muslim, albeit this is too often elided in this scholarship. The point here is that the incorporation of the figure of the Jew – racially and religiously, politically as well as culturally, civilizationally as well as existentially – into the West simultaneously reconstructs the figure of the Muslim as the enemy of the Jews, as has been the case during these very same decades that preceded the global war.

A number of critical scholars have sought to rethink the West's relations with Jews and Muslims by, for example, asking whether 'Judeo-Christian' or 'the Abrahamic' are more appropriate in dealing with the religious traditions and (dis) affiliations that have shaped the West. The Abrahamic allows for a more inclusive and pluralist conception of the West, is the view of some of them. Be that as it may, the issue I focus on in the rest of the chapter is how a recasting of Islam and the figure of the Muslim grounds the formulation of the 'Judeo-Christian'. A seminal moment in this remaking is the Nazi camp, for the religio-racial politics of the Holocaust produced there a figure – that of the *Muselmann* – which reflects the devastating effects of Europe's religio-racial politics for European Jews as well as their devastating consequences that soon followed for Palestinians with the post-Holocaust founding of the state of Israel.

This figure of the Muselmann, described as a symbol of death in the camp, terrified the camp's Jewish inmates. The figure, as Agamben and other scholars have argued, is to be found in the Holocaust literature as a spectre that haunted the camps' survivors for the rest of their lives. Agamben names this the 'limit figure', the one who demonstrates the limits of ethics after Auschwitz. The Germans used the term 'Muselmann' to refer to Muslims, a term also used by Jews in the camps. Asking why it would be the case that it was *this* term that was used to refer to the Jews who died in the camps, a question not taken up by Agamben, I read his study of the Muselmann against the grain by situating it in the context of the Orientalism as well as the racial politics of whiteness that structured the idea of Europe during that period.

My reading demonstrates how, among other things, the figure of the *Muselmann* functions to fracture the category 'Semite/Oriental' in the Nazi camp. My argument here is that the deadly religio-racial politics of the camp resulted in the splitting of the figure of the Jew – that is, the one who perished in the camp as *Muselmann* – from the one who survived the camp as European to become integrated into the whiteness of the West. Yet this splitting also has its 'external' aspects, for it simultaneously split the category 'Oriental/Semite' such that the burden of this designation would henceforth be borne by the figure of the Muslim as a quintessential symbol of decay and death.

The post-Nazi integration of Euro-American Jews into whiteness was related to, and accompanied by, the founding of the settler society of Israel and its colonization of Palestine. The strategic location of Israel in the heart of the Middle East, and its establishment at a moment when most of the colonized world was in the throes of revolutionary change, rendered the former uniquely situated to destabilize the region and fracture the possibility of radical transformation of the Muslim world. These two factors, the production of the *Muselmann* as the figure of death in the camp, and the establishment of Israel to advance Western colonialism in a 'post-independence' Third World, set into motion the transformation of the religio-racial politics of the West that would produce the present formation of the 'Judeo-Christian'.

Europe's enmities, Europe's friends

Pointing to the absence of a history of the 'enemy' in the Western philosophical tradition, Gil Anidjar makes a distinction between the Other and the Enemy in his discussion of Europe's relations with the Jew and the Arab.[23] Both Jew and Arab have been constituted as 'enemy' in Europe's theologio-political tradition, such that this relation is indispensable to the very making of Europe, he argues. However, according to Anidjar, these 'enemies' are of a different sort: the constitution of the Jew as enemy is grounded in religion and that of the Arab in politics.[24] Drawing on Mamdani's thesis that an enemy has to be constituted politically *before* it can be marked for elimination, Anidjar shows how the Jew is produced as the 'enemy of God'[25] and the Arab the enemy 'par excellence' of a political Europe.[26]

Anidjar's reading of the construction of the theological enemy draws on Levinas, who argued that 'the state of war suspends morality; it divests eternal institutions and obligations of their eternity and rescinds ad interim the unconditional imperative,' such that war informs 'the mind's openness upon the true'.[27] Expanding on this idea that 'foreseeing the art of war and winning it by every means' constitutes 'politics,' which depends upon 'the very exercise of reason,' that is, philosophy, Anidjar explains that war 'is what philosophy – the exercise of reason – thinks', such that 'politics is philosophy, and its thinking is a thinking of war, and a thinking at war'.[28] Here, an integral link is established between *politics* and *philosophy*, such that both are constituted in and through war in the making of Europe.

Paul's Letter to the Romans (55–57CE – the New Testament), which advocates Christian salvation through the gospel of Jesus Christ, was crucial to the construction of the Jew as an enemy, Anidjar goes on. He points out that this letter was considered 'a political declaration of war' by Jacob Taubes, scholar of religion, philosophy and Judaism. A contradictory view of Jews is identified at work here, for they are 'God's and God's Beloved' people (ancient Israel) and also 'God's enemies'[29] in their rejection of Christ as Messiah. Paul's letter thus produces 'the Jew' as the theological enemy, 'at once under the law and excluded from it'.[30]

Tracing this figuration of Jews through the writings of St. Augustine and Thomas Aquinas, Anidjar argues that although the Jew and the Arab sometimes overlapped as the 'enemy' in this line of Christian thought, Jews nevertheless remained the 'internal' enemy of Christianity.

The Arab, however, is constituted as the 'political' enemy in this making of Europe. Following the idea of the 'political' as defined by war as well as the presence of an enemy, Anidjar turns to Derrida's reading of Carl Schmitt's distinction between the 'political' and the 'theological' in the teachings of the gospels, particularly the passage that is '"at the source of Western theology"' with the injunction, "love your enemies"'. Although Schmitt is known for identifying the continuity between theology and politics, Anidjar shows how the distinction between them breaks down in Schmitt's own discussion when he turns to Islam as an example of the 'political' enemy in 'the thousand-year struggle between Christians and Moslems'.[31] Schmitt's argument is that the theological injunction 'Love your enemies' cannot be read as political for it identifies no 'political enemy' as such, and that it is the entry of Islam as the 'enemy' that produced the 'political'. Yet in Derrida's view, Schmitt's own distinction of the 'political' is problematized in this use of the example of Islam – an enemy that is simultaneously both 'political' and 'non-political'. Derrida therefore took Schmitt's reading of the injunction to mean that 'Christ's teachings would thus be moral or psychological, even metaphysical, but not political'.[32] In Schmitt's view, the political emerges in the struggle with the enemy, which he identifies in Christo-Europe's war with Islam ('determinate enemy') as *the* ('determinate') war through which Europe itself 'becomes' political.[33] It is in becoming 'an organized power in this world' that a religious community (Christian) becomes a political one (Europe), argued Schmitt, 'Its holy wars and crusades are actions which presuppose an enemy decision.'[34]

Derrida's *Politics of Friendship*, according to Anidjar, interprets Schmitt's distinction between theology and politics to mean that, 'without an enemy, Europe would be a subject that would lose its being-political', that Europe is a subject that 'would purely and simply depoliticize itself' in the absence of war.[35] Concurring with Derrida's reading, Anidjar goes on to explain that 'without this enemy par excellence that is Islam, Europe, Christian Europe would not or would no longer exist'.[36] In Schmitt's view then, 'Europe, and with it, the political, "nothing more and nothing less than the political as such . . . would no longer exist without the figure of the enemy"', and as Anidjar puts it, '*this* figure of the enemy . . . is Islam. If such is indeed the case, it would demonstrate, were it still needed, that Islam is not only at the source of "our history", but also that it is one of the "conditions" of the history that I am trying to read', that is, the history of the enemy.[37] These discussions, in my view, elide the 'religious' as well as the 'political', in for example, taking 'Western theology' as 'religious' in the injunction, 'Love your enemies'. Such an approach depoliticizes the construction of the 'Western', for there can be no "Western theology" before the formation of the West, which, in this view, comes into being through war with Islam. Likewise, the existence of the 'religious community' – that becomes political through war – is taken for granted, whereas this 'religious community' that is and is not Europe is itself produced through the 'holy war', that is, through the Christianization of the heterogeneous 'pagan' communities that constituted themselves as Christian in this 'holy war'.

Moreover, one finds no actual engagement with Islam here, nor with the Muslim, the embodiment of the 'political enemy' par excellence that produces this 'Europe'. This enemy that is the Muslim is identified in Anidjar's reading not by their concrete and historical relation to Islam, but following European convention, is defined, for the main, as 'Arab'.

Given that Anidjar's objective is to trace the relations of enmity that produce Europe, when he looks at the relations between the Jew and the Arab, he does so in this context. He therefore explains (by way of Guenoun) that while the Jew becomes the 'theological' enemy, 'Europe gives itself a face, a *figure*, by way of Islam', that 'Europe fabricates for itself a site where it will be able to protect itself from itself, protect itself from what it projects and imagines as and its end . . . for Europe, Europe and Islam are intimately involved in a "specular formation of mirror images" that is "the primordial identitarian rapport, constitutive of Europeanness"'.[38] In this 'primordial . . . rapport', which is 'an originary structure of Europe', Islam becomes exteriorized[39] for it is the site not only for the constitution of Europe-as-Christian, but also the site of Europe's constitution of itself as political entity. In other words, Europe's political identity is indelibly marked in a curious relation of exteriority and interiority with Islam. Why then the Jew, the Arab, and not the Jew, the Muslim? Why a 'primordial identitarian rapport'?

Let me highlight here the point that the separations being made here between the theological and the political, between religion and philosophy, between enemy and friend that are being tracked by Anidjar are, of course, those made by Christian-Europe. These are alien to the Islam that is supposedly the object of their concern.[40] This 'Islam' of the Christo-European imaginary is spectral and it haunts the West from its very inception as such.

Anidjar follows the link between the Jew and Arab as figures of absolute subjection – the Jew to the unchanging dictates of religious law (theology), the Arab to the fanatic dictates of terror and violence (politics) – in the development of the tradition of the West (via Kant, Montesquieu, Hegel, Freud, etc.); he argues that the Jew and the Arab are here defined as both the same and also not the same. Islam's construction as military and political denies its identity as 'religion', for 'as a condition of the political', Islam is 'not political through and through', such that the Arab becomes 'a figure of the beyond, beyond the political'.[41] Derrida's reading of Schmitt likewise signals that this Islam is the 'beyond',

> because . . . the war with Islam is 'more than a political war.' It is 'a struggle with the political at stake, a struggle for politics' where the political itself is therefore put under question from a certain outside. As paradoxical as it seems, Islam remains the exemplary political enemy, but it is also an enemy that 'would no longer even be a political enemy but an enemy of *the* political'. The site of Islam – its interiority and exteriority vis-à-vis Europe and vis-à-vis 'the political' – is therefore troubled and unsettled insofar as this site is both political and non-political.[42]

This Islam becomes a totalizing force that allows no room for the category of politics, it is both the condition of politics and the negation of politics. If first religion, and then politics, makes the Christian-European human in the theological and then the secular paradigm, what is this zone of the 'beyond' that is inhabited by Islam, by the Muslim? Beyond the political? Beyond the human?

Yet if Islam is indeed 'intimately involved in a "specular formation of mirror images"', why does it remain 'outside' Derrida's, not to mention Anidjar's 'rewriting' of Europe from the 'point of view of the enemy'? If war *with* Islam is *the* beginning of *politics*, as Anidjar reads Schmitt and Derrida to say, if Islam is embedded in the very structures by which Europe *thinks* itself, why then not engage this 'enemy' who embodies this tradition by her proper name, the one she claims for herself, Muslim? Why the ongoing collapse of the 'Moslem', the enemy named by Schmitt, into the racializing category 'Arab'? From which point of view, and of which enemy, is this 'rewriting' of Europe to be understood? What possibilities do such erasures and collapsings open up, what possibilities do they render impossible? I read – perhaps too hastily – the collapsing of the 'Moslem', as Schmitt defines *this* enemy, into the category 'Arab' as reluctance to engage with Islam, with this enemy, *except* as abstraction, except as racial abstraction.

When asked in an interview about the use of the categories Jew (religious) and Arab (ethnic), not the Muslim (religious) in this study of the Enemy, Anidjar explains that he wanted to 'submit' to the 'force of these names'. He explains that, 'In the media, in Israeli political discourse, in discussions about institutions, on Israeli ID cards, everywhere practically, "Jew" and "Arab" are the terms that persist.'[43] He goes on to note a 'confusion', a 'slippage', in the 'the broad range of terms' used in 'Western languages' to refer to the Muslim, and that these terms do not have a 'referent' as Europe uses them in a 'self-referential manner' to 'speak to itself'. The obvious question arises: why re-inscribe such 'self-referentiality', for the violence that is done to the Muslim in/by the names Europe has given her, including the most recent, 'radical terrorist', is not inconsequential. Yet another series of points, banal perhaps, are in order here: the Muslim insists in her self-naming that Islam is central to her world; it is this insistence that constructs her as an 'enemy' in contemporary Western discourses. The centring of Israeli political discourse to name this Muslim an Arab can perhaps be (mis)read as less Anidjar's 'submission' to the 'force' of the latter name than a clearly unintended reiteration of the subjugation of the Muslim to this name. Anidjar is, of course, highly mindful of the racial/ethnic politics of Europe, including the politics of naming, yet the link between the religio-racial and coloniality, although referenced a number of times, remains to be substantively integrated into his analysis. As does an interrogation of the Israeli practice of privileging 'religion' in the designation 'Jew' and 'race' in the designation 'Arab'.

Anidjar's reading of the 'enemy' can be complicated further on two more counts: first, the 'pre-European' Christian construction of Islam and its configuration of the Muslim in theological (evil, satanic) as well as *racial* (degenerate) terms persist in the contemporary discourses of enmity of Israel as well as Euro-America; second, this particular configuration of *this* enemy is constitutive of a West that is now widely identified as Judeo-Christian and embraces the figure of the Jew as Self-same, not enemy.

War *with* Islam as the beginning of *politics* is embedded in the very structures by which Europe *thinks* itself, Anidjar emphasizes via his readings of Derrida, Schmitt and so forth. War *with* Palestine/Islam as the beginning of *politics* is likewise embedded in the very structures by which Zionism/Israel thinks *itself*. Anidjar's placing of the figure of the Jew in the same analytic frame as that of the Arab to emphasize their construction-in-common as 'enemies' of Europe is well taken. Yet that historical 'construction-in-common' is shattered by the 'Judeo-Christian', by this formation's construction-in-common of the figure of the Jew with that of the Christian, in political as well as theological terms.

Let me follow here Anidjar's unpacking of the 'passage' between 'the Jew, the Arab' in his use of the example of Derrida. Anidjar begins with the question, 'What, indeed, could be more important, more urgent, than the Jew, the Arab' today?[44] Between 'the Jew, the Arab' is the Abrahamic, according to Derrida, albeit 'between' them is also to be found the Christian. But Anidjar identifies yet another question that is also important here, 'is "the Jew, the Arab" an empirical or a transcendental question'?, that is, is this 'philosophical, rhetorical, political, religious, or autobiographical', he asks, for 'it can no longer be simply empirical, identitarian, or historicist'.[45] Making the extraordinary claim, 'the Abrahamic is also Derrida's name', Anidjar takes up the various names of Derrida, including his self-naming, his identity, as it were.[46] The naming of Derrida is no easy task (he will assert and not assert his name/s or even the semblance of an 'I' for these names), nor are the names themselves stable (he will also claim distance, affinity, identification, disidentification with/through these names), Anidjar explains. Yet Anidjar persists in following 'the Arab, the Jew', indeed 'the Abrahamic', as conceptualized by, and in the figure of, Derrida.

Derrida's self and externally ascribed names and identities include 'uprooted African . . . born in Algiers';[47] 'sort of African';[48] 'Judeo-Algerian';[49] 'Egyptian' (by way of 'North African');[50] 'the trace of so-called identities (African, Algerian, Arab Jew, Hispano-Moor . . . Franco-Maghrebin, . . . animal)';[51] as well as the 'shadow/specter' of 'a little black and very Arab Jew' as enigmatic site of his "life", his "religion", and of the Abrahamic'.[52] 'The Jew, the Arab' – when the comma is replaced with hyphen – has an 'explosive dimension', Anidjar explains. With the hyphen, the term 'surrounds itself with bombs', and Derrida states that the hyphen's 'silence' 'does not pacify or appease anything, not a single torment, not a single torture . . . is never enough to conceal protests, cries of anger or suffering, the noise of weapons and bombs'.[53] Derrida, Anidjar argues, is here 'preoccupied with ethical concerns . . . an "ethics of memory" . . .' as well as with 'exposing' 'a reading field that is a minefield' ('incineration, suffering').[54] The Abrahamic 'doubles' Derrida's identity, the names 'the Jew, the Arab', as well as Derrida's 'I', to 'explode over this minefield . . . resists all localization. . . . The name occurs rather in the proximity of an explosion that maintains its unreadability. It is an event that, in troubling simultaneity, exposes and explodes the name of Derrida, the names of the Abrahamic, while founding them'.[55] Anidjar points to the complexity of 'identity' in his richly layered reading of Derrida's deconstruction of even the possibility of such a thing; yet the name 'Derrida', even as this is being 'exploded' by the 'Abrahamic', is also defined as 'founding' this 'Abrahamic'.

Identity is without doubt an immensely complex, not to mention, messy thing. Yet a thing it is, and contend with it one must.

Let me turn to Derrida's conversation with Mustapha Cherif, described by Borradori as 'one of the only moderate Islamic voices speaking up today', on the possibilities of 'reconciling' the divide, West and Islam to follow this question of identity and affiliations.⁵⁶ Here too, Derrida draws on his multifaceted identity, identifications, affiliations and relationalities (proximity and distance, fraternity, even rejection). These avowals and disavowals complicate Anidjar's reading of 'Derrida'; they do, however, provide a valuable insight into the question I have raised earlier: What does the collapsing of the Muslim into the Arab enable? I amend the question here to ask: What does the collapsing of the Muslim *and* the Jew into the name Arab enable *here*?

In his conversation with Mustapha Cherif, Derrida discusses how, as a ten-year-old Jewish-Algerian, he lost his French citizenship and as a consequence, could no longer attend the French school. Although he mentions receiving more support from Algerians than from the Algerian-French, Derrida describes this loss of French citizenship as 'one of the earth-shattering experiences of my existence, one of the earth-shattering Algerian experiences of my existence'.⁵⁷ The name-identity 'French citizen' is, hence, one that mattered, and mattered deeply, to Derrida. The Jew, the Arab, the French citizen. Derrida then explains that of 'all the cultural wealth' he has received/inherited, 'my Algerian culture has sustained me the most'.⁵⁸ When asked whether his proximity to Muslims in Algeria contributed to his 'philosophical orientation', 'vocation and work'?⁵⁹, Derrida responds that this cultural heritage 'probably inspired' his philosophical work, for 'all of that had to have come out of a reference to an elsewhere whose place and language were unknown and forbidden to me'.⁶⁰ Derrida then points out that Algiers became the 'French literary capital in exile' after the landing of the Allies (1942) to explain how 'in the brilliant wake of this strange moment of glory, I was essentially harpooned by French literature and philosophy'.⁶¹

When pressed on the question of his relation to the Muslim, Derrida responds, 'Arab language, that other was unknown or forbidden to me by the established order', so that although he lived on 'the edge of an Arab neighbourhood', this was segregated, its borders 'almost uncrossable': 'Close and infinitely far away – that was the distance that was inculcated into us', he explains.⁶² So, the Jew, the French, the not-Arab? On the question of the Arabic language, this was available in school as an 'optional', a 'foreign' language, and Derrida goes on to reflect, 'I sometimes wonder whether this language, unknown for me, is not my favourite language. The first of my preferred languages . . . I like to hear it above all outside of any communication, in the poetic solemnity of song or prayer.'⁶³ The Jew, the French. The Arab, muted? 'Unknown'? Named as 'favourite' only under condition of non-intelligibility?

The Jew, the Algerian, Derrida explains, was the victim of a tripled separation: from the Arab and the Berber ('actually the language and the culture'); from the French/European language and culture ('viewed as distant poles, unrelated to history'); and from Jewish memory, history and language. In this condition, 'The arrogant specificity, the traumatizing brutality of what is called the colonial war, colonial cruelty – some, including myself, experienced it from both sides, if I may say so'.[64] The Jew, then. Not Arab, not Algerian, not French. Traumatizing brutality from 'both sides'. Caught in the middle. The Jew, not colonized nor colonizer, the victim of a colonized Algeria then. This colonized Algeria Derrida has elsewhere described as 'an environment about which it will always be difficult to say whether it was colonizing or colonized'.[65]

Cherif pushes the question of the violence of the West against the Muslim world, of the 'dehumanization and despiritualization' of the West, of the triptych – 'secularism, scientism, capitalism' – that is the 'emblem of the modern West'[66]. Derrida responds by questioning whether this is indeed a 'Western triptych' as he goes on to criticize scientism ('positivist allegation of scientific power') as 'a detestable thing'; argues that secularism is 'calling for its own transformation' ('I believe this is occurring in France today'); and notes that the State 'can oppose economic forces, abusive economic concentrations, international forces of economic powers'.[67] He then calls for 'an authentic secularization of the political, that is, the separation between the theocratic and the political', going on to clarify,

> I believe that we must – here I am speaking as a Frenchman, a Westerner, a Western philosopher – I believe that what we must consider as our first task is to *ally* ourselves to that in the Arab and Muslim world which is trying to advance the idea of a secularization of the political, the idea of a separation between the theocratic and the political – this both out of respect for the political and for democratization and out of respect for faith and religion.[68]

There it is, the secularizing-colonizing mentality of Europe. The Jew, the Frenchman, the Westerner. The Abrahamic as Westerity? The Westerner as the Self globalized? Names do have meanings. They encode even as they connote power. Despite the best of intentions in disavowals of the self, this Self does not quite so readily let go.

The Jew, the Muslim: The religio-racial politics of the camp

The 'enemy' of political Europe, the Jew, who is defined as not political, Anidjar points out in *The Jew, the Arab*, becomes defined as 'weak' by this Europe, as deserving of elimination. Anidjar turns again to Schmitt, to his pronouncement on this enemy who is 'non-political': 'If a people no longer possesses the energy or the will to maintain itself in the sphere of politics, the latter will not thereby vanish from the world. Only a weak people will disappear.'[69] These comments on such a 'weak people . . . recall the Jewish people', notes Anidjar; 'in what is almost a call for the disappearance of a weak people hints of a *dehumanization* to come, a prefiguration of what was going to happen to entire communities, religious and non-religious, of European Jews', for it is these people who had no state, no land.[70] Islam and Christian-Europe are both engaged in the 'political' in Schmitt's discussion, while the Jew remains outside this field, defined by lack of the 'political' in the eyes of a 'political' Europe. Being outside of the 'political' becomes here a rationale for genocide. Anidjar's analysis of the constitution of the Jew, the Arab as 'enemy' of Europe is nowhere more powerful than in his discussion of Auschwitz, where he addresses the terrible proximity between the Jew and the Muslim as signalled by the *Muselmann*.

I will return to Anidjar's discussion of the *Muselmann* below, let me take up first Agamben's insightful reading of this figure. As I show in my reading of both Agamben's and Anidjar's treatment of the *Muselmann*, this figure marks a critical moment in the making of the 'Judeo-Christian', in religious, racial as well as secular terms. This figure of the *Muselmann* is hence crucial to tracking the subsequent transformation of the figure of the Jew into the Westerner, no longer 'enemy' in either theologio-racial or politico-cultural terms.

The genocidal violence of the camp speaks to the force of this integration of the Jews into the West, yet the cost of this fraternal embrace of Jews – as Friend, as co-civilizationalist in/of the West – was borne by the Jews who perished there, and subsequently, the Palestinians who were subjected to the *Naqba* and its ongoing effects. These two developments are internally related, that is, the Nazi camp and the occupation of Palestine. The figure of the Muselmann stands at their interstice.

In *Remnants of Auschwitz*, Agamben describes the concentration camp as a 'limit situation' to argue that Auschwitz is the 'decisive lesson of the century'.[71] The 'limit figure' at the heart of the extreme institution that was the Nazi camp is the one known to the Jewish inmates and their German captors as the *Muselmann*. This *Muselmann* was a figure visibly on the verge of death, a condition evident in its utter abjection; in other words, the *Muselmann* signified death. The relation of the camp's survivor to this figure, Agamben points out, was fraught with fear, terror and horror. As personification of death, the *Muselmann* was a broken and degraded figure, lifeless yet at the limit of the human and the inhuman. In this condition of utter hopelessness, of giving up on life itself, the Jew was interpellated as the *Muselmann*.

In *Man's Search for Meaning*, Viktor E. Frankl, a survivor of Auschwitz, describes a visit from a colleague in the morning following his first night in the camp. This colleague was previously known, and he came to comfort Frankl and the other newly arrived inmates to advise them on how to survive in the camp,

> But one thing I beg of you . . . shave daily, even if you have to use a piece of glass to do it . . . even if you have to give your last piece of bread for it. You will look younger and the scraping will make your cheeks look ruddier. If you want to stay alive, there is only one way: look fit for work. If you even limp, because, let us say, you have a small blister on your heel, and an SS man spots this, he will wave you aside and the next day you are sure to be gassed. Do you know what we mean by a 'Moslem'? A man who looks miserable, down and out, sick and emaciated, and who cannot manage hard physical labor any longer . . . that is a 'Moslem.' Sooner or later, usually sooner, every 'Moslem' goes to the gas chambers. Therefore, remember, shave, stand and walk smartly, then you need not be afraid of gas.[72]

Avoid 'looking' like the 'Moslem', the one who was sure to perish in the death chambers, this was the strategy for survival in the camp.

Agamben's reading of the *Muselmann* draws on studies of the Nazi camp by Zdislaw Ryn and Stanislaw Klodzinski, in which the two scholars conclude that the *Muselmann* 'documents [the] total triumph of power over the human being'.[73] Agamben concurs that the figure does indeed mark 'the moving threshold in which man passed into non-man'.[74] In the terrible space of the camp, suspended between life and death, living death-in-life, the Jew came to name him/herself the Muslim. Apparently the starved and emaciated figure, its eyes glazed and its movements stunted, recalled for the Jewish survivors and the German guards the image of a Muslim in prayer.[75] Why this may be the case is a question Agamben does not pursue. Indeed, as Parvez Manzoor has noted, not many scholars have sought to engage this memory of the *Muselmann*, which 'lies buried under Islamophobic myths'.[76]

The *Muselmann*, Anidjar points out, is to be found 'everywhere' in the Holocaust literature, the figure is described by him as 'something like a theologio-political history of absolute subjection'.[77] Inge Clendinnen describes this figure in a similar manner:

> Many of those assaulted relinquished the struggle and became Muselmanner, 'Muslims', men and women reduced to staring, listless creatures, no longer responding even to beatings, who for a few days or weeks existed, barely – and who then collapsed and were sent to the gas. We can guess [sic] that the term Muselmanner refers to the docile acceptance of one's destiny popularly ascribed to Islam and 'the East'.[78]

These *Muselmann* 'were dead but they didn't know it', recalled Elie Wiesel.[79]

This idea that the Muslim submits to 'destiny' in a mindless docility prescribed by Islam is a staple of the Western imaginary, wherein this phantasm of the Muslim overrides the actual historical Muslim who relates to her faith as a lifelong call to the active pursuit of justice, of the ethical life. Muslims are repeatedly admonished in the Qur'anic text for submission to earthly powers and are instead constantly reminded to submit to none in their fidelity to the transcendental divine.[80] As Manzoor points out, the 'authentic Muslim of history' could not have been the model of this 'Muselmann' of the camp.[81] Who then is this *Muselmann*? Indeed, who is this Jew who dies as the *Muselmann*? And who is the Jew who found life in the abandonment of the *Muselmann*?

The visceral identification felt by the Jewish survivor with the *Muselmann* that is mentioned 'everywhere' in the literature, traumatizing as this was, did not give rise to a positive expression of shared experience, shared struggle, it did not lead to an affiliation based on recognition of cultural, religious or historical commonality (despite both Jew and Muslim having been being racialized as Semites and Orientals in Europe's racializing discourses). The testimonies of the camps' survivors clarify how total was this lack of affiliation:

> No one felt compassion for the Muslim, and no one felt sympathy for him either. The other inmates, who continually feared for their lives, did not even judge him worthy of being looked at. For the prisoners who collaborated, the Muslims were

a source of anger and worry; for the SS they were merely useless garbage. Every group thought about eliminating them, each in its own way.[82]

The Muslim. Useless garbage. The genocidal conditions that structured the camp rendered impossible fraternal identification with the Muslim, one gleans this view very clearly from such statements: the stakes were life itself.

The Jewish survivors turned in horror from this monstrous figure, for the emotions recounted by the survivors towards this 'Muslim' included the terror invoked by the figure's warning of who/what it was that they themselves could become. Indeed, what they *had* become in the camps. It was thus with terror-turned-hatred, not empathy, that the Jewish survivor turned away from the *Muselmann* who perished in the camp. As Agamben so astutely points out, 'with a kind of ferocious irony, the Jews knew that they would not die at Auschwitz as Jews'.[83] What such an extraordinary insight may reveal about the politics of race and religion that were encapsulated in the figure of the *Muselmann*, in this constitution of 'bare life' in the Nazi camp, is left unexamined.

What would it mean to take this insight seriously, that the Jew who died at Auschwitz did so as a *Muselmann*? That the Jew who survived the camp did so by using every psychic and social resource available to wrench him/herself away from this figure? The camp's survivors speak of their conviction that the condition of possibility for their survival was to avoid the *Muselmann*; survivors attest to doing whatever was necessary to expunge this Muslim-in-the-Jew to protect their own humanity. In the deadly conditions of the camp, any affiliation, or identification, with this dreaded figure heralded certain death. The conditions of life and death, the question of survival in the camp is clearly a terrible, highly fraught and complicated matter, I do not claim to unpack such a terrible situation here. But what the survivors have to say about their experience, about their understanding of who the figure of the *Muselmann* meant, and did not mean, to them is important to understand.

The *Muselmann* of the Nazi camp was not, of course, the actual, empirical, historical Muslim, yet this figure was a symbol, even if phantom like, of the actual, empirical, historical Muslim. This figure was a reminder of the Semite in the Jew, fashioned in the starkest Orientalist manner. The *Muselmann* was thus also the Muslim, read as the sign of a submission to fate that was total, a submission defined even now as characteristic of Islam, as signifying the antithesis of the West, its reason, its secular-modernity, its self-owning Subject. That the association of the abject figure of living-death with the actual, historical Muslim was not racially innocent becomes evident as soon as one attends to the other names that were also used to refer to this 'complete witness' of the camp. These other names for the *Muselmann* included 'mummy-man', 'donkey', 'camel', 'cretin', 'useless garbage', 'cripple' and 'tired sheik'.[84] In the women's camps, the figure was known as the 'Muselweiber' (female Muslim), the 'trinket'.[85] While one could argue that the Orientalist chain of signification that binds these names to the actual, historical Muslim is unmistakable, it would do well to remember that Orientalism is not a discourse that originated from among Jewish peoples, but subsumed them also in its grasp.

The designation Oriental included Jews as well as Muslims into Western power until well into the first half of the twentieth century.[86] It was this religio-racial proximity between Jews and Muslims, both 'enemies' of Europe, that was fractured in the camp. It is worth taking the time to further unpack this moment that inaugurated the 'new' West, that remade its deadly religio-racial politics.

In Hannah Arendt's view, 'there was not the slightest doubt that Jews had been killed qua Jews' in the camps. However, Anidjar complicates and contests such a reading by highlighting the racial, not only religious, politics of the Nazi regime.[87] For the Nazis defined the Jews in Europe as a 'race' apart as well as religiously degraded.[88] Anidjar explains that the Nazi definition of Jews was 'more elaborate' than Arendt allows as they identified 'as 'Jews' scores of people who had absolutely no relation to Jews, people who made no claims to Jewishness, not because they were hiding, afraid, ashamed or self-hating, but because it would never have occurred to them to identify with any Jewishness whatsoever'.[89] Indeed, many of these Europeanized 'Jews' could not even conceive of the 'death sentence – Jew' as being applicable to them, he argues.[90] In Anidjar's view, Arendt's claim is 'unexpected, indeed surprising because it collapses two distinct discursive moments in the extension of the Nazi death sentence'.[91] The first moment is 'the recognition by the persecuted addressees that there is no escape from that sentence'; the second moment comes with the realization 'that that to which one is reduced at that moment is what one is'.[92] Arendt holds to the significance of the second moment as a political principle, namely, 'one can resist only in terms of the identity that is under attack'.[93] It is notable that Anidjar's critique of Arendt is supported by the statements of the survivors who attested differently to their experience than Arendt's perspective might suggest. Indeed, this racial designation of Jews-as-race, as Orientals, was shared across Western nation-states, the violence organized by such designation written into their immigration policies and citizenship rights, including in the United States, Britain, Canada, and so forth, into the mid-twentieth century.

Although Anidjar attends to the racial politics of the Nazi regime, he does not directly address the relation of the *Muselmann* to the actual Muslim: 'the question raised by the Muslims has a pervasive, if vanishing aspect, since the "ferocious irony" of which Agamben speaks has made it impossible to know whether the Muslim is an Arab, a Jew, a Christian, and even a man or a woman.'[94] Consequently, the *Muselmann* collapses into illegibility. The possibility that the *Muselmann* references what it names, the Muslim, is thus occluded.

The testimonies of survivors as referenced by Agamben reveal that the burden of the Jewish survivors' rejection of the 'racial' (Oriental, Semitic) – not religious (Jewish) – designation imposed upon them by the Nazis was borne by the figure of the *Muselmann*. If this was indeed the case, the survivors' turning away from this figure can be read as a projection – born of terror and desperation – of the 'internal' 'racial/Oriental' aspect of the figure of the Jew onto the *Muselmann*, a projection that confirmed to the Jewish survivors that the *Muselmann*, not the Jew, was the 'real' racial object of Nazi hatred. For the Jews who identified as Europeans, turning on, and away from, the figure symbolizing the 'real' Oriental/Semite was the psychic means to physical survival. Read in this light, could the

Muselmann be considered to have underwritten Jewish survival, which depended on the expunging of the racial difference of the Jew? Such 'internal' purging of their 'race' was understood by the survivors to be the condition of their survival, and of protecting their identity as European. Put differently, turning away from the *Muselmann* became a literal turning away from the horizon of death towards that of life, a turning away that allowed the possibility of escape from certain death. Such a turning away from the 'internal' racial difference of the Jew by displacing this onto the figure of the Muslim made this the name of those who *really* carried the racial difference of Europe, those who were destined to die. The *Muselmann* was thus a doubled figuration of racial difference, first, marked as the object of the racial hatred of Europe, and second, marked as the object of the terror-ridden hatred of the Jews who staked their claim to Europe's whiteness. In a perverse manner, the Muslim became both the hated 'Semite' of Europe as well as the hate-filled 'anti-Semite' who symbolized the death of the Jews in the camp.

It remains unclear whether the use of the name *Muselmann* in the camp originated among the Jews or the Germans.[95] This figure, too, is a legacy of the camp; left behind by the Jewish survivor who emerged from the camp as European, that is, into the status of the sovereign Subject. However, the racial object that carried the name *Muselmann* would be no less hated in what would become this sovereign Subject's waging of its own forms of genocidal violence.

As Gilman and others have documented, many European Jews were assimilated, even converted to Christianity, decades before the rise of Nazism. Indeed, the early Zionists debated the consequences of such assimilation. In the United States, Rabbi Meyer, a Semitic Studies scholar, stated that Jews in the United States had more in common with American whites than with 'the Arab of the desert, the true representative of the Semitic world of yore' or with Middle Eastern Jews; this Reform Rabbi made the case that 'today, but little of that original Semitic blood will be found in the veins of any of us'.[96] Another Reform Rabbi, Sale, likewise argued that 'we can not get away from the bald fact, based on anatomical measurements, that only about five percent of all Jews bear the characteristic mark of the Semitic origin on their body', and as Massad concludes from such statements, the Jewish disavowal of the Semite-as-Arab was physiological, not only psychic.[97] If the refiguration of the Jew in the camp in relation to the *Muselmann* is tied to, and facilitates, the acceptance of the camps' survivors as European by Western nation-states, the camp can be read as the site of the racial death of the Jew-as-Semite and the racial rebirth of the Jew-as-white.

Agamben argues that ethics 'begins' in the figure of the *Muselmann*, hated-by-German-and-Jew-alike, 'in Auschwitz, ethics begins precisely at the point where the Muselmann, the "complete witness", makes it forever impossible to distinguish between man and non-man.'[98] However, both 'man' and 'non-man' remain stubbornly 'Western' in this analysis, the historical Muslim, in his/her onto-epistemological specificity, is barred from appearance in this invocation of her name. In an act of epistemic erasure, Agamben too turns away from the *Muselmann*, ready to accept the seemingly innocent explanation that the *Muselmann* reminded the camp's survivors of Muslims in prayer. Treating the *Muselmann* as simply concept-metaphor, Agamben re-inscribes the disappearance of the empirical and historical Muslim, a nonentity in-and-for him/herself. For his part, Anidjar struggles to come to terms with this figure of the *Muselmann*, insisting on naming him Muslim, yet unable to engage with this Muslim in his/her own terms, that is, Islam, such that he collapses the Muslim into the category 'Arab'.

How then, did this violent severing of the Jew-as-European survivor and the Jew-as-Muselmann who perished in the camps impact the – highly politicized – post-Holocaust status of the survivors? Their testimonies reveal the immense pain, guilt and shame they felt at the perishing of the *Muselmanner* among them. Identification with this figure led to a 'complete collapse[d] as far as [my] psychological life was concerned',[99] testified one survivor, but dis-identification proved no less painful, the attempt to do so led to a lifetime of anguished haunting by the tortured figure.

The fraught figure of the Muselmann, the embodiment of the innermost secrets and terrors of the camp, raises crucial questions, as Agamben and Anidjar both emphasize in their readings of the figure. My reading leads me to make the case that the 'Oriental' Jew had been constructed as very much like the Oriental 'Muslim' in the European imaginary for centuries, except of course, for the difference of 'religion' between them. Does the significance of this religious difference hold the clue to the Jewish association of the *Muselmann* with the Muslim at prayer? Would such an association not accentuate this 'religious' difference between the two? For the act of prayer would attest to, in the clearest manner, the difference between the Jew and the Muslim, a 'religious' difference that had the power to rupture their racial 'sameness'. Such religious difference had the potential to eclipse racial affinity, such that the *Muselmann* remained archetype of the non-human in the Orientalist lexicon, with the Jew who, as European, was to become not quite so abject/object/alien.

Anidjar's study of the 'enemy' of Europe tracks how Jews were written out of history as 'theological' enemy, located also outside the realm of politics. The projection of this status onto the hated figure of the *Muselmann* opened up the possibility for the assertion of the status of the Jew-as-European, as Human, oriented towards life, towards the future, not death. The Jewish survivors were to emerge from Auschwitz into history and politics, into the Western construction of these terms that were already deeply steeped in war with Islam and Muslims.

In the aftermath of the Holocaust, the Zionist project culminated in the founding of the Jewish state, Israel, and in its acquisition of its 'national' territory in historic Palestine. Many survivors of the Holocaust, Massad has pointed out, 'left the shores of Europe as refugees, but arrived on the shores of Palestine as armed colonial settlers'.[100] Many among them joined the Haganah and 'participated in the expulsion of the Palestinians and in the many massacres of the 1948 war'.[101] They terrorized Palestinians into leaving their homes and communities, built their Kibbutzim on the lands of destroyed Palestinian villages, looted Palestinian property and in the process, became a sovereign people in the well-trodden path of Europe. Claiming the right to colonize Palestine as their very birthright, ordained by their Covenant with their God, Euro-American Jews thus acquired the form of political agency that was now ordained by the West – sovereignty as the right to colonize. In the process, Euro-American Jews became the Self-same of the Western Subject, the figure of the Jew was now that of a Westerner, the settler. Confirmation of such racial remaking was evidenced by the realization of Zionism as the postcolonial incarnation of settler colonialism.

Agamben recognizes that the relation of the 'witness' to the 'Muselmann' was one that split the self; however, neither he nor Anidjar address the racial logic at work in this 'splitting'. The construction of the post-Nazi era, of the constitution of the figure of the Jew as thoroughly political – sovereign and the only 'democrat' in the Middle East – became tied to the figure of the Muslim as thoroughly 'religious', hate-filled and death-oriented fanatic in this racial logic. Anidjar considers the catastrophe 'that the Jew became a Muslim' to be 'unaccountable'.[102] Yet, as noted by Pugliese in his study of Guantanamo Bay, 'whoever is designated as a Muselmann/Musalman/Muslim is compelled to wear the burden of absolute alterity.'[103]

Is the figure of the Muslim, doubled in its raciality – as death-oriented enemy of the West and anti-Semitic hater of the Jew – destined to remain the dreaded spectre that now haunts the formation, the Judeo-Christian? Anidjar, drawing on Derrida, reads Europe's casting of Islam as 'political' and also 'the enemy of *the* political'. But what might engaging the Muslim in the historical specificity of the colonization of their world *do* to these formations of 'religion' and 'politics', 'theology' and 'philosophy', that are so vital to the Western tradition, to its claim to singularity?

These distinctions are unfortunately reconstructed by Derrida, his deconstruction of the Western tradition notwithstanding, by replicating its refusal to engage Islam on its own terms, by insisting on the secularization of the Muslim world as the condition for its 'freedom', its acceptance into the fraternity of the Abrahamic.

The Judeo-Christian: Making friendship, remaking enmity

As is well documented, Jewish colonists began arriving in Palestine in the 1880s, but it was during the First World War, and in its aftermath that the idea of creating the state of Israel in Palestine gained support as a political proposition. The Balfour Declaration (1917) advanced the possibility and as the British and the Zionists negotiated this, Palestinians were written out of the land. As is also well documented, the claim of the Zionists (Congress founded in 1897) over Palestine was made – as it is defended even now – on the idea of the Jewish covenant with their God. This movement to establish the state of Israel divided Jewish communities: some of the opposition was based on the project's racial ideology (confirmation of Jewish racial alterity, identification of European Jews as descendants of the ancient 'Semitic' Hebrews, etc.), political positioning (alliance with imperialism, anti-communism), contending nationalism (assimilated Jews defined themselves as American, British, German, French etc.), as well as religion (anti-Jewish heresy).[104] The British interest in supporting the establishment of Israel was with an eye to the future, as stated emphatically by Lord Balfour in a memorandum (1919), 'The four great powers are committed to Zionism, and Zionism, be it right or wrong, good or bad, is rooted in age-long tradition, in present needs, in future hopes, *of far profounder import than the desire and prejudices of the 700,000 Arabs who now inhabit that ancient land. In my opinion that is right*.'[105] The British had no interest in consulting Palestinians about this future. If such was the political sentiment and strategy of the British – still an Empire – in the early twentieth century, it has prevailed the in post-Empire political calculus of the UK, and is now a cornerstone in the policies – foreign and domestic – of the Western nation-states. Balfour's views could well have been expressed by any US president with regard to the present and future needs of that country. Indeed, it has been. Repeatedly, as is also well documented.

Founded in the partition of Palestine, the state of Israel was established through the massacre, dispossession and exile of the Palestinians. The ideology of the Zionist state, Massad has argued, appropriated Jewish history and the experience of the Holocaust to this end, such that this event 'was not seen as a break with Jewish history but rather as its legitimate, continuation'; Zionism tied European Jewish history to Palestinian lands, in a relation of domination that sought to erase Palestine, its peoples, its history.[106] In Anidjar's view, Zionism presented Jewish communities with a contradiction, that is, Zionism brought about a radical transformation of Judaism, and thus, of what it meant to be Jewish. Defining Zionism's association with Judaism as 'peculiar', even 'paradoxical', Anidjar argues that on the one hand, Zionism 'affirms the connection between Judaism and Zionism' as it is an expression, and a culmination of Jewish nationalism,[107] but on the other hand, Zionism is also the 'end' of Judaism, for it brings to an end the exile of the Jews, thus producing a 'new Jew', the one that is 'opposed to the exilic "old Jew"'.[108]

The establishment of the Zionist state in the post-Holocaust moment took place at the culminating point in two trajectories of European history – European anti-Semitism and European colonialism. The merging of these trajectories in the new settler colony allowed Euro-America to redeem some of its 'moral legitimacy' and simultaneously extend its reach deep into the Middle East.

In post-Second World War Europe, Goldberg has argued, the Holocaust was transformed into the singular racial tragedy of Europe, standing above and pushing aside the preceding and concurrent histories of racial genocides across the colonized world. In the Middle East and Asia, the new nation-states that emerged from the anti-colonial struggles of the late nineteenth and twentieth century were born of such violence, shaped as they were by the idea of the modern nation as based on shared characteristics of race, religion, ethnicity, culture and/or language, regulated by a centralized state. This formation was foreign to the Islamic world, an antithesis to the concept of the *ummah* and of the cosmopolitan societies of the Muslim empires. The homogeneity of the nation-state was carved out of the heterogeneous Islamic world by nationalist movements through partitions, genocides, expulsions (the partition of South Asia; the genocide of the Armenians; the Partition of Greater Syria, etc.). The partition of Palestine was thus of apiece with the religio-racial politics reworking the post-independence world that eventually resulted in the creation of postcolonial nation-states where none had previously existed.

In this post-independence context, Israel, with its westward orientation, ensured a disruptive presence in the region to destabilize it for decades to come. Israel's creation was a transnational project, supported by the 'old' European imperial powers (the UK, France and Germany) as well as the 'old' settler states (the United States, Canada, Australia, etc.). With this backing, Zionist ideology institutionalized the religio-racial logic of the West; the Euro-American-ness of this Jewish nation-state legitimized its status as democratic, secular-nationalist and even socialist. Gone was the (theological) enmity with the Jew that is traced by Anidjar, gone also was the proximity of the Jew to the Muslim/Arab.

Said, Massad and others have pointed out that among the other effects of the *Naqba*, the burden of European anti-Semitism was now placed onto Palestinians, who were held morally and politically responsible for the European genocide of Jewish populations. The colonization of the Palestinians was thus transmuted into both the Western 'atonement' for the Holocaust and the Western retribution for the anti-Semitism now ascribed to the Muslim/Arab world. Europe's fraternity with Israel/Jews thus transformed the Palestinian resistance into existential enmity. The older denigration and violence directed by the West against the Oriental/Semite was now turned with full force onto the Palestinians, the categories 'Oriental/Arab/Muslim' soon conflated with that of 'terrorist'. The Palestinian resistance contests these religio-racial logics of the West, exposing the dehumanization that is to be found at its core:

> But we are not just cannon fodder for Israeli soldiers. We are not just victims trying to save our children. We have our memories of the olive trees we left behind, the warmth of the earth and the smell of the zaa'tar and marameyya on the hillside of the West Bank. We have the keys to our homes and the 'knowledge' that this land is our land. We are here and we will not be ignored, nor will we be exterminated. We are the rightful owners of this land and we will pass on this heritage to the next generation.[109]

I close this chapter with a number of points pertinent to the relation between the formation of the 'Judeo-Christian' and the transformation of Palestine into the site for advancing the West's religio-racial technologies of violence – colonization and dispossession; terrorism and anti-terrorism; sovereignty and subjectivity. That this transformation was unfolding in the age of Third-World revolution speaks to the necessity of situating this 'national' within the imperial 'global', for Western power relies on the erasure of the historical consciousness of colonized peoples as the condition of aligning them with a future projected as Westernity. Confining this consciousness in the post-independence period to the parameters of the nation-state, and reading this 'present' – in terms of identity and culture – into its own past as always already the same is how the state of coloniality is reproduced. Such governance of the historical consciousness of colonized-cum-independent peoples becomes destabilized as soon as the racial-colonial nature of the global order and the religio-political logic that shapes it – is brought into focus, as is presently the case with the revolutionary movements that mark the early twenty-first century.

Said argued that Palestinian writers, intellectuals and political organizations, involved in the larger nineteenth-century anti-colonial Arab awakening in the Middle East,

> formed great national blocks among the population, directed the energies of the 'non-Jewish' Palestinian community, created a Palestinian identity opposed equally to British rule and to Jewish colonization, and solidified the Palestinian sense of belonging by whichever continuity of residence to a distinct national group with a language (the Palestinian Arab dialect) and a specific communal sense (threatened particularly by Zionism) of its own.[110]

These comments underscore the importance of the vastly divergent interests mobilized by, and invested in, building 'great national blocks', and 'national identity' as oppositional to Western domination (the Judeo-Christian as the secular-colonial in the present). This is not the modernization project in thrall with Westernization, the internalization of which was warned against by Fanon in what he called 'the pitfalls of national consciousness'.

Said's intellectual and political commitments in deconstructing Orientalism and its links to anti-Semitism, as well as in the struggle for Palestine, were secular in nature. He had earlier however, recognized, even if only in passing, the place of Islam in the Orientalist paradigm, 'what has not been sufficiently stressed in histories of modern anti-Semitism has been the legitimation of such atavistic designations by Orientalism, and . . . the way this academic and intellectual legitimation has persisted right through the modern age in discussion of Islam, the Arabs, or the Near Orient.'[111] My reading of the *Muselmann* in this chapter identifies this figure as signalling the internal rupture within the communities of European Jews and the religio-racial politics of Europe, within the Orientalist discourse itself, such that the Muslim/Arab came to signify terror, death and violence. This transformation – mediated by the *Muselmann* – underwrites the formation of the Judeo-Christian that enabled the passage of Jewish communities into their newly sanctioned identity as Israeli, white and hence modern. This figure of the Muselmann signals also the passage of the submerged Islamophobia within the Orientalist worldview into the position of dominance.

The history of Palestinian resistance to Western domination is, and always was, multifaceted and heterogeneous. The range, breadth and depth of the political perspectives that have shaped this resistance can be seen in some of the significant moments that mark its trajectory – the first Palestinian war of resistance led by the Qadiriya Sufi, Sheikh 'Izz ad-Din al-Qassam, and his Palestinian mujahids (1936–9); the formation of the Palestine Liberation Organization – with the different political factions it represented; the post-Oslo Palestinian Authority; and formation of Hamas (The Islamic Resistance Movement of Palestine) whose military wing takes its name from the Sufi Sheikh, etc. This trajectory has been shaped as much by the Palestinian resistance to the expansionary nature of the Israeli occupation as by the changing politico-social conditions within Palestine and the greater Middle East, which includes the awakening of revolutionary Islamist movements. The Orientalism studied by Said morphed during these moments into the Islamophobia that now underwrites the global war on terror, fuelling the conflicts across the region in tandem with the Israeli wars in Gaza, the West Bank, and other parts of the region. The structural link between these wars and the formation of the 'Judeo-Christian' cannot be overlooked, for these are internally linked. The question of Palestine is thus also a frontline in the Islamophobic politics of the global war on terror.

A major military power among the most militarized nation-states in the world, Israel is the biggest single recipient of US foreign assistance on an annual basis (over $81.3 billion in fifty years), it is also the largest importer of US arms.[112] This settler state is thus equipped – ideologically, materially and constitutionally – to render its services to the larger Western alliance battling 'Islamic terror' in the global war. Strategically included at the centre of US foreign policy, Israel in turn provides 'counter-terror' expertise – intelligence, security, weaponry and military – to United States, Canada, India, even Greece, among many others.[113] If such 'Israelization' speaks to the religio-racial politics of the Judeo-Christian West, Palestine symbolizes the revolutionary resistance of the Islamic, Arab secular, as well as larger anti-colonial resistance to Westernity. If the Westernizing Subject once again propels the figure of the Muslim – emblematic of the wretched of the earth – towards the horizon of death, this Muslim reaches yet again towards Islam.

NOTES

Introduction

1. Malcom X, quoted in Zain Abdullah, 'Malcolm X, Islam, and the Black Self', in *Malcolm X's Michigan Worldview: An Exemplar for Contemporary Black Studies*, ed. Rita Kiki Edozie and Curtis Stokes, 1st edn (East Lansing: Michigan State University Press, 2015), 212, 215.
2. Salman Sayyid, *Recalling the Caliphate: Decolonisation and World Order* (London: Hurst Publishers, 2014), 43.
3. Gil Anidjar, *The Jew, the Arab: A History of the Enemy*, Cultural Memory in the Present (Stanford: Stanford University Press, 2003).
4. Anidjar, *The Jew, the Arab*, 49.
5. Europe's encounter with Islam made Islam the 'political enemy par excellence' of Europe, explains Anidjar, the 'determinate struggle' between them for a thousand years could be read as 'the source of Europe's political existence, a Europe that thinks itself Christian, that grants itself its Christianity and its Christendom, its "Christian politics," insofar as it is engaged in this struggle'. The existence of Europe is thus 'political', as defined in the political-philosophical tradition studied by Anidjar, *The Jew, the Arab*, 48.
6. Ian Almond, *The New Orientalists: Postmodern Representations of Islam from Foucault to Baudrillard* (London: I. B. Tauris, 2007), 59.
7. 'St. John of Damascus: Critique of Islam', Orthodox Christian Information Centre, accessed 1 June 2018, http://orthodoxinfo.com/general/stjohn_islam.aspx.
8. '1095 Pope Urban II Launches the First Crusade', Christianity Today, accessed 1 June 2018, https://www.christianitytoday.com/history/issues/issue-28/1095-pope-urban-ii-launches-first-crusade.html.
9. The term *Blackamoor* was used by Europeans to refer to Muslims, Arabs, Berbers and North Africans. For an excellent collection of writings on the multiple meanings of 'race' in the early-modern period, see: Frederick Quinn, *The Sum of All Heresies: The Image of Islam in Western Thought* (Oxford: Oxford University Press, 2008); John Victor Tolan, *Saracens: Islam in the Medieval European Imagination* (New York: Columbia University Press, 2002); Anouar Majid, *We Are All Moors: Ending Centuries of Crusades against Muslims and Other Minorities* (Minneapolis: University of Minnesota Press, 2009).
10. Ziauddin Sardar, *Orientalism*, Concepts in the Social Sciences (Philadelphia: Open University Press, 1999); Edward Said, *Orientalism* (London: Penguin, 1995).
11. Viktor Frankl, *Man's Search for Meaning*, Young readers edition (Boston: Beacon Press, 2017); Giorgio Agamben, *Remnants of Auschwitz: The Witness and the Archive*, trans. Daniel Heller-Roazen (New York: Zone Books, 2000).
12. Michael Omi and Howard Winant, *Racial Formation in the United States: From the 1960s to the 1990s*, 2nd edn (New York: Routledge, 1994); Les Back and John Solomos, eds, *Theories of Race and Racism: A Reader*, 2nd edn, Routledge Student

Readers (London: Routledge, 2009); Ambalavaner Sivanandan, *A Different Hunger: Writings on Black Resistance* (London: Pluto Press, 1982); Jodi Melamed, *Represent and Destroy: Rationalizing Violence in the New Racial Capitalism* (Minneapolis: University of Minnesota Press, 2011); Walter Mignolo, *The Darker Side of Western Modernity: Global Futures, Decolonial Options* (Durham: Duke University Press, 2011).

13   See Melamed, *Represent and Destroy*; Himani Bannerji, *Dark Side of the Nation: Essays on Multiculturalism, Nationalism, and Gender* (Toronto: Canadian Scholars' Press, 2000); Sunera Thobani, *Exalted Subjects: Studies in the Making of Race and Nation in Canada* (Toronto: University of Toronto Press, 2007).

14   See Andrew Lebovich, 'The Real Reason U.S. Troops Are in Niger', *Foreign Policy*, 27 October 2017, https://foreignpolicy.com/2017/10/27/the-real-reason-u-s-troops-are-in-niger/. Also see Charlie Savage, Eric Schmitt and Thomas Gibbons-Neff, 'U.S. Kept Silent about Its Role in Another Firefight in Niger', *The New York Times*, 14 March 2018, https://www.nytimes.com/2018/03/14/world/africa/niger-green-berets-isis-firefight-december.html. Also see Steven Lee Myers, 'Lasers and Missiles Heighten U.S.-China Military Tensions', *The New York Times*, 7 August 2018, sec. World, https://www.nytimes.com/2018/05/04/world/asia/china-united-states-lasers-pilots.html.

15   Here is how President Bush described this crisis in the United States: 'We've seen nationalism distorted into nativism, forgotten the dynamic that immigration has always brought to America. We see a fading confidence in the value of free markets and international trade, forgetting that conflict, instability and poverty follow in the wake of protectionism. We've seen the return of isolationist sentiments, forgetting that American security is directly threatened by the chaos and despair of distant societies.' Peter Baker, 'Without Saying "Trump," Bush and Obama Deliver Implicit Rebukes', *The New York Times*, 19 October 2017, sec. U.S., https://www.nytimes.com/2017/10/19/us/politics/george-bush-trump.html.

16   My study draws on Stuart Hall's reading of the concept of the 'West' as not so much a reference to geography as to the historical phenomenon known as 'modernity'. Hall argued that the idea of the 'West' is defined in relation to 'the Rest', that is, the 'non-West', to highlight the relationality between these concepts Four major functions are served by the concept of the West, which Hall defined as classificatory (Western vs non-Western); representational (urban, industrialized, etc.); comparative ('West' as advanced, 'Rest' as not so); and evaluative (developed, modern, good, etc.). The concept of the West thus 'produces a certain kind of *knowledge* about a subject and certain attitudes towards it', was Hall's view. As ideology, the concept of the West was central to the development of Enlightenment philosophy, and hence to its construction of Reason and Modernity, in which European society was defined as 'the most advanced type of society on earth' and 'European man [*sic*] the pinnacle of human achievement'.

See Stuart Hall, 'The West and The Rest: Discourse and Power', in *The Formations of Modernity*, ed. Stuart Hall and Bram Gieben, Understanding Modern Societies: An Introduction (Cambridge: Polity Press and the Open University, 1992), 186, 187

I also draw on Talal Asad's point that although 'spatially discontinuous and internally diverse, "the West" is not a mere Hegelian myth . . . it informs innumerable intentions, practices and discourses in systemic ways'. Conceiving thus of the 'West' is not, as he explains, to attribute to it a 'fixed Western identity or a single Western way of thinking'; rather, it is to recognize that 'a singular collective identity defines itself in terms of a unique historicity in contrast to all others, a historicity that shifts from place to place – Greece, Rome, Latin Christendom, the Americas – until it embraces the world'.

If such historicity shifts from place to place as Asad describes, the elements that constitute its exalted status also change accordingly. It is therefore the processes of fabrication and appropriation of particular features that become designated as central to the West's historicity as 'organic continuity' that are of interest to me. See Talal Asad, *Genealogies of Religion: Discipline and Reasons of Power in Christianity and Islam* (Baltimore: Johns Hopkins University Press, 1993), 18.

17 Frantz Fanon, *The Wretched of the Earth*, trans. Richard Philcox (New York: Grove Press, 2007); Frantz Fanon, *Black Skin, White Masks*, trans. Charles Lam Markmann (London: Pluto Press, 1986).
18 Mitchell Dean, *Governmentality: Power and Rule in Modern Society* (London: SAGE Publications, 2006); Michel Foucault, *Discipline and Punish: The Birth of the Prison*, trans. Alan Sheridan, A Peregrine Book (Harmondsworth: Penguin, 1979); Judith Butler, *Gender Trouble: Feminism and the Subversion of Identity* (London: Routledge, 2011).
19 See Olivier Roy, *The Failure of Political Islam* (Cambridge: Harvard University Press, 1994).
20 Leila Ahmed, *A Quiet Revolution: The Veil's Resurgence, from the Middle East to America* (New Haven: Yale University Press, 2011); Miriam Cooke, *Women Claim Islam: Creating Islamic Feminism through Literature* (New York: Routledge, 2001), xii, xix.
21 Cooke, *Women Claim Islam*, xiii.
22 Nilüfer Göle, *The Forbidden Modern: Civilization and Veiling* (Ann Arbor: University of Michigan Press, 1996).
23 Some of these conflicts include those between the so-called moderate Muslims and militant movements; the Egyptian state and the Muslim Brotherhood; Iran and Saudi Arabia and the UAE; the Gulf States and Qatar; the Syrian rebel organizations and the Asad regime, etc.
24 See, for example, Fanon's famous critique of Sartre in Fanon, *Black Skin, White Masks*. See also Michael Hardt and Antonio Negri, *Empire* (Cambridge: Harvard University Press, 2000); Slavoj Žižek, 'Europe Must Move beyond Mere Tolerance', *The Guardian*, 25 January 2011, sec. Opinion, https://www.theguardian.com/commentisfree/2011/jan/25/european-union-slovenia.
25 See, for example, Žižek, 'Europe Must Move beyond Mere Tolerance'; Tariq Ali, *The Clash of Fundamentalisms: Crusades, Jihads and Modernity* (London: Verso, 2002). See also Deepa Kumar's response to the criticism from the left regarding her discussion of the Danish Cartoons. Kumar notes that what is 'deeply troubling is that the majority of comments, presumably from progressives, are hostile to Islam and Muslims'. She argues that these comments, with 'the wholesale demonization of Arabs and Muslims is racist and unacceptable', serve to 'bolster US foreign policy goals in the Middle East' and 'weaken' the ability of the left to organize opposition to the US wars. Deepa Kumar, 'Fighting Islamophobia: A Response to Critics', *MR Online*, 3 April 2006, https://mronline.org/2006/04/03/fighting-islamophobia-a-response-to-critics/.
26 See, for example, Cedric Robinson, *Black Marxism: The Making of the Black Radical Tradition* (Chapel Hill: University of North Carolina Press, 2000); Angela Yvonne Davis, *Women, Race & Class* (London: The Women's Press, 1982). Also see Hamid

Dabashi, 'Can Non-Europeans Think?', *Aljazeera*, 15 January 2013, https://www.alj azeera.com/indepth/opinion/2013/01/20131114142638797542.html.

27 See, for example, Judith Butler, *Precarious Life: The Powers of Mourning and Violence* (London: Verso, 2004); Giorgio Agamben, *Homo Sacer: Sovereign Power and Bare Life*, trans. Daniel Heller-Roazen, Meridian, 1st edn (Stanford: Stanford University Press, 1998).

28 Alastair Crooke, *Resistance: The Essence of the Islamist Revolution* (London: Pluto Press, 2009), 1. This quote comes from a cleric in Iran, but the same critique of Western thought is to be found in Sayyid Quṭb, *Social Justice in Islam* (Washington: American Council of Learned Societies, 1953); and Ali Shariati, *Man and Islam* (North Haledon: Islamic Publications International, 1981). See William Shepard, *Sayyid Qutb and Islamic Activism: A Translation and Critical Analysis of Social Justice in Islam*, vol. 54 (Leiden: E. J. Brill, 1996).

29 See Joan Wallach Scott, ed., *Women's Studies on the Edge* (Durham: Duke University Press, 2008).

30 Kimberle Crenshaw, 'Mapping the Margins: Intersectionality, Identity Politics, and Violence against Women of Color', *Stanford Law Review* 43, no. 6 (1991): 1241–99, https://doi.org/10.2307/1229039.

31 Mohammad Salama, 'Arabic and the Monopoly of Theory', *ARCADE: Literature, the Humanities and the World*, 13 April 2015, https://arcade.stanford.edu/blogs/arabic-and-monopoly-theory.

32 J. Luchte, 'A Rupture in Colonial Reason: Spivak, Fanon, and The Question of Subalternity', *Continental Philosophy*, 2014, http://www.continental-philosophy.org/2014/11/05/a-rupture-in-colonial-reason-spivak-fanon-and-the-question-of-subalternity.

33 Kuan-Hsing Chen, *Asia as Method: Toward Deimperialization* (Durham: Duke University Press, 2010), 2.

34 Salama, 'Arabic and the Monopoly of Theory'.

35 Although critical race theory is most commonly associated with the tradition of Critical Legal Studies that emerged in the 1970s (Delgado, Aylward), I am approaching CRT as the tradition was earlier shaped in the anti-racist and anti-colonial movements of the late nineteenth and twentieth centuries (Du Bois, Fanon, etc.).

36 See for example, Melamed, *Represent and Destroy*; Pankaj Mishra, *From the Ruins of Empire: The Revolt against the West and the Remaking of Asia* (London: Allen Lane, 2012); Vijay Prashad, *The Darker Nations: A People's History of the Third World* (New York: The New Press, 2008).

37 See Salman Sayyid, *A Fundamental Fear: Eurocentrism and the Emergence of Islamism*, 2nd edn (London: Zed Books, 2003).

38 Talal Asad, *Formations of the Secular: Christianity, Islam, Modernity*, 1st edn (Stanford: Stanford University Press, 2003).

39 As Massad points out, the task of cultivating a pro-Western 'moderate' Islam was a long-standing colonial ambition. In the late nineteenth century, French colonial settlers in North Africa discussed the strategy, and Edmond Douttee, one of the settlers, stated that 'rather than repress "the exaggerated religious manifestations" of extant Islam, the task before Europeans was more productive: "we could, on the contrary, favor the birth of a new Islam more inclined towards compromise and tolerance of Europe; to encourage the young generation of *ulama* who are working in that direction, and to increase the number of mosques, madrasas, and Muslim

universities, ensuring that we staff them with adherents of the new theories."' Joseph Andoni Massad, *Islam in Liberalism* (Chicago: University of Chicago Press, 2015), 71.
40 Hasan Azad, 'Muslims and the Path of Intellectual Slavery: An Interview with Wael Hallaq (Part Two)', *Jadaliyya*, 7 June 2014, http://www.jadaliyya.com/Details/30782.
41 The crisis of late capitalism has been described as a condition wherein '[s]uperfluous production and consumerism corrode labour, with the correlation of more precarious employment and structural unemployment, as well as a level of destruction of nature never before seen on such a global scale'. Ricardo Antunes, 'Introduction: The Substance of the Crisis', in *The Structural Crisis of Capital*, by Istvan Meszaros (New York: Monthly Review Press, 2009), 13–22.
42 See Bernard Lewis, *Islam and the West* (New York: Oxford University Press, 1993). The approach taken by Lewis is not only typical, but has set the pattern for subsequent studies of relations between Islam and the West.
43 A recent study of Islam and European empires frames the relation between these in the following terms: 'The expansion of Europe engulfed vast parts of the Islamic world, gradually subjugating Muslims around the globe, from the West African savannah to the shores of Southeast Asia, under non-Muslim imperial rule. In the heyday of empire, Britain, France, Russia, and the Netherlands each governed more Muslim subjects than any independent Muslim state. European politicians and colonial officials believed Islam to be of considerable political significance, and were quite cautious when it came to matters of the religious life of their Muslim subjects.' David Motadel, 'Introduction', in *Islam and the European Empires* (Oxford: Oxford University Press, 2014), 1.
44 This is how Bernard Lewis describes Europe: 'Europe is a European notion, as is the whole geographical system of continents, of which Europe was the first. Europe conceived and made Europe; Europe discovered, named, and in a sense, made America. Centuries earlier, Europe had invented both Asia and Africa, the inhabitants of which, until the age of European world supremacy in the nineteenth century, were unaware of these names, these identities, even of these classifications which Europeans had devised for them. Even in Europe, the notion of Europe as a cultural and political entity was relatively modern – a postmedieval secularized restatement of what had previously been known as Christendom.' Lewis, *Islam and the West*, 3.

See also Hichem Djaït, *Europe and Islam*, trans. Peter Heinegg (Berkeley: University of California Press, 1985); Franco Cardini, *Europe and Islam*, Making of Europe (Oxford: Blackwell, 2001). For more recent examples that likewise conceive of Europe as internally self-forming entity but differ from Lewis in their reading of the meaning of this Europe, see Peter O'Brien, *European Perceptions of Islam and America from Saladin to George W. Bush: Europe's Fragile Ego Uncovered* (New York: Palgrave Macmillan, 2009).

A welcome departure in this field is the recent study by Joseph Massad, which examines how the projection by Western societies of totalitarianism, misogyny and homophobia onto Islam enables these societies to constitute themselves as liberal, democratic, tolerant and egalitarian. Islam, Massad argues, is 'at the heart of liberalism, at the heart of Europe; it was there at the moment of the birth of liberalism and the birth of Europe. . . . It is an internal constituent of liberalism, not merely an external other, though liberalism often projects it as the latter'. Massad, *Islam in Liberalism*, 1. Massad's study takes up many of the topics that animate my study, and while I have learned much from this study, its focus is on Western liberalism.

Moreover, he does not take up the question of race, nor its internal relation to 'religion', which is key in my study.

45 It is noteworthy that Stuart Hall's work on the historical construction of the 'West' is largely ignored in most studies of 'Islam and Europe', and of 'Islam and the West'. Hall has drawn ample attention to how the narrative of Western modernity relied on its production as having an 'internalist story', one which credits its own 'self-generating capacity' for its transition from feudalism to capitalism. See Stuart Hall et al., eds, *Modernity: An Introduction to Modern Societies* (Cambridge: Blackwell, 1996).

46 See Rana Kabbani, *Europe's Myths of Orient: Devise and Rule* (London: Macmillan, 1986); Sardar, *Orientalism*; Tolan, *Saracens*; O'Brien, *European Perceptions of Islam and America from Saladin to George W. Bush*.

47 See 'Pope Urban II's Speech Calling for the First Crusade', *CBN.Com – The Christian Broadcasting Network*, 25 September 2013, http://www1.cbn.com/spirituallife/callin g-for-the-first-crusade.

48 Mir Tamim Ansary, *Destiny Disrupted: A History of the World through Islamic Eyes*, 1st edn (New York: PublicAffairs, 2009).

49 O'Brien, *European Perceptions of Islam and America from Saladin to George W. Bush*, 7.

50 Sarah Lambert, 'Crusading or Spinning', in *Gendering the Crusades*, ed. Susan Edgington and Sarah Lambert (Cardiff: University of Wales Press, 2001), 1.

51 Miriam Rita Tessera, 'Philip Count of Flanders and Hildegard of Bingen: Crusading against the Saracens or Crusading Against Deadly Sin?', in *Gendering the Crusades*, ed. Susan Edgington and Sarah Lambert (Cardiff: University of Wales Press, 2001), 79.

52 Tessera, 'Philip Count of Flanders and Hildegard of Bingen', 84.

53 Tessera, 'Philip Count of Flanders and Hildegard of Bingen', 84.

54 Tessera, 'Philip Count of Flanders and Hildegard of Bingen', 82.

55 Tessera, 'Philip Count of Flanders and Hildegard of Bingen', 83.

56 Quoted in Tolan, *Saracens*, 106–7.

57 Heath Dillard, *Daughters of the Reconquest: Women in Castilian Town Society, 1100-1300*, Cambridge Iberian and Latin American Studies (Cambridge and New York: Cambridge University Press, 1984); Susan Edgington and Sarah Lambert, eds, *Gendering the Crusades* (Cardiff: University of Wales Press, 2001).

58 P. Chatterjee, 'Colonialism, Nationalism, and Colonized Women: The Contest in India', *American Ethnologist* 16, no. 4 (1989): 622–33.

59 Jinthana Haritaworn, *Queer Lovers and Hateful Others: Regenerating Violent Times and Places* (London: Pluto Press, 2015).

60 Zillah Eisenstein, *Against Empire: Feminisms, Racism, and the West* (London: Zed Books, 2004); Kelly Oliver, *Women as Weapons of War: Iraq, Sex, and the Media* (New York: Columbia University Press, 2007); Susan Faludi, *The Terror Dream: Fear and Fantasy in Post-9/11 America* (New York: Metropolitan Books, 2007); Katha Pollitt, 'After the Taliban', *The Nation*, 29 November 2001, https://www.thenation.com/arti cle/after-taliban/.

61 S. Thobani, 'White Wars: Western Feminisms and the War on Terror', *Feminist Theory* 8, no. 2 (2007): 169–85.

62 See Valerie Amos and Pratibha Parmar, 'Challenging Imperial Feminism', *Feminist Review*, no. 80 (2005): 44–63; Chandra Talpade Mohanty, Lourdes Torres and Ann Russo, eds, *Third World Women and the Politics of Feminism* (Bloomington: Indiana University Press, 1991); Davis, *Women, Race & Class*.

63 Irshad Manji, *The Trouble with Islam: A Muslim's Call for Reform in Her Faith* (New York: St. Martin's Press, 2004); Ayaan Hirsi Ali, *The Caged Virgin: An Emancipation Proclamation for Women and Islam* (New York: Free Press, 2006); Azar Nafisi, *Reading Lolita in Tehran: A Memoir in Books* (New York: Random House, 2003).
64 Davis, *Women, Race & Class*; Chandra Talpade Mohanty, *Feminism without Borders: Decolonizing Theory, Practicing Solidarity* (London: Duke University Press Books, 2003); Amos and Parmar, 'Challenging Imperial Feminism'.
65 See, for example, Joan Wallach Scott, *The Politics of the Veil* (Princeton: Princeton University Press, 2007); Ahmed, *A Quiet Revolution*; Lila Abu-Lughod, *Do Muslim Women Need Saving?* (Cambridge: Harvard University Press, 2015).
66 See Karen Brodkin Sacks, 'How Did Jews Become White Folks?', in *How Did Jews Become White Folks & What That Says about America* (New Brunswick: Rutgers University Press, 1998), 274–83.Quoteonp.274. https://nelsonssociology101.weebly.com/uploads/2/6/1/1/6/26165328/jews.pdf
67 Anidjar, *The Jew, the Arab*; J. Kameron Carter, *Race: A Theological Account* (Oxford: Oxford University Press, 2008).
68 See Back and Solomos, *Theories of Race and Racism*; Goldberg, David Theo.
69 See Melani McAlister, *Epic Encounters: Culture, Media, and U.S. Interests in the Middle East since 1945*, Updated edn, with a post-9/11 chapter, American Crossroads 6 (Berkeley: University of California Press, 2005).

Chapter 1

1 For an example of how the category 'enemy combatant' played out in the lives of the Muslims caught up in its dragnet, see Moazzam Begg and Victoria Brittain, *Enemy Combatant: My Imprisonment at Guantánamo, Bagram, and Kandahar* (New York: New Press, 2006).
2 These cardboard cut-outs were removed after the Council on American Islamic Relations lobbied the Pentagon to address 'the Islamophobia in military training'. See Allison Deger, 'Military "Kill House" Training Base Used Muslim Women Targets', *Mondoweiss*, 6 July 2012, https://mondoweiss.net/2012/07/military-kill-house-training-base-used-muslim-women-targets/.
3 Scott, *The Politics of the Veil*, 5.
4 Antony Anghie, *Imperialism, Sovereignty and the Making of International Law*, Cambridge Studies in International and Comparative Law 37 (Cambridge and New York: Cambridge University Press, 2005).
5 Francisco de Victoria, quoted in Antony Anghie, 'The Evolution of International Law: Colonial and Postcolonial Realities', *Third World Quarterly* 27, no. 5 (2006): 744.
6 Sir Arthur Hirtzel, quoted in Anghie, 'The Evolution of International Law', 747.
7 For my discussion of exaltation, see Thobani, *Exalted Subjects*.
8 For an example of this 'invasion' into modern times, see the ruckus following the appearance of the Muslim student leader, Maryam Pougetoux, on French television wearing a hijab. Aida Alami, 'The College Student Who Has France's Secularists Fulminating', *The New York Times*, 1 June 2018, sec. World, https://www.nytimes.com/2018/06/01/world/europe/maryam-pougetoux-islam-france.html.
9 Michael Hastings, 'The Runaway General: The Profile That Brought Down McChrystal', *Rolling Stone*, 22 June 2010, 93.

10. Ann Scott Tyson, 'McChrystal Faces Raft of Issues as New Commander in Afghanistan', *The Washington Post*, 13 May 2009, sec. Nation, http://www.washingtonpost.com/wp-dyn/content/article/2009/05/12/AR2009051203679.html.
11. The war strategy is publicly supported in the regular celebration of US troops at events as mundane as preferential treatment at airports and on commercial air flights to the more excitement generating community breakfasts, rallies, etc. to 'honour our troops'.
12. Hastings, 'The Runaway General', 96.
13. Elisabeth Bumiller and Mark Mazzetti, 'A General Steps from the Shadows', *The New York Times*, 12 May 2009, sec. AsiaPacific, https://www.nytimes.com/2009/05/13/world/asia/13commander.html.
14. Bumiller and Mazzetti, 'A General Steps from the Shadows'.
15. The Bureau of Investigative Journalism found that it is mostly civilians who are killed by drone attacks in Pakistan. Consider, for example, these drones strikes were found to kill 'militants' in 12 per cent of such attacks in Pakistan, with only 4 per cent of these being members of Al-Qaeda, the 'enemy' at the launch of this war. See Rozina Ali, 'Are US Drone Strikes in Pakistan War Crimes? Only 12% of Those Killed Are Known Militants', *Informed Comment*, 25 October 2014, https://www.juancole.com/2014/10/strikes-pakistan-militants.html.
16. Andrew Cockburn, *Kill Chain: The Rise of the High-Tech Assassins* (New York: Henry Holt and Company, 2015), 214.
17. Mark Landler and Michael Gordon, 'President Cedes Afghan Strategy to the Pentagon: A Quiet Shift of Power', *The New York Times*, 19 June 2017, National edition.
18. See Agamben, *Homo Sacer*.
19. Cockburn, *Kill Chain*, 8. The 'kill list' prepared by President Obama and other leaders 'effectively considers men of military age as legitimate targets'; Ali, 'Are US Drone Strikes in Pakistan War Crimes?' A decade and a half after the launch of the War on Terror, and with all the horrors of the torture of detainees exposed in the notorious Abu Ghraib photographs, the majority (59 per cent) of Americans polled continued to support the use of torture by the CIA. Jeffrey St Clair, 'When Torturers Walk', *Counterpunch*, 20 March 2015, https://www.counterpunch.org/2015/03/20/when-torturers-walk/.
20. Fanon, *Black Skin, White Masks*.
21. Fanon, *Black Skin, White Masks*, 110.
22. Fanon, *Black Skin, White Masks*, 10.
23. Achille Mbembé, 'Necropolitics', trans. Libby Meintjes, *Public Culture* 15, no. 1 (Winter 2003): 11–40.
24. Ziauddin Sardar mentions Fanon's full name in the Foreword to the 2008 edition of *Black Skin, White Masks*. See Fanon, *Black Skin, White Masks*, ix.
25. For an excellent discussion of the role of Islam in shaping the revolutionary politics of the Algerian peasantry, see Fouzi Slisli, 'Islam: The Elephant in Fanon's The Wretched of the Earth', *Critique: Critical Middle Eastern Studies* 17, no. 1 (Spring 2008): 97–108.
26. Slisli, 'Islam', 97.
27. Slisli revisits Fanon's chapter on 'Spontaneity: Its Strengths and Weaknesses' to make this argument. See Slisli, 'Islam'.

28 Marnia Lazreg, *Torture and the Twilight of Empire: From Algiers to Baghdad*, Human Rights and Crimes against Humanity (Princeton: Princeton University Press, 2008).
29 Richard Wood, 'Vicious Circles: Fanon, Islamism and Decolonization', *Counterpunch*, 20 March 2015, https://www.counterpunch.org/2015/03/20/vicious-circles-fanon-islamism-and-decolonization/.
30 Knut Vikør, 'Religious Revolts in Colonial North Africa', in *Islam and the European Empires*, ed. David Motadel (Oxford: Oxford University Press, 2014), 170–86.
31 Vikør, 'Religious Revolts in Colonial North Africa', 171.
32 Ricardo René Laremont, *Islam and the Politics of Resistance in Algeria, 1783-1992* (Trenton: Africa World Press, 2000), 6.
33 Reiland Rabaka, *Forms of Fanonism: Frantz Fanon's Critical Theory and the Dialectics of Decolonization* (Lanham: Lexington Books, 2010), 32.
34 See Julia Clancy-Smith, 'Islam and the French Empire in North Africa', in *Islam and the European Empires*, ed. David Motadel (Oxford: Oxford University Press, 2014), 90–111.
35 Marnia Lazreg, 'Gender and Politics in Algeria: Unraveling the Religious Paradigm', *Signs* 15, no. 4 (1990): 758.
36 Lazreg, 'Gender and Politics in Algeria', 758.
37 Frantz Fanon, *A Dying Colonialism*, trans. Haakon Chevalier (New York: Grove Press, 1967).
38 See Edward Said, *Covering Islam: How the Media and the Experts Determine How We See the Rest of the World* (New York: Pantheon Books, 1981).
39 Clinton Bennett, *Studying Islam: The Critical Issues* (New York: A&C Black, 2010), 3.
40 See Arvind-Pal Mandair, *Religion and the Specter of the West: Sikhism, India, Postcoloniality, and the Politics of Translation* (New York: Columbia University Press, 2009), for an excellent critique of the postcolonial treatment of the question of religion.
41 Asad, *Genealogies of Religion*; Asad, *Formations of the Secular*; Wael Hallaq, *The Impossible State: Islam, Politics, and Modernity's Moral Predicament* (New York: Columbia University Press, 2013); Sayyid, *A Fundamental Fear*; Shahab Ahmed, *What Is Islam? The Importance of Being Islamic* (Princeton: Princeton University Press, 2016); Ovamir Anjum, *Politics, Law, and Community in Islamic Thought: The Taymiyyan Movement* (New York: Cambridge University Press, 2012).
42 *Islamophobia* is defined here as a discourse inciting public hatred of Islam and violence towards Muslims, its present embedded-ness in political culture is evidenced in the perennial upswing in reported hate crimes against Muslims across North America and Europe. Not surprising, the majority of these target Muslim women.

The term 'Islamophobia' is defined as originating in the UK Runnymede Trust Report on discrimination against, and harassment of, Muslims during the 1990s. Chris Allen points out that although the American periodical *Insight* first used the term in its contemporary form, he credits the Runnymeade Trust report, 'British Muslims and Islamophobia' (1997) as the 'first source to posit a firm definition of Islamophobia – the "shorthand" way of referring to dread or hatred of Islam – and, therefore, to dislike all or most Muslims'. See Christopher Allen, *Islamophobia* (Surrey: Ashgate, 2010), 15.). Presently, critical scholars define the term in a number of ways, including as 'the disciplining of Muslims by reference to an antagonistic Western horizon'. See Salman Sayyid, 'Out of the Devil's Dictionary', in *Thinking through Islamophobia: Global Perspectives*, ed. Salman Sayyid and AbdoolKarim

Vakil (London: C. Hurst, 2010), 15. Tariq Modood has written about anti-Muslim and anti-Islam discrimination in the UK as 'a cultural sickness' and Ziauddin Sardar links this term to the historical anti-Islamic perspective of the West. Although the term itself is of recent origin, the social, cultural and political phenomena it names clearly has much earlier antecedents whose ideological as well as material consequences reverberate into the present.

It is not my intention here to suggest that Islamophobia is static nor that it has a historically unbroken lineage. Rather my use of this term links it to forms of hatred directed towards Islam at previous junctures to draw attention to its productivity during those earlier historical moments. Mindful of Said's comments on the resilience of the structures that reproduce the object of his concern, my discussion of Islamophobia emphasizes the continuities as well as discontinuities in this discourse. Said's view was that the structures of representation that produce Orientalism did not remain unchanged, that their repetition at different moments could be considered as recurrence, as re-appropriation, which, he explained, 'doesn't mean it's the same'. (Edward Said, quoted in Ania Loomba, 'Remembering Said', *Comparative Studies of South Asia, Africa and the Middle East* 23, no. 1 (2003): 13.) My study of repetition in the representational tropes of Western fascination with Islam demonstrates how this has not always been 'the same' in its expression, yet such fascination does have an underlying logic to it. Moreover, although I consider it necessary that contemporary studies of national and global politics take some account of Islamophobia, I also believe studies of Islamophobia call for some level of engagement with Islam itself, which, unfortunately, is not the case often enough.

43   My use of the term 'Islamophobia' follows Salman Sayyid's suggestion to focus on the use that has been made of this term: 'This is not to produce an idea of Islamophobia that corresponds to an analytical definition based on a single property or essence capable of unifying the multiple uses of this term in all possible situations, but rather to think it through the notion of a family resemblance based on overlapping similarities.' Salman Sayyid, 'Thinking through Islamophobia', in *Thinking through Islamophobia: Global Perspectives*, ed. Salman Sayyid and AbdoolKarim Vakil (London: C. Hurst, 2010), 2.

44   Karen Armstrong, *Islam: A Short History* (London: Phoenix, 2001); Vernon Egger, *A History of the Muslim World since 1260: The Making of a Global Community* (Upper Saddle River: Pearson Prentice Hall, 2008); Fazlur Rahman, *Islam* (Chicago: University of Chicago Press, 1979).

45   Omid Safi, *Memories of Muhammad: Why the Prophet Matters* (Harper Collins, 2009); Armstrong, *Islam*; Ziauddin Sardar and Zafar Abbas Malik, *Muhammad for Beginners* (Cambridge: Icon Books, 1999).

46   Islam integrated the pilgrimage to Mecca as well as reverence for the Ka'ba (pre-Islamic in origin) into the centre of its ritualistic life; recognized Jewish and Christian Prophets as also Prophets of Islam; and accepted the Bible and the Jewish scriptures along with the adherents of these faiths as 'people of the book'. See Armstrong, *Islam*; Tariq Ramadan, *In the Footsteps of the Prophet: Lessons from the Life of Muhammad* (Oxford: Oxford University Press, 2007); Ziauddin Sardar, *Desperately Seeking Paradise: Journeys of a Sceptical Muslim* (London: Granta Books, 2004). It is significant that the Islamic rituals and practices (some shared in common with Jews and Christians) as developed by the Prophet continue even now to reflect this Islamic openness to its pre-Islamic past in the daily lives of Muslims. Examples

include the retention of the pre-Islamic name, 'Allah', for Islam's naming of the divine power; the rituals of daily prayers facing Mecca, where the Ka'ba, that 'pre-eminent symbol' of Islam, rests in a site sacred to Muslims but believed to have been dedicated by Abraham; and the Hajj, 'the apex of Muslim spiritual experience', which Muslims are required to perform at least once in their lifetime is a pilgrimage that predates Islam. Sardar, *Desperately Seeking Paradise*, 128. In these most spiritually significant of their rituals, Muslims are reminded daily of the pre-Islamic origins of their faith.

See Kecia Ali and Oliver Leaman, *Islam: The Key Concepts* (London: Routledge, 2007), 6. Furthermore, as Ziauddin Sardar explains about these continuities, and about the place of the Ka'ba in Muslim life: 'The Ka'ba is the pre-eminent symbol of Islam.... From every point on earth a Muslim seeks orientation towards this central place, the starting point of dedication to The God and his guidance of values and ethics, to which they must constantly return on the daily journey through life.' Sardar, *Desperately Seeking Paradise*, 127.

47 See Armstrong, *Islam*; Minou Reeves, *Muhammad in Europe: A Thousand Years of Western Myth-Making* (New York: New York University Press, 2003); Safi, *Memories of Muhammad*; Ramadan, *In the Footsteps of the Prophet*.
48 'One important account of creation is found at the beginning of Surah 4 ("Woman")'. Q.4:1 commands people: 'Revere your lord who created you from a single soul (**nafs wahidah**) and created from it its mate and from them brought forth many men and women.' Ali and Leaman, *Islam*, 23.
49 See Armstrong, *Islam*; Amina Wadud, *Qur'an and Woman: Rereading the Sacred Text from a Woman's Perspective* (New York: Oxford University Press, 1999); Asma Barlas, *'Believing Women' in Islam: Unreading Patriarchal Interpretations of the Qur'an* (Austin: University of Texas Press, 2002).
50 Armstrong, *Islam*, 36.
51 Ali and Leaman, *Islam*, 113.
52 Armstrong, *Islam*; Safi, *Memories of Muhammad*.
53 Ali and Leaman, *Islam*; Egger, *A History of the Muslim World since 1260*; Armstrong, *Islam*.
54 Muhammad Asad, *The Message of the Qur'an* (London: The Book Foundation, 2003), xi.
55 Armstrong, *Islam*, 7–9. Muhammad Asad's translation of the *ahl al-kitab* as 'followers of earlier revelation', and of Muslims as those who 'self-surrender to God' would support such a reading of Islam's openness towards what are now called 'other religions'. Asad, *The Message of the Qur'an*, xi. Certainly the example of the rulers who ruled in the name of Islam in *al-Andalus*, and the Ottoman and Mughal empires would substantiate such a claim. For example, the Mughals continued to define their society as *Dar ul Islam* even in the context of a majority Hindu community. See Ayesha Jalal, *Self and Sovereignty: Individual and Community in South Asian Islam since 1850* (London: Routlege, 2000).
56 Armstrong, *Islam*; Reeves, *Muhammad in Europe*; Asad, *The Message of the Qur'an*; Barlas, *'Believing Women' in Islam*; Fazlur Rahman, *Islam*; Wadud, *Qur'an and Woman*.
57 Reeves, *Muhammad in Europe*, 23.
58 See Armstrong, *Islam*; Safi, *Memories of Muhammad*; Mohammad Abu-Hamdiyyah, *The Qur'an: An Introduction* (London: Routledge, 2000).
59 See Armstrong, *Islam*.

For example, the Prophet is known to have engaged in debate and dialogue on Jewish and Christian theology during his lifetime; the first constitution of Medina specifically sought to institute an alliance between Muslims and Jews (guaranteeing their 'civil' as well as 'religious' rights, in modern parlance) in the face of the impending attacks on the city by the non-Muslim Arabs of Mecca; and the Prophet secured refuge for a community of Muslims, which included his daughter Ruqayya, under the protection of the Christian Negus Armah in Ethiopia. See Minou Reeves, 'Muhammad's Rule in Medina: The Making of Islam', in *Muhammad in Europe: A Thousand Years of Western Myth-Making* (New York: NYU Press, 2003), 31–56.

60 Fazlur Rahman, *Islam*, 1.
61 Fazlur Rahman, *Islam*, 2–3.
62 As Rahman explains it, 'Although it would not be correct to say that the Umayyad state had become secular and that a full cleavage had occurred between religion and state, nevertheless it is true that the state life no longer possessed that kind of relationship with religious developments which it had had hitherto. Whereas previously the Caliph had enjoyed a religious and moral pre-eminence and his decisions had been subservient to a religious end, the Umayyads, though their state basically retained the Islamic framework, were largely lay rulers who exercised political authority but lost a large measure of religious prestige'. Fazlur Rahman, *Islam*, 3.
63 Sardar, *Orientalism*, 66.
64 Egger, *A History of the Muslim World since 1260*.
65 Egger, *A History of the Muslim World since 1260*, xx.
66 For a discussion of these developments, see Chapter One, 'The Formative Period, 610–950', in Egger, *A History of the Muslim World since 1260*.
67 Marshall Hodgson, quoted in John Voll, 'Islam as a Community of Discourse and a World-System', in *The Sage Handbook of Islamic Studies*, ed. Akbar Ahmed and Tamara Sonn (London: SAGE Publications, 2010).
68 Voll, for example, has used world systems theory to advance 'a concept of the global Muslim community as a multicivilizational and cosmopolitan community of discourse'. See Voll. Also see Immanuel Wallerstein, 'Islam in the Modern World-System', *Sociologisk Forskning* 43, no. 4 (2006): 66–74.
69 This is how Karen Armstrong describes the Prophet Muhammad's approach to the two monotheistic traditions in the region, Judaism and Christianity: 'Muhammad's message was simple: He taught the Arabs no new doctrines about God: most of the Quraysh were already convinced that Allah had created the world and would judge humanity in the Last Days, as Jews and Christians believed. Muhammad did not think that he was founding a new religion, but that he was merely bringing the old faith in the One God to the Arabs, who had never had a prophet before'. Armstrong, *Islam*, 4. See also Egger, *A History of the Muslim World since 1260*. This is a view not shared by Rahman.
70 Fazlur Rahman, *Islam*, 12. Rahman's reading of the 'newness' of Islam as a departure from earlier monotheism is echoed in Massad's recent reference to the Qur'an, in which he finds the assertion of 'an originary Islam which Abraham, Moses, and Jesus preached and to which they belonged and from which Jews and Christians had departed'. Massad, *Islam in Liberalism*, 328–9. As Massad explains, while 'inclusive' of the Prophets of Jews and Christians, the Qur'an states that 'Abraham was neither Jew nor Christian, but was a Hanif, a Muslim, and he did not associate anyone with God'. Massad, 329. Massad further notes that the Qur'an 'sublates' the scriptures of

Judaism and Christianity, but calls on Muslims to 'include' Jews and Christians as 'people of the book'. Massad, *Islam in Liberalism*, 329.
71 Karen Armstrong highlights the Qur'an's message of social and economic justice; so do Amina Wadud and Asma Barlas who have engaged in two of the most influential women-centred readings of the Qur'an that highlight this egalitarian commitment.
72 The Qur'an's thesis, Asad explains, is 'that all life, being God-given, is a unity, and that problems of the flesh and of the mind, of sex and economics, of individual righteousness and social equity are intimately connected with the hopes which man may legitimately entertain with regard to his life after death'. Asad, *The Message of the Qur'an*, viii.
73 Ahmed, *What Is Islam?*, 348.
74 Ahmed, *What Is Islam?*, 348.
75 Ahmed, *What Is Islam?*, 348.
76 Asad, *Genealogies of Religion*, 1. Asad recently revisited the question in an interview for *Qui Parle*. See Basit Kareem Iqbal, 'Thinking about Method: A Conversation with Talal Asad', *Qui Parle* 26, no. 1 (June 2017): 195–218.
77 Asad, *Genealogies of Religion*.
78 Talal Asad, 'The Idea of an Anthropology of Islam', Occasional Papers Series (Washington, DC: Center for Contemporary Arab Studies, Georgetown University, 1986), 7.
79 Iqbal, 'Thinking about Method', 198.
80 Iqbal, 'Thinking about Method', 198.
81 Talal Asad, 'Thinking about Tradition, Religion, and Politics in Egypt Today', *Critical Inquiry* 42, no. 1 (1 September 2015): 166–214.
82 Asad, 'The Idea of an Anthropology of Islam', 14.
83 Iqbal, 'Thinking about Method', 196.
84 Asad, 'The Idea of an Anthropology of Islam', 15.
85 It should be noted that Asad's formulation of Islam as a discursive tradition raises its own limitations. As Ovamir Anjum points out in his insightful reading of Asad, the relation between the 'historical tradition' and contemporary practice requires further elaboration. For although Asad's notion of 'orthodoxy' is localized and configured by the power relations that constitute it as such, the tension between the idea of a singular discursive tradition (Orthodox) and its local (orthodox) articulations remains unresolved. Ovamir Anjum, 'Islam as a Discursive Tradition: Talal Asad and His Interlocutors', *Comparative Studies of South Asia, Africa and the Middle East* 27, no. 3 (4 December 2007): 656–72.
86 Sayyid, *A Fundamental Fear*, 45. As Sayyid explains it, 'The master signifier is the signifier to which other signifiers refer, and are unified by – and it fixes their identity. It is the unique point of symbolic authority that guarantees and sustains the coherence of the whole ensemble.'
87 Sayyid, *A Fundamental Fear*, 43.
88 Sayyid, *A Fundamental Fear*, 43–4.
89 Sayyid describes Islam in the following manner: 'In a totalized universe of meaning we find a multiplicity of nodal points operating to structure the chains of signification, but among them we find one specific signifier – the master signifier – which functions at the level of the totality (that is, it retrospectively constitutes that universe of meaning as a unified totality). This master signifier is a paradoxical signifier in so far as it is a particularity that functions as a metonymy for the whole discursive universe. As such, it acquires a universal dimension and functions

as a place of inscription for other signifiers. It is the signifier of the totality that guarantees and sanctions that unity: it designates the whole by its very presence. It functions as the place of inscription of all the other signifiers of that totality.' Sayyid, *A Fundamental Fear*, 45.
90 Sayyid, *A Fundamental Fear*, 44.
91 Sayyid, *A Fundamental Fear*, 44.
92 Sayyid, *A Fundamental Fear*, 46. Sayyid makes the useful observation that Islamists 'attempt to transform Islam from a nodal point in a variety of discourses into the master signifier'.
93 Faisal Devji, *Landscapes of the Jihad: Militancy, Morality, Modernity* (Ithaca: Cornell University Press, 2005), 162.
94 Ovamir Anjum, 'Do Islamists Have an Intellectual Deficit?', Rethinking Political Islam (Brookings Institute, 20 April 2016), https://www.brookings.edu/research/do-islamists-have-an-intellectual-deficit/.
95 Anjum, 'Do Islamists Have an Intellectual Deficit?'.
96 Anjum, 'Do Islamists Have an Intellectual Deficit?', 5.
97 Sherman A. Jackson, *Islam and the Blackamerican: Looking Toward the Third Resurrection* (New York: Oxford University Press, 2005), 11.
98 Jackson, *Islam and the Blackamerican*, 9.
99 Michael Gomez, *Black Crescent: The Experience and Legacy of African Muslims in the Americas* (New York: Cambridge University Press, 2005), xi.
100 Gomez, *Black Crescent*, x.
101 See 'Religious Landscape Study', Religion & Public Life Project (Pew Research Center, 11 May 2015), http://www.pewforum.org/religious-landscape-study/racial-and-ethnic-composition/.
102 Gomez, *Black Crescent*, x.
103 Sohail Daulatzai, *Black Star, Crescent Moon: The Muslim International and Black Freedom beyond America* (Minneapolis: University of Minnesota Press, 2012), xi.
104 Daulatzai, *Black Star, Crescent Moon*, xiv–xv.
105 Daulatzai, *Black Star, Crescent Moon*, xiii–xiv.
106 Jeffrey Guhin, 'Colorblind Islam: The Racial Hinges of Immigrant Muslims in the United States', *Social Inclusion* 6, no. 2 (2018): 87–97.
107 Rosemary Corbett, *Making Moderate Islam: Sufism, Service, and the 'Ground Zero Mosque' Controversy* (Stanford: Stanford University Press, 2017).
108 Ahmed, *What Is Islam?*, 520.
109 Faisal Devji, *The Terrorist in Search of Humanity: Militant Islam and Global Politics*, Crises in World Politics (London: Hurst & Co., 2008).
110 Devji, *Landscapes of the Jihad*, x.
111 Devji, *The Terrorist in Search of Humanity*, x.
112 Devji, *The Terrorist in Search of Humanity*, 9.
113 Devji, *The Terrorist in Search of Humanity*, x.
114 See Crooke, *Resistance*. Devji also argues that Islamic 'militancy' has emerged as a global phenomenon with attacks like those of 9/11 better understood on the grounds of ethics rather than politics, for he considers these attacks as symbolic acts which are notable more for their effects than their causes. Such attacks have outcomes well beyond the intentionality or control of the perpetrators, argues Devji, hence they present a certain ambiguity in terms of their causes, similar to the ambiguity about how the factor of 'risk' works in the global economy. If globalization has deepened the integration of the economy, it has also created the

conditions of possibility for the emergence of radical Jihadi groups as global agents, argues Devji. See Devji, *Landscapes of the Jihad*.
115 Crooke, *Resistance*, 274.
116 In the rhetoric of the Islamists, argues Devji, 'The Muslim community . . . has broken its theological bounds to stand in for humanity, but by doing so it has also created a bond with all the world's people, who are no longer asked simply to convert to Islam, but rather to identify with Muslim suffering to achieve their own potential humanity.' Devji, *The Terrorist in Search of Humanity*, 30.
117 Fanon, *Black Skin, White Masks*; Paul Gilroy, *Race and the Right to Be Human* (Utrecht: Universiteit Utrecht, 2009).
118 Fanon, *Black Skin, White Masks*, 92.
119 William Brustein, *Roots of Hate: Anti-Semitism in Europe before the Holocaust* (Cambridge: Cambridge University Press, 2003), xi.
120 In his study of anti-Semitism in France, Germany, Great Britain, Italy and Romania during the period 1879–1939, Brustein argues that 'anti-Semitism is a multifaceted form of prejudice' whose manifestations 'had become embedded in Western culture generally over the centuries' and 'would periodically erupt at moments of large-scale Jewish immigration, severe economic crisis or revolutionary challenge to the existing social and political order'. Brustein, *Roots of Hate*, xii.
121 Brustein, *Roots of Hate*, 5.
122 Steven Beller, *Antisemitism: A Very Short Introduction* (Oxford: Oxford University Press, 2007), 1.
123 Brustein, *Roots of Hate*, 6–7.
124 Beller, *Antisemitism*, 15.
125 Brustein, *Roots of Hate*, 35–40.
126 Brustein, *Roots of Hate*, 46.
127 See also Joseph Massad and Gil Anidjar for further discussion of this point.
128 Tomoko Masuzawa, *The Invention of World Religions, or, How European Universalism Was Preserved in the Language of Pluralism* (Chicago: University of Chicago Press, 2005).
129 As noted in the section, this point is also made by Goldberg.
130 Sardar, *Desperately Seeking Paradise*, 309.
131 The pro-Israeli site of the American-Israeli Cooperative Enterprise, Jewish Virtual Library, refers positively to the Muslim treatment of the Jews who were expelled from Spain. 'Modern Jewish History: The Spanish Expulsion (1492)', Jewish Virtual Library, A Project of AICE, accessed 15 September 2018, https://www.jewishvirtual library.org/the-spanish-expulsion-1492.
132 See 'Modern Jewish History: The Spanish Expulsion (1492)'.
133 See Walter Mignolo, Maureen Quilligan and Margaret Greer, eds, *Rereading the Black Legend: The Discourses of Religious and Racial Difference in the Renaissance Empires* (Chicago: University of Chicago Press, 2008), which traces the religious and racial dynamics of the Reconquista.
134 Tomoko Masuzawa, 'Islam, a Semitic Religion', in *The Invention of World Religions, or, How European Universalism Was Preserved in the Language of Pluralism* (Chicago: University of Chicago Press, 2005).
135 Massad identifies Renan as a key figure in the racialization of the category of the Semite: 'Ernest Renan was perhaps one of the most illustrious Orientalists who helped bring about this transformation.' For Renan, the 'Semitic Spirit' had two forms: 'The Hebraic or Mosaic form, and the Arabic or Muslim form', Massad

explains. Said summarized such representations as follows, 'The Semites are rabid monotheists who produced no mythology, no art, no commerce, no civilization; their consciousness is a rigid and narrow one; all in all they represent an "inferior combination of human nature"', and Massad argues that in Renan's view, the Jew and the Arab were similar in nature. Massad, *Islam in Liberalism*, 316.
136 Dorothy Figueira, *Aryans, Jews, Brahmins: Theorizing Authority through Myths of Identity* (New Delhi: Navayana, 2015), viii.
137 Figueira, *Aryans, Jews, Brahmins*, viii.
138 Massad, *Islam in Liberalism*, 316.
139 Massad, *Islam in Liberalism*, 324.
140 Massad, *Islam in Liberalism*, 318.
141 While I do not wish to contribute to the erasure of the millions of non-Jews who were also put to death in the Nazi camps, including gender/sexual minorities, Roma and communists, my focus here is on one particular aspect of this genocide, namely the racial killing and remaking of Jewish communities.
142 Freud in 'The Future of an Illusion', quoted in Massad, *Islam in Liberalism*, 299.
143 Massad, *Islam in Liberalism*, 21.
144 Massad, *Islam in Liberalism*, 31.
145 As the editorial secretary of the National Conference, who wrote the introduction to the book, stated: 'In entitling the book *The Religions of Democracy*, we have in mind the belief in the worth and rights of the individual which characterizes all three of the faiths with which it deals. Based upon religion, it repudiates all forms of tyranny. This affirmation of the supreme importance of the individual lies at the foundation of all true democracy'. Quoted in Massad, *Islam in Liberalism*, 31.
146 Massad, *Islam in Liberalism*, 31.
147 Beller, *Antisemitism*, 11.
148 Beller, *Antisemitism*, 11.
149 'An American soldier boasts of having tortured Iraqis and making a 15 year old Iraqi girl commit suicide after she had been raped.' See *I've Tortured and Raped in Iraq*, accessed 14 September 2018, https://www.youtube.com/watch?v=qFOF-jv32dA.
150 Donald McNeil Jr, 'The Long, Dusky Trek toward Tolerance', *The New York Times*, 13 February 2009, sec. Movies, https://www.nytimes.com/2009/02/15/movies/15mcne.html.
151 This is how Akbar Ahmed describes the pilgrimage: 'Stripped to the regulation dress, two unstitched pieces of white cloth worn in a specific manner, no jewellery allowed, princes and paupers, presidents and pick pockets jostle and are jostled anonymously in the unending crowds. The different colours, heights and sizes of Muslims reflect the diversity of Muslim society; and here all barriers of caste, class, and colour are removed. Overweight, pale Egyptian scholars, tall, lean, black Sudanese, blue-eyed blonds from Europe, small, brown, slant-eyed Malays – all creatures of God, Muslims are one in the house of God. All are pilgrims – some scurrying from prayer site to site, greedily adding up merit; others lost in meditation, suspended in some dream-like world; still others unconsciously weeping tears of ecstasy. The live dynamism and power of a world religion are here amply displayed.' Akbar Ahmed, *Discovering Islam: Making Sense of Muslim History and Society* (London: Routledge, 1988), 145.
152 Sardar, *Desperately Seeking Paradise*, 127–8.
153 Kathryn Babayan, '"In Spirit We Ate Each Other's Sorrow": Female Companionship in Seventeenth-Century Safavi Iran', in *Islamicate Sexualities: Translations across*

Temporal Geographies of Desire, ed. Kathryn Babayan and Afsaneh Najmabadi, Harvard Middle Eastern Monographs 39 (Cambridge: Center for Middle Eastern Studies of Harvard University, Harvard University Press, 2008), 243.
154 Asad, *Formations of the Secular*, 90.
155 Cooke, *Women Claim Islam*, xxiv.
156 This is what Malcolm X had to say of his experience of the Hajj: 'When I was in ... on the pilgrimage, I had close contact with Muslims whose skin would in America be classified as white, and with Muslims who would themselves be classified as white in America. But these particular Muslims didn't call themselves white. They looked upon themselves as human beings, as part of the human family, and therefore they looked upon all other segments of the human family as part of that same family'. Describing the 'different attitudes' and 'air' of these light-skinned Muslims, Malcolm X went on to say, 'if Islam had done that for them, perhaps if the white man in America would study Islam, perhaps it could do the same thing for him'. *El-Hajj Malek Shabazz Malcolm X – 1964 Post-Hajj Interview*, 1964, https://www.youtube.com/watch?v=zCwOn32IqXo.
157 See Dirk van den Berg, *The Siege of Mecca* (PBS International), accessed 14 September 2018, http://pbsinternational.org/programs/siege-of-mecca/.
158 *I've Tortured and Raped in Iraq*.
159 Georgiana Banita, 'Raymond Williams and Online Video: The Tragedy of Technology', in *About Raymond Williams*, ed. Monika Seidl, Roman Horak and Lawrence Grossberg (London: Routledge, 2009), 102–3.
160 Banita, 'Raymond Williams and Online Video', 102.
161 Banita, 'Raymond Williams and Online Video', 98.
162 Paul von Zielbauer, '3rd U.S. Soldier Sentenced for Rape and Murder in Iraq', *The New York Times*, 5 August 2007, sec. Americas, https://www.nytimes.com/2007/08/05/world/americas/05iht-soldier.1.6986906.html.
163 Paul Harris, 'US Soldier Admits Killing Unarmed Afghans for Sport', *The Guardian*, 23 March 2011, sec. US news, https://www.theguardian.com/world/2011/mar/23/us-soldier-admits-killing-afghans.
164 Harris, 'US Soldier Admits Killing Unarmed Afghans for Sport'.
165 Harris, 'US Soldier Admits Killing Unarmed Afghans for Sport'.
166 Alex Spillius, 'General Who Said Killing Is a Hoot Lands Top Job', *The Montreal Gazette*, 9 July 2010.
167 Thom Shanker, 'Petraeus's Successor Is Known for Impolitic Words', *The New York Times*, 19 July 2010, sec. World, https://www.nytimes.com/2010/07/20/world/20mattis.html.
168 Tom Turnipseed, 'Killing for Fun; Military Madness', *Common Dreams*, 13 July 2010, https://www.commondreams.org/views/2010/07/13/killing-fun-military-madness.
169 Shanker, 'Petraeus's Successor Is Known for Impolitic Words'.
170 Dunham Will, 'General: It's "Fun to Shoot Some People"', *CNN.Com*, 4 February 2005, http://www.cnn.com/2005/US/02/03/general.shoot/.
171 Luke Harding, 'The Other Prisoners', *The Guardian*, 20 May 2004, sec. World News, https://www.theguardian.com/world/2004/may/20/iraq.gender.
172 This incident is described in Joseph Pugliese, *State Violence and the Execution of Law: Biopolitcal Caesurae of Torture, Black Sites, Drones* (London: Routledge, 2013).
173 Ms. Haspel was directly linked to the 'enhanced interrogations' (including waterboarding and the infliction of pain to the point of death) used by the CIA and was reported to have 'direct, first hand knowledge about' this torture. She is

also reported to have run 'the black site at which Abu Zubaydah was detained and interrogated' in court documents filed by attorneys representing a number of the torture victims and to 'have personally signed the order to destroy the videotapes of the Thai site interrogations'. See Larry Siems, 'The Truth about Torture: Trump's CIA Pick Can't Lead without Facing Her Past', *The Guardian*, 14 March 2018, sec. US news, https://www.theguardian.com/us-news/2018/mar/14/gina-haspel-torture-trump-cia-director-pick-has-to-face-past.

174 Anne McClintock, *Imperial Leather: Race, Gender, and Sexuality in the Colonial Contest* (London: Routledge, 1995), 22.
175 Thomas Hendriks, 'Race and Desire in the Porno-Tropics: Ethnographic Perspectives from the Post-Colony', *Sexualities* 17, nos. 1–2 (1 January 2014): 214.
176 Hendriks, 'Race and Desire in the Porno-Tropics', 215.
177 Hendriks, 'Race and Desire in the Porno-Tropics', 218.
178 Hendriks, 'Race and Desire in the Porno-Tropics', 218.
179 Hendriks, 'Race and Desire in the Porno-Tropics', 220.
180 Frances Perraudin, 'David Cameron Lacked "balls" to Head off the Rise of Isis, Says Former Defence Chief', *The Guardian*, 30 August 2015, sec. Politics, https://www.theguardian.com/politics/2015/aug/30/david-cameron-lacked-balls-to-head-off-the-rise-of-isis-says-former-defence-chief.
181 Jeffrey St Clair, 'Israeli Tunnel Vision', *Counterpunch*, 5 September 2014, https://www.counterpunch.org/2014/09/05/israeli-tunnel-vision/.
182 Will, 'General: It's "Fun to Shoot Some People"'.
183 Meyda Yeğenoğlu, *Colonial Fantasies: Towards a Feminist Reading of Orientalism*, Cambridge Cultural Social Studies (Cambridge: Cambridge University Press, 1998); Scott, *The Politics of the Veil*.
184 Fanon, *Black Skin, White Masks*, 170.
185 Robert Aldrich, *Colonialism and Homosexuality* (London: Routledge, 2003), 18.
186 Aldrich, *Colonialism and Homosexuality*, 18.
187 Fanon, *Black Skin, White Masks*, 169–70.
188 See, for example, Ida B. Wells-Barnett, *On Lynchings*, Classics in Black Studies Series (Amherst: Humanity Books, 2002); Trudier Harris, *Exorcising Blackness: Historical and Literary Lynching and Burning Rituals* (Bloomington: Indiana University Press, 1984); Graham Dawson, *Soldier Heroes: British Adventure, Empire, and the Imagining of Masculinities* (London: Routledge, 1994); Darlene Clark Hine and Earnestine Jenkins, eds, *A Question of Manhood: A Reader in U.S. Black Men's History and Masculinity*, Blacks in the Diaspora (Bloomington: Indiana University Press, 1999).
189 This is how a feature article reported the impact of the 9/11 attacks on media consumption in the United States: 'After days of watching the catastrophic events of Sept. 11, many Americans patriotically marched to their video stores to rent movies in which U.S. action heroes, in the words of one radio announcer, "kick terrorist butt."' The most watched videos were reported to be replete with Orientalist tropes. Kamal Al-solaylee, 'All Arabs Are Not Alike', *The Globe and Mail*, 3 October 2001, sec. News flash.
190 See Jean Baudrillard, *The Spirit of Terrorism*, trans. Chris Turner, Revised edition (London: Verso, 2003).
191 In an interesting choice of terminology, Juan Cole noted that American dependence on 'Islamic oil' has also shaken the nation's sense of self: 'Being reliant on foreign lands for gasoline, and having its price determined by faraway events, is galling and

even perhaps felt as castrating. The foreigners who control the sources of American manhood and liberty of movement are largely Arabs and Iranians, among the more disliked ethnicities in the United States.' Juan Ricardo Cole, *Engaging the Muslim World* (New York: Palgrave Macmillan, 2009).
192 See Joseph Massad, *Desiring Arabs* (Chicago: University of Chicago Press, 2007); Jasbir Puar, *Terrorist Assemblages: Homonationalism in Queer Times*, Next Wave (Durham: Duke University Press, 2007); Haritaworn, *Queer Lovers and Hateful Others*; Fatima El-Tayeb, *European Others: Queering Ethnicity in Postnational Europe* (Minneapolis: University of Minnesota Press, 2011).
193 Puar, *Terrorist Assemblages*.
194 Massad, *Desiring Arabs*.
195 Haritaworn, *Queer Lovers and Hateful Others*.
196 Piyel Haldar, *Law, Orientalism and Postcolonialism: The Jurisdiction of the Lotus-Eaters* (London: Routledge, 2007); Kabbani, *Europe's Myths of Orient*; Sardar, *Orientalism*.
197 Haldar, *Law, Orientalism and Postcolonialism: The Jurisdiction of the Lotus-Eaters*; McClintock, *Imperial Leather*.
198 While the invasion of Iraq was less readily supported by some of these states, for example Canada, none broke off their ties with the United States in the larger 'War on Terror', nor did they refuse to engage in other aspects of the occupation of Iraq, such as intelligence gathering and sharing and implementing the 'anti-terrorism' measures developed by the United States for adoption at the global level.

Chapter 2

1 Vincent Lloyd, ed., *Race and Political Theology* (Stanford: Stanford University Press, 2012).
2 Lloyd, ed., *Race and Political Theology*, 8.
3 Lloyd, ed., *Race and Political Theology*, 8.
4 Lloyd, ed., *Race and Political Theology*, 5–6.
5 In the Fourth Crusade, the Pope and the city-state of Venice orchestrated the decade-long occupation (1204) of the Byzantine capital, Constantinople, that eroded the influence of the Orthodox Church for centuries. See John Godfrey, 'Venice and the Fourth Crusade', *History Today* 26, no. 1 (January 1976), https://www.historytoday.com/john-godfrey/venice-and-fourth-crusade.
6 Mandair, *Religion and the Specter of the West*, xii. Mandair traces the imposition of this category, and its consequences, into South Asia as part of the colonial episteme.
7 Mandair, *Religion and the Specter of the West*, xiv.
8 Massad's reading of the Qur'an finds the text 'asserts an originary Islam which Abraham, Moses, and Jesus preached and to which they belonged and from which Jews and Christians had deviated (the Qur'an announces that "Abraham was neither Jew nor Christian but was a Hanif, a Muslim, and he did not associate anyone with God"). In fact, the Qur'an never uses the word "din" in the plural at all, restricting it to the singular.' Joseph Massad, 'Forget Semitism', in *Living Together: Jacques Derrida's Communities of Violence and Peace*, ed. Elisabeth Weber (New York: Fordham University Press, 2012), 71.
9 Mandair explains that 'The active forgetting of the ontotheological continuity between religion and secularism – the religious nature of the formation called

secular or the secular nature of the formation called religion – has, however, been thoroughly probed by the discipline that has come to be called "continental philosophy of religion"'. Mandair, *Religion and the Specter of the West*, xiii.
10 Mandair, *Religion and the Specter of the West*, 2.
11 Mandair, *Religion and the Specter of the West*, xiv.
12 Mandair, *Religion and the Specter of the West*, 128.
13 See Masuzawa, *The Invention of World Religions*.
14 Cheikh Anta Diop, *The African Origin of Civilization: Myth or Reality*, trans. Mercer Cook (New York: Lawrence Hill, 1974).
15 Martin Bernal's book, *Black Athena*, sparked a bitter academic controversy regarding the relation between Afro-Asiatic traditions and Greek civilization, with Bernal defining the former as the 'roots' of the latter. See Martin Bernal, *Black Athena: Afroasiatic Roots of Classical Civilization; Volume III: The Linguistic Evidence* (New Brunswick: Rutgers University Press, 1987). Greg Thomas provides an engaging critique of Bernal, whose book, Thomas notes, elides the earlier work of Black scholars on this topic. Although Cheikh Anta Diop had decisively demonstrated the African roots of civilization in his many publications, Diop's work was sidelined by Bernal, as it has been within academic scholarship in general. Thomas also argues that Bernal's identification of the eighteenth- and nineteenth-century European appropriation of a Greek tradition shorn of its Afro-Asiatic grounding leaves unproblematized the much longer history of the practices of racialization of the West and its forms of imperialism. See Chapter One, Greg Thomas, *The Sexual Demon of Colonial Power: Pan-African Embodiment and Erotic Schemes of Empire* (Bloomington: Indiana University Press, 2007). Also see Diop, *The African Origin of Civilization*.
16 See Bernal, *Black Athena* and the controversy surrounding its publication.
17 Egger, *A History of the Muslim World since 1260*, xxix.
18 See 'Presentation', *Universidad de Castilla – La Mancha*, n.d., https://www.uclm.es/escueladetraductores/english/history/.
19 See Kamaly's excellent review of Greek Thought and Arabic Culture, by Dimitri Gutas. Hossein Kamaly, *Review of Greek Thought, Arabic Culture: The Graeco-Arabic Translation Movement in Baghdad and Early 'Abbasid Society (2nd-4th/8th-10th Centuries),'* by Dimitri Gutas, *International Society for Iranian Studies* 32, no. 4 (Autumn 1999): 575–8.
20 Egger, *A History of the Muslim World since 1260*, xx–xxi.
21 Jonathan Lyons, *Islam through Western Eyes: From the Crusades to the War on Terrorism* (New York: Columbia University Press, 2012), 193.
22 Graham Hammill, Julia Reinhard Lupton and Etienne Balibar, eds, 'Introduction', in *Political Theology and Early Modernity* (Chicago: University of Chicago Press, 2012), 1.
23 Maria Rosa Menocal, *The Ornament of the World: How Muslims, Jews, and Christians Created a Culture of Tolerance in Medieval Spain* (Boston: Little, Brown and Company, 2002).
24 Menocal, *The Ornament of the World*.
25 Pál, P. Z. 'The Shifting of International Trade Routes in the 15th-17th Centuries', *Acta Historica Academiae Scientiarum Hungaricae* 14, no. 3/4 (1968): 287–321.
26 See Max Weber, *The Protestant Ethic and the Spirit of Capitalism*, trans. Talcott Parsons (London: Routledge, 2005), https://doi.org/10.4324/9780203995808.
27 Sardar, *Orientalism*; Ivan Kalmar, *Early Orientalism: Imagined Islam and the Notion of Sublime Power* (London: Routledge, 2013).

28 Murat İyigün, 'Luther and Suleyman', *The Quarterly Journal of Economics* 123, no. 4 (2008): 1465–94.
29 İyigün, 'Luther and Suleyman', 1472.
30 Loomba, *Shakespeare, Race, and Colonialism*, 25.
31 Loomba, *Shakespeare, Race, and Colonialism*, 81.
32 This difference between 'religious' and 'irreligious' Blacks can be seen in the depictions of Muslims, who 'are still often pictured as physically as well as morally "black", but the difference between them and the irreligious Moor is marked, and expressed in terms of class, culture and location. North African or Arab Moors, being Muslims, are allowed a cultural lineage, religious traditions, and occasionally, a lighter skin colour. Sub-Saharan Africans are increasingly associated with a lack of religion and culture, and painted as low-born.' Loomba, *Shakespeare, Race, and Colonialism*, 81.
33 Kabbani, *Europe's Myths of Orient*, 14.
34 Tolan, *Saracens*.
35 Jacob Pandian, *Anthropology and the Western Tradition: Toward an Authentic Anthropology* (Prospect Heights: Waveland Press, 1985), 8.
36 Pandian, *Anthropology and the Western Tradition*.
37 Carter, *Race*, 3–4.
38 Carter, *Race*, 4.
39 Walter Mignolo, 'Afterword: What Does the Black Legend Have to Do with Race?', in *Rereading the Black Legend: The Discourses of Religious and Racial Difference in the Renaissance Empires*, ed. Walter Mignolo, Maureen Quilligan and Margaret Greer (Chicago: University of Chicago Press, 2008).
40 Mignolo, 'Afterword', 312.
41 Loomba, *Shakespeare, Race, and Colonialism*, 26.
42 Loomba, *Shakespeare, Race, and Colonialism*, 68.
43 Gil Anidjar, *Blood: A Critique of Christianity* (New York: Columbia University Press, 2014), 34.
44 Anidjar, *Blood*, 32.
45 Anidjar, *Blood*, 32.
46 Anidjar, *Blood*, 32.
47 See Mignolo, Quilligan and Margaret Greer, eds, *Rereading the Black Legend*.
48 Mignolo, Quilligan, and Greer, eds, *Rereading the Black Legend*, 313.
49 Mignolo, Quilligan, and Greer, eds, *Rereading the Black Legend*, 316.
50 See Gomez, *Black Crescent*.
51 Hortense Spillers, 'Mama's Baby, Papa's Maybe: An American Grammar Book', *Diacritics* 17, no. 2 (1987): 70, https://doi.org/10.2307/464747.
52 See Chapter One. Willie James Jennings, *The Christian Imagination: Theology and the Origins of Race* (New Haven: Yale University Press, 2010).
53 Jennings, *The Christian Imagination*.
54 Jennings, *The Christian Imagination*.
55 Jennings, *The Christian Imagination*.
56 Spillers, 'Mama's Baby, Papa's Maybe', 70.
57 Spillers, 'Mama's Baby, Papa's Maybe', 71.
58 Jennings, *The Christian Imagination*.
59 Spillers, 'Mama's Baby, Papa's Maybe', 70.
60 Jennings, *The Christian Imagination*.
61 James Sweet, 'Spanish and Portuguese Influences on Racial Slavery in British North America, 1492-1619', in *Proceedings of the Fifth Annual Gilder Lehrman Center*

International Conference at Yale University (Collective Degradation: Slavery and the construction of race, New Haven, 2003), 5–6.
62. Sweet, 'Spanish and Portuguese Influences on Racial Slavery in British North America, 1492–1619', 7.
63. Jerald Dirks, *Muslims in American History: A Forgotten Legacy* (Beltsville: Amana Publications, 2006). Also see Gomez, *Black Crescent*.
64. Sylvia Wynter, 'Unsettling the Coloniality of Being/Power/Truth/Freedom: Towards the Human, After Man, Its Overrepresentation – An Argument', *CR: The New Centennial Review* 3, no. 3 (2003): 260, https://doi.org/10.1353/ncr.2004.0015.
65. Wynter, 'Unsettling the Coloniality of Being/Power/Truth/Freedom', 263.
66. Wynter, 'Unsettling the Coloniality of Being/Power/Truth/Freedom', 263.
67. Sylvia Wynter, 'On How We Mistook the Map for the Territory, and Re-Imprisoned Ourselves in Our Unbearable Wrongness of Being, of Désêtre: Black Studies toward the Human Project', in *Not Only the Master's Tools: African-American Studies in Theory and Practice*, ed. Lewis Gordon and Jane Anna Gordon, Cultural Politics & the Promise of Democracy (Boulder: Paradigm, 2006), 107–69.
68. Wynter, 'Unsettling the Coloniality of Being/Power/Truth/Freedom', 264.
69. Said, *Orientalism*, 119.
70. Philip Rossi, 'Kant's Philosophy of Religion', in *The Stanford Encyclopedia of Philosophy*, ed. Edward Zalta and Edward Zalta, Fall 2013 (forthcoming, 2013), URL=http// http://plato.stanford.edu/cgi-bin/encyclopedia/archinfo.cgi?entry=kant-religion.
71. Rossi, 'Kant's Philosophy of Religion'.
72. Rossi, 'Kant's Philosophy of Religion'.
73. Rossi, 'Kant's Philosophy of Religion'.
74. Rossi, 'Kant's Philosophy of Religion'.
75. See Emmanuel Chukwudi Eze, *Race and the Enlightenment: A Reader* (Cambridge: Wiley-Blackwell, 1997).
76. Robert Bernasconi, ed., *Race* (Oxford: Blackwell Publishers, 2001); Eze, *Race and the Enlightenment*; Mark Larrimore, 'Antinomies of Race: Diversity and Destiny in Kant', *Patterns of Prejudice* 42, nos. 4–5 (1 September 2008): 341–63.
77. Larrimore, 'Antinomies of Race', 342.
78. Eze, *Race and the Enlightenment*; Bernasconi, *Race*.
79. Eze, *Race and the Enlightenment*, 5.
80. Eze, *Race and the Enlightenment*, 5.
81. Ian Almond, *History of Islam in German Thought: From Leibniz to Nietzsche*, Routledge Studies in Cultural History 11 (New York: Routledge, 2010).
82. Almond, *History of Islam in German Thought*, 36–7.
83. Larrimore, 'Antinomies of Race', 347.
84. Larrimore, 'Antinomies of Race', 347.
85. Larrimore, 'Antinomies of Race', 349.
86. Larrimore, 'Antinomies of Race', 349.
87. Larrimore, 'Antinomies of Race', 341.
88. Wynter, 'On How We Mistook the Map for the Territory, and Re-Imprisoned Ourselves in Our Unbearable Wrongness of Being, of Désêtre', 139.
89. Stephen Palmquist, 'Could Kant's Jesus Be God?', *International Philosophical Quarterly* 52, no. 4 (December 2012): 424.
90. Palmquist, 'Could Kant's Jesus Be God?', 426.
91. Palmquist, 'Could Kant's Jesus Be God?', 431, note 19.
92. Palmquist, 'Could Kant's Jesus Be God?', 431, note 19.
93. Palmquist, 'Could Kant's Jesus Be God?' 432, note 20.

94   Palmquist, 'Could Kant's Jesus Be God?', 432, note 21.
95   Sunera Thobani, *Exalted Subjects: Studies in the Making of Race and Nation in Canada* (Toronto: University of Toronto Press, 2007).
96   Carter, *Race*, 16.
97   Carter, *Race*, 6–7.
98   Almond, *History of Islam in German Thought*, 123.
99   Palmquist argues that the divinity of Christ is compatible with Kant's notion of reason: 'Kant is not arguing that it is *irrational* to believe that a person whose actions appear to be completely consistent with a moral disposition is "divine" (or "good"); rather, he is affirming that such a belief can have a genuine practical use by providing "encouragement" inasmuch as it can "put beyond doubt the feasibility of what the law commands" by making "visible that which the practical rule expresses more generally"'. Palmquist, 'Could Kant's Jesus Be God?', 436.
100 Almond, *History of Islam in German Thought*, 4.
101 Almond, *History of Islam in German Thought*, 2.
102 Almond, *History of Islam in German Thought*, 3.
103 Almond, *History of Islam in German Thought*, 3.
104 The report was written by N. Bisani, quoted in Massad, *Islam in Liberalism*, 106.
105 See, for one example, Menocal, *The Ornament of the World*.
106 See Masuzawa, *The Invention of World Religions*; Mandair, *Religion and the Specter of the West*.
107 See Almond, *History of Islam in German Thought*.
108 Almond, *History of Islam in German Thought*, 130–1.
109 Almond, *History of Islam in German Thought*, 131.
110 Almond, *History of Islam in German Thought*, 131.
111 Mandair, *Religion and the Specter of the West*, 152.
112 Mandair, *Religion and the Specter of the West*, 152.
113 Kumkum Sangari and Sudesh Vaid, eds, *Recasting Women: Essays in Colonial History* (New Delhi: Kali for Women, 1989).
114 Mandair, *Religion and the Specter of the West*, 128.
115 Almond, *History of Islam in German Thought*.
116 Almond, *History of Islam in German Thought*; Eze, *Race and the Enlightenment*.
117 See Susan Buck-Morss, 'Hegel and Haiti', *Critical Inquiry* 26, no. 4 (2000): 821.
118 Almond, *History of Islam in German Thought*, 123.
119 Michael Hoffheimer, 'Race and Law in Hegel's Philosophy of Religion', in *Race and Racism in Modern Philosophy*, ed. Andrew Valls (Ithaca: Cornell University Press, 2005), 199.
120 Almond, *History of Islam in German Thought*, 124.
121 Almond, *History of Islam in German Thought*, 124.
122 Gerrit Steunebrink, 'A Religion after Christianity? Hegel's Interpretation of Islam between Judaism and Christianity', in *Hegel's Philosophy of the Historical Religions*, ed. Bart Labuschagne and Timo Slootweg (Leiden: Brill, 2012), 207.
123 Steunebrink, 'A Religion after Christianity? Hegel's Interpretation of Islam between Judaism and Christianity', 208.
124 Anidjar, *The Jew, the Arab*, 131.
125 Almond, *History of Islam in German Thought*.
126 Steunebrink, 'A Religion after Christianity? Hegel's Interpretation of Islam between Judaism and Christianity', 224.
127 See Steunebrink, 'A Religion after Christianity? Hegel's Interpretation of Islam between Judaism and Christianity', 224.

128 Steunebrink, 'A Religion after Christianity? Hegel's Interpretation of Islam between Judaism and Christianity', 215.
129 Steunebrink, 'A Religion after Christianity? Hegel's Interpretation of Islam between Judaism and Christianity', 216. This is how Steunebrink describes Hegel's assessment of Islam as fanatical 'Because Christianity has Trinity, the history of man is a concrete history. However, Islam hates and condemns all concreteness. . . . Hegel wants to say that because of its abstract conception of divine unity, Islam cannot cope with concrete unity and plurality in man of his passions either. Because no reflexion can bring the passions into unity, there is the extremism of either following the passions wildly or doing nothing, fatalism. Next to fatalism comes fanaticism. For man is still a practical being wanting to realize goals. Therefore, the only goal of a Muslim life can be to evoke in all human beings the feeling of the veneration of the One. Therefore, the Islamic religion is essentially fanatic.' Steunebrink, 'A Religion after Christianity? Hegel's Interpretation of Islam between Judaism and Christianity', 216–17.
130 Almond, *History of Islam in German Thought*, 127.
131 As Almond notes of Hegel, 'For the thinker who was able to leave Islam out of his study of world religions – and the Ottomans out of history – it remains significant that only in an *aesthetic* sense could the contemporaneity of the Muslim world be acknowledged for Hegel. The realm of poetry, unlike those of economy, history or theology, was a relatively safe one, where a foreign culture might be allowed to share a moment of teleological influence without too many problematic implications.' Almond, *History of Islam in German Thought*, 129.
132 Almond, *History of Islam in German Thought*, 114.
133 For Hegel, Islam was 'primitive' in contrast to Christianity, it 'would forever be this monochrome amorphous, expansive entity, a monodimensional power whose explosive growth in the Mediterranean lay precisely in an absence of complexity'. Almond, *History of Islam in German Thought*, 118.
134 Steunebrink, 'A Religion after Christianity? Hegel's Interpretation of Islam between Judaism and Christianity', 225.
135 Anidjar, *The Jew, the Arab*, 131.
136 Anidjar, *The Jew, the Arab*, 132.
137 Almond, *History of Islam in German Thought*, 122.
138 Almond, *History of Islam in German Thought*, 118–19.
139 Almond, *History of Islam in German Thought*, 118.
140 Masuzawa, *The Invention of World Religions*, xii.
141 Masuzawa, *The Invention of World Religions*, xii.
142 Masuzawa, *The Invention of World Religions*, xii.
143 Masuzawa, *The Invention of World Religions*, 179.
144 Sardar, *Orientalism*, 2.

Chapter 3

1 'Sworn Statements by Abu Ghraib Detainees', *The Washington Post*, accessed 19 January 2014, http://www.washingtonpost.com/wp-srv/world/iraq/abughraib/swornstatements042104.html.
2 President Obama's address to the UN General Assembly (2011), quoted by Todd Larson, Senior LGBT Coordinator, U.S. Agency for International Development. See

Todd Larson, 'President Obama and the Global Fight for LGBT Rights', *Huffington Post*, 5 November 2012, https://www.huffingtonpost.com/todd-larson/president-obama-and-the-global-fight-for-lgbt-rights_b_2060883.html.

3   Paul Joseph Watson, 'U.S. Military Investigator Confirms Women and Children Were Raped at Abu Ghraib', 28 May 2009, https://www.infowars.com/us-military-investigator-confirms-women-and-children-were-raped-at-abu-ghraib/.
4   Christina Sharpe, *Monstrous Intimacies: Making Post-Slavery Subjects* (Durham: Duke University Press, 2010).
5   Sherene Razack, *Casting Out: The Eviction of Muslims from Western Law and Politics* (Toronto: University of Toronto Press, 2008); Hazel Carby, 'US/UK's Special Relationship: The Culture of Torture in Abu Ghraib and Lynching Photographs', *Nka Journal of Contemporary African Art* 2006, no. 20 (1 May 2006): 60–71; Thompson et al., eds, *Modernity*; Puar, *Terrorist Assemblages*; Massad, *Desiring Arabs*.
6   Puar, *Terrorist Assemblages*, xxiv.
7   Puar, *Terrorist Assemblages*, xiv.
8   Puar, *Terrorist Assemblages*, xxiii.
9   Puar, *Terrorist Assemblages*, xxiii.
10 Puar, *Terrorist Assemblages*, xxiv.
11 Massad, *Desiring Arabs*, 37.
12 Massad, *Desiring Arabs*, 37.
13 Massad, *Islam in Liberalism*, 203.
14 Massad, *Desiring Arabs*, 41.
15 E. W. Lane, quoted in Kabbani, *Europe's Myths of Orient*, 67.
16 Evan Goldstein, 'Osama Bin Laden Made Me Famous', *The Chronicle of Higher Education*, 22 April 2012, https://www.chronicle.com/article/Osama-bin-Laden-Made-Me/131584.
17 Lewis, quoted in Lyons, *Islam through Western Eyes*, 157.
18 Goldstein, 'Osama Bin Laden Made Me Famous'.
19 The relation of the United States with Islam predates the founding of the Confederation, given the significant presence of Muslim slaves of African descent. Islam was suppressed in this history with the conversion of slaves to Christianity. See Gomez.
20 John Ernest Merrill, 'Of the Tractate of John of Damascus on Islam', in *Classical and Medieval Literature Criticism*, ed. Jelena Krstovic, vol. 27 (Detroit: Gale, 1998), http://link.galegroup.com/apps/doc/H1420015175/LitRC?sid=googlescholar.
21 'St. John of Damascus: Critique of Islam',.
22 Reeves, *Muhammad in Europe*, 4.
23 Kabbani, *Europe's Myths of Orient*; Sardar, *Orientalism*; Tolan, *Saracens*.
24 Rudi Bleys, *The Geography of Perversion: Male-To-Male Sexual Behavior Outside the West and the Ethnographic Imagination, 1750-1918* (New York: New York University Press, 1995), 20.
25 Bleys, *The Geography of Perversion*.
26 Edward Said, *Orientalism* (New York: Pantheon Books, 1978), 190.
27 Michel Foucault, *The History of Sexuality: Volume 1: An Introduction*, Reissue edition (New York: Vintage, 1990).
28 Kabbani, *Europe's Myths of Orient*, 6.
29 Peter Gardella, *Innocent Ecstasy: How Christianity Gave America an Ethic of Sexual Pleasure* (New York: Oxford University Press, 1985). Cardella's study of the Christian influence in contemporary American approaches to sexuality, and the pursuit of 'ecstasy' in the form of sexual orgasm begins by noting that 'For fifteen hundred

years, from the time of St. Augustine (d 430) to the twentieth century, Christians believed that original sin corrupted every aspect of life. Theologians did not simplemindedly identify sex with sin; the "concupiscence," or the insatiable desire, of human beings expressed itself in many ways. But no one, whether reborn in Christ or not, was regarded as exempt from the "infection of nature." Christians hoped for forgiveness, not innocence. In this life, the most saintly human would remain, in Martin Luther's phrase, "*simul peccator ac justus*" – both justified and a sinner. Luther himself seems to have enjoyed sex, and he taught that men and women had a fundamental right to sexual enjoyment; but Luther also said that, ever since Eden, the act of intercourse was "horribly marred" by "the hideousness inherent in our flesh, namely, the bestial desire and lust," and that intercourse even in marriage was never free from sin.' Gardella, *Innocent Ecstasy*, 5–6.

30 Anidjar, *The Jew, the Arab*.
31 Paul, quoted in Anidjar, *The Jew, the Arab*, 6.
32 Anidjar, *The Jew, the Arab*, 6.
33 Anidjar, *The Jew, the Arab*, 6–7.
34 Kecia Ali, *Sexual Ethics and Islam: Feminist Reflections on Qur'an, Hadith and Jurisprudence* (Oxford: Oneworld Publications, 2006), 13.
35 Ali, *Sexual Ethics and Islam*, 12.
36 Ali, *Sexual Ethics and Islam*, 40.
37 Kabbani, *Europe's Myths of Orient*, 14–15.
38 Kabbani, *Europe's Myths of Orient*, 5.
39 See Lyons, *Islam through Western Eyes*, 66–8.
40 Kabbani, *Europe's Myths of Orient*, 16.
41 See Karen Armstrong, *Muhammad: A Prophet for Our Time* (San Francisco: HarperOne, 2007); Ramadan, *In the Footsteps of the Prophet*.
42 Tolan, *Saracens*, 152.
43 For an excellent study of these fantasies, see Kabbani, *Europe's Myths of Orient*.
44 Kabbani, *Europe's Myths of Orient*, 15.
45 Kabbani, *Europe's Myths of Orient*, 34.
46 See Bleys, *The Geography of Perversion*.
47 See Joseph Massad, 'The Empire of Sexuality: An Interview with Joseph Massad', *Jadaliyya*, March 2013, http://www.jadaliyya.com/Details/28167.
48 Jasbir Puar, 'Mapping US Homonormativities', *Gender, Place & Culture* 13, no. 1 (1 February 2006): 32.
49 Benjamin Doherty, 'War Sporno: How the Israeli Army Uses Sex and Instagram to Sell Its Racism and Violence', *The Electronic Intifada*, 26 December 2012, https://electronicintifada.net/blogs/benjamin-doherty/war-sporno-how-israeli-army-uses-sex-and-instagram-sell-its-racism-and.
50 Tolan, *Saracens*, 106–7.
51 In her poem glorifying the Christian boy-martyr's rejection of King Abdrahemen's alleged sexual advances, Hrotsvitha of Gandersheim has the boy, Pelagius, proclaim:

> '*It is not proper for a man purified through baptism in Christ*
> *To bow down his unsullied neck to a barbarous love*
> *Nor for a Christian anointed with holy oil*
> *To be captured by the kiss of the Demon's filthy associate.*
> *Therefore embrace licitly the stupid men*

> *Insane and rich, who frolic with you on the lawn;*
> *Let the slaves which are your idols be your friends.'*
>
> Quoted in Tolan, Saracens, 106–7.

52 Tolan, *Saracens*, 108.
53 Tolan, *Saracens*, 107–8. Tolan explains that 'the earliest vivid description of Saracen idolatry predates the first Crusade by a century; it comes from the pen of a nun writing about a Cordovan martyr'. Earlier writers had described Muslims as pagans, '[y]et none of these earlier authors imagined Saracen religion in such vivid terms. . . . Many earlier authors assumed that the Saracens or Arabs continued to observe the same cults as had their pagan ancestors. Yet Hrotsvitha is the first Latin author to describe this paganism in lurid detail and to use it to justify resistance against the Saracen rule.' See Tolan, *Saracens*, 108.
54 Kenneth Wolf, 'Convivencia and the "Ornament of the World"', *Pomona Faculty Publications and Research*, 1 January 2007, https://scholarship.claremont.edu/pomona_fac_pub/43.
55 Revathi Krishnaswamy, *Effeminism: The Economy of Colonial Desire* (Ann Arbor: University of Michigan Press, 1998), 20–1.
56 Krishnaswamy, *Effeminism*, 21.
57 Krishnaswamy, *Effeminism*, 21.
58 Daniel Boyarin, 'The Double Mark of the Male Muslim', in *Race and Political Theology*, ed. Vincent Lloyd (Stanford: Stanford University Press, 2012), 177. Important to note is that 'the African here is clearly not the (pagan) sub-Saharan black African, but the Muslim Moor of North Africa', an identification 'that is . . . quite decisive for the play'. See Boyarin, 'The Double Mark of the Male Muslim', 177. Boyarin suggests that a painting of the ambassador of Morocco would likely have influenced how Shakespeare and his audience would have imaged Moors. See Boyarin, 'The Double Mark of the Male Muslim', 186, note 13.
59 Boyarin, 'The Double Mark of the Male Muslim', 175.
60 Boyarin, 'The Double Mark of the Male Muslim', 177.
61 Boyarin underscores the graphic nature of this biblical allusion to Ezekiel: 'The chapter [Ezekiel] tells a parable of two sisters, Aholah and Aholibah, who both went whoring after foreign lovers (one is, as we are told, Samaria; and the other, Jerusalem). Their lovers, in both cases, were profoundly attractive young military men: "She doted upon the Assyrians her neighbours, captains and rulers clothed most gorgeously, horsemen riding upon horses, all of them desirable young men" (23:12). It is of these young men that it is said that their penises are like the penises of asses and their ejaculations like those of horses. And the consequences are predictable (at least for Ezekiel): "Therefore, O Aholibah, thus saith the Lord GOD; Behold, I will raise up thy lovers against thee, from whom thy mind is alienated, and I will bring them against thee on every side" (23:22)'. See Boyarin, 'The Double Mark of the Male Muslim', 178.
62 Boyarin, 'The Double Mark of the Male Muslim', 178. Desdemona's tragedy is that she has loved a Moor, which presents the threat of miscegenation, 'the monstrous image of the rampant black penis entering the lily-white female body (as well as the specter of a grandchild with horns and black skin) is raised with all its fascinating, arousing horror'. Boyarin, 'The Double Mark of the Male Muslim', 176. The Jew is the other figure with a circumcised penis.

63 Boyarin explains that Desdemona's fate is '[n]o more a punishment than the downfalls of any other tragic heroes and with equal (if not greater) admiration of and deep sympathy for the tragic hero whose flaw causes his downfall, Desdemona's loving not wisely but too well also is the author of her destruction, for, as in the Biblical text, it is the very male partner in an "improper" love who becomes the enemy who destroys the female lover'. Boyarin, 'The Double Mark of the Male Muslim', 178.
64 Boyarin, 'The Double Mark of the Male Muslim', 174.
65 Boyarin's reading of race, religion and sex recognizes that 'in it we encounter a system of differences that are neither racial nor religious, neither sexuality generated not quite gendered, but all of these aggregated, laid on one another in ways that make nonsense of (or rather demonstrate the recent construction of) our own social and critical litanies'. Boyarin, 'The Double Mark of the Male Muslim', 175.
66 Boyarin, 'The Double Mark of the Male Muslim', 179.
67 Muslims ruled significant parts of Europe for eight centuries, Boyarin reminds his readers, 'and the anxiety about the Christianness of Christian Europe itself is at stake in Othello's penis, a circumcised penis penetrating to the very centre of Europe: that "old black ram" tupping/topping, conquering, defeating your white you'. Boyarin, 'The Double Mark of the Male Muslim', 175.
68 Boyarin, 'The Double Mark of the Male Muslim', 178.
69 Boyarin, 'The Double Mark of the Male Muslim', 185.
70 Boyarin, 'The Double Mark of the Male Muslim', 175.
71 The play provides 'an exemplary early instance of the queering of the very identity markers that form our contemporary mantras of race, gender or religion' to the constructed-ness of 'our most naturalized of differences, the differences between differences'. Boyarin, 'The Double Mark of the Male Muslim', 176.
72 Kaja Silverman points out that the 'differentiation of the white man from the black man on the basis of the black man's hyperbolic penis . . . places the white man on the side of "less" rather than "more", and so, threatens to erase the distinction between him and the white woman', concluding that '[t]his is the primary reason . . . why the body of the black man disrupts the unity of the white male corporeal ego'. Kaja Silverman, quoted in David Eng, *Racial Castration: Managing Masculinity in Asian America*, Perverse Modernities (Durham: Duke University Press, 2001), 150–1. My point, however, is different. I am interested in the relation between the white man's and the white woman's desire for the Moor.
73 Julia Clancy-Smith and Frances Gouda, eds, *Domesticating the Empire: Race, Gender, and Family Life in French and Dutch Colonialism* (Charlottesville: University of Virginia Press, 1998), 5.
74 Richard Burton, quoted in Kabbani, *Europe's Myths of Orient*, 51.
75 Robert Aldrich discusses at some length the book, *L'art d'aimer aux colonies*, written by a French Doctor Jacobus X in 1893. In this book, which records the sexual practices in the colonies, the Doctor 'was especially assiduous in phalloplethysmography, measuring the size of penises and comparing dimensions across races'. Aldrich, *Colonialism and Homosexuality*, 14.
76 Aldrich, *Colonialism and Homosexuality*, 1.
77 Aldrich, *Colonialism and Homosexuality*; Anton Gill, *Ruling Passions: Sex, Race and Empire* (London: BBC Books, 1995).
78 Aldrich, *Colonialism and Homosexuality*, 9. Alrich explains that these men reproduced 'though to much varying degrees, accepted ideas current in the colonial

age about "natives". Racialist and racist stereotypes abounded. Romanticism and idealisation of foreign cultures – or conversely, denigration of them – were common, along with wild fantasies about the luxuriance of the hammam, Africans' generous genital endowments. Asians' passivity and the beauty and virility of half-naked "savages". Aldrich, *Colonialism and Homosexuality*, 9.
79 Aldrich, *Colonialism and Homosexuality*, 16.
80 Aldrich, *Colonialism and Homosexuality*, 16.
81 Piyel Haldar, *Law, Orientalism and Postcolonialism: The Jurisdiction of the Lotus-Eaters* (London: Routledge, 2007), xii.
82 Haldar, *Law, Orientalism and Postcolonialism*, 99.
83 Haldar, *Law, Orientalism and Postcolonialism*, xi.
84 Massad, 'The Empire of Sexuality'.
85 Malek Alloula, *The Colonial Harem*, trans. Myrna Godzich and Wlad Godzich (Minneapolis: University of Minnesota Press, 1986), 7–14.
86 Alloula, *The Colonial Harem*, 19.
87 Almond, *The New Orientalists*, 113.
88 Almond, *The New Orientalists*, 118.
89 Almond, *The New Orientalists*, 120.
90 Almond, *The New Orientalists*, 120–1.
91 Almond, *The New Orientalists*, 121.
92 Almond, *The New Orientalists*, 121.
93 Billie Melman, quoted in Lyons, *Islam through Western Eyes*, 156.
94 Kabbani, *Europe's Myths of Orient*, 67.
95 Yeğenoğlu, *Colonial Fantasies*, 85.
96 Amira Jarmakani, '"The Sheik Who Loved Me": Romancing the War on Terror', *Signs: Journal of Women in Culture and Society* 35, no. 4 (1 June 2010): 996.
97 Jarmakani, '"The Sheik Who Loved Me"', 997.
98 Jarmakani, '"The Sheik Who Loved Me"', 1004.
99 Jarmakani, '"The Sheik Who Loved Me"', 996–7.
100 Kabbani, *Europe's Myths of Orient*, 20–1.
101 Kabbani, *Europe's Myths of Orient*, 22.
102 Kabbani, *Europe's Myths of Orient*, 68.
103 Sharon Churcher, 'How I Killed Bin Laden: Story of Navy Seal America Tried to Gag', *The Mail on Sunday*, 2 September 2012, 20.
104 The Seal had this to say about Osama bin Laden: 'In all of my deployments, we routinely saw this phenomenon. The higher up the food chain the targeted individual was, the bigger a pussy he was'. Churcher, 'How I Killed Bin Laden', 20.
105 Eng, *Racial Castration*.
106 Craig Smith, 'Kandahar Journal; Shh, It's an Open Secret: Warlords and Pedophilia', *The New York Times*, 21 February 2002, sec. World, https://www.nytimes.com/2002/0 2/21/world/kandahar-journal-shh-it-s-an-open-secret-warlords-and-pedophilia.html.
107 Lionel Tiger, quoted in Puar, 'Mapping US Homonormativities', 73.
108 See Susan Block, 'Inside the Two Heads of the Crotch Bomber', *Counterpunch*, 4 January 2010, https://www.counterpunch.org/2010/01/04/inside-the-two-heads -of-the-crotch-bomber/.
109 Christopher Torchia, 'There Really Is Something in the Water, Kandahar Men Say', *The Globe and Mail*, 10 April 2002, sec. A12.
110 Susan Bordo, *The Male Body: A New Look at Men in Public and in Private* (New York: Farrar, Straus and Giroux, 1999), 87–91.

Chapter 4

1. Barbara Ehrenreich, "Foreword: Feminism's Assumptions Upended", in *One of the Guys: Women as Aggressors and Torturers*, ed. Tara McKelvey (Emeryville: Seal Press, 2007), 1.
2. Ilene Feinman, "Shock and Awe: Abu Ghraib, Women Soldiers, and the Racially Gendered Torture", in *One of the Guys: Women as Aggressors and Torturers*, ed. Tara McKelvey (Emeryville: Seal Press, 2007), 62.
3. Barbara Ehrenreich, for one example, writes that despite her opposition to the first Gulf War (1991), 'I was proud of our servicewomen and delighted that their presence irked their Saudi hosts.' Ehrenreich, 'Foreword: Feminism's Assumptions Upended', 2.
4. For a collection of essays by feminists on revelations of the Abu Ghraib torture, see Tara McKelvey, ed., *One of the Guys: Women as Aggressors and Torturers* (Emeryville: Seal Press, 2007).
5. These claims can be found in the essays penned by feminists in McKelvey.
6. Lucinda Marshall discusses the rape and torture of Iraqi women and men, and ties this to the misogynist practices of the US military. However, even she capitulates to the power of the culturalist framing of the violence. 'In Iraqi culture, abuse, intimidation, and sexual assault of a woman is considered to be a reflection on the manhood of her husband and male family members.' The rape and torture of Iraqi women is tied to the violence and death at the hands of their family in the name of cultural difference. See Lucinda Marshall, 'The Misogynist Implications', in *One of the Guys: Women as Aggressors and Torturers*, ed. Tara McKelvey (Emeryville: Seal Press, 2007), 55–6.
7. I am describing here the response of white feminists to the release of the Abu Ghraib photographs. The response of Black women/feminists, as of women/feminists of colour was in sharp contrast. I have already discussed some of these responses in Chapter 2. See Ayanna Thompson, *Performing Race and Torture on the Early Modern Stage*, Routledge Studies in Renaissance Literature and Culture 9 (New York: Routledge, 2008); Carby, 'US/UK's Special Relationship', 60–71.
8. In keeping with this imperial feminist phantasy, Chesler reveals that her own feminism was spurred by the hyper-patriarchy of the Muslim world as she witnessed this during her travels to Afghanistan. Phyllis Chesler, *The New Anti-Semitism: The Current Crisis and What We Must Do about It* (San Francisco: Jossey-Bass, 2003), 16.
9. Noreen Shanahan, 'Armstrong Continues Chronicles of Afghanistan Women', *Herizons* 23, no. 2 (Fall 2009): 45.
10. Wente Margaret, 'We're in Afghanistan for This?', *The Globe and Mail*, 2 April 2009, sec. A 13.
11. For example, speaking on behalf of 'more than 220 leading human rights and women's organizations in the U.S. and around the world', the Washington-based Feminist Majority Foundation backed the US invasion of Afghanistan and called on the Bush Administration to increase the level of troops and extend the occupation across the country. See 'Eleanor Smeal Urges President to Fulfill Promise to Afghan Women', *Feminist Majority Foundation, Online*, 22 May 2002, http://feminist.org/news/newsbyte/uswirestory.asp?id=6544.
12. 'Women Leaders Call for Expansion of International Peace Troops and More U.S. Funds to Restore the Rights of Afghan Women', *Feminist Majority Foundation Online*, 8 April 2002, http://www.feminist.org/news/pressstory.asp?id=6449.

13 'Violence against Iraqi Women Continues Unabated', *Electronic Iraq*, 1 December 2008, http://electroniciraq.net/news/newsanalysis/Violence_aginst_Iraqi_women_continues unabated_1/22/2009.
14 See Sedef Arat-Koc, 'Hot Potato Imperial Wars or Benevolent Interventions? Reflections on "Global Feminism" Post September 11th', *Atlantis* 26, no. 2 (2002): 53–65; Saba Mahmood and Charles Hirschkind, 'Feminism, the Taliban, and Politics of Counter-Insurgency', *Anthropological Quarterly* 75, no. 2 (2002): 339–54.
15 Canadian feminist and human rights activist, Sally Armstrong, called for a similar expansion of the occupation by US, Canadian and NATO forces in the celebrated documentary, Robin Bender, *Daughters of Afghanistan* (Choices, 2004).
16 Christine Stolba, 'Feminists Go to War', *The Women's Quarterly*, 19 February 2002, http://freerepublic.com/focus/f-news/631259/posts.
17 See Manji, *The Trouble with Islam*; , Ali, *The Caged Virgin*.
18 Chesler, *The New Anti-Semitism*, 41.
19 For a critique of this caricatured use of words during war time, see: The War of the World: Conversation with Niall Ferguson, interview by Lawrence Tisch, Institute for International Studies, University of California-Berkeley, 2006, http://globetrotter.berkeley.edu/people6/Ferguson/ferguson06-con5.html.
20 Chesler, *The New Anti-Semitism*, 88.
21 Chesler, *The New Anti-Semitism*, 12.
22 Irshad Manji's attack on Islam and Muslims is an example of the attempts of some Muslim feminists to give credence to the 'clash of civilizations' narrative. See Irshad Manji, *The Trouble with Islam : A Wake-up Call for Honesty and Change* (Toronto: Random House of Canada, Limited, 2003). For an excellent analysis of the writings of Irshad Manji, Pyllis Chesler and Orianna Fallaci on the War on Terror, see Sherene Razack, 'Unassimilable Muslims and Civilized White People: The Race/Culture Divide in Law', *The Annual Meeting of The Law and Society Association, Renaissance Hotel, Chicago*, 27 May 2004. Also see Razack, *Casting Out*.
23 Chesler, *The New Anti-Semitism*, 16.
24 Phyllis Chesler, *The Death of Feminism: What's Next in the Struggle for Women's Freedom* (New York: Palgrave Macmillan, 2005).
25 Chesler, *The Death of Feminism*, 2.
26 Chesler, *The New Anti-Semitism*, 213.
27 This is how Chesler presents the relations between Jews, Christians and Islam: 'I do not wish to alarm you but I am fairly and accurately describing how most Islamic extremists have treated "the infidel" for centuries (even when life was still soft and easy). Unlike the Catholic Church, which has evolved and begun to rethink and regret some of its earlier positions, fundamentalist Islam has not yet evolved. With some exceptions, it is exactly the same today as it was when Muhammad was alive. Sameness is what is valued; difference is feared and hated.' Chesler, *The New Anti-Semitism*, 21. She further discusses the relationship between these two groups in the following terms: 'Please understand: I am not quarreling with the rights of Catholics or Christians to worship Christ as the Messiah in any way they so choose. I am horrified, saddened, outraged – a mite prickly – about the Church's centuries-long mistreatment of Jews, its acts of both omission and commission. I am not saying that because the Church persecuted Jews – or did too little to rescue Jews endangered by the princes of the Church – that all Christians are therefore evil (I do agree, however, with Harvard political scientist Daniel Jonah Goldhagen that it is time for the living Catholic Church to acknowledge its role in the persecution of the Jews that

culminated in the Holocaust and to make serious retribution). I am not saying that each and every Christian persecuted Jews as God-killers. Many did, some did not; some saved Jews, but most chose not to endanger themselves to prevent pogroms or Jewish extermination.' Chesler, *The New Anti-Semitism*, 29.
28 See, Betsy Reed and Katha Pollitt, eds., *Nothing Sacred: Women Respond to Religious Fundamentalism and Terror* (New York: Nation Books, 2002).
29 The essay in which Butler argues for the need to confront anti-Semitism and oppose Israeli state violence without equating the two is part of a debate she had with Lawrence Summers, president of Harvard University.
30 Butler, *Precarious Life*, xi.
31 Butler, *Precarious Life*, xi.
32 Butler, *Precarious Life*, xiv.
33 Butler, *Precarious Life*, xii.
34 Butler, *Precarious Life*, 20.
35 Butler, *Precarious Life*, 31.
36 Butler, *Precarious Life*, 31.
37 Fanon, *Black Skin, White Masks*.
38 Fanon, *Black Skin, White Masks*, 13.
39 Butler, *Precarious Life*, 149–50.
40 Hamid Dabashi, ed., *Dreams of a Nation: On Palestinian Cinema* (London: Verso, 2006), 11.
41 Dabashi, *Dreams of a Nation*, 11.
42 Eisenstein, *Against Empire*, xv.
43 Eisenstein, *Against Empire*, xix.
44 Eisenstein argues that '[T]he downsizing and corporate restructuring of the US economy through the 1980s and 1990s has now been accompanied by a restructuring of the CIA, FBI, and Pentagon. . . . This new security-state monitors and conducts surveillance in the name of democracy.' Eisenstein, *Against Empire*, xix.
45 This is how Eisenstein traces the beginnings of the Iraq war: 'The US war against Iraq preceded the post-September 11 "war on terrorism". It has been a more-than-decade-long war with three noted episodes: Desert Storm, in 1991, orchestrated by Bush Sr.; the renewed bombing of 1998 designed by Bill Clinton and Madeleine Albright; and the "war on terrorism"/Operation Iraqi Freedom of 2003 led by Bush Jr and Donald Rumsfeld. Economic sanctions were in place this entire time, devastating the country as a whole, while Saddam amassed incredible wealth for himself. Through the sanctions, the US blocked shipments of milk, yogurt, printing equipment for schools, dialysis and dental supplies, chlorine for purifying water, and textbooks for medical schools. Children suffered the most: hundreds of thousands died of malnutrition and radiation poisoning.' Eisenstein, *Against Empire*, 12.
46 Eisenstein takes the Bush Administration and its 'women helpmates' to task for taking 'the post September-11 moment and appropriat[ing] the language of women's rights for a right-wing and neoliberal imperial agenda', Eisenstein, *Against Empire*, 148.
47 Eisenstein, *Against Empire*, 151.
48 Eisenstein, *Against Empire*, 152.
49 See also, Smeeta Mishra, '"Saving" Muslim Women and Fighting Muslim Men: Analysis of Representations in The New York Times', *Global Media Journal* 6, no. 11 (Fall 2007); Lila Abu-Lughod, 'Do Muslim Women Really Need Saving?

Anthropological Reflections on Cultural Relativism and Its Others', *American Anthropologist* 104, no. 3 (2002): 783–90; and Sherene H. Razack, 'Imperilled Muslim Women, Dangerous Muslim Men and Civilised Europeans: Legal and Social Responses to Forced Marriages', *Feminist Legal Studies* 12, no. 2 (October 2004): 129–74.

50 Eisenstein, *Against Empire*, 150.
51 There are, of course, some exceptions to this general tendency. See, for example, Ruth Frankenberg, *White Women, Race Matters: The Social Construction of Whiteness*, 5th edn (Minneapolis: University of Minnesota Press, 1993).
52 Eisenstein, *Against Empire*, 156.
53 See Adrien Katherine Wing, ed., *Global Critical Race Feminism: An International Reader* (New York: NYU Press, 2000); Mohanty, *Feminism without Borders*.
54 Talal Asad et al., *Is Critique Secular?: Blasphemy, Injury, and Free Speech* (Berkeley: University of Berkeley, 2009).
55 The essays in the volume studied in this section were presented at a symposium, 'Is Critique Secular?', organized at the Townsend Center for Humanities, University of California, Berkeley, at the launch of a new programme in critical theory (2007). Asad et al.
56 Wendy Brown, 'Introduction', in *Is Critique Secular?: Blasphemy, Injury, and Free Speech*, ed. Talal Asad et al. (Berkeley: University of Berkeley, 2009), 7.
57 Brown, 'Introduction', 7.
58 Sara Ahmed, *Queer Phenomenology: Orientations, Objects, Others* (Durham: Duke University Press, 2006), 6–7.
59 Ahmed, *Queer Phenomenology*, 9.
60 Brown, 'Introduction', 17.
61 Brown, 'Introduction', 9.
62 Brown, 'Introduction', 10.
63 Brown, 'Introduction', 10.
64 Brown, 'Introduction', 10.
65 Brown, 'Introduction', 11.
66 Brown, 'Introduction', 13.
67 Talal Asad, 'Free Speech, Blasphemy, and Secular Criticism', in *Is Critique Secular?: Blasphemy, Injury, and Free Speech*, ed. Talal Asad et al. (Berkeley: University of Berkeley, 2009), 20.
68 Asad, 'Free Speech, Blasphemy, and Secular Criticism', 21.
69 Asad, 'Free Speech, Blasphemy, and Secular Criticism', 24.
70 Asad, 'Free Speech, Blasphemy, and Secular Criticism', 25.
71 Asad, 'Free Speech, Blasphemy, and Secular Criticism', 28.
72 Asad, 'Free Speech, Blasphemy, and Secular Criticism', 29.
73 Asad, 'Free Speech, Blasphemy, and Secular Criticism', 56.
74 Asad, 'Free Speech, Blasphemy, and Secular Criticism', 46–7.
75 Asad, 'Free Speech, Blasphemy, and Secular Criticism', 47.
76 Asad, 'Free Speech, Blasphemy, and Secular Criticism', 48.
77 Saba Mahmood, 'Religious Reason and Secular Affect: An Incommensurable Divide?', in *Is Critique Secular?: Blasphemy, Injury, and Free Speech*, ed. Talal Asad et al. (Berkeley: University of Berkeley, 2009), 70.
78 Mahmood, 'Religious Reason and Secular Affect', 68.
79 Mahmood, 'Religious Reason and Secular Affect', 89.
80 Mahmood, 'Religious Reason and Secular Affect', 92.

81 Judith Butler, 'The Sensibility of Critique: Response to Asad and Mahmood', in *Is Critique Secular?: Blasphemy, Injury, and Free Speech*, ed. Talal Asad et al. (Berkeley: University of Berkeley, 2009), 117–18.
82 Butler, 'The Sensibility of Critique', 102.
83 As Butler explains, 'A certain critical perspective emerges as a consequence of comparative work', Butler, 'The Sensibility of Critique', 105.
84 Butler, 'The Sensibility of Critique', 104.
85 Butler, 'The Sensibility of Critique', 104–5.
86 Butler, 'The Sensibility of Critique', 106.
87 Butler, 'The Sensibility of Critique', 105.
88 Butler, 'The Sensibility of Critique', 107.
89 Butler, 'The Sensibility of Critique', 107.
90 Butler, 'The Sensibility of Critique', 100.
91 Butler, 'The Sensibility of Critique', 113. This is one way in which Butler considers Foucault to have 'rewrought' Kant: 'Kant, of course, sought to understand the universal and timeless features of cognition in his effort to articulate the preconditions of judgement, but it is surely possible to transpose a Kantian procedure onto a historical scheme, as Foucault sought to do.' Butler, 'The Sensibility of Critique', 115.
92 Butler, 'The Sensibility of Critique', 126.
93 Butler, 'The Sensibility of Critique', 126.
94 'Definition of CODA', in *Merriam-Webster: An Encyclopaedia Britannica Company*, n.d., https://www.merriam-webster.com/dictionary/coda.
95 Butler, 'The Sensibility of Critique', 127.
96 Butler, 'The Sensibility of Critique', 127.
97 Butler, 'The Sensibility of Critique', 129.
98 Butler, 'The Sensibility of Critique', 128.
99 Butler, 'The Sensibility of Critique', 128.
100 Butler, 'The Sensibility of Critique', 134.
101 Butler, 'The Sensibility of Critique', 134.
102 Brown, 'Introduction', 15.
103 Brown, 'Introduction', 16.
104 Brown, 'Introduction', 18.

Chapter 5

1 George Bush, 'Address to the Nation on the Terrorist Attacks', The American Presidency Project, 11 September 2001, http://www.presidency.ucsb.edu/ws/?pid=58057.
2 Richard Gamble, the First World War historian, has this to say about the American sense of manifest destiny: 'With surprising consistency, though to varying degrees over time and with shifting emphases . . . Americans have been habitually drawn to language that is redemptive, apocalyptic, and expansive. Americans have long experienced and articulated a sense of urgency, of hanging on the precipice of great change. . . . They have fallen easily into the Manichean habit of dividing the world into darkness and light, Evil and Good, past and future, Satan and Christ. They have seen themselves as a progressive, redemptive force, waging war in the ranks of

Christ's army, or have imagined themselves even as Christ Himself, liberating those in bondage and healing the afflicted.' Quoted by Talal Asad, *On Suicide Bombing*, Wellek Library Lectures (New York: Columbia University Press, 2007), 86–7.
3   See President Obama's speech in response to the controversy sparked by the comments of Reverend Wright: Barack Obama, 'Transcript of Obama Speech', *Politico*, 18 March 2008, https://www.politico.com/news/stories/0308/9100.html.
4   Dan Merica, 'Trump: "We Are Stopping Cold the Attacks on Judeo-Christian Values,"' *CNN*, 13 October 2017, https://www.cnn.com/2017/10/13/politics/trump-values-voters-summit/index.html.
5   Sander L. Gilman, *Jewish Self-Hatred: Anti-Semitism and the Hidden Language of the Jews* (Baltimore: Johns Hopkins University Press, 1986), 6–7.
6   Gilman, *Jewish Self-Hatred*, 7.
7   Carter, *Race*, 4.
8   Carter, *Race*, 25.
9   Here is how Carter defines his task of re-reading Kant's philosophical work: 'My attention centers on his [Kant's] account of the question that on his own admission was at the core of his philosophical research: *Was ist der Mensch?* – What is man? As Kant's late work *Conflict of the Faculties* (1798) made clear, this question of philosophical anthropology and, indeed, of thought itself was nothing less than an account of the "great drama of religion."' Carter, *Race*, 80.
10 Masuzawa has found that the category of 'world religion', first referencing Christianity's 'unique universality', then including Buddhism in the late nineteenth century, shifted significantly in the early decades of the twentieth century to include Islam and Judaism. At this point, Judaism was redefined from a 'national' to a world religion, coinciding 'with the inception of a new concept of the West defined as Judeo-Christian'. Masuzawa, *The Invention of World Religions, or, How European Universalism Was Preserved in the Language of Pluralism*, 28.
11 Masuzawa, *The Invention of World Religions, or, How European Universalism Was Preserved in the Language of Pluralism*.
12 As Masuzawa explains in regard to this new configuration of the Aryan and the Semite: 'Whatever fascination and promise the science of language might have held for the pioneering scholars of Oriental languages, one driving passion of comparative philology was the exaltation of a particular grammatical apparatus: inflection. Metaphysically and abstractly imagined rather than historically documented, inflection was construed as a syntactical structure resulting naturally from and directly from the innermost spiritual urge of as a people (Volk), and as such, it was said to attest to the creativity and the spirit of freedom of those who originated from this linguistic form. Not surprisingly, these attributes, together with the grammatical form itself, were touted as the defining characteristic of the family of Indo-European (Aryan) languages, the family comprising Sanskrit as its "eldest daughter" in the East, Persian as her close kin, but also with the Western siblings Greek, Latin, Teutonic, Slavonic, and so forth, of which the most modern European languages were unmistakable descendants. The ancient broad band of the Indo-European language family, stretched across from east to west, had been intersected, in both space and time, by another linguistic family. This other group, the Semitic languages, included Arabic and Hebrew, which were well known to Europeans because they were the language of the Qur'an and of the Old Testament respectively. The great majority of nineteenth-century philologists maintained that, in comparison to the first family, this second tribe of languages was decidedly

imperfect and inchoate in inflectional capability, and with this imperfection came all the limitations that characterized their native speakers as a race. Muller's contemporary and longtime correspondent, Ernest Renan, is among the most celebrated exponent of this view.' Masuzawa, *The Invention of World Religions, or, How European Universalism Was Preserved in the Language of Pluralism*, 24–5.
13 Masuzawa, *The Invention of World Religions, or, How European Universalism Was Preserved in the Language of Pluralism*, 179.
14 Masuzawa, *The Invention of World Religions, or, How European Universalism Was Preserved in the Language of Pluralism*, 301.
15 Mark Silk, 'Notes on the Judeo-Christian Tradition in America', *American Quarterly* 36, no. 1 (1984): 66.
16 Silk, 'Notes on the Judeo-Christian Tradition in America', 66.
17 Silk, 'Notes on the Judeo-Christian Tradition in America', 66.
18 Silk, 'Notes on the Judeo-Christian Tradition in America', 67.
19 Silk, 'Notes on the Judeo-Christian Tradition in America', 69.
20 Silk, 'Notes on the Judeo-Christian Tradition in America', 83.
21 Silk, 'Notes on the Judeo-Christian Tradition in America', 83.
22 Peter Berger, 'Judeo-Christian or Abrahamic?', *The American Interest*, 23 December 2015, https://www.the-american-interest.com/2015/12/23/judeo-christian-or-abrahamic/.
23 As Anidjar explains it, 'The movement of the enemy thus has to be distinguished from the other who comes from afar, the neighbour or *prochain* who, before the subject, comes. Symmetrically opposed – rather than asymmetrically approaching, the enemy departs and vanishes, which is to say that the enemy also *remains* as departing and vanishing. The space within which this movement takes place is defined by Levinas as the space of the political, as the space of war.' Anidjar, *The Jew, the Arab*, 3.
24 Anidjar, *The Jew, the Arab*, xvii.
25 Anidjar, *The Jew, the Arab*.
26 Anidjar, *The Jew, the Arab*, 5.
27 Anidjar, *The Jew, the Arab*, 3.
28 Anidjar, *The Jew, the Arab*, 4.
29 Anidjar, *The Jew, the Arab*, 4–7.
30 Anidjar, *The Jew, the Arab*, 9.
31 Anidjar, *The Jew, the Arab*, 48.
32 Derrida, quoted in Anidjar, *The Jew, the Arab*, 48.
33 Anidjar, *The Jew, the Arab*, 48.
34 Carl Schmitt, quoted in Anidjar, *The Jew, the Arab*, 49.
35 Anidjar, *The Jew, the Arab*, 49.
36 Anidjar, *The Jew, the Arab*, 49.
37 Anidjar, *The Jew, the Arab*, 49.
38 Anidjar, *The Jew, the Arab*, xxi.
39 Anidjar, *The Jew, the Arab*, xxi.
40 This recognition of the interconnectedness of all aspects of human social and spiritual life is underscored in most writings on Islam from Muslim perspectives. See, for example, Asad, *The Message of the Qur'an*; Sayyid, *Recalling the Caliphate*; Crooke, *Resistance*. Even scholars working within the Western tradition have to engage with this interconnectedness, as noted by Roxanne Euben in her study of Islamic 'fundamentalism', 'Perhaps the most common observation in Middle

Eastern scholarship concerns the intimacy between religion and politics: the Prophet was both the recipient of the Qur'anic revelation and the founder of the first political community in Islamic history. The first year of the Islamic calendar is not the year of Muhammad's birth or the date God's word was revealed but rather marks the ascendance of the Muslim community in Medina. This actualization of God's will on earth is the prototype for all Muslim political communities, the ideal in whose shadow Islamic political theory, jurisprudence and ethics developed.' Euben's somewhat Eurocentric discussion of this interlinking of politics with religion in Islam, including that of 'fundamentalisms', as amounting to a form of essentialism does not negate the interlinked nature of these spheres in complex and shifting articulation of the Islamic tradition. See Roxanne Euben, *Enemy in the Mirror: Islamic Fundamentalism and the Limits of Modern Rationalism: A Work of Comparative Political Theory* (Princeton: Princeton University Press, 1999), 49.
41 Anidjar, *The Jew, the Arab*, 49.
42 Anidjar, *The Jew, the Arab*, 49.
43 The Jew, the Arab: An Interview with Gil Anidjar, accessed 24 May 2020, https://asiasociety.org/jew-arab-interview-gil-anidjar.
44 Anidjar, *The Jew, the Arab*, 40.
45 Anidjar, *The Jew, the Arab*, 41.
46 Anidjar, *The Jew, the Arab*, 42.
47 Derrida, Zabus, quoted in Anidjar, *The Jew, the Arab*, 42.
48 Derrida, quoted in Anidjar, *The Jew, the Arab*, 44.
49 Derrida, quoted in Anidjar, *The Jew, the Arab*, 43.
50 Bennington, quoted in Anidjar, *The Jew, the Arab*, 42.
51 Derrida, quoted in Anidjar, *The Jew, the Arab*, 44.
52 Anidjar, *The Jew, the Arab*, 46.
53 Anidjar, *The Jew, the Arab*, 46.
54 Anidjar, *The Jew, the Arab*, 46.
55 Anidjar, *The Jew, the Arab*, 46–7.
56 Giovanna Borradori, 'Foreword', in *Islam and the West: A Conversation with Jacques Derrida*, ed. Mustapha Cherif, trans. Teresa Lavender Fagan, Religion and Postmodernism (Chicago: The University of Chicago Press, 2008), x.
57 Derrida, in Mustapha Cherif, *Islam and the West: A Conversation with Jacques Derrida*, trans. Teresa Lavender Fagan, Religion and Postmodernism (Chicago: The University of Chicago Press, 2008), 29.
58 Derrida, in Cherif, *Islam and the West*, 30.
59 Cherif, *Islam and the West*, 31.
60 Derrida in Cherif, *Islam and the West*, 32.
61 Derrida, in Cherif, *Islam and the West*, 32.
62 Derrida, in Cherif, *Islam and the West*, 33.
63 Derrida, in Cherif, *Islam and the West*, 34.
64 Derrida, in Cherif, *Islam and the West*, 35.
65 Derrida, quoted in Anidjar, *Islam and the West*, 43.
66 Cherif, *Islam and the West*, 49.
67 Derrida, quoted in Cherif, *Islam and the West*, 52.
68 Derrida, quoted in Cherif, *Islam and the West*, 53–4.
69 Schmitt, quoted in Anidjar, *The Jew, the Arab*, 50–1.
70 Anidjar, *The Jew, the Arab*, 51.
71 Agamben, *Remnants of Auschwitz*, 14.

72 Viktor Frankl, *Man's Search for Meaning: The Classic Tribute to Hope from the Holocaust* (London: Rider Books, 2004), 32.
73 Sofsky, quoted by Agamben, *Remnants of Auschwitz*, 47.
74 Agamben, *Remnants of Auschwitz*, 48.
75 Ryn and Klodzinski offer the following explanation with regard to the use of the name 'Muslim' for the most dejected of the Jewish inmates of the camps, 'They excluded themselves from all relations to their environment. If they could still move around, they did so in slow motion, without bending their knees. They shivered since their body temperature usually fell below 98.7 degrees. Seeing them from afar, one had the impression of seeing Arabs praying. This image was the origin of the term used at Auschwitz for people dying of malnutrition: Muslims.' Quoted in Agamben, *Remnants of Auschwitz*, 43.
76 Parvez Manzoor, 'Turning Jews into Muslims: The Untold Saga of the Muselmänner', *Islam* 21, no. 28 (2001): 12.
77 Anidjar notes that the 'Musselman' appears in the works of David Rousset, Eugen Kogon, Primo Levi, Elie Wiesel, Bruno Betterlheim, among many other writers, yet there remains a silence regarding this figure and its meaning in much of the Holocaust literature. Anidjar, *The Jew, the Arab*, 141.
78 Anidjar, *The Jew, the Arab*, 140 and Clendinnen, quoted in Anidjar, *The Jew, the Arab*, 140.
79 Elie Wiesel, 'Stay Together Always', quoted in Anidjar, *The Jew, the Arab*, 140.
80 Sardar, *Orientalism*.
81 Manzoor, 'Turning Jews into Muslims: The Untold Saga of the Muselmänner', 12.
82 Ryn and Klodzinski, quoted in Agamben, *Remnants of Auschwitz*, 43.
83 Agamben, *Remnants of Auschwitz*, 45.
84 Agamben, *Remnants of Auschwitz*, 44, 47.
85 Cited from the *Encyclopaedia Judaica* by Manzoor, 'Turning Jews into Muslims: The Untold Saga of the Muselmänner'.
86 Gilman, *Jewish Self-Hatred*.
87 Arendt, quoted by Gil Anidjar, *Semites: Race, Religion, Literature* (Stanford, CA: Stanford University Press, 2007), 23.
88 Aberbach's position supports Anidjar's when he explains that in Germany, the 'Church had always legitimized hatred of the Jews as the killers of Christ; German political leaders since Bismarck had used anti-Semitism as a political tool to gain power; popular German literature was full of virulently racist ideas that Hitler drew upon. When in 1920 the anti-Semitic forgery *The Protocols of the Elder of Zion* appeared in German, it sold 120,000 copies by the end of the year', in his study of pre-Holocaust German society. See David Aberbach, *Charisma in Politics, Religion and the Media: Private Trauma, Public Ideals* (Houndsmills: Macmillan, 1996), 31.
89 Anidjar, *Semites*, 24.
90 Anidjar, *Semites*, 24.
91 Anidjar, *Semites*, 24.
92 Anidjar, *Semites*, 24.
93 Arendt, quoted in Anidjar, *Semites*, 25.
94 Anidjar, *The Jew, the Arab*, 146.
95 Anidjar, *Semites*.
96 Joseph Massad, 'Forget Semitism', in *Living Together: Jacques Derrida's Communities of Violence and Peace*, ed. Elisabeth Weber (New York: Fordham University Press, 2012), 65.

97 Massad, 'Forget Semitism', 65.
98 Agamben, *Remnants of Auschwitz*, 47.
99 Feliksa Piekarska, quoted in Agamben, *Remnants of Auschwitz*, 166.
100 Joseph Massad, 'Palestinians and Jewish History: Recognition or Submission?', *Journal of Palestine Studies* 30, no. 1 (2000): 52–67.
101 Massad, 'Palestinians and Jewish History', 55.
102 Anidjar, *The Jew, the Arab*, 161.
103 Joseph Pugliese, 'Apostrophe of Empire: Guantanamo Bay, Disneyland', *Borderlands* 8, no. 3 (2009): 17.
104 See Joseph Massad, *100 Years after the Balfour Declaration* (Vienna: Verein Dar Al Janub, 2017), https://www.youtube.com/watch?v=TXzktQKBGxY.
105 Edward Said, *The Question of Palestine* (New York: Times Books, 1979), 16–17.
106 Massad, 'Palestinians and Jewish History', 52.
107 Gil Anidjar, 'Mal de Sionisme (Zionist Fever)', in *Living Together: Jacques Derrida's Communities of Violence and Peace*, ed. Elisabeth Weber (New York: Fordham University Press, 2012), 49.
108 Anidjar, 'Mal de Sionisme (Zionist Fever)', 49.
109 Haidar Eid, 'Gaza, the Goy!', *Aljazeera*, 27 August 2014, sec. Opinion/Human Rights, https://www.aljazeera.com/indepth/opinion/2014/08/gaza-goy-2014827104730724557.html.
110 Said, *The Question of Palestine*, 12.
111 Said, Quoted in Massad, 'Forget Semitism', 66.
112 Jim Lobe, 'Israel Ranked World's Most Militarised Nation', *Inter Press Service*, 14 November 2012, http://www.ipsnews.net/2012/11/israel-ranked-as-worlds-most-militarised-nation/; BBC News, 'US in Major Arms Deal with Israel', 22 April 2013, sec. Middle East, https://www.bbc.com/news/world-middle-east-22244832; William Hartung and Frida Berrigan, 'Report: U.S. Arms Transfers and Security Assistance to Israel', World Policy Institute, 6 May 2002, https://worldpolicy.org/report-u-s-arms-transfers-and-security-assistance-to-israel-world-policy-institute-research-project/.
113 Eitan Shamir, 'Rethinking Operation Protective Edge', *Middle East Quarterly* 22, no. 2 (1 March 2015), https://www.meforum.org/articles/2015/rethinking-operation-protective-edge.

BIBLIOGRAPHY

Abdullah, Zain. 'Malcolm X, Islam, and the Black Self'. In *Malcolm X's Michigan Worldview: An Exemplar for Contemporary Black Studies*, edited by Rita Kiki Edozie and Curtis Stokes, 205–26. East Lansing: Michigan State University Press, 2015.

Aberbach, David. *Charisma in Politics, Religion and the Media: Private Trauma, Public Ideals*. Houndsmills: Macmillan, 1996.

Abuelaish, Izzeldin. *I Shall Not Hate: A Gaza Doctor's Journey on the Road to Peace and Human Dignity*. London: Bloomsbury, 2011.

Abu-Hamdiyyah, Mohammad. *The Qur'an: An Introduction*. London: Routledge, 2000.

Abu-Lughod, Lila. *Do Muslim Women Need Saving?* Cambridge: Harvard University Press, 2015.

Abu-Lughod, Lila. 'Do Muslim Women Really Need Saving? Anthropological Reflections on Cultural Relativism and Its Others'. *American Anthropologist* 104, no. 3 (2002): 783–90.

Agamben, Giorgio. *Homo Sacer: Sovereign Power and Bare Life*. Translated by Daniel Heller-Roazen. Meridian. Stanford: Stanford University Press, 1998.

Agamben, Giorgio. *Remnants of Auschwitz: The Witness and the Archive*. Translated by Daniel Heller-Roazen. New York: Zone Books, 2000.

Agamben, Giorgio. *State of Exception*. Translated by Kevin Attell. Chicago: University of Chicago Press, 2005.

Ahmed, Akbar. *Discovering Islam: Making Sense of Muslim History and Society*. London: Routledge, 1988.

Ahmed, Azam, and Nicole Perlroth. 'Using Texts as Lures, Government Spyware Targets Mexican Journalists and Their Families', *The New York Times*, 19 June 2017. https://www.nytimes.com/2017/06/19/world/americas/mexico-spyware-anticrime.html.

Ahmed, Leila. *A Quiet Revolution: The Veil's Resurgence, from the Middle East to America*. New Haven: Yale University Press, 2011.

Ahmed, Leila. 'Western Ethnocentrism and Perceptions of the Harem'. *Feminist Studies* 8, no. 3 (1982): 521–34.

Ahmed, Sara. *On Being Included: Racism and Diversity in Institutional Life*. Durham: Duke University Press, 2012.

Ahmed, Sara. *Queer Phenomenology: Orientations, Objects, Others*. Durham: Duke University Press, 2006.

Ahmed, Shahab. *What Is Islam? The Importance of Being Islamic*. Princeton: Princeton University Press, 2016.

Ahren, Raphael. 'Will Goldstone 2 Be as Bad as the First One?' *The Times of Israel*, 26 July 2014, sec. Analysis. http://www.timesofisrael.com/will-goldstone-2-be-as-bad-as-the-first-one/.

Alami, Aida. 'The College Student Who Has France's Secularists Fulminating', *The New York Times*, 1 June 2018, sec. World. https://www.nytimes.com/2018/06/01/world/europe/maryam-pougetoux-islam-france.html.

Alderson, Andrew. 'Iraq: Investigation into New Claims of Torture by British Soldiers', *The Telegraph*, 14 November 2009, sec. World. https://www.telegraph.co.uk/news/worldnews/middleeast/iraq/6567529/Iraq-Investigation-into-new-claims-of-torture-by-British-soldiers.html.

Aldrich, Robert. *Colonialism and Homosexuality*. London: Routledge, 2003.

Ali, Kecia. *Sexual Ethics and Islam: Feminist Reflections on Qur'an, Hadith and Jurisprudence*. Oxford: Oneworld Publications, 2006.

Ali, Kecia, and Oliver Leaman. *Islam: The Key Concepts*. London: Routledge, 2007.

Ali, Rozina. 'Are US Drone Strikes in Pakistan War Crimes? Only 12% of Those Killed Are Known Militants', *Informed Comment*, 25 October 2014. https://www.juancole.com/2014/10/strikes-pakistan-militants.html.

Ali, Tariq. *The Clash of Fundamentalisms: Crusades, Jihads and Modernity*. London: Verso, 2002.

Allen, Christopher. *Islamophobia*. Surrey: Ashgate, 2010.

Alloula, Malek. *The Colonial Harem*. Translated by Myrna Godzich and Wlad Godzich. Minneapolis: University of Minnesota Press, 1986.

Almond, Ian. *History of Islam in German Thought: From Leibniz to Nietzsche*. Routledge Studies in Cultural History 11. New York: Routledge, 2010.

Almond, Ian. *The New Orientalists: Postmodern Representations of Islam from Foucault to Baudrillard*. London: I.B. Tauris, 2007.

Al-solaylee, Kamal. 'All Arabs Are Not Alike'. *The Globe and Mail*. 3 October 2001, sec. News flash.

Amanpour, Christiane. *In the Footsteps of Bin Laden*. Documentary. CNN, 2006.

Amer, Sahar. 'Cross-Dressing and Female Same-Sex Marriage in Medieval French and Arabic Literatures'. In *Islamicate Sexualities: Translations across Temporal Geographies of Desire*, edited by Afsaneh Najmabadi and Kathryn Babayan, 72–113. Harvard Middle Eastern Monographs 39. Cambridge: Harvard University Press, 2008.

Amos, Valerie, and Pratibha Parmar. 'Challenging Imperial Feminism'. *Feminist Review*, no. 80 (2005): 44–63.

Anghie, Antony. *Imperialism, Sovereignty and the Making of International Law*. Cambridge Studies in International and Comparative Law 37. Cambridge, UK; New York, NY: Cambridge University Press, 2005.

Anghie, Antony. 'The Evolution of International Law: Colonial and Postcolonial Realities'. *Third World Quarterly* 27, no. 5 (2006): 739–53.

Anghie, Antony, ed. *The Third World and International Order: Law, Politics and Globalization*. Developments in International Law 45. Leiden: Brill Academic Publishers, 2003.

Anidjar, Gil. *Blood: A Critique of Christianity*. New York: Columbia University Press, 2014.

Anidjar, Gil. 'Mal de Sionisme (Zionist Fever)'. In *Living Together: Jacques Derrida's Communities of Violence and Peace*, edited by Elisabeth Weber, 45–58. New York: Fordham University Press, 2012.

Anidjar, Gil. *Semites: Race, Religion, Literature*. Stanford, CA: Stanford University Press, 2007.

Anidjar, Gil. *The Jew, the Arab: A History of the Enemy*. Cultural Memory in the Present. Stanford: Stanford University Press, 2003.

Anjum, Ovamir. 'Do Islamists Have an Intellectual Deficit?' Rethinking Political Islam. Brookings Institute, 20 April 2016. https://www.brookings.edu/research/do-islamists-have-an-intellectual-deficit/.

Anjum, Ovamir. 'Islam as a Discursive Tradition: Talal Asad and His Interlocutors'. *Comparative Studies of South Asia, Africa and the Middle East* 27, no. 3 (4 December 2007): 656–72.

Anjum, Ovamir. *Politics, Law, and Community in Islamic Thought: The Taymiyyan Movement*. New York: Cambridge University Press, 2012.

Ansary, Mir Tamim. *Destiny Disrupted: A History of the World through Islamic Eyes*. 1st edn. New York: PublicAffairs, 2009.

Antunes, Ricardo. 'Introduction: The Substance of the Crisis'. In *The Structural Crisis of Capital*, edited by Istvan Meszaros, 13–22. New York: Monthly Review Press, 2009.

Arat-Koc, Sedef. 'Hot Potato Imperial Wars or Benevolent Interventions? Reflections on "Global Feminism" Post September 11th'. *Atlantis* 26, no. 2 (2002): 53–65.

Armour, Ellen, and Susan St Ville, eds. *Bodily Citations: Religion and Judith Butler*. New York: Columbia University Press, 2006.

Armstrong, Karen. *Islam: A Short History*. London: Phoenix, 2001.

Armstrong, Karen. *Muhammad: A Prophet for Our Time*. San Francisco: HarperOne, 2007.

Asad, Muhammad. *The Message of the Qur'an*. London: The Book Foundation, 2003.

Asad, Talal. *Formations of the Secular: Christianity, Islam, Modernity*. Stanford: Stanford University Press, 2003.

Asad, Talal. *Genealogies of Religion: Discipline and Reasons of Power in Christianity and Islam*. Baltimore: Johns Hopkins University Press, 1993.

Asad, Talal. 'Muhammad Asad, Between Religion and Politics'. *Islam & Science* 10, no. 1 (Summer 2012): 77–88.

Asad, Talal. *On Suicide Bombing*. Wellek Library Lectures. New York: Columbia University Press, 2007.

Asad, Talal. 'The Idea of an Anthropology of Islam'. *Georgetown University: Center for Contemporary Arab Studies*, Occasional Papers Series, 1986.

Asad, Talal. 'Thinking about Tradition, Religion, and Politics in Egypt Today'. *Critical Inquiry* 42, no. 1 (1 September 2015): 166–214.

Asad, Talal, Judith Butler, Saba Mahmood, and Wendy Brown. *Is Critique Secular? Blasphemy, Injury, and Free Speech*. Berkeley: University of Berkeley, 2009.

Austen, Ian, and Megan Specia. 'Canadian Held Hostage in Afghanistan Says Militants Killed His Child'. *The New York Times*, 15 October 2017, sec. World. https://www.nytimes.com/2017/10/14/world/canada/canadian-american-hostages-daughter.html.

Azad, Hasan. 'Muslims and the Path of Intellectual Slavery: An Interview with Wael Hallaq (Part Two)'. *Jadaliyya*, 7 June 2014. http://www.jadaliyya.com/Details/30782.

Babayan, Kathryn. '"In Spirit We Ate Each Other's Sorrow": Female Companionship in Seventeenth-Century Safavi Iran'. In *Islamicate Sexualities: Translations across Temporal Geographies of Desire*, edited by Kathryn Babayan and Afsaneh Najmabadi, 239–96. Harvard Middle Eastern Monographs 39. Cambridge: Center for Middle Eastern Studies of Harvard University, Harvard University Press, 2008.

Bacevich, Andrew. 'Prepare, Pursue, Prevail! Onward and Upward with U.S. Central Command'. *Salon.Com*, 26 March 2017. https://www.salon.com/2017/03/26/prepare-pursue-prevail-onward-and-upward-with-u-s-central-command_partner/.

Back, Les, and John Solomos, eds. *Theories of Race and Racism: A Reader*. 2nd edn. Routledge Student Readers. London: Routledge, 2009.

Baker, Peter. 'Without Saying "Trump," Bush and Obama Deliver Implicit Rebukes'. *The New York Times*, 19 October 2017, sec. U.S. https://www.nytimes.com/2017/10/19/us/politics/george-bush-trump.html.

Banita, Georgiana. 'Raymond Williams and Online Video: The Tragedy of Technology'. In *About Raymond Williams*, edited by Monika Seidl, Roman Horak, and Lawrence Grossberg. London: Routledge, 2009.

Bannerji, Himani. *Dark Side of the Nation: Essays on Multiculturalism, Nationalism, and Gender*. Toronto: Canadian Scholars' Press, 2000.

Barlas, Asma. *'Believing Women' in Islam: Unreading Patriarchal Interpretations of the Qur'an*. Austin: University of Texas Press, 2002.

Barnard, Anne. 'Red Cross Warns of "Dehumanizing" Rhetoric in ISIS Fight'. *The New York Times*, 27 October 2017, sec. World. https://www.nytimes.com/2017/10/26/world/middleeast/red-cross-islamic-state.html.

Baudrillard, Jean. *The Spirit of Terrorism*. Translated by Chris Turner. Revised edition. London: Verso, 2003.

BBC News. 'US in Major Arms Deal with Israel'. 22 April 2013, sec. Middle East. https://www.bbc.com/news/world-middle-east-22244832.

Beck, Glenn. *USAMA BIN LADEN Muslim Monster KILLED! :: AMERICA THANKS U.S. ARMED FORCES!!*, 2011. https://www.youtube.com/watch?v=uovBp-laFWc.

Begg, Moazzam, and Victoria Brittain. *Enemy Combatant: My Imprisonment at Guantánamo, Bagram, and Kandahar*. New York: New Press, 2006.

Beinin, Joel. 'The Israelization of American Middle East Policy Discourse'. *Social Text* 21, no. 2 (16 June 2003): 125–39.

Beller, Steven. *Antisemitism: A Very Short Introduction*. Oxford: Oxford University Press, 2007.

Bender, Robin. *Daughters of Afghanistan*. Choices, 2004.

Bennett, Clinton. *Studying Islam: The Critical Issues*. London: Continuum International Publishing Group, 2010.

Berg, Dirk van den. *The Siege of Mecca*. PBS International. Accessed 14 September 2018. http://pbsinternational.org/programs/siege-of-mecca/.

Bergen, Peter. *Manhunt: The Ten-Year Search for Bin Laden from 9/11 to Abbottabad*. New York: Broadway Books, 2013.

Berger, Peter. 'Judeo-Christian or Abrahamic?' *The American Interest*, 23 December 2015. https://www.the-american-interest.com/2015/12/23/judeo-christian-or-abrahamic/.

Bernal, Martin. *Black Athena: Afroasiatic Roots of Classical Civilization; Volume III: The Linguistic Evidence*. New Brunswick: Rutgers University Press, 1987.

Bernasconi, Robert, ed. *Race*. Oxford: Blackwell Publishers, 2001.

Bleys, Rudi. *The Geography of Perversion: Male-To-Male Sexual Behavior Outside the West and the Ethnographic Imagination, 1750–1918*. New York: NYU Press, 1995.

Block, Susan. 'Inside the Two Heads of the Crotch Bomber'. *Counterpunch*, 4 January 2010. https://www.counterpunch.org/2010/01/04/inside-the-two-heads-of-the-crotch-bomber/.

'Body Count: Casualty Figures after 10 Years of the "War on Terror"'. Washington: Physicians for Social Responsibility, 2015. https://www.psr.org/blog/resource/body-count/.

Bordo, Susan. *The Male Body: A New Look at Men in Public and in Private*. New York: Farrar, Straus and Giroux, 1999.

Borger, Julian. 'Chilcot Inquiry: Tony Blair Decided on Iraq War a Year before Invasion – Ambassador'. *The Guardian*, 26 November 2009, sec. UK news. https://www.theguardian.com/uk/2009/nov/26/iraq-war-chilcot-inquiry-tonyblair.

Borradori, Giovanna. 'Foreword'. In *Islam and the West: A Conversation with Jacques Derrida*, edited by Mustapha Cherif, translated by Teresa Lavender Fagan. Religion and Postmodernism. Chicago: The University of Chicago Press, 2008.

Boyarin, Daniel. 'The Double Mark of the Male Muslim'. In *Race and Political Theology*, edited by Vincent Lloyd, 174–87. Stanford: Stanford University Press, 2012.
Bronner, Ethan. 'Israel Completing Rebuttal to Goldstone Report'. *The New York Times*, 23 January 2010, sec. Middle East. https://www.nytimes.com/2010/01/24/world/middleeast/24goldstone.html.
Brustein, William. *Roots of Hate: Anti-Semitism in Europe before the Holocaust*. Cambridge: Cambridge University Press, 2003.
Buckley, Chris, and Paul Mozur. 'What Keeps Xi Jinping Awake at Night'. *The New York Times*, 11 May 2018, sec. World. https://www.nytimes.com/2018/05/11/world/asia/xi-jinping-china-national-security.html.
Buck-Morss, Susan. 'Hegel and Haiti'. *Critical Inquiry* 26, no. 4 (2000): 821–65.
Bumiller, Elisabeth, and Mark Mazzetti. 'A General Steps from the Shadows'. *The New York Times*, 12 May 2009, sec. Asia Pacific. https://www.nytimes.com/2009/05/13/world/asia/13commander.html.
Bureau of Public Affairs, Department of State. 'U.S.-Afghan Women's Council'. Accessed 15 September 2018. https://2001-2009.state.gov/g/wi/57232.htm.
Burton, Richard. *Wanderings in Three Continents*. Reading: Garnet Publishing, 2010.
Bush, George. 'Address to the Nation on the Terrorist Attacks'. The American Presidency Project, 11 September 2001. http://www.presidency.ucsb.edu/ws/?pid=58057.
Butler, Judith. 'Desire'. In *Critical Terms for Literary Study*, edited by Frank Lentricchia and Thomas McLaughlin, Second edition. Chicago: University of Chicago Press, 1995.
Butler, Judith. *Gender Trouble: Feminism and the Subversion of Identity*. London: Routledge, 2011.
Butler, Judith. *Precarious Life: The Powers of Mourning and Violence*. London: Verso, 2004.
Carby, Hazel. 'US/UK's Special Relationship: The Culture of Torture in Abu Ghraib and Lynching Photographs'. *Nka Journal of Contemporary African Art* 2006, no. 20 (1 May 2006): 60–71.
Cardini, Franco. *Europe and Islam*. Making of Europe. Oxford: Blackwell, 2001.
Carter, J. Kameron. *Race: A Theological Account*. Oxford: Oxford University Press, 2008.
CBC. 'Colvin's Testimony True: Former Afghan MP'. 26 November 2009. https://www.cbc.ca/news/world/colvin-s-testimony-true-former-afghan-mp-1.850389.
Chatterjee, Partha. 'Colonialism, Nationalism, and Colonialized Women: The Contest in India'. *American Ethnologist* 16, no. 4 (1989): 622–33.
Chen, Kuan-Hsing. *Asia as Method: Toward Deimperialization*. Durham: Duke University Press, 2010.
Cherif, Mustapha. *Islam and the West: A Conversation with Jacques Derrida*. Translated by Teresa Lavender Fagan. Religion and Postmodernism. Chicago: The University of Chicago Press, 2008.
Chesler, Phyllis. *The Death of Feminism: What's Next in the Struggle for Women's Freedom*. New York: Palgrave Macmillan, 2005.
Chesler, Phyllis. *The New Anti-Semitism: The Current Crisis and What We Must Do about It*. San Francisco: Jossey-Bass, 2003.
Christianity Today. '1095 Pope Urban II Launches the First Crusade'. Accessed 1 June 2018. https://www.christianitytoday.com/history/issues/issue-28/1095-pope-urban-ii-launches-first-crusade.html.
Churcher, Sharon. 'How I Killed Bin Laden: Story of Navy Seal America Tried to Gag'. *The Mail on Sunday*, 2 September 2012.
Churchill, Ward. *Kill the Indian, Save the Man: The Genocidal Impact of American Indian Residential Schools*. San Francisco: City Lights, 2004.

Cirilli, Kevin. '10 Facts about Enemy Combatants'. *Politico*, 22 April 2013. https://www.politico.com/story/2013/04/what-is-an-enemy-combatant-90436.html.
Clancy-Smith, Julia. 'Islam and the French Empire in North Africa'. In *Islam and the European Empires*, edited by David Motadel, 90–111. Oxford: Oxford University Press, 2014.
Clancy-Smith, Julia, and Frances Gouda, eds. *Domesticating the Empire: Race, Gender, and Family Life in French and Dutch Colonialism*. Charlottesville: University of Virginia Press, 1998.
Clarence-Smith, William Gervase. *Islam and the Abolition of Slavery*. London: C. Hurst & Company, 2006.
Coates, Ta-Nehisi. 'We Should Have Seen Trump Coming | Ta-Nehisi Coates'. *The Guardian*, 29 September 2017, sec. News. https://www.theguardian.com/news/2017/sep/29/we-should-have-seen-trump-coming.
Cockburn, Andrew. *Kill Chain: The Rise of the High-Tech Assassins*. New York: Henry Holt and Company, 2015.
Cole, Juan Ricardo. *Engaging the Muslim World*. New York: Palgrave Macmillan, 2009.
Cook, Jonathan. 'They Aren't Hiding It Anymore: Calls for Genocide, Rape of Palestinian Women Enter Israeli Mainstream'. *Global Research*, 22 July 2014. http://www.globalresearch.ca/they-arent-hiding-it-anymore-calls-for-genocide-rape-of-palestinian-women-enters-israeli-mainstream/5392634.
Cooke, Miriam. *Women Claim Islam: Creating Islamic Feminism through Literature*. New York: Routledge, 2001.
Corbett, Rosemary. *Making Moderate Islam: Sufism, Service, and the 'Ground Zero Mosque' Controversy*. Stanford: Stanford University Press, 2017.
Crenshaw, Kimberle. 'Mapping the Margins: Intersectionality, Identity Politics, and Violence against Women of Color'. *Stanford Law Review* 43, no. 6 (1991): 1241–99. https://doi.org/10.2307/1229039.
Crooke, Alastair. *Resistance: The Essence of the Islamist Revolution*. London: Pluto Press, 2009.
Dabashi, Hamid. 'Can Non-Europeans Think?' *Aljazeera*, 15 January 2013. https://www.aljazeera.com/indepth/opinion/2013/01/2013114142638797542.html.
Dabashi, Hamid, ed. *Dreams of a Nation: On Palestinian Cinema*. London: Verso, 2006.
Daulatzai, Sohail. *Black Star, Crescent Moon: The Muslim International and Black Freedom beyond America*. Minneapolis: University of Minnesota Press, 2012.
Davis, Angela Yvonne. *Women, Race & Class*. London: The Women's Press, 1982.
Dawson, Graham. *Soldier Heroes: British Adventure, Empire, and the Imagining of Masculinities*. London: Routledge, 1994.
Dean, Mitchell. *Governmentality: Power and Rule in Modern Society*. London: SAGE Publications, 2006.
'Definition of CODA'. In *Merriam-Webster: An Encyclopaedia Britannica Company*, n.d. https://www.merriam-webster.com/dictionary/coda.
Deger, Allison. 'Military "Kill House" Training Base Used Muslim Women Targets'. *Mondoweiss*, 6 July 2012. https://mondoweiss.net/2012/07/military-kill-house-training-base-used-muslim-women-targets/.
Devji, Faisal. *Landscapes of the Jihad: Militancy, Morality, Modernity*. Ithaca: Cornell University Press, 2005.
Devji, Faisal. *The Terrorist in Search of Humanity: Militant Islam and Global Politics*. Crises in World Politics. London: Hurst & Co., 2008.

Dillard, Heath. *Daughters of the Reconquest: Women in Castilian Town Society, 1100–1300*. Cambridge Iberian and Latin American Studies. Cambridge, New York: Cambridge University Press, 1984.

Diop, Cheikh Anta. *The African Origin of Civilization: Myth or Reality*. Translated by Mercer Cook. New York: Lawrence Hill, 1974.

Dirks, Jerald. *Muslims in American History: A Forgotten Legacy*. Beltsville: Amana Publications, 2006.

Djaït, Hichem. *Europe and Islam*. Translated by Peter Heinegg. Berkeley: University of California Press, 1985.

Doherty, Benjamin. 'War Sporno: How the Israeli Army Uses Sex and Instagram to Sell Its Racism and Violence'. *The Electronic Intifada*, 26 December 2012. https://electronicintifada.net/blogs/benjamin-doherty/war-sporno-how-israeli-army-uses-sex-and-instagram-sell-its-racism-and.

Edge, Dan, and Stephen Grey. *Frontline: Kill/Capture*. PBS, 2011. https://www.pbs.org/wgbh/frontline/film/kill-capture/.

Edgington, Susan, and Sarah Lambert, eds. *Gendering the Crusades*. Cardiff: University of Wales Press, 2001.

Egger, Vernon. *A History of the Muslim World since 1260: The Making of a Global Community*. Upper Saddle River: Pearson Prentice Hall, 2008.

Ehrenreich, Barbara. 'Foreword: Feminism's Assumptions Upended'. In *One of the Guys: Women as Aggressors and Torturers*, edited by Tara McKelvey, 1–6. Emeryville: Seal Press, 2007.

Ehrenreich, Barbara. 'What Abu Ghraib Taught Me'. *AlterNet*, 19 May 2004. https://www.alternet.org/story/18740/what_abu_ghraib_taught_me.

Eid, Haidar. 'Gaza, the Goy!'. *Aljazeera*, 27 August 2014, sec. Opinion/Human Rights. https://www.aljazeera.com/indepth/opinion/2014/08/gaza-goy-2014827104730724557.html.

Eisenstein, Zillah. *Against Empire: Feminisms, Racism, and the West*. London: Zed Books, 2004.

'Eleanor Smeal Urges President to Fulfill Promise to Afghan Women'. *Feminist Majority Foundation, Online*, 22 May 2002. http://feminist.org/news/newsbyte/uswirestory.asp?id=6544.

El-Hajj Malek Shabazz Malcolm X - 1964 Post-Hajj Interview, 1964. https://www.youtube.com/watch?v=zCwOn32IqXo.

Eltahawy, Mona. *Headscarves and Hymens: Why the Middle East Needs a Sexual Revolution*. London: Weidenfeld & Nicolson, 2016.

El-Tayeb, Fatima. *European Others: Queering Ethnicity in Postnational Europe*. Minneapolis: University of Minnesota Press, 2011.

El-Tayeb, Fatima. '"Gays Who Cannot Properly Be Gay": Queer Muslims in the Neoliberal European City'. *European Journal of Women's Studies* 19, no. 1 (2012): 79–95.

Eng, David. *Racial Castration: Managing Masculinity in Asian America*. Perverse Modernities. Durham: Duke University Press, 2001.

Englehardt, Tom. '"Bug Splat": Body Counts, Drones, and "Collateral Damage"'. *Informed Comment*, 4 May 2015. https://www.juancole.com/2015/05/drones-collateral-damage.html.

Euben, Roxanne. *Enemy in the Mirror: Islamic Fundamentalism and the Limits of Modern Rationalism: A Work of Comparative Political Theory*. Princeton: Princeton University Press, 1999.

Eze, Emmanuel Chukwudi. *Race and the Enlightenment: A Reader*. Cambridge: Wiley-Blackwell, 1997.
Falk, Richard. 'Iraq, the United States, and International Law: Beyond the Sanctions'. In *Iraq: The Human Cost of History*, edited by Tareq Ismael and William Haddad, 16–33. London: Pluto Press, 2004.
Faludi, Susan. *The Terror Dream: Fear and Fantasy in Post-9/11 America*. New York: Metropolitan Books, 2007.
Fanon, Frantz. *A Dying Colonialism*. Translated by Haakon Chevalier. New York: Grove Press, 1967.
Fanon, Frantz. *Black Skin, White Masks*. Translated by Charles Lam Markmann. London: Pluto Press, 1986.
Fanon, Frantz. *The Wretched of the Earth*. Translated by Richard Philcox. New York: Grove Press, 2007.
Fazlur, Rahman. *Islam*. Chicago: University of Chicago Press, 1979.
Feinman, Ilene. 'Shock and Awe: Abu Ghraib, Women Soldiers, and the Racially Gendered Torture'. In *One of the Guys: Women as Aggressors and Torturers*, edited by Tara McKelvey, 57–80. Emeryville: Seal Press, 2007.
Ferguson, Niall. 'Turning Points'. *The New York Times*, 30 November 2012, sec. Global Opinion. https://www.nytimes.com/2012/11/30/opinion/global/niall-ferguson-turning-points.html.
Fick, Nathaniel, and John Nagl. 'Counterinsurgency Field Manual: Afghanistan Edition'. *Foreign Policy*, 1 October 2009. https://foreignpolicy.com/2009/10/01/counterinsurgency-field-manual-afghanistan-edition/.
Figueira, Dorothy. *Aryans, Jews, Brahmins: Theorizing Authority through Myths of Identity*. New Delhi: Navayana, 2015.
Foucault, Michel. *Discipline and Punish: The Birth of the Prison*. Translated by Alan Sheridan. A Peregrine Book. Harmondsworth: Penguin, 1979.
Foucault, Michel. *The History of Sexuality: Volume 1: An Introduction*. Reissue edition. New York: Vintage, 1990.
Frankenberg, Ruth. *White Women, Race Matters: The Social Construction of Whiteness*. 5th edition. Minneapolis: University of Minnesota Press, 1993.
Frankl, Viktor. *Man's Search for Meaning: The Classic Tribute to Hope from the Holocaust*. London: Rider Books, 2004.
Franks, Mary Anne. 'Obscene Undersides: Women and Evil between the Taliban and the United States'. *Hypatia* 18, no. 1 (2003): 135–56.
Gardella, Peter. *Innocent Ecstasy: How Christianity Gave America an Ethic of Sexual Pleasure*. New York: Oxford University Press, 1985.
Gibbons-Neff, Thomas, Eric Schmitt, and Adam Goldman. 'C.I.A. to Expand Its Covert Role in Afghanistan'. *The New York Times*, 23 October 2017, Late edition.
Gill, Anton. *Ruling Passions: Sex, Race and Empire*. London: BBC Books, 1995.
Gilley, Bruce. 'The Case for Colonialism'. *Third World Quarterly*, 2017: 1–17.
Gilman, Sander. *Difference and Pathology: Stereotypes of Sexuality, Race, and Madness*. Ithaca: Cornell University Press, 1985.
Gilman, Sander L. *Jewish Self-Hatred: Anti-Semitism and the Hidden Language of the Jews*. Baltimore: Johns Hopkins University Press, 1986.
Gilroy, Paul. *Race and the Right to Be Human*. The Netherlands: Universiteit Utrecht, 2009.
Godfrey, John. 'Venice and the Fourth Crusade'. *History Today* 26, no. 1 (January 1976). https://www.historytoday.com/john-godfrey/venice-and-fourth-crusade.

Goldberg, David Theo. 'Racial Europeanization'. *Ethnic and Racial Studies* 29, no. 2 (1 March 2006): 331–64.
Goldstein, Evan. 'Osama Bin Laden Made Me Famous'. *The Chronicle of Higher Education*, 22 April 2012. https://www.chronicle.com/article/Osama-bin-Laden-Made-Me/13 1584.
Goldstone, Richard. 'Reconsidering the Goldstone Report on Israel and War Crimes'. *Washington Post*, 1 April 2011. https://www.washingtonpost.com/opinions/reconsider ing-the-goldstone-report-on-israel-and-war-crimes/2011/04/01/AFg111JC_story.html.
Göle, Nilüfer. *The Forbidden Modern: Civilization and Veiling*. Ann Arbor: University of Michigan Press, 1996.
Gomez, Michael. *Black Crescent: The Experience and Legacy of African Muslims in the Americas*. New York: Cambridge University Press, 2005.
Gordon, Lewis. 'African-American Philosophy, Race, and the Geography of Reason'. In *Not Only the Master's Tools: African-American Studies in Theory and Practice*, edited by Lewis Gordon and Jane Anna Gordon, 3–50. Cultural Politics & the Promise of Democracy. Boulder: Paradigm, 2006.
Graham, Stephen, ed. *Cities, War, and Terrorism: Towards an Urban Geopolitics*. Studies in Urban and Social Change. Oxford: Blackwell Publishing, 2004.
Greenberg, Cheryl Lynn. *Troubling the Waters: Black-Jewish Relations in the American Century*. Princeton: Princeton University Press, 2010. http://muse.jhu.edu/book/30108.
Guhin, Jeffrey. 'Colorblind Islam: The Racial Hinges of Immigrant Muslims in the United States'. *Social Inclusion* 6, no. 2 (2018): 87–97.
Gupta, Rahila. 'Mona Eltahawy and Sexual Revolution in the Middle East'. *OpenDemocracy*, 18 January 2016. https://www.opendemocracy.net/5050/rahila-gupta/ mona-eltahawy-and-sexual-revolution-in-middle-east.
Halberstam, Judith. *Female Masculinity*. Durham: Duke University Press, 1988.
Haldar, Piyel. *Law, Orientalism and Postcolonialism: The Jurisdiction of the Lotus-Eaters*. London: Routledge, 2007.
Hall, Stuart. 'The West and The Rest: Discourse and Power'. In *The Formations of Modernity*, edited by Stuart Hall and Bram Gieben, 275–332. Understanding Modern Societies: An Introduction. Cambridge: Polity Press & the Open University, 1992.
Hallaq, Wael. *The Impossible State: Islam, Politics, and Modernity's Moral Predicament*. New York: Columbia University Press, 2013.
'Hamas Calls for Gaza Truce'. *Newshour*. BBC World Service, 27 July 2014. https://ww w.bbc.co.uk/programmes/p0239l48.
Hammill, Graham, Julia Reinhard Lupton, and Etienne Balibar, eds. 'Introduction'. In *Political Theology and Early Modernity*, 1–21. Chicago: University of Chicago Press, 2012.
Harding, Luke. 'The Other Prisoners'. *The Guardian*, 20 May 2004, sec. World news. https ://www.theguardian.com/world/2004/may/20/iraq.gender.
Hardt, Michael, and Antonio Negri. *Empire*. Cambridge: Harvard University Press, 2000.
Hardy, Paul. 'Islam and the Race Question'. Accessed 23 September 2018. http://www.masu d.co.uk/ISLAM/misc/race.htm.
Haritaworn, Jinthana. *Queer Lovers and Hateful Others: Regenerating Violent Times and Places*. London: Pluto Press, 2015.
Haritaworn, Jinthana, Adi Kuntsman, and Silvia Posocco, eds. *Queer Necropolitics*. London: Routledge, 2014. https://www-taylorfrancis-com.ezproxy.library.ubc.ca/bo oks/e/9781136005282.

Harris, Kathleen. 'Anti-Muslim Crimes in Canada up 60%, StatsCan Reports'. *CBC*, 13 June 2017. https://www.cbc.ca/news/politics/hate-crimes-muslims-statscan-1.4158042.

Harris, Paul. 'US Soldier Admits Killing Unarmed Afghans for Sport'. *The Guardian*, 23 March 2011, sec. US news. https://www.theguardian.com/world/2011/mar/23/us-soldier-admits-killing-afghans.

Harris, Trudier. *Exorcising Blackness: Historical and Literary Lynching and Burning Rituals*. Bloomington: Indiana University Press, 1984.

Hartung, William, and Frida Berrigan. 'Report: U.S. Arms Transfers and Security Assistance to Israel'. World Policy Institute, 6 May 2002. https://worldpolicy.org/report-u-s-arms-transfers-and-security-assistance-to-israel-world-policy-institute-research-project/.

Hastings, Michael. 'The Runaway General: The Profile That Brought Down McChrystal'. *Rolling Stone*, 22 June 2010.

Hendriks, Thomas. 'Race and Desire in the Porno-Tropics: Ethnographic Perspectives from the Post-Colony'. *Sexualities* 17, no. 1–2 (1 January 2014): 213–29.

Hess, Pamela. '"Enemy Combatant" Added to DOD Doctrine'. *UPI*, 8 April 2005. https://www.upi.com/Enemy-combatant-added-to-DOD-doctrine/52081112993349/.

Hine, Darlene Clark, and Earnestine Jenkins, eds. *A Question of Manhood: A Reader in U.S. Black Men's History and Masculinity*. Blacks in the Diaspora. Bloomington: Indiana University Press, 1999.

Hirsi Ali, Ayaan. *The Caged Virgin: An Emancipation Proclamation for Women and Islam*. New York: Free Press, 2006.

Hoffheimer, Michael. 'Race and Law in Hegel's Philosophy of Religion'. In *Race and Racism in Modern Philosophy*, edited by Andrew Valls, 194–216. Ithaca: Cornell University Press, 2005.

Huckerby, Jayne. 'A Decade Lost: Locating Gender in U.S. Counter-Terrorism'. Center for Human Rights and Global Justice, NYU School of Law, 1 July 2011. https://chrgj.org/document-center/a-decade-lost-locating-gender-in-u-s-counter-terrorism/.

'Human Rights in Palestine and Other Occupied Arab Territories: Report of the United Nations Fact Finding Mission on the Gaza Conflict'. UN Human Rights Council, 15 September 2009. https://www.un.org/ruleoflaw/blog/document/human-rights-in-palestine-and-other-occupied-arab-territories-report-of-the-united-nations-fact-finding-mission-on-the-gaza-conflict/.

Ignatieff, Michael. *The Lesser Evil: Political Ethics in an Age of Terror*. The Gifford Lectures. Princeton: Princeton University Press, 2004.

Iqbal, Basit Kareem. 'Thinking about Method: A Conversation with Talal Asad'. *Qui Parle* 26, no. 1 (June 2017): 195–218.

'Israel Pays UN for Gaza War Damage'. *Aljazeera*, 24 January 2010. http://english.aljazeera.net/news/middleeast/2010/01/201012371243624144.html.

@IsraeliPM. Tweet, 29 August 2018. https://twitter.com/IsraeliPM/status/1034849460344573952.

I've Tortured and Raped in Iraq. Accessed 14 September 2018. https://www.youtube.com/watch?v=qFOF-jv32dA.

Iveković, Rada, and Julie Mostov, eds. *From Gender to Nation*. New Delhi: Zubaan, 2004.

İyigün, Murat. 'Luther and Suleyman'. *The Quarterly Journal of Economics* 123, no. 4 (2008): 1465–94.

Jackson, Sherman. *Islam and the Problem of Black Suffering*. New York: Oxford University Press, 2009.

Jackson, Sherman A. *Islam and the Blackamerican: Looking Toward the Third Resurrection*. New York: Oxford University Press, 2005.

Jalal, Ayesha. *Self and Sovereignty: Individual and Community in South Asian Islam since 1850*. London: Routlege, 2000.

Jarmakani, Amira. '"The Sheik Who Loved Me": Romancing the War on Terror'. *Signs: Journal of Women in Culture and Society* 35, no. 4 (1 June 2010): 993–1017.

Jennings, Willie James. *The Christian Imagination: Theology and the Origins of Race*. New Haven: Yale University Press, 2010.

Jewish Virtual Library, A Project of AICE. 'Modern Jewish History: The Spanish Expulsion (1492)'. Accessed 15 September 2018. https://www.jewishvirtuallibrary.org/the-spanish-expulsion-1492.

Jordan, Winthrop D. *White over Black: American Attitudes toward the Negro, 1550–1812*. Second edition. Chapel Hill: University of North Carolina Press, 2012.

Kabbani, Rana. *Europe's Myths of Orient: Devise and Rule*. London: Macmillan, 1986.

Kalmar, Ivan. *Early Orientalism: Imagined Islam and the Notion of Sublime Power*. London: Routledge, 2013.

Kamaly, Hossein. 'Review of *Greek Thought, Arabic Culture: The Graeco-Arabic Translation Movement in Baghdad and Early Abbasid Society (2nd–4th/8th–10th Centuries)*, by Dimitri Gutas'. *International Society for Iranian Studies* 32, no. 4 (Autumn 1999): 575–8.

Kelly, Oliver. *Women as Weapons of War: Iraq, Sex, and the Media*. Vanderbilt University. Accessed 19 July 2010. https://www.youtube.com/watch?v=yEkljySp9ds.

Kershner, Isabel, and David M. Halbfinger. 'Israelis Reflect on Gaza: "I Hope at Least That Each Bullet Was Justified"'. *The New York Times*, 17 May 2018, sec. World. https://www.nytimes.com/2018/05/15/world/middleeast/israelis-gaza-protests.html.

Khalidi, Rashid. *The Iron Cage: The Story of the Palestinian Struggle for Statehood*. Boston: Beacon Press, 2006.

Khan, Naveeda. *Muslim Becoming: Aspiration and Skepticism in Pakistan*. Durham: Duke University Press, 2012.

Khanna, Ranjana. *Dark Continents: Psychoanalysis and Colonialism*. Durham: Duke University Press, 2003.

Kotb, Sayed. *Social Justice in Islam*. Translated by John B. Hardie. Washington: American Council of Learned Societies, 1953.

Krishnaswamy, Revathi. *Effeminism: The Economy of Colonial Desire*. Ann Arbor: University of Michigan Press, 1998.

Kumar, Deepa. 'Fighting Islamophobia: A Response to Critics'. *MR Online*, 3 April 2006. https://mronline.org/2006/04/03/fighting-islamophobia-a-response-to-critics/.

Lambert, Sarah. 'Crusading or Spinning'. In *Gendering the Crusades*, edited by Susan Edgington and Sarah Lambert, 1–15. Cardiff: University of Wales Press, 2001.

Landler, Mark, and Michael Gordon. 'President Cedes Afghan Strategy to the Pentagon: A Quiet Shift of Power'. *The New York Times*, 19 June 2017, National edition.

Laremont, Ricardo René. *Islam and the Politics of Resistance in Algeria, 1783–1992*. Trenton: Africa World Press, 2000.

Larrimore, Mark. 'Antinomies of Race: Diversity and Destiny in Kant'. *Patterns of Prejudice* 42, no. 4–5 (1 September 2008): 341–63.

Larson, Todd. 'President Obama and the Global Fight for LGBT Rights', *Huffington Post*, 5 November 2012. https://www.huffingtonpost.com/todd-larson/president-obama-and-the-global-fight-for-lgbt-rights_b_2060883.html.

Lawrence, Bruce, ed. *Messages to the World: The Statements of Osama Bin Laden*. Annotated edition. London: Verso, 2005.

Lazreg, Marnia. 'Gender and Politics in Algeria: Unraveling the Religious Paradigm'. *Signs* 15, no. 4 (1990): 755–80.

Lazreg, Marnia. *Torture and the Twilight of Empire: From Algiers to Baghdad*. Human Rights and Crimes against Humanity. Princeton: Princeton University Press, 2008.

Lebovich, Andrew. 'The Real Reason U.S. Troops Are in Niger'. *Foreign Policy*, 27 October 2017. https://foreignpolicy.com/2017/10/27/the-real-reason-u-s-troops-are-in-niger/.

Lentin, Ronit. *Thinking Palestine*. London: Zed Books, 2008.

Lewis, Bernard. *Islam and the West*. New York: Oxford University Press, 1993.

Lloyd, Vincent, ed. *Race and Political Theology*. Stanford: Stanford University Press, 2012.

Lobe, Jim. 'Israel Ranked World's Most Militarised Nation'. *Inter Press Service*. 14 November 2012. http://www.ipsnews.net/2012/11/israel-ranked-as-worlds-most-militarised-nation/.

Loomba, Ania. 'Remembering Said'. *Comparative Studies of South Asia, Africa and the Middle East* 23, no. 1 (2003): 12–14.

Loomba, Ania. *Shakespeare, Race, and Colonialism*. Oxford Shakespeare Topics. Oxford: Oxford University Press, 2002.

Loomba, Ania, and Jonathan Burton, eds. *Race in Early Modern England: A Documentary Companion*. New York: Palgrave Macmillan, 2007.

Luchte, J. 'A Rupture in Colonial Reason: Spivak, Fanon, and The Question of Subalternity'. *Continental Philosophy*, 2014. http://www.continental-philosophy.org/2014/11/05/a-rupture-in-colonial-reason-spivak-fanon-and-the-question-of-subalternity.

Lunat, Ziyaad, and Max Ajl. 'A Glimmer of Hope'. *The Electronic Intifada*, 12 November 2009. https://electronicintifada.net/content/glimmer-hope/8531.

Lyons, Jonathan. *Islam Through Western Eyes: From the Crusades to the War on Terrorism*. New York: Columbia University Press, 2012.

Maalouf, Amin. *The Crusades Through Arab Eyes*. London: Al Saqi Books, 2012.

Mahmood, Saba, and Charles Hirschkind. 'Feminism, the Taliban, and Politics of Counter-Insurgency', *Anthropological Quarterly* 75, no. 2 (2002): 339–54.

Majid, Anouar. *We Are All Moors: Ending Centuries of Crusades against Muslims and Other Minorities*. Minneapolis: University of Minnesota Press, 2009.

Malcolm, X. *By Any Means Necessary*. Takoma Park: Pathfinder, 1992.

Mandair, Arvind-Pal. *Religion and the Specter of the West: Sikhism, India, Postcoloniality, and the Politics of Translation*. New York: Columbia University Press, 2009.

Manji, Irshad. *The Trouble with Islam: A Muslim's Call for Reform in Her Faith*. New York: St. Martin's Press, 2004.

Manji, Irshad. *The Trouble with Islam: A Wake-up Call for Honesty and Change*. Toronto: Random House of Canada, Limited, 2003.

Manzoor, Parvez. 'Turning Jews into Muslims: The Untold Saga of the Muselmänner'. *Islam* 21, no. 28 (2001): 8–12.

Maracle, Lee. *I Am Woman*. North Vancouver: Write-On Press, 1988.

Marchand, Suzanne. 'Review of History of Islam in German Thought: From Leibniz to Nietzsche'. *Reviews in History*, no. 939 (n.d.). https://www.history.ac.uk/reviews/review/939.

Margaret, Wente. 'We're in Afghanistan for This?' *The Globe and Mail*, 2 April 2009, sec. A 13.

Marshall, Lucinda. 'The Misogynist Implications'. In *One of the Guys: Women as Aggressors and Torturers*, edited by Tara McKelvey, 51–6. Emeryville: Seal Press, 2007.

Massad, Joseph. *100 Years after the Balfour Declaration*. Vienna: Verein Dar Al Janub, 2017. https://www.youtube.com/watch?v=TXzktQKBGxY.
Massad, Joseph. 'Blaming the Lobby'. *Al Ahram*, 23 March 2006. http://weekly.ahram.org.eg/2006/787/op35.htm.
Massad, Joseph. *Desiring Arabs*. Chicago: University of Chicago Press, 2007.
Massad, Joseph. 'Forget Semitism'. In *Living Together: Jacques Derrida's Communities of Violence and Peace*, edited by Elisabeth Weber, 59–79. New York: Fordham University Press, 2012.
Massad, Joseph. *Islam in Liberalism*. Chicago: University of Chicago Press, 2015.
Massad, Joseph. 'Israel's Right to Be Racist'. *The Electronic Intifada*, 15 March 2007. https://electronicintifada.net/content/israels-right-be-racist/6813.
Massad, Joseph. 'Palestinians and Jewish History: Recognition or Submission?' *Journal of Palestine Studies* 30, no. 1 (2000): 52–67.
Massad, Joseph. 'Re-Orienting Desire: The Gay International and the Arab World'. *Public Culture* 14, no. 2 (1 May 2002): 361–85.
Massad, Joseph. 'The Empire of Sexuality: An Interview with Joseph Massad'. *Jadaliyya*, March 2013. http://www.jadaliyya.com/Details/28167.
Masuzawa, Tomoko. *The Invention of World Religions, or, How European Universalism Was Preserved in the Language of Pluralism*. Chicago: University of Chicago Press, 2005.
Mbembé, Achille. 'Necropolitics'. Translated by Libby Meintjes. *Public Culture* 15, no. 1 (Winter 2003): 11–40.
Mbembé, Achille. *On the Postcolony*. Berkeley: University of California Press, 2001.
McAlister, Melani. *Epic Encounters: Culture, Media, and U.S. Interests in the Middle East since 1945*. Updated edition, with A post-9/11 chapter. American Crossroads 6. Berkeley: University of California Press, 2005.
McClintock, Anne. *Imperial Leather: Race, Gender, and Sexuality in the Colonial Contest*. London: Routledge, 1995.
McGreal, Chris. 'Death on the Beach: Seven Palestinians Killed as Israeli Shells Hit Family Picnic'. *The Guardian*, 10 June 2006, sec. World news. https://www.theguardian.com/world/2006/jun/10/israel.
McKelvey, Tara, ed. *One of the Guys: Women as Aggressors and Torturers*. Emeryville: Seal Press, 2007.
McLeod, Laura. 'Well, What Is the Feminist Perspective on Iraq?' *Political Studies Review* 10, no. 3 (1 September 2012): 385–93.
McNeil Jr., Donald. 'The Long, Dusky Trek toward Tolerance'. *The New York Times*, 13 February 2009, sec. Movies. https://www.nytimes.com/2009/02/15/movies/15mcne.html.
Melamed, Jodi. *Represent and Destroy: Rationalizing Violence in the New Racial Capitalism*. Minneapolis: University of Minnesota Press, 2011.
Menocal, Maria Rosa. *The Ornament of the World: How Muslims, Jews, and Christians Created a Culture of Tolerance in Medieval Spain*. Boston: Little, Brown and Company, 2002.
Merica, Dan. 'Trump: "We Are Stopping Cold the Attacks on Judeo-Christian Values"'. *CNN*, 13 October 2017. https://www.cnn.com/2017/10/13/politics/trump-values-voters-summit/index.html.
Merrill, John Ernest. 'Of the Tractate of John of Damascus on Islam'. In *Classical and Medieval Literature Criticism*, edited by Jelena Krstovic, Vol. 27. Detroit: Gale, 1998. http://link.galegroup.com/apps/doc/H1420015175/LitRC?sid=googlescholar.

Mignolo, Walter. *The Darker Side of Western Modernity: Global Futures, Decolonial Options*. Durham: Duke University Press, 2011.
Mignolo, Walter, Maureen Quilligan, and Margaret Greer, eds. *Rereading the Black Legend: The Discourses of Religious and Racial Difference in the Renaissance Empires*. Chicago: University of Chicago Press, 2008.
Miller, Stuart. 'Do Not Resist: New Film Shows How US Police Have Become an Occupying Army'. *The Guardian*, 30 September 2016, sec. Film. https://www.theguardian.com/film/2016/sep/30/do-not-resist-film-documentary-us-police-militarization.
Mishra, Pankaj. *From the Ruins of Empire: The Revolt against the West and the Remaking of Asia*. London: Allen Lane, 2012.
Mishra, Smeeta. '"Saving" Muslim Women and Fighting Muslim Men: Analysis of Representations in The New York Times'. *Global Media Journal* 6, no. 11 (Fall 2007): 1.
Mitter, Partha. *Much Maligned Monsters: A History of European Reactions to Indian Art*. Chicago: University of Chicago Press, 1992.
Mohanty, Chandra Talpade. 'Under Western Eyes: Feminist Scholarship and Colonial Discourses'. In *Feminism without Borders: Decolonizing Theory, Practicing Solidarity*. Durham: Duke University Press, 2003.
Mohanty, Chandra Talpade, Lourdes Torres, and Ann Russo, eds. *Third World Women and the Politics of Feminism*. Bloomington: Indiana University Press, 1991.
Monture, Patricia, and Brenda Conroy. *Thunder in My Soul: A Mohawk Woman Speaks*. Halifax: Fernwood Publishing, 1995.
Morgan, Robin. *The Demon Lover: On the Sexuality of Terrorism*. 1st edition. New York, NY: Norton, 1989.
Morie Sileo. *Talal Asad and Abdullahi An'Naim on Islam and Human Rights*. Berkeley, 2009. https://www.youtube.com/watch?v=PyeDj1iUSms.
Morrow, Adrian. 'Killing of Nabra Hassanen Leaves Virginia Muslim Community Shaken', *The Globe and Mail*, 22 June 2017. https://www.theglobeandmail.com/news/world/killing-of-nabra-hassanen-leaves-virginia-muslim-community-shaken/article35442848/.
Motadel, David. 'Introduction'. In *Islam and the European Empires*, 1–34. Oxford: Oxford University Press, 2014.
Myers, Steven Lee. 'Lasers and Missiles Heighten U.S.-China Military Tensions'. *The New York Times*, 7 August 2018, sec. World. https://www.nytimes.com/2018/05/04/world/asia/china-united-states-lasers-pilots.html.
Nafisi, Azar. *Reading Lolita in Tehran: A Memoir in Books*. New York: Random House, 2003.
Najmabadi, Afsaneh. *Women with Mustaches and Men without Beards: Gender and Sexual Anxieties of Iranian Modernity*. Berkeley: University of California Press, 2005.
Najmabadi, Afsaneh, and Kathryn Babayan, eds. *Islamicate Sexualities: Translations across Temporal Geographies of Desire*. Harvard Middle Eastern Monographs 39. Cambridge: Center for Middle Eastern Studies of Harvard University, 2008.
Nicholson, Helen. *Love, War, and the Grail*. History of Warfare 4. Leiden: Brill, 2001.
Niewyk, Donald, and Francis Nicosia. *The Columbia Guide to the Holocaust*. New York: Columbia University Press, 2000.
Norton, Ben. 'Netanyahu Appoints Ayelet Shaked—Who Called for Genocide of Palestinians—as Justice Minister in New Government'. *Mondoweiss*, 6 May 2015. https://mondoweiss.net/2015/05/netanyahu-palestinians-government/.
Obama, Barack. 'Transcript of Obama Speech'. *Politico*, 18 March 2008. https://www.politico.com/news/stories/0308/9100.html.
O'Brien, Peter. *European Perceptions of Islam and America from Saladin to George W. Bush: Europe's Fragile Ego Uncovered*. New York: Palgrave Macmillan, 2009.

Oliver, Kelly. *Women as Weapons of War: Iraq, Sex, and the Media*. New York: Columbia University Press, 2007.
Omi, Michael, and Howard Winant. *Racial Formation in the United States: From the 1960s to the 1990s*. 2nd edition. New York: Routledge, 1994.
Orthodox Christian Information Centre. 'St. John of Damascus: Critique of Islam,' n.d. http://orthodoxinfo.com/general/stjohn_islam.aspx.
Pach, Zs P. 'The Shifting of International Trade Routes in the 15th–17th Centuries'. *Acta Historica Academiae Scientiarum Hungaricae* 14, no. 3/4 (1968): 287–321.
Palmquist, Stephen. 'Could Kant's Jesus Be God?' *International Philosophical Quarterly* 52, no. 4 (December 2012): 421–37.
Pandian, Jacob. *Anthropology and the Western Tradition: Toward an Authentic Anthropology*. Prospect Heights: Waveland Press, 1985.
Pappé, Ilan. *The Ethnic Cleansing of Palestine*. Oxford: Oneworld, 2006.
Patel, Khadija. 'Q&A: Exploring Sweden's 'feminist' Foreign Policy'. *Al Jazeera*, 15 June 2015, sec. Africa. https://www.aljazeera.com/indepth/features/2015/06/southafrica-au-sweden-feminism-foreign-policy-150615140028265.html.
Patterson, Orlando. *Slavery and Social Death: A Comparative Study*. Cambridge: Harvard University Press, 1982.
Pease, Donald. 'Between the Homeland and Abu Ghraib: Dwelling in Bush's Biopolitical Settlement'. In *Exceptional State: Contemporary U.S. Culture and the New Imperialism*, edited by Ashley Dawson and Malini Johar Schueller, 60–87. New Americanists. Durham: Duke University Press, 2007.
Perera, Suvendrini. 'What Is a Camp'. *Borderlands* 1, no. 1 (2002): 14–21.
Perera, Suvendrini, and Sherene Razack, eds. *At the Limits of Justice: Women of Colour on Terror*. Toronto: University of Toronto Press, 2014.
Peritz, Ingrid. 'Quebec Veil Law Bill 62 Sparks Protests and Confusion'. *The Globe and Mail*, 20 October 2017. https://www.theglobeandmail.com/news/national/in-quebec-veil-law-bill-62-sparks-protests-and-confusion/article36680954/.
Peritz, Ingrid, and Daniel Leblanc. 'RCMP Accused of Racial Profiling over "Interview Guide" Targeting Muslim Border Crossers'. *The Globe and Mail*, 12 October 2017. https://www.theglobeandmail.com/news/national/rcmp-halts-use-of-screening-questionnaire-aimed-at-muslim-asylum-seekers/article36560918/.
Perraudin, Frances. 'David Cameron Lacked "balls" to Head off the Rise of Isis, Says Former Defence Chief', *The Guardian*, 30 August 2015, sec. Politics. https://www.theguardian.com/politics/2015/aug/30/david-cameron-lacked-balls-to-head-off-the-rise-of-isis-says-former-defence-chief.
Pollitt, Katha. 'After the Taliban', *The Nation*, 29 November 2001. https://www.thenation.com/article/after-taliban/.
'Pope Urban II's Speech Calling for the First Crusade'. *CBN.Com - The Christian Broadcasting Network*, 25 September 2013. http://www1.cbn.com/spirituallife/calling-for-the-first-crusade.
Prashad, Vijay. 'Mediterranean Refugee Crisis Escalating'. *The Real News Network*, 29 August 2015. https://therealnews.com/stories/vprashad0828refugees.
Prashad, Vijay. *The Darker Nations: A People's History of the Third World*. New York: The New Press, 2008.
Pregill, Michael. 'I Hear Islam Singing: Shahab Ahmed's What Is Islam? The Importance of Being Islamic'. *Harvard Theological Review* 110, no. 1 (January 2017): 149–65.
Presentation'. *Universidad de Castilla – La Mancha*. n.d. https://www.uclm.es/escueladetraductores/english/history/.

Puar, Jasbir. 'Mapping US Homonormativities'. *Gender, Place & Culture* 13, no. 1 (1 February 2006): 67–88.
Puar, Jasbir. *Terrorist Assemblages: Homonationalism in Queer Times*. Next Wave. Durham: Duke University Press, 2007.
Pugliese, Joseph. 'Apostrophe of Empire: Guantanamo Bay, Disneyland'. *Borderlands* 8, no. 3 (2009): 1–26.
Pugliese, Joseph. *State Violence and the Execution of Law: Biopolitcal Caesurae of Torture, Black Sites, Drones*. London: Routledge, 2013.
Quinn, Frederick. *The Sum of All Heresies: The Image of Islam in Western Thought*. Oxford: Oxford University Press, 2008.
Rabaka, Reiland. *Forms of Fanonism: Frantz Fanon's Critical Theory and the Dialectics of Decolonization*. Lanham: Lexington Books, 2010.
Rāhnamā, ʻAlī. *An Islamic Utopian: A Political Biography of Ali Shariʻati*. London: I.B. Tauris, 1998.
Ramadan, Tariq. *In the Footsteps of the Prophet: Lessons from the Life of Muhammad*. Oxford: Oxford University Press, 2007.
Rashid, Naaz. *Veiled Threats: Representing the Muslim Woman in Public Policy Discourses*. Bristol: Policy Press, 2016.
Razack, Sherene. *Casting Out: The Eviction of Muslims from Western Law and Politics*. Toronto: University of Toronto Press, 2008.
Razack, Sherene. 'Unassimilable Muslims and Civilized White People: The Race/Culture Divide in Law'. *The Annual Meeting of the The Law and Society Association, Renaissance Hotel, Chicago*, 27 May 2004.
Razack, Sherene H. 'Imperilled Muslim Women, Dangerous Muslim Men and Civilised Europeans: Legal and Social Responses to Forced Marriages'. *Feminist Legal Studies* 12, no. 2 (October 2004): 129–74.
Reed, Betsy, and Katha Pollitt, eds. *Nothing Sacred: Women Respond to Religious Fundamentalism and Terror*. New York: Nation Books, 2002.
Reeves, Minou. *Female Warriors of Allah: Women and the Islamic Revolution*. New York: Dutton, 1989.
Reeves, Minou. *Muhammad in Europe: A Thousand Years of Western Myth-Making*. New York: NYU Press, 2003.
'Religious Landscape Study'. Religion & Public Life Project. Pew Research Center, 11 May 2015. http://www.pewforum.org/religious-landscape-study/racial-and-ethnic-composi tion/.
Reuters. 'A Crisis that Has Europe in Its Grip'. *The Globe and Mail*, 3 September 2015.
Robinson, Cedric. *Black Marxism: The Making of the Black Radical Tradition*. Chapel Hill: University of North Carolina Press, 2000.
Ross, Alice, and James Ball. 'GCHQ Documents Raise Fresh Questions over UK Complicity in US Drone Strikes'. *The Guardian*, 24 June 2015, sec. UK news. https://www.theguardian.com/uk-news/2015/jun/24/gchq-documents-raise-fresh-questions-over-uk-complicity-in-us-drone-strikes.
Rossi, Philip. 'Kant's Philosophy of Religion'. In *The Stanford Encyclopedia of Philosophy*, edited by Edward Zalta and Edward Zalta, Fall 2013. forthcoming, 2013. http://plato.st anford.edu/cgi-bin/encyclopedia/archinfo.cgi?entry=kant-religion.
Roy, Olivier. *Secularism Confronts Islam*. New York: Columbia University Press, 2007.
Roy, Olivier. *The Failure of Political Islam*. Cambridge: Harvard University Press, 1994.
Sacco, Joe. *Palestine*. Reprint. London: Jonathan Cape, 2003.

Safi, Omid. *Memories of Muhammad: Why the Prophet Matters*. New York: Harper Collins, 2009.
Said, Edward. *Covering Islam: How the Media and the Experts Determine How We See the Rest of the World*. New York: Pantheon Books, 1981.
Said, Edward. *Orientalism*. London: Penguin, 1995.
Said, Edward. *Peace and Its Discontents: Essays on Palestine in the Middle East Peace Process*. New York: Vintage Books, 1996.
Said, Edward. *The Question of Palestine*. New York: Times Books, 1979.
Salama, Mohammad. 'Arabic and the Monopoly of Theory'. *ARCADE: Literature, the Humanities and the World*, 13 April 2015. https://arcade.stanford.edu/blogs/arabic-and-monopoly-theory.
Sangari, Kumkum, and Sudesh Vaid, eds. *Recasting Women: Essays in Colonial History*. New Delhi: Kali for Women, 1989.
Sardar, Ziauddin. *Desperately Seeking Paradise: Journeys of a Sceptical Muslim*. London: Granta Books, 2004.
Sardar, Ziauddin. *Orientalism*. Concepts in the Social Sciences. Buckingham: Open University Press, 1999.
Sardar, Ziauddin, and Zafar Abbas Malik. *Muhammad for Beginners*. Cambridge: Icon Books, 1999.
Savage, Charlie, Eric Schmitt, and Thomas Gibbons-Neff. 'U.S. Kept Silent about Its Role in Another Firefight in Niger'. *The New York Times*, 14 March 2018. https://www.nytimes.com/2018/03/14/world/africa/niger-green-berets-isis-firefight-december.html.
Sayyid, Salman. *A Fundamental Fear: Eurocentrism and the Emergence of Islamism*. 2nd edition. London: Zed Books, 2003.
Sayyid, Salman. 'Out of the Devil's Dictionary'. In *Thinking through Islamophobia: Global Perspectives*, edited by Salman Sayyid and AbdoolKarim Vakil, 5–18. London: C. Hurst, 2010.
Sayyid, Salman. *Recalling the Caliphate: Decolonisation and World Order*. London: Hurst Publishers, 2014.
Sayyid, Salman. 'Thinking through Islamophobia'. In *Thinking through Islamophobia: Global Perspectives*, edited by Salman Sayyid and AbdoolKarim Vakil, 1–4. London: C. Hurst, 2010.
Scahill, Jeremy. *Dirty Wars: The World Is a Battlefield*. New York: Nation Books, 2013. http://ebookcentral.proquest.com/lib/ubc/detail.action?docID=1113900.
Scahill, Jeremy. 'The Assassination Complex: Secret Military Documents Expose the Inner Workings of Obama's Drone Wars'. *The Intercept*, The Drone Papers, Article No. 1 of 8, 15 October 2015. https://theintercept.com/drone-papers/the-assassination-complex/.
Scott, Joan Wallach. *The Politics of the Veil*. Princeton: Princeton University Press, 2007.
Scott, Joan Wallach, ed. *Women's Studies on the Edge*. Durham: Duke University Press, 2008.
Shamir, Eitan. 'Rethinking Operation Protective Edge'. *Middle East Quarterly* 22, no. 2 (1 March 2015). https://www.meforum.org/articles/2015/rethinking-operation-protective-edge.
Shanahan, Noreen. 'Armstrong Continues Chronicles of Afghanistan Women'. *Herizons* 23, no. 2 (Fall 2009): 45.
Shane, Scott, and Eric Schmitt. 'C.I.A. Deaths Prompt Surge in U.S. Drone Strikes'. *The New York Times*, 22 January 2010, sec. Asia Pacific. https://www.nytimes.com/2010/01/23/world/asia/23drone.html.

Shanker, Thom. 'Petraeus's Successor Is Known for Impolitic Words'. *The New York Times*, 19 July 2010, sec. World. https://www.nytimes.com/2010/07/20/world/20mattis.html.

Shariati, Ali. *Man and Islam*. Translated by Fatollah Marjani. North Haledon: Islamic Publications International, 1981.

Sharoni, Simona, and Rabab Abdulhadi. 'Transnational Feminist Solidarity in Times of Crisis'. *International Feminist Journal of Politics* 17, no. 4 (2 October 2015): 654–70.

Sharp, Jeremy. 'U.S. Foreign Aid to Israel'. *Congressional Research Service*. RL 33222, 22 December 2016. www.crs.gov.

Sharpe, Christina. *Monstrous Intimacies: Making Post-Slavery Subjects*. Durham: Duke University Press, 2010.

Shepard, William. *Sayyid Qutb and Islamic Activism: A Translation and Critical Analysis of Social Justice in Islam*, Vol. 54. Leiden: E. J. Brill, 1996.

Sheth, Falguni. *Toward a Political Philosophy of Race*. Albany: State University of New York, 2009.

Siems, Larry. 'The Truth about Torture: Trump's CIA Pick Can't Lead without Facing Her Past'. *The Guardian*, 14 March 2018, sec. US news. https://www.theguardian.com/us-news/2018/mar/14/gina-haspel-torture-trump-cia-director-pick-has-to-face-past.

Silk, Mark. 'Notes on the Judeo-Christian Tradition in America'. *American Quarterly* 36, no. 1 (1984): 65–85.

Sivanandan, Ambalavaner. *A Different Hunger: Writings on Black Resistance*. London: Pluto Press, 1982.

Slisli, Fouzi. 'Islam: The Elephant in Fanon's The Wretched of the Earth'. *Critique: Critical Middle Eastern Studies* 17, no. 1 (Spring 2008): 97–108.

Smith, Craig. 'Kandahar Journal; Shh, It's an Open Secret: Warlords and Pedophilia'. *The New York Times*, 21 February 2002, sec. World. https://www.nytimes.com/2002/02/21/world/kandahar-journal-shh-it-s-an-open-secret-warlords-and-pedophilia.html.

Smith, Marie-Danielle. 'Senate Passes Bill to Remove Mention of "Barbaric Cultural Practices" from Harper-Era Law'. *National Post*, 12 December 2017. https://nationalpost.com/news/politics/senate-passes-bill-to-remove-mention-of-barbaric-cultural-practices-from-law-passed-by-harper-conservatives.

'Snapshot'. Accessed 22 September 2018. https://www-taylorfrancis-com.ezproxy.library.ubc.ca/books/9780203995808.

Spillers, Hortense. 'Mama's Baby, Papa's Maybe: An American Grammar Book'. *Diacritics* 17, no. 2 (1987): 65–81. https://doi.org/10.2307/464747.

Spillius, Alex. 'General Who Said Killing Is a Hoot Lands Top Job'. *The Montreal Gazette*, 9 July 2010.

St Bernard of Clairvaux. *In Praise of the New Knighthood: A Treatise on the Knights Templar and the Holy Places of Jerusalem*. Translated by M. Conrad Greenia. Monastic Studies Series 25. Piscataway: Gorgias Press, 2010.

St Clair, Jeffrey. 'Israeli Tunnel Vision'. *Counterpunch*, 5 September 2014. https://www.counterpunch.org/2014/09/05/israeli-tunnel-vision/.

St Clair, Jeffrey. 'When Torturers Walk'. *Counterpunch*, 20 March 2015. https://www.counterpunch.org/2015/03/20/when-torturers-walk/.

Steet, Linda. *Veils and Daggers: A Century of National Geographic's Representation of the Arab World*. Philadelphia: Temple University Press, 2000.

Steunebrink, Gerrit. 'A Religion after Christianity? Hegel's Interpretation of Islam between Judaism and Christianity'. In *Hegel's Philosophy of the Historical Religions*, edited by Bart Labuschagne and Timo Slootweg, 207–42. Leiden: Brill, 2012.

Stolba, Christine. 'Feminists Go to War'. *The Women's Quarterly*, 19 February 2002. http://freerepublic.com/focus/f-news/631259/posts.
Stoler, Ann Laura. *Race and the Education of Desire: Foucault's History of Sexuality and the Colonial Order of Things*. Durham: Duke University Press Books, 1995.
Stratton, Jon. 'Zombie Trouble: Zombie Texts, Bare Life and Displaced People'. *European Journal of Cultural Studies* 14, no. 3 (1 June 2011): 265–81.
'Submission to the Canadian Parliamentary Coalition to Combat Anti-Semitism'. *Faculty for Palestine Canada*, 31 August 2009. http://www.faculty4palestine.ca/submission-to-the-cpcca/.
Sweet, James. 'Spanish and Portuguese Influences on Racial Slavery in British North America, 1492–1619'. In *Proceedings of the Fifth Annual Gilder Lehrman Center International Conference at Yale University*. New Haven: Yale University, 2003.
'Sworn Statements by Abu Ghraib Detainees'. *The Washington Post*. Accessed 19 January 2014. http://www.washingtonpost.com/wp-srv/world/iraq/abughraib/swornstatements042104.html?noredirect=on.
Tessera, Miriam Rita. 'Philip Count of Flanders and Hildegard of Bingen: Crusading against the Saracens or Crusading Against Deadly Sin?' In *Gendering the Crusades*, edited by Susan Edgington and Sarah Lambert, 77–93. Cardiff: University of Wales Press, 2001.
The Jew, the Arab: An Interview with Gil Anidjar. Accessed 24 May 2020. https://asiasociety.org/jew-arab-interview-gil-anidjar.
The War of the World: Conversation with Niall Ferguson. Interview by Lawrence Tisch. Institute for International Studies, University of California-Berkeley, 2006. http://globetrotter.berkeley.edu/people6/Ferguson/ferguson06-con5.html.
Thobani, Sunera. 'Empire, Bare Life and the Constitution of Whiteness: Sovereignty in the Age of Terror'. *Borderlands* 11, no. 1 (2012): 1–26.
Thobani, Sunera. *Exalted Subjects: Studies in the Making of Race and Nation in Canada*. Toronto: University of Toronto Press, 2007.
Thobani, Sunera. 'Gender and Empire: Veilomentaries and the War on Terror'. In *Global Communications: Toward a Transcultural Political Economy*, edited by Paula Chakravartty and Yuezhi Zhao, 219–42. Critical Media Studies. Lanham: Rowman & Littlefield Publishers, 2008.
Thobani, Sunera. 'White Wars: Western Feminisms and the "War on Terror"'. *Feminist Theory* 8, no. 2 (2007): 169–85.
Thomas, Greg. *The Sexual Demon of Colonial Power: Pan-African Embodiment and Erotic Schemes of Empire*. Bloomington: Indiana University Press, 2007.
Thompson, Ayanna. *Performing Race and Torture on the Early Modern Stage*. Routledge Studies in Renaissance Literature and Culture 9. New York: Routledge, 2008.
Thompson, Kenneth, Stuart Hall, David Held, and Don Hubert, eds. *Modernity: An Introduction to Modern Societies*. Cambridge: Blackwell, 1996.
Tolan, John Victor. *Saracens: Islam in the Medieval European Imagination*. New York: Columbia University Press, 2002.
Torchia, Christopher. 'There Really Is Something in the Water, Kandahar Men Say'. *The Globe and Mail*, 10 April 2002, sec. A12.
'Transcript: Trump's First State of the Union Speech, Annotated'. *The New York Times*, 30 January 2018, sec. U.S. https://www.nytimes.com/interactive/2018/01/30/us/politics/state-of-the-union-2018-transcript.html.
Trumbull IV, George. *An Empire of Facts: Colonial Power, Cultural Knowledge, and Islam in Algeria, 1870–1914*. Critical Perspectives on Empire. Cambridge: Cambridge University Press, 2009.

Turnipseed, Tom. 'Killing For Fun; Military Madness'. *Common Dreams*, 13 July 2010. https://www.commondreams.org/views/2010/07/13/killing-fun-military-madness.
Tyson, Ann Scott. 'McChrystal Faces Raft of Issues as New Commander in Afghanistan'. *The Washington Post*, 13 May 2009, sec. Nation. http://www.washingtonpost.com/wp-dyn/content/article/2009/05/12/AR2009051203679.html.
Vanaik, Achin. 'Introduction'. In *Selling US Wars*, 1–24. Northampton: Olive Branch Press, 2007.
Vikør, Knut. 'Religious Revolts in Colonial North Africa'. In *Islam and the European Empires*, edited by David Motadel, 170–86. Oxford: Oxford University Press, 2014.
'Violence against Iraqi Women Continues Unabated'. *Electronic Iraq*. 1 December 2008. http://electroniciraq.net/news/newsanalysis/Violence_aginst_Iraqi_women_continues unabated_1/22/2009.
Voll, John. 'Islam as a Community of Discourse and a World-System'. In *The Sage Handbook of Islamic Studies*, edited by Akbar Ahmed and Tamara Sonn. London: SAGE Publications, 2010.
Wadud, Amina. *Qur'an and Woman: Rereading the Sacred Text from a Woman's Perspective*. New York: Oxford University Press, 1999.
Wallerstein, Immanuel. 'Islam in the Modern World-System'. *Sociologisk Forskning* 43, no. 4 (2006): 66–74.
Watson Institute International. 'Costs of War'. Brown University. Accessed 7 September 2018. https://watson.brown.edu/costsofwar/costs/human/refugees/iraqi.
Watson Institute International. 'Costs of War'. Brown University. Accessed 7 September 2018. https://watson.brown.edu/costsofwar/costs/human/refugees/afghan.
Watson, Paul Joseph. 'U.S. Military Investigator Confirms Women and Children Were Raped At Abu Ghraib'. 28 May 2009. https://www.infowars.com/us-military-investig ator-confirms-women-and-children-were-raped-at-abu-ghraib/.
Weber, Elisabeth, ed. *Living Together: Jacques Derrida's Communities of Violence and Peace*. New York: Fordham University Press, 2012.
Weber, Max. *The Protestant Ethic and the Spirit of Capitalism*. Translated by Talcott Parsons. London: Routledge, 2005. https://doi.org/10.4324/9780203995808.
Wells-Barnett, Ida B. *On Lynchings*. Classics in Black Studies Series. Amherst: Humanity Books, 2002.
Will, Dunham. 'General: It's "Fun to Shoot Some People"'. *CNN.Com*, 4 February 2005. http://www.cnn.com/2005/US/02/03/general.shoot/.
Wing, Adrien Katherine, ed. *Global Critical Race Feminism: An International Reader*. New York: NYU Press, 2000.
Winstanley, Asa. '"Liberal" Guardian to Print pro-Genocide Ad'. *The Electronic Intifada*, 9 August 2014. https://electronicintifada.net/blogs/asa-winstanley/liberal-guardian-p rint-pro-genocide-ad.
Wolf, Kenneth. 'Convivencia and the "Ornament of the World"'. *Pomona Faculty Publications and Research*, 1 January 2007. https://scholarship.claremont.edu/pomona _fac_pub/43.
'Women Leaders Call for Expansion of International Peace Troops and More U.S. Funds to Restore the Rights of Afghan Women'. *Feminist Majority Foundation* Online, 8 April 2002. http://www.feminist.org/news/pressstory.asp?id=6449.
Wood, Richard. 'Vicious Circles: Fanon, Islamism and Decolonization'. *Counterpunch*, 20 March 2015. https://www.counterpunch.org/2015/03/20/vicious-circles-fanon-isl amism-and-decolonization/.

Wynter, Sylvia. 'On How We Mistook the Map for the Territory, and Re-Imprisoned Ourselves in Our Unbearable Wrongness of Being, of Désêtre: Black Studies toward the Human Project'. In *Not Only the Master's Tools: African-American Studies in Theory and Practice*, edited by Lewis Gordon and Jane Anna Gordon, 107–69. Cultural Politics & the Promise of Democracy. Boulder: Paradigm, 2006.

Wynter, Sylvia. 'Unsettling the Coloniality of Being/Power/Truth/Freedom: Towards the Human, After Man, Its Overrepresentation – An Argument'. *CR: The New Centennial Review* 3, no. 3 (2003): 257–337. https://doi.org/10.1353/ncr.2004.0015.

Yanay, Niza. *The Ideology of Hatred: The Psychic Power of Discourse*. New York: Fordham University Press, 2013.

Yeğenoğlu, Meyda. *Colonial Fantasies: Towards a Feminist Reading of Orientalism*. Cambridge Cultural Social Studies. Cambridge: Cambridge University Press, 1998.

Yuval-Davis, Nira. *Gender and Nation*. London: SAGE Publications, 2013.

Zakaria, Rafia. 'Writing While Muslim: The Freedom to Be Offended'. Los Angeles *Review of Books*, 8 May 2015. https://lareviewofbooks.org/article/writing-while-muslim-the-freedom-to-be-offended-charlie-hebdo/.

Zielbauer, Paul von. '3rd U.S. Soldier Sentenced for Rape and Murder in Iraq'. *The New York Times*, 5 August 2007, sec. Americas. https://www.nytimes.com/2007/08/05/world/americas/05iht-soldier.1.6986906.html.

Žižek, Slavoj. 'Europe Must Move beyond Mere Tolerance'. *The Guardian*, 25 January 2011, sec. Opinion. https://www.theguardian.com/commentisfree/2011/jan/25/european-union-slovenia.

INDEX

Abrahamic 50, 174, 179, 181
Abu Ghraib 9, 23, 65–7, 72–3, 107–9, 113–14, 137, 139–40, 143, 157
Afghanistan 3, 7, 9, 26, 35, 39–40, 58–9, 67, 71, 73, 129, 132, 135, 142–4, 146, 148, 151, 153–6
Afro-asiatic 82
Agamben 31–2, 63, 174, 181–8
Ahmed, Leila 11
Ahmed, Sara 155, 158
Ahmed, Shahab 57–8
Al-Andalus 6, 18, 22, 30–1, 62–2, 83, 121–2
Aldrich, Robert 72, 127–8
Algeria 10, 40–4, 73, 104, 129, 179–80
Algerian revolution 40–4
Ali, Kecia 119–20
Alloula, Malek 129
Almond, Ian 5, 94, 97–8, 101–3, 130–1
Al-Qaeda 11, 58, 135, 139, 143, 148–9, 155, 168
America 14, 30–4, 38, 55–6, 61–3, 69, 74, 83, 85, 87–8, 90–2, 105–6, 116, 121–2, 146, 153, 157, 166, 169–70, 173–4, 178, 186–90
Anghie, Antony 38–9
Anidjar, Gil 4–5, 31, 88, 101, 119, 175–81, 183, 185–90
Anjum, Ovamir 53–4
anti-colonial 5–6, 10, 12–13, 27, 29, 32–3, 40, 42–4, 52, 56–9, 76, 80, 111, 143, 145–6, 150–1, 156–7, 174, 189–90
Arab 4–5, 14, 17, 31–4, 36, 39, 41, 46–9, 53, 63–5, 72, 99, 101, 103, 111–2, 116, 122, 127–8, 133–4, 145, 172, 175–81, 185–92
Arendt, Hannah 7, 37, 164, 185
Aryan 30, 33, 62, 93, 103, 170
Asad, Muhammad 46–7, 50

Asad, Talal 15, 49, 51–2, 54, 65, 79, 157–67
attraction 6, 70, 72, 75, 101, 113–14, 122–6, 134, 136
Auschwitz 32, 174, 181–2, 184, 186–7

barbarism 7, 9, 20–1, 28–9, 37, 76, 105, 112, 117, 136, 141, 145
Barlas, Asma 46
Bin Laden 40, 122, 135, 154–5
Black 3, 7–8, 12–13, 22–3, 27, 30, 37, 41, 55–7, 65, 68–9, 72–3, 77, 85–7, 89–92, 95, 104, 108–11, 117–18, 124–7, 134, 140–1, 143, 150, 155–7, 170, 179
Blackamoor 5–6
Black Legend 88
Blackness 56, 85, 87, 92, 170
blasphemy 157, 159–62, 167
Boyarin, Daniel 125–6, 131
Brown, Wendy 157–9, 163, 167
Bush Administration 9, 17, 26, 41, 147, 151, 153, 156, 169–70
Bush Jr., George 151, 169
Butler, Judith 147–53, 157–8, 162–8

camp 30–3, 63–4, 130, 173–5, 181–7
Canada 7, 146, 185, 190, 192
capitalism 6, 12, 79, 84, 153–6, 160, 181
Carter, J. Kameron 86, 96, 170–1
castration (racial) 71, 114–15, 135–6
Cherif, Mustapha 17, 179–81
Chesler, Phyllis 145–7, 153, 168
Christ 30–1, 60, 63–4, 86, 88–90, 95–6, 100, 122–3, 170–2, 175
Christendom 4, 16–21, 38, 45, 78, 82, 84–6, 105, 108–9, 115, 120–1
Christianity 18, 30, 34, 36, 46, 51, 54, 60–3, 77–80, 82, 84–7, 90, 92–7, 99–102, 104, 119, 121, 125–6, 145, 159, 167, 170–2, 174–5, 186

Christians 18, 20–2, 47–9, 62–3, 82–90, 95, 97–9, 101, 115–17, 119, 121–2, 169–71, 176
civilization 7, 9, 18–19, 22–3, 25, 37, 41, 48–9, 63, 68, 80–2, 94, 99, 103, 105, 114, 117, 159, 171, 173–4, 182
colonialism 1, 13, 27, 31, 33, 40, 54, 58, 63, 78, 116, 122, 145–7, 150, 153–4, 159, 175, 187, 189
  anti- 14, 76, 118, 145
  settler 6–7, 31–3, 63, 83, 85, 114, 146, 150, 175, 187, 189–90, 192
colonizing 13, 16, 29, 36, 50, 54, 64, 71, 76, 79–80, 85, 115, 117, 136, 150, 152, 168, 180–1
Cooke, Miriam 11, 65
crisis–political, economic 1–3, 8, 15, 28, 32, 73
critical theory 9–10, 12, 159
criticism 151–2, 156–60, 164–5, 167
critique 11–14, 27–9, 40–1, 44–5, 51, 54–6, 76, 79–81, 91, 93, 100, 113, 141, 150, 156–60, 162, 164–7, 185
Crooke, Alistair 59
Crusades 17–21, 23, 31, 82, 85, 88, 142, 176
cultural politics 3, 8, 23, 29, 35, 45–6, 68, 71
culture 3, 14, 16–19, 23–5, 28, 30, 33, 35, 37–9, 44, 49, 56, 60–1, 63, 66–8, 72–3, 75, 77–8, 80, 85, 94, 99, 102, 107–9, 113, 117, 128–9, 133–5, 137, 141, 144, 155, 163–4, 172–3, 180, 189–90

decolonization 34, 36, 63
Derrida, Jacques 4–5, 17, 176–81, 188
desire 1, 5–6, 8–9, 15–17, 20–2, 36, 43, 45, 57, 59, 67–9, 71–2, 74–5, 82, 102–5, 108–10, 112–17, 119–34, 136, 141–2, 149, 153, 156–7, 188
Devji, Faisal 58
Diop, Cheikh Anta 81
disgust 23, 46, 67, 69–70, 75, 113–14

Eisenstien, Zillah 153–6
enemy combatant 37–8, 40–1, 64
enemy/enmity 2–5, 9–10, 16, 18–19, 30–1, 35, 37–8, 40–1, 45, 59–60, 64, 70, 77, 86, 89, 105, 111, 116, 119, 126, 145, 168, 174–8, 181–2, 187–8, 190
Eng, David 71, 115
Enlightenment 48, 61, 78, 87, 93–4, 97–8, 100, 102, 105, 131, 158, 160, 164, 171
epistemology 172, 174–81, 183–5
Europe 3–6, 10, 13, 15–25, 30–3, 38–9, 49, 54, 57, 60–4, 69–70, 72, 74, 78–95, 97–105, 115–17, 119, 121–32, 134–6, 146, 157, 159–65, 170–2, 174–81, 183–91

Fanon 9–11, 14, 37, 40–4, 58–60, 72, 76, 100, 150, 191
fear 6, 9, 22, 46, 72, 76, 116, 121–2, 124, 130–1, 144, 148, 151, 155, 169, 182–3
femininity 23–5, 69–71, 74–5, 110, 117–18, 121–2, 129, 134, 136
feminism 13, 23, 26–9, 36, 40, 72, 119, 121, 133, 139–43, 145–8, 153–6, 168
feminist 8, 12–14, 16, 20, 22–9, 36, 69–70, 73, 76, 113, 117–18, 122, 131–4, 137, 139–48, 150, 153–7, 167–8
feminist theory 13, 117
feminized 24–5, 113–15, 118
Foucault, Michel 20, 116–17, 160, 164
Frankl, Viktor 182

gay 33, 74, 107, 109–12, 122, 145, 165–6
Gay International 74, 111–12
gender 1–4, 6, 8, 13, 16, 19–29, 35–6, 37, 40, 46, 67–8, 70–1, 73–5, 94, 107–15, 117–18, 120, 122, 124–6, 132–6, 141–3, 145–6, 148–9, 151, 153–7, 166, 168
Gilman, Sander 170–1, 186
globalization 1–2, 7, 10, 15, 35, 52, 58, 133, 145
Gomez, Michael 55–6
Greece (ancient) 49, 61, 63, 80–2, 102, 125, 192

harem 23, 26, 74, 121, 129, 131–2, 136
Haritaworn, Jin 73, 111–12

hatred 4, 9, 14, 16–17, 26, 31, 34, 46, 64, 68, 77, 113, 129, 143–4, 155, 171, 184–6
Hegel 80, 94, 97–102, 130–1, 158, 177
Hendriks, Thomas 69
heteronormativity 13, 25, 110
heterosexuality 20–2, 26, 36, 71–4, 108–9, 111–13, 115–18, 122, 126, 128–9, 133, 136
hijab 1, 6, 23, 37, 39, 45, 77, 108
Hildegard of Bingen 20–1
Holocaust 30–3, 36, 61, 63, 173–4, 183, 187, 189–90
homonationalism 73, 109–10, 112
homophobia 21, 165–6, 168
homosexuality 22, 36, 72–4, 108–12, 116–18, 126–30, 135–6, 140
Hrotsvitha of Gandersheim 22, 122–5

imperialism 12, 15, 23, 26–9, 33–4, 38, 58, 74, 77, 109–12, 127, 132, 140–3, 146–50, 153–9, 161, 167–8, 188
international law 38–9, 85
invasion 2, 7, 9, 18, 26, 34, 39, 43, 65, 69, 77, 141, 143–4, 147, 149, 151, 157
Iraq 3, 7, 9, 39–40, 60, 65–8, 139, 144, 147–9, 151–2
Islamic Studies 15, 52, 57–8, 76, 79, 163
Islamist 1–2, 6–8, 10–15, 21, 28–9, 34–5, 42, 49, 52–3, 58–9, 73, 135, 143, 159, 168, 174, 191
Israel 6, 17–18, 30–6, 61, 63–4, 70, 114, 122, 145–7, 152, 170, 174–5, 178, 187–92

Jackson, Sherman 55–6
Jennings, Willie James 89–90
Jews 4, 18, 30–3, 47, 49, 60–4, 83, 86–8, 94, 98, 105, 116, 119, 121, 145–7, 170–5, 181–2, 184–91
Judaism 30–1, 46, 60, 62–3, 86, 94, 97, 101–2, 119, 145–6, 170–5, 189
Judeo-Christian 16, 30–1, 34–6, 60, 61, 64, 145, 147, 161, 169–75, 178–9, 182, 188, 190–2

Kant, Immanuel 87, 93–9, 102–3, 105, 160, 164, 177
Lambert, Sarah 19
left 3, 8, 12, 14, 16, 61, 139, 141, 146, 165
Lewis, Bernard 17, 113–15
liberal, liberal-democratic 3, 6–8, 10, 14, 29–30, 40, 56, 63, 111, 133, 137, 141, 146, 149, 154, 159–61, 166–7, 173
liberalism 3–4, 6, 14, 30, 43, 63, 160
logics 3–4, 8, 16–17, 19, 30, 33, 35–6, 39, 45, 52, 54, 61, 63, 69, 71, 75, 79, 81–2, 89–92, 94–6, 104, 121, 135, 142, 146, 151, 171, 188, 190
Loomba, Ania 85, 87

McChrystal, Stanley 40
McClintock, Anne 69
Malcolm X 1, 34, 56, 65
man 1, 6, 24–5, 38, 40–1, 64–72, 75, 86, 91–5, 97, 100, 112, 114–15, 117–18, 120, 126–7, 129, 132–6, 150, 155, 169, 182, 184–6
Mandair, Arvind-Pal 54, 78–80, 82, 92, 98
manhunt 40
masculinity 23–5, 67, 69–74, 109–10, 115, 117–18, 122, 125, 129, 131, 134, 136, 142–3, 156
Massad, Joseph 3, 30, 32, 46, 62–4, 73, 97, 111–12, 128, 186–7, 189–90
Masuzawa, Tomoko 54, 62, 80, 92, 98, 102, 171–3
Mignolo, Walter 87–8, 91
militarism 109, 114
militarization 15, 153
modernity 1, 5, 11–12, 15, 17–18, 21, 30, 36, 39, 41–2, 44, 54, 60, 77–9, 82, 84–6, 91, 94, 100, 102–5, 112, 133, 149, 160–1, 171, 174, 184, 191
monogenesis 95
monstrosity 16, 20, 110, 122
monstrous 45, 70, 72, 85–6, 101, 108, 117, 121, 126, 129, 135, 184
Moor 1, 17, 21, 45, 83–4, 88–90, 121–2, 124–6, 170, 179
multiculturalism 3, 7, 27, 111, 146

Muselmann 1, 6, 17, 30–2, 45, 174–5, 181–8, 191

nation-state 2–3, 6–7, 14–15, 17, 27, 29–34, 41, 53, 61, 74, 77, 83–5, 103, 139, 141, 147, 150, 156–7, 163, 166, 169–71, 185, 189–90
Nazism 31, 186
neoliberalism 3, 7–10, 27, 35, 52, 57–8, 111, 133, 147, 153

Obama, Barack 56, 67, 107, 169–70
Obama Administration 9, 41
occupation 2, 7, 9, 11, 24, 26, 34–5, 39, 41–2, 44, 58, 64, 69, 77, 141–4, 146, 151, 153–4, 157, 182, 192
orient 24, 26, 45, 62, 68, 70, 74, 92, 102, 105, 107, 113–15, 117–18, 127–9, 131–2, 134, 136, 191
oriental 1, 3–4, 6, 17, 21, 23–5, 30–2, 44–5, 61–4, 74, 80, 99, 101, 114–15, 117, 121, 127, 129–37, 170, 183, 185, 187, 190
orientalism 5, 8, 12, 17, 23–4, 37, 40, 44–6, 61, 63, 70, 73, 92, 97, 99, 103, 113–18, 130, 133, 146, 174, 184, 187, 191
orientalizing 18, 24–5, 33, 40, 50, 109, 136, 142, 153
other, the 3–4, 9, 12–13, 24, 28, 73–4, 79, 86, 90, 92–3, 99, 102, 111–12, 147–53, 170, 175
Ottoman 23, 39, 62, 81, 84–5, 88, 98, 101

pagan 20, 38, 45, 62, 86, 89–90, 116, 121, 123–4
Palestine 9, 17, 30, 32–4, 36, 43–5, 59–60, 64–65, 148, 152, 175, 178, 187–92
pathological 42, 110
perverse/perversion 6, 19, 21–3, 25, 36, 46, 68, 70–1, 75, 108–11, 113, 115–18, 120–5, 127, 135–6, 142, 170, 186
philosophy 4, 51, 78, 80–2, 84, 87, 91–4, 96–7, 99–101, 103, 130, 163, 175, 177, 180, 188

phobogenic 5, 8, 37, 59, 68
political 4, 77–9, 82, 126
political culture 3, 28, 56, 60, 63, 70
political philosophy 4
political theology, *see* political; theology
porno-tropics 69
postmodernism 5, 12, 41, 79, 111, 148
poststructuralism 12–13
precarious 12, 28, 39, 143, 147, 153
Puar, Jasbir 73, 109–10, 112, 122

queer 14, 16, 24, 26–9, 36, 68, 74–5, 109–13, 116, 130, 134, 141, 165–8
queerness 74, 109–11, 134
queer-phobia 113
queer theory 36

race, racial 1–9, 12–19, 22–36, 37–41, 44–6, 52, 54–6, 59–64, 67–8, 70–3, 75, 77–100, 102–5, 109–11, 113–18, 122, 124–31, 135–7, 141–2, 145–6, 149–50, 153–7, 161, 163–4, 169–72, 174–5, 178, 181–2, 184–92
racial 6, 30
racial castration, *see* castration (racial); racial
racialization 2, 5, 13, 15, 25, 40, 62, 76, 91, 153, 155–6, 188
racial liberalism, *see* liberalism; racial
racism 14, 33, 55, 60, 65, 145–6, 153, 156–7, 161, 165–6, 170
Rahman, Fazlur 48–50
Reconquista 5, 17, 23, 83, 87, 91, 142
religion 1–2, 4–6, 9, 14–16, 18–19, 35–6, 39, 43–5, 47, 49–51, 54–6, 59–61, 63–4, 67, 76, 77–80, 82–7, 91, 93, 95–105, 118, 121, 124–6, 130, 157–60, 163, 165, 170, 172–3, 175, 177–9, 181, 184, 187–89
religio-racial 4, 8, 12, 17–19, 22–3, 25, 28, 30, 32–3, 35–6, 38, 44–5, 59, 63–4, 70–1, 75, 82–5, 90–4, 104, 114–15, 117–18, 125, 135, 142–3, 146, 170–1, 174–5, 178, 181, 184, 189–92

revulsion 9, 20, 46, 70, 72, 74, 101, 109, 113, 121, 134
rights (civil, political, liberal) 6–8, 14, 26, 29, 35, 37–8, 40, 58, 63, 107–9, 111–12, 133, 142–4, 148

Safavid 85
Said, Edward 14, 23–4, 30, 32, 40, 44–6, 62–3, 70, 92, 97, 114–18, 190–2
salvation 19–20, 22, 39, 47–8, 86, 90–1, 95, 118–19, 175
Saracen 1, 5, 17, 19, 38, 45, 83, 85, 90, 121–3
Sardar, Ziauddin 105
Sayyid, Salman 2, 52–3
secular 1–2, 4, 6, 10–1, 16–17, 30, 35–6, 39, 42, 44–5, 61–4, 78, 81–2, 86–7, 90–3, 96–7, 100, 104–5, 116–17, 147, 156–65, 167, 169–70, 174, 177, 182, 184, 190–2
secularization 5–6, 14, 17, 19, 35, 91–2, 127, 142, 181, 188
securitization 15, 58, 77, 109
security 12, 35, 39, 58, 70, 135, 143–4, 147, 159, 192
Semite 1, 17, 30–2, 45, 61–4, 103, 170, 172, 174, 183–6, 190
Semitic (Semitism) 54, 103–4, 172, 185–6, 188
  anti-Semitism 30–4, 60–1, 63, 143, 145–7, 170–2, 173, 186, 188–91
settler colonialism, *see* colonialism, settler
sex 1, 13, 16, 19–21, 23, 26, 36, 46, 67, 69, 71–2, 107–9, 112–13, 118–21, 123–5, 127–8, 132, 134–5, 140
sexuality 1–2, 13, 20–1, 23, 36, 68, 70, 72, 76, 107–12, 114–22, 124–31, 134–7, 154–5, 168
Sheikh 132–3, 191
sin (original sin) 20–1, 86, 91, 95–6, 114, 116–19
slavery (slaves, transatlantic slave trade, racial slavery) 6, 11, 14–15, 25, 38, 47, 55–6, 69–70, 73–5, 83–6, 89–92, 95, 100, 105, 117–22, 135, 142, 153–4, 160

sovereign subject 32, 39–40, 94, 101, 186, 188
sovereignty 1, 8, 15–16, 32, 36, 38–40, 68, 85, 94, 101, 104, 106, 149, 153, 168, 169, 171, 186–8, 190
sovereignty doctrine 38–9, 83
Spillers, Hortense 89
subjectivity 1, 8, 15, 22, 36, 39–40, 68, 76, 80, 101, 104, 106, 110, 112, 124, 133, 142–3, 168, 169, 190

Tessera, Miriam Rita 20–1
theology 4–5, 18–22, 31, 38, 45, 61, 77–8, 80, 84, 86–93, 97, 104, 108, 115, 117, 121, 160, 169, 171, 175–9, 182–3, 187–8, 190
Third World 6, 12, 14, 27, 29, 32–6, 42, 56, 175, 192
Third World project 32, 34
Third World revolution 42
Tolan, John Victor 85
torture 9, 66–8, 107–9, 113, 128, 139–40, 157, 169, 179, 187
Trump Administration 9, 41, 64, 67, 141, 170

US 3, 6–7, 12, 29–30, 33–5, 37, 40–1, 44, 55–6, 58, 64, 66–7, 70, 73–5, 84, 107, 109–11, 114, 139–41, 144–51, 153–6, 168–70, 172–3, 189, 192

veil 11, 21, 25, 37, 44, 67, 70–3, 108, 113, 115, 121, 129, 134–6, 158
violence 2–3, 7–9, 11–12, 14–15, 21, 23, 25, 28–9, 32, 36, 40–2, 45, 54, 58–60, 63, 65–8, 71, 73, 75, 79, 84, 88, 94, 104, 107–9, 112, 117–18, 121–6, 128–31, 134–7, 139–40, 143–5, 147–57, 160, 163, 165, 167–71, 177–8, 181–2, 185–6, 190–1

war on terror (Afghan war, Iraq war) 6–8, 10, 15–17, 26, 28, 31, 33, 37–9, 64, 103, 107, 109, 112–13, 122, 133, 136, 145, 147–8, 150, 153–5, 169–70, 173, 191–2
Westernity 13, 29, 35, 44, 105, 111, 141, 181, 190, 192

Westernizing 6–7, 12, 14–16, 20, 22, 26, 28–9, 50, 68, 75, 80, 104, 110–11, 129, 136–7, 142–3, 192
white supremacy 3, 6–7, 9–10, 12, 29, 32, 56, 58, 64, 76, 80, 86, 137, 141–2, 146–7, 154–5, 171
woman 6, 13, 20, 22–6, 28–9, 37, 40, 44, 50, 66–75, 93, 112–13, 115, 117–18, 121, 126, 129, 131–6, 141–5, 155–6, 168, 185
world religions 54, 77, 80, 93, 99, 101–3, 171–2
wretched of the earth, the 8–9, 59, 192
Wynter, Sylvia 91–2, 95

Yeğenoğlu, Meyda 23, 132

Zionism 63, 145–7, 171, 173, 178–9, 187–91

www.ingramcontent.com/pod-product-compliance
Lightning Source LLC
Chambersburg PA
CBHW072135290426
44111CB00012B/1877